Lecture Notes in Computer Science 12292

More information about this series at http://www.springer.com/series/7408

Anton Jansen · Ivano Malavolta ·
Henry Muccini · Ipek Ozkaya ·
Olaf Zimmermann (Eds.)

Software Architecture

14th European Conference, ECSA 2020
L'Aquila, Italy, September 14–18, 2020
Proceedings

 Springer

Editors
Anton Jansen
Koninklijke Philips N.V.
Eindhoven, The Netherlands

Ivano Malavolta 🄳
VU Amsterdam
Amsterdam, The Netherlands

Henry Muccini 🄳
University of L'Aquila
L'Aquila, Italy

Ipek Ozkaya 🄳
Carnegie Mellon University
Pittsburg, PA, USA

Olaf Zimmermann
University of Applied Sciences
of Eastern Switzerland
Rapperswil, Switzerland

ISSN 0302-9743   ISSN 1611-3349 (electronic)
Lecture Notes in Computer Science
ISBN 978-3-030-58922-6   ISBN 978-3-030-58923-3   (eBook)
https://doi.org/10.1007/978-3-030-58923-3

LNCS Sublibrary: SL2 – Programming and Software Engineering

This Springer imprint is published by the registered company Springer Nature Switzerland AG
The registered company address is: Gewerbestrasse 11, 6330 Cham, Switzerland

Preface

The European Conference on Software Architecture (ECSA) is the premier European conference that provides researchers and practitioners with a platform to present and discuss the most recent, innovative, and significant findings and experiences in the field of software architecture research and practice. This 14th edition of ECSA builds upon a series of successful European workshops on software architecture held during 2004–2006, as well as a series of European software architecture conferences during 2007–2019. This edition of ECSA had a unique nature as due to the novel coronavirus, COVID-19, it was the first ECSA conference that was originally to be held in L'Aquila, Italy, but convened the participants around the globe virtually during September 14–18, 2020.

This year's technical program included a main research track, three keynote talks, and an industry track (included in this volume), as well as a doctoral symposium track with its own keynote, a gender diversity in software architecture track with its own keynote, and a tool demos track. In addition, ECSA 2020 also offered nine workshops on diverse topics related to the software architecture discipline, such as automotive architectures, quality-aware DevOps, and IoT systems. In addition, ECSA 2020 featured a journal first track partnering with the *Journal of Software and Systems*, Elsevier, and the IEEE Software Magazine. The contributions of all these other meetings are included in the companion proceedings, published in a volume by Springer CCIS.

ECSA 2020 received 103 contributions to all tracks. For the main research track, we received 60 submissions in the two main categories: full and short research papers. Based on the recommendations of the Program Committee, we accepted 12 papers as full papers and 5 additional papers as short papers. Hence the acceptance rate for full research papers was 20% for ECSA 2020. For the industrial track, we received 11 submissions and accepted 6 of them. The conference attracted papers (co-)authored by researchers, practitioners, and academia from 24 countries (Austria, Australia, Brazil, Canada, Chile, Columbia, Denmark, Ecuador, Finland, France, Germany, Italy, the Netherlands, New Zealand, Spain, Pakistan, Poland, Portugal, Romania, Sweden, Switzerland, Tunisia, the UK, and the USA).

The main ECSA program had three keynotes. Professor Ivica Crnkovic from Chalmers University, Sweden, talked about "AI engineering—new challenges in system and software architecting and managing lifecycle for AI-based systems." Professor Diomidis Spinellis, from Athens University of Economics and Business, Greece, gave a presentation on "Fifty years of sustained progress: Form, forces, and lessons of Unix architectural evolution." The industry keynote was delivered by Michael Keeling, an experienced software engineer and the author of the book "Design It! From Programmer to Software Architect."

We are grateful to the members of the Program Committee for helping us to seek submissions and provide valuable and timely reviews. Their efforts enabled us to put together a high-quality technical program for ECSA 2020. We would like to thank the members of the Organizing Committee of ECSA 2020 for playing an enormously important role in successfully organizing the event with several tracks and collocated events, as well as the workshop organizers, who made significant contributions to this year's successful event.

We also thank our sponsors who provided financial support for the event: the University of L'Aquila, Italy, provided the technology infrastructure and the support needed, nExpecto, and Springer.

The ECSA 2020 submission and review process was supported by the EasyChair conference management system. We acknowledge the prompt and professional support from Springer who published these proceedings in electronic volumes as part of the *Lecture Notes in Computer Science* series. Finally, we would like to thank the authors of all the ECSA 2020 submissions and the attendees of the conference for their participation.

ECSA 2020 planning and execution took place during an unprecedented time in our history, globally we had to face a pandemic as well as understand and react to consequences of systematic racism and intolerance. As the ECSA community, we pledge to stand against racism and intolerance and strive to elevate the ideas and voices of black, indigenous, and people of color who have been historically excluded because of systemic racism.

We thank the support of the software architecture community, they reacted by continuing to advance the field of software architecture through their scientific submissions to ECSA, while staying flexible as the Organizing Committee had to pivot several times from an in-person, to hybrid, to an all-online conference.

July 2020

Anton Jansen
Ivano Malavolta
Henry Muccini
Ipek Ozkaya
Olaf Zimmermann

Organization

General Chair

Henry Muccini   University of L'Aquila, Italy

Steering Committee

Muhammad Ali Babar	The University of Adelaide, Australia
Paris Avgeriou	University of Groningen, The Netherlands
Tomas Bures	Charles University, Czech Republic
Rogério de Lemos	University of Kent, UK
Laurence Duchien	CRIStAL, University of Lille, France
Carlos E. Cuesta	Rey Juan Carlos University, Spain
David Garlan	Carnegie Mellon University, USA
Paola Inverardi	University of L'Aquila, Italy
Patricia Lago	Vrije Universiteit Amsterdam, The Netherlands
Antónia Lopes	University of Lisbon, Portugal
Ivano Malavolta	Vrije Universiteit Amsterdam, The Netherlands
Raffaela Mirandola	Politecnico di Milano, Italy
Henry Muccini	University of L'Aquila, Italy
Flavio Oquendo (Chair)	IRISA, University of South Brittany, France
Ipek Ozkaya	Carnegie Mellon University, USA
Jennifer Pérez	Technical University of Madrid, Spain
Bedir Tekinerdogan	Wageningen University, The Netherlands
Danny Weyns	KU Leuven, Belgium
Uwe Zdun	University of Vienna, Austria

Research Track

Program Committee Chairs

Ivano Malavolta	Vrije Universiteit Amsterdam, The Netherlands
Ipek Ozkaya	Carnegie Mellon University, USA

Program Committee

Jesper Andersson	Linnaeus University, Sweden
Paris Avgeriou	University of Groningen, The Netherlands
Rami Bahsoon	University of Birmingham, UK
Luciano Baresi	Politecnico di Milano, Italy
Thais Batista	Federal University of Rio Grande do Norte, Brazil
Steffen Becker	University of Stuttgart, Germany
Stefan Biffl	TU Wien, Austria

Patrizio Pelliccione	Chalmers University of Technology, Sweden
Jennifer Perez	Universidad Politécnica de Madrid, Spain
Claudia Raibulet	University of Milano-Bicocca, Italy
Maryam Razavian	Eindhoven University of Technology, The Netherlands
Ralf Reussner	Karlsruhe Institute of Technology, Germany
Bradley Schmerl	Carnegie Mellon University, USA
Romina Spalazzese	Malmö University, Sweden
Girish Suryanarayana	Siemens Corporate Technology, India
Bedir Tekinerdogan	Wageningen University, The Netherlands
Chouki Tibermacine	University of Montpellier, France
Rainer Weinreich	Johannes Kepler University Linz, Austria
Danny Weyns	KU Leuven, Belgium
Uwe Zdun	University of Vienna, Austria
Liming Zhu	The University of New South Wales, Australia
Olaf Zimmermann	Hochschule für Technik Rapperswill, Switzerland

Additional Reviewers

Anastase Adonis	Axel Legay
Abdulatif Alabdulatif	Samir Ouchani
Maria Istela Cagnin	Eduardo Silva
Everton Cavalcante	Roberto Verdecchia
Milena Guessi	

Industry Track

Program Committee Chairs

| Anton Jansen | Philips, The Netherlands |
| Olaf Zimmermann | Hochschule für Technik Rapperswil, Switzerland |

Program Committee

Mohsen Anvaari	Independent Consultant, Norway
Andrei Furda	Hitachi Rail STS, Australia
Heiko Koziolek	ABB Corporate Research, Germany
Thomas Kurpick	Trusted Shops, Germany
Xabier Larrucea	Tecnalia, Spain
Daniel Lübke	iQuest GmbH, Germany
Željko Obrenović	Incision, The Netherlands
Eltjo Poort	CGI, The Netherlands
Daniele Spinosi	Micron Technology, Italy
Michael Stal	Siemens, Germany
Johannes Wettinger	Bosch, Germany
Erik Wittern	IBM T.J. Watson Research Center, USA
Eoin Woods	Endava, UK

Additional Reviewers

Stefan Kapferer
Mirko Stocker

Organizing Committee

Proceedings Chair

Mirco Franzago   University of L'Aquila, Italy

Web Chair

Karthik Vaidhyanathan   Gran Sasso Science Institute, Italy

Tool Demos Chairs

Paris Avgeriou   University of Groningen, The Netherlands
Barbora Buhnova   Masaryk University, Czech Republic

Gender Diversity in SA Chairs

Javier Camara   University of York, UK
Catia Trubiani   Gran Sasso Science Institute, Italy

Doctoral Symposium Chairs

Patrizia Scandurra   DIIMM, University of Bergamo, Italy
Danny Weyns   KU Leuven, Belgium

Workshops Chairs

Mauro Caporuscio   Linnaeus University, Sweden
Anne Koziolek   Karlsruhe Institute of Technology, Germany

Journal First Chair

Uwe Zdun   University of Vienna, Austria

Publicity Chairs

Stéphanie Challita   Inria, France
Juergen Musil   TU Wien, Austria

Student Volunteer Chairs

Roberta Capuano   University of L'Aquila, Italy
Jamal El Hecham   IRISA, France

Virtualization Chairs

Claudio Di Sipio   University of L'Aquila, Italy
Luca Traini   University of L'Aquila, Italy

Keynotes

AI Engineering — New Challenges in System and Software Architecting and Managing Lifecycle for AI-based Systems

Ivica Crnkovic

Chalmers University, Gothenburg, Sweden
ivica.crnkovic@chalmers.se

Abstract. Artificial Intelligence based on Machine Learning, and in particular Deep Learning, is today the fastest growing trend in software development, and literally used in all other research disciplines, with a very high impact on the modern society. However, a wide use of AI in many systems, in particular dependable systems, is still far away of being widely used. On the one hand there is a shortage of expertise, on the other hand the challenges for managing AI-based complex and dependable systems are enormous, though less known, and in general underestimated. Some aspects of these challenges are based on management of resources, including computational, data storage capacity, performance, and real-time constraints. Introduction of AI-based components, i.e. components that includes AI algorithms, require significant changes in system and software architecture, and its successful deployment is based on many architectural decisions and on changes of the development process.

This talk discusses some of these challenges, illustrate a case of Cyber-physical systems, and gives some ideas for new research in software engineering inducing software architecture, i.e. for AI engineering.

Short Bio

Ivica Crnkovic is a professor of software engineering at Chalmers University, Gothenburg, Sweden. He is the director of ICT Area of Advance at Chalmers University, and the director of Chalmers AI Research Centre (CHAIR). His research interests include, software architecture, software development processes, software engineering for large complex systems, component-based software engineering, and recently Software engineering for AI. Professor Crnkovic is the author of more than 200 refereed publications on software engineering topics, and guest editor of a number of special issues in different journals and magazines, such as IEEE Software, and Elsevier JSS. He was the general chair of 40th International Conference on Software Engineering (ICSE) 2018, held in Gothenburg, 2018. Before Chalmers, Ivica Crnkovic was affiliated with Mälardalen University, Sweden, and before that he was employed at ABB company, Sweden, where he was responsible for software development environments and tools.

More information is available on http://www.ivica-crnkovic.net

Fifty Years of Sustained Progress: Form, Forces, and Lessons of Unix Architectural Evolution

Diomidis Spinellis

Department of Management Science and Technology,
Athens University of Economics and Business, Greece
dds@aueb.gr

Abstract. Unix has evolved over five decades, shaping modern operating systems, key software technologies, and development practices. Studying the evolution of this remarkable system from an architectural perspective can provide insights on how to manage the growth of large, complex, and long-lived software systems. Along main Unix releases leading to the FreeBSD lineage we examine core architectural design decisions, the number of features, and code complexity, based on the analysis of source code, reference documentation, and related publications. We see that the growth in size has been uniform, with some notable outliers, while cyclomatic complexity has been religiously safeguarded. A large number of Unix-defining design decisions were implemented right from the very early beginning, with most of them still playing a major role. Unix continues to evolve from an architectural perspective, but the rate of architectural innovation has slowed down over the system's lifetime. Architectural technical debt has accrued in the forms of functionality duplication and unused facilities, but in terms of cyclomatic complexity it is systematically being paid back through what appears to be a self-correcting process. Some unsung architectural forces that shaped Unix are the emphasis on conventions over rigid enforcement, the drive for portability, a sophisticated ecosystem of other operating systems and development organizations, and the emergence of a federated architecture, often through the adoption of third-party subsystems. These findings allow us to form an initial theory on the architecture evolution of large, complex operating system software.

Short Bio

Diomidis Spinellis is a Professor in the Department of Management Science and Technology at the Athens University of Economics and Business, Greece. His research interests include software engineering, IT security, and cloud systems engineering. He has written two award-winning, widely- translated books: "Code Reading" and "Code Quality: The Open Source Perspective". His most recent book is "Effective Debugging: 66 Specific Ways to Debug Software and Systems". Dr. Spinellis has also published more than 300 technical papers in journals and refereed conference proceedings, which have received more than 8000 citations. He served for a decade as a member of the

IEEE Software editorial board, authoring the regular "Tools of the Trade" column, and as the magazine's Editor-in- Chief over the period 2015–2018. He has contributed code that ships with Apple's macOS and BSD Unix and is the developer of UMLGraph, CScout, git-issue, and other open-source software packages, libraries, and tools. Dr. Spinellis is a senior member of the ACM and the IEEE.

Mighty Methods: Four Essential Tools for Every Software Architect's Silver Toolbox

Michael Keeling

LendingHome, USA
mkeeling@neverletdown.net

Abstract. It is an oversimplification to say that we are living in extraordinary times. When my team was first asked to work from home back in February we were happy to do our part in attempting to stem the tide of an inevitable global pandemic. While we were eager to help, we were also nervous about how suddenly distributing our co-located team would affect our way of working. And yet, after several months we've settled into a "new normal" that looks surprisingly similar to our way of working from Before. Much about how we worked changed, in some cases dramatically, but a handful of design methods that were central to our team remained effective even after the shift from a co-located to fully distributed context. In particular, mob programming, example mapping, architecture decision records, and visual thinking are consistently among the most versatile and reliable tools in my silver toolbox.

In this talk we'll briefly explore these four methods and speculate about what makes them effective tools for software architects in such a broad range of contexts and situations. While this is not a talk about remote work per se, we'll attempt to use the shifting context of work we've all experienced to further isolate variables that might help us identify other potential mighty methods waiting for software architects to adopt.

Short Bio

Michael Keeling is a software engineer at LendingHome and the author of Design It!: From Programmer to Software Architect. Prior to LendingHome, Keeling worked at IBM on the Watson Discovery Service, Vivisimo, BuzzHoney, and Black Knight Technology. Keeling has also served as an Adjunct Faculty member at Carnegie Mellon University in the Master of Software Engineering Distance Program since 2009. He holds a Master in Software Engineering from Carnegie Mellon University in Pittsburgh, PA and a Bachelor of Science in Computer Science from the College of William and Mary in Williamsburg, VA.

Keeling's current research interests include software architecture design methods, agile software development, and human factors of software engineering. He is a regular speaker in the architecture and agile communities, presenting papers and talks, and facilitating workshops for both national and international audiences. Keeling is a two-time winner of the SEI/IEEE Software "Architecture in Practice" Best Presentation Award for talks given at the 2012 and 2014 SATURN conferences. A full list of his talks and workshops are available on his website:

http://www.neverletdown.net/p/speaking-and-writing.html.

Contents

Microservices

Assessing Architecture Conformance to Coupling-Related Patterns
and Practices in Microservices 3
    Evangelos Ntentos, Uwe Zdun, Konstantinos Plakidas,
    Sebastian Meixner, and Sebastian Geiger

Formal Software Architectural Migration Towards Emerging
Architectural Styles...................................... 21
    Nacha Chondamrongkul, Jing Sun, and Ian Warren

Monolith Migration Complexity Tuning Through the Application
of Microservices Patterns.................................... 39
    João Franscisco Almeida and António Rito Silva

Uncertainty, Self-adaptive, and Open System

Decentralized Architecture for Energy-Aware Service Assembly 57
    Mauro Caporuscio, Mirko D'Angelo, Vincenzo Grassi,
    and Raffaela Mirandola

Continuous Experimentation for Automotive Software on the Example
of a Heavy Commercial Vehicle in Daily Operation 73
    Federico Giaimo and Christian Berger

Towards Using Probabilistic Models to Design Software Systems
with Inherent Uncertainty...................................... 89
    Alex Serban, Erik Poll, and Joost Visser

Model-Based Approaches

Empowering SysML-Based Software Architecture Description with Formal
Verification: From SysADL to CSP............................ 101
    Fagner Dias, Marcel Oliveira, Thais Batista, Everton Cavalcante,
    Jair Leite, Flavio Oquendo, and Camila Araújo

A Flexible Architecture for Key Performance Indicators Assessment
in Smart Cities 118
    Martina De Sanctis, Ludovico Iovino, Maria Teresa Rossi,
    and Manuel Wimmer

Performance and Security Engineering

A Multi-objective Performance Optimization Approach
for Self-adaptive Architectures 139
  Davide Arcelli

Data Stream Operations as First-Class Entities in Component-Based
Performance Models 148
  Dominik Werle, Stephan Seifermann, and Anne Koziolek

Architecture-Centric Support for Integrating Security Tools
in a Security Orchestration Platform 165
  Chadni Islam, Muhammad Ali Babar, and Surya Nepal

VisArch: Visualisation of Performance-based Architectural Refactorings 182
  *Catia Trubiani, Aldeida Aleti, Sarah Goodwin, Pooyan Jamshidi,
  Andre van Hoorn, and Samuel Gratzl*

Architectural Smells and Source Code Analysis

An Initial Study on the Association Between Architectural Smells
and Degradation 193
  Sebastian Herold

Architectural Technical Debt: A Grounded Theory 202
  Roberto Verdecchia, Philippe Kruchten, and Patricia Lago

Does BERT Understand Code? – An Exploratory Study on the Detection
of Architectural Tactics in Code 220
  Jan Keim, Angelika Kaplan, Anne Koziolek, and Mehdi Mirakhorli

Education and Training

Teaching Students Software Architecture Decision Making. 231
  *Rafael Capilla, Olaf Zimmermann, Carlos Carrillo,
  and Hernán Astudillo*

The PDEng Program on Software Technology: Experience Report
on a Doctorate Level Architecture Training Program 247
  Ad T. M. Aerts and Yanja Dajsuren

Experiences and Learnings from Industrial Case Studies

Architectural Concerns for Digital Twin of the Organization. 265
  *Mauro Caporuscio, Farid Edrisi, Margrethe Hallberg,
  Anton Johannesson, Claudia Kopf, and Diego Perez-Palacin*

Quick Evaluation of a Software Architecture Using the Decision-Centric
Architecture Review Method: An Experience Report   281
  Pablo Cruz, Luis Salinas, and Hernán Astudillo

The Quest for Introducing Technical Debt Management in a Large-Scale
Industrial Company   296
  Somayeh Malakuti and Sergey Ostroumov

Architecting Contemporary Distributed Systems

Determining Microservice Boundaries: A Case Study Using Static
and Dynamic Software Analysis   315
  Tiago Matias, Filipe F. Correia, Jonas Fritzsch, Justus Bogner,
  Hugo S. Ferreira, and André Restivo

IAS: An IoT Architectural Self-adaptation Framework   333
  Mahyar T. Moghaddam, Eric Rutten, Philippe Lalanda,
  and Guillaume Giraud

A Comparison of MQTT Brokers for Distributed IoT Edge Computing   352
  Heiko Koziolek, Sten Grüner, and Julius Rückert

Author Index   369

Microservices

Assessing Architecture Conformance to Coupling-Related Patterns and Practices in Microservices

Evangelos Ntentos[1]([✉]), Uwe Zdun[1], Konstantinos Plakidas[1],
Sebastian Meixner[2], and Sebastian Geiger[2]

[1] Faculty of Computer Science, Research Group Software Architecture,
University of Vienna, Vienna, Austria
{Evangelos.Ntentos,Uwe.Zdun,Konstantinos.Plakidas}@univie.ac.at
[2] Siemens Corporate Technology, Vienna, Austria
{Sebastian.Meixner,Sebastian.Geiger}@siemens.com

Abstract. Microservices are the go-to architectural style for building applications that are polyglot, support high scalability, independent development and deployment, and are rapidly adaptable to changes. Among the core tenets for a successful microservice architecture is high independence of the individual microservices, i.e. loose coupling. A number of patterns and best practices are well-established in the literature, but most actual microservice-based systems do not, as a whole or in part, conform to them. Assessing this conformance manually is not realistically possible for large-scale systems. This study aims to provide the foundations for an automated approach for assessing conformance to coupling-related patterns and practices specific for microservice architectures. We propose a model-based assessment based on generic, technology-independent metrics, connected to typical design decisions encountered in microservice architectures. We demonstrate and assess the validity and appropriateness of these metrics by performing an assessment of the conformance of real-world systems to patterns through statistical methods.

1 Introduction

Microservice architectures [14,15,22] describe an application as a collection of autonomous and loosely coupled services, typically modeled around a domain. Key microservice tenets are development in independent teams, cloud-native technologies and architectures, polyglot technology stacks including polyglot persistence, lightweight containers, loosely coupled service dependencies, high releasability, and continuous delivery [22]. Many architectural patterns that reflect recommended "best practices" in a microservices context have already been published in the literature [18,19,23]. The fact that microservice-based systems are complex and polyglot means that an automatic or semi-automatic assessment of their conformance to these patterns is difficult: real-world systems feature combinations of these patterns, and different degrees of violations of the

© Springer Nature Switzerland AG 2020
A. Jansen et al. (Eds.): ECSA 2020, LNCS 12292, pp. 3–20, 2020.
https://doi.org/10.1007/978-3-030-58923-3_1

same; and different technologies in different parts of the system implement the patterns in different ways, making the automatic parsing of code and identification of the patterns a haphazard process.

This work focuses on describing a method for assessing architecture conformance to coupling-related patterns and practices in microservice architectures. Coupling between microservices is caused by existence of dependencies, e.g. whenever one service calls another service to fulfill a request or share data. Loose coupling is an established topic in service-oriented architectures [22] but the application to the specific context of microservice architectures has not, to our knowledge, been examined so far.

Strong coupling is conflicting with some of the key microservice tenets mentioned above. In particular, releasability, which is a highly desirable characteristic in modern systems due to the emergence of DevOps practices, relies on the rapid and independent release of individual microservices, and is compromised by strong dependencies between them. For the same reason, development in independent teams becomes more difficult, and independent deployment of individual microservices in lightweight containers is also impeded. This work covers three broad coupling aspects: *Coupling through Databases*, resulting from reliance on commonly accessed data via shared databases; *Coupling through Synchronous Invocations*, resulting from synchronous communication between individual services; and *Coupling through Shared Services*, which arises through the dependence on common shared services (for details see Sect. 3).

In reality, of course, no microservice system can support *all* microservice tenets well at the same time. Rather the *architectural decisions* for or against the use of specific patterns and practices must reflect a trade-off between ensuring the desired tenets and other important quality attributes [12,22]. From these considerations, this paper aims to study the following research questions:

- **RQ1** How can we automatically assess conformance to loose coupling-related patterns and practices in the context of microservice architecture decision options?
- **RQ2** How well do measures for assessing coupling-related decision options and their associated tenets perform?
- **RQ3** What is a set of minimal elements needed in a microservice architecture model to compute such measures?

In pursuing of these questions, we surveyed the relevant literature (Sect. 2) and gathered knowledge sources about established architecture practices and patterns, their relations and tenets in form of a *qualitative study on microservice architectures*. This enabled us to create a meta-model for the description of microservice architectures, which was verified and refined through iterative application in modelling a number of real-world systems, as outlined in Sect. 4. We manually assessed all models and model variants on whether each decision option is supported, thereby deriving an objective *ground truth* (Sect. 5). As the basis for an automatic assessment, we defined a number of generic, technology-independent metrics to measure architecture conformance to the decision options, i.e. at least one metric per major decision option (Sect. 6).

These metrics (and combinations thereof) were applied on the models and model variants to derive a numeric assessment, and then compared to the ground truth assessment via an ordinal regression analysis (Sect. 7). Section 8 discusses the results of our approach, as well as its limitations and potential threats to validity. Finally, in Sect. 9 we draw our conclusions and discuss options for future work.

2   Related Work

Many studies focus on best practices for microservice architectures. Richardson [18] has published a collection of microservice patterns related to major design and architectural practices. Patterns related to microservice APIs have been introduced by Zimmermann et al. [23], while Skowronski [19] collected best practices for event-driven microservice architectures. Microservice fundamentals and best practices are also discussed by Fowler and Lewis [14], and are summarized in a mapping study by Pahl and Jamshidi [16]. Taibi and Lenarduzzi [20] study microservice "bad smells", i.e. practices that should be avoided (which would correspond to violations in our work).

Many software metrics-related studies for evaluating the system architecture and individual architectural components exist, but most of them are not specific to the microservices domain. Allen et al. [1,2] study component metrics for measuring a number of quality attributes, e.g. size, coupling, cohesion, dependencies of components, and the complexity of the architecture. Additional studies for assessing quality attributes related to coupling and cohesion have been proposed and validated in the literature [3,4,6,11]. Furthermore, a small number of studies [5,17,21] propose metrics specifically for assessing microservice-based software architectures. Although these works study various aspects of architecture, design metrics, and architecture-relevant tenets such as coupling and independent deployment, their approach is usually generic. None of the works covers all the related software aspects for measuring coupling in a microservice context: the use of databases, system asynchronicity, and shared components. This is the overarching perspective of our work, and the chief contribution of this paper.

3   Decisions

In this section, we briefly introduce the three coupling-related decisions along with their decision options (i.e. the relevant patterns and practices) which we study in this paper. We also discuss the impact on relevant microservice tenets, which we later on use as an argumentation for our manual ground truth assessment in Sect. 5.

Inter-Service Coupling Through Databases. One important decision in microservice-based systems is data persistence, which needs to take into account qualities such as reliability and scalability, but also adhere to microservice-specific best practices, which recommend that each microservice should be loosely coupled and thus able to be developed, deployed, and scaled independently [14]. At one extreme of the scale, one option is *No Persistent Data Storage*, which is applicable only for services whose functions are performed on transient data. Otherwise, the most recommended option is the *Database per Service* pattern [18]: each service has its own database and manages its own data independently. Another option, which negatively affects *loose coupling*, is to use a *Shared Database* [18]: a service writes its data in a common database and other services can read these data when required. There are two different ways to implement this pattern: in *Data Shared via Shared Database* multiple services share the same table, resulting in a strongly coupled system, whereas in *Databased Shared but no Data Sharing* each service writes to and reads from its own tables, which has a lesser impact on coupling.

Inter-Service Coupling Through Synchronous Invocations. Service integration is another core decision when building a microservice-based system. A theoretically optimal system of independent microservices would feature no communication between them. Of course, services need to communicate in reality, and so the question of integrating them so as to not result in tight inter-service coupling becomes paramount. The recommended practice is that communication between the microservices should be, as much as possible, asynchronous. This can be achieved through several patterns which are widely implemented in typical technology stacks: the *Publish/Subscribe* [13] pattern, in which services can subscribe to a channel to which other services can publish; the use of a *Messaging* [13] middleware, which decouples communication by using a queue to store messages sent by the producer until they are received by the consumer; the *Data Polling* [18] pattern, in which services periodically poll other services for data changes; and the *Event Sourcing* [18] pattern, that ensures that all changes to application state are stored as a sequence of events; *Asynchronous Direct Invocation* technique, in which services communicate asynchronously via direct invocations. Applying these patterns ensures loose coupling (to different degrees), and increases the system reliability.

Inter-Service Coupling Through Shared Services. Many of the microservice patterns focus on system structure, i.e. avoiding services sharing other services altogether, or at least not in a strongly coupled way. An optimal system in terms of architecture quality should not have any shared service. In reality, this is often not feasible, and in larger systems service sharing leads to chains of transitive dependencies between services. This is problematic when a service is unaware of its transitive dependencies, and of course for the shared service itself, where the needs of its dependents must always be taken into account during its evolution. We define three cases: a *Directly Shared Service* is a microservice which is directly linked to and required by more than one other service; a *Transitively Shared Service* is a microservice which is linked to other services via at least one intermediary service; and a *Cyclic Dependency* [10] which is formed when there is a direct or transitive path that leads back to its origin, i.e. that allows a service to be ultimately dependent on itself after a number of intermediary services. Cyclic dependencies often emerge inadvertently through increasing complexity over the system's lifecycle, and require extensive refactoring to resolve. All three cases are inimical to the principle of *loose coupling* as well as to system qualities such as *performance*, *modifiability*, *reusability*, and *scalability*.

4   Research and Modeling Methods

In this section, we summarize the research and modeling methods applied in our study. The code and models used in and produced as part of this study have been made available online for reproducibility[1].

4.1   Research Method

Figure 1 shows the research steps from initial data collection to final data analysis. For the data collection phase we conducted a multi-vocal literature study using *web resources*, *public repositories*, and *scientific papers* as sources [9]. We then analyzed the data collected using qualitative methods based on *Grounded Theory* [7] coding methods, such as open and axial coding, and extracted the three core architectural decisions described in the previous section along with their corresponding decision drivers and impacts. As data for our further research we used generated models taken from the *Model Generation* process, described below. We defined a rating scheme for systematic assessment based on support or violation of core practices and tenets. From these we derived a ground truth for our study (the ground truth and its calculation rules are described in Sect. 5) as well as a set of metrics for automatically calculating conformance to each individual pattern or practice per decision. We then used the ground truth data to assess how well the hypothesized metrics can possibly predict the ground truth data by performing an ordinal regression analysis. Ordinal regression is a widely used method for modeling an ordinal response's dependence on a set of independent predictors, which is applicable in a variety of domains. For the ordinal regression analysis we used the *lrm* function from the *rms* package in R [8].

4.2   Model Generation

We began by performing an iterative study of a variety of microservice-related knowledge sources, and we gradually refined a meta-model which contains all the required elements to help us reconstruct existing microservice-based systems. In order to investigate the ontology, and to evaluate the meta-model's efficiency, we gathered a number of microservice-based systems, summarized in Table 1. Each is either a system published by practitioners (on GitHub and/or practitioner blogs) or a system variant adapted from a published example according to discussions in the relevant literature in order to explore the possible decision space. Apart from the specific variations described in Table 1 all other system aspects remained the same as in the base models.

---

[1] https://bit.ly/2WmFP3N.

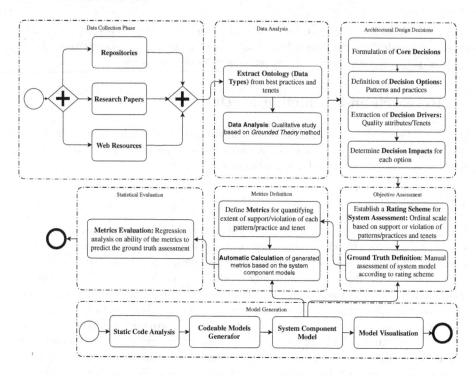

Fig. 1. Overview diagram of the research method followed in this study

The systems were taken from 9 independent sources in total. They were developed by practitioners with microservice experience, and they are representative of the best practices summarized in Sect. 3. We performed a fully manual static code analysis for those models where the source code was available (7 of our 9 sources; two were modeled from documentation published by the practitioners).

To create our models, we used our existing modeling tool CodeableModels[2], a Python implementation for the precise specification of meta-models, models, and model instances in code. Based on CodeableModels, we specified meta-models for components, connectors and relationships. We then manually created model instances for each of the systems in Table 1. In addition, we realized automated constraint checkers and PlantUML code generators to generate graphical visualizations of all meta-models and models.

The result is a set of precisely modeled component models of the examined software systems (modeled using the techniques described below). This resulted in a total of 27 models summarized in Table 1. We assume that our evaluation systems are, or reflect, real-world practical examples of microservice architectures. As many of them are open source systems with the purpose of demonstrating practices or technologies, they are at most of medium size and modest complexity, though.

---

[2] https://github.com/uzdun/CodeableModels.

4.3   Methods for Modeling Microservice Component Architectures

From an abstract point of view, a microservice-based system is composed of components and connectors, with a set of component types for each component and a set of connector types for each connector. For modeling microservice architectures we followed the method reported in our previous work [21].

5   Ground Truth Calculations

In this section, we present and describe the calculation of the ground truth assessment for each of the decisions from Sect. 3. The results of those assessments are reported in Table 2. The assessment begins with a manual evaluation by the authors on whether each of the relevant patterns (decision options) is either Supported, Partially Supported, or Not Supported (**S**, **P**, **N** in Table 2). Based on this and informed by the description of the impacts of the various decision options in Sect. 3, we combined the outcome of all decision options to derive an ordinal assessment on how well the decision as a whole is supported in each model, using the ordinal scale: [**++**: very well supported, **+**: well supported, **o**: neutral, **-**: badly supported, **--**: very badly supported]. This was done according to best practices documented in literature. For instance, following the ordinal scale the assessment for the model BM1 is **+**: well supported, since a) option *Database per Service* is not supported, b) some services have a shared database, but c) they do not share data via the shared database.

For the *Inter-Service Coupling through Databases* decision, we derive the following scoring scheme for our ground truth assessment:

- **++**: All services (which require data persistence) have individual databases *Database per Service*.
- **+**: Some services have *Shared Databases* and no *Data Shared via the Shared Databases*.
- **o**: All services have *Shared Databases* and no *Data Shared via the Shared Databases*.
- **-**: Some services have *Shared Databases* and *Data Shared via the Shared Databases*.
- **--**: All services have *Shared Databases* and *Data Shared via the Shared Databases*.

From the *Inter-Service Coupling through Synchronous Invocations* decision, we derive the following scoring scheme for our ground truth assessment:

- **++**: All services communicate asynchronously via *Message Brokers* or *Publish/Subscribe* or *Stream Processing*
- **+**: All services communicate asynchronously via *API Gateway* or *HTTP Polling* or *Direct Asynchronous calls*, or (some) via *Message Brokers* or *Publish/Subscribe* or *Stream Processing*.
- **o**: None or some services communicate asynchronously and all other services communicate asynchronously via *Data Sharing* (e.g. Shared DB).

Table 1. Overview of modelled systems (size, details, and sources)

Model ID	Model Size	Description / Source
BM1	10 components 14 connectors	Banking-related application based on CQRS and event sourcing (from `https://github.com/cer/event-sourcing-examples`).
BM2	8 components 9 connectors	Variant of BM1 which uses direct RESTful completely synchronous service invocations instead of event-based communication.
BM3	8 components 9 connectors	Variant of BM1 which uses direct RESTful completely asynchronous service invocations instead of event-based communication.
CO1	8 components 9 connectors	The common component model E-shop application implemented as microservices directly accessed by a Web frontend (from `https://github.com/cocome-community-case-study/cocome-cloud-jee-microservices-rest`).
CO2	11 components 17 connectors	Variant of CO1 using a SAGA orchestrator on the order service with a message broker. Added support for Open Tracing. Added an API gateway.
CO3	9 components 13 connectors	Variant of CO1 where the reports service does not use inter-service communication, but a shared database for accessing product and store data. Added support for Open Tracing.
CI1	11 components 12 connectors	Cinema booking application using RESTful HTTP invocations, databases per service, and an API gateway (from `https://codeburst.io/build-a-nodejs-cinema-api-gateway-and-deploying-it-to-docker-\part-4-703c2b0dd269`).
CI2	11 components 12 connectors	Variant of CI1 routing all interservice communication via the API gateway.
CI3	10 components 11 connectors	Variant of CI1 using direct client to service invocations instead of the API gateway.
CI4	11 components 12 connectors	Variant of CI1 with a subsystem exposing services directly to the client and another subsystem routing all traffic via the API gateway.
EC1	10 components 14 connectors	E-commerce application with a Web UI directly accessing microservices and an API gateway for service-based API (from `https://microservices.io/patterns/microservices.html`).
EC2	11 components 14 connectors	Variant of EC1 using event-based communication and event sourcing internally.
EC3	8 components 11 connectors	Variant of EC1 with a shared database used to handle all but one service interactions.
ES1	20 components 36 connectors	E-shop application using pub/sub communication for event-based interaction, a middleware-triggered identity service, databases per service (4 SQL DBs, 1 Mongo DB, and 1 Redis DB), and backends for frontends for two Web app types and one mobile app type (from `https://github.com/dotnet-architecture/eShopOnContainers`).
ES2	14 components 35 connectors	Variant of ES1 using RESTful communication via the API gateway instead of event-based communication and one shared SQL DB for all 6 of the services using DBs. No service interaction via the shared database occurs.
ES3	16 components 35 connectors	Variant of ES1 using RESTful communication via the API gateway instead of event-based communication and one shared database for all 4 of the services using SQL DB in ES1. However, no service interaction via the shared database occurs.
FM1	15 components 24 connectors	Simple food ordering application based on entity services directly linked to a Web UI (from `https://github.com/jferrater/Tap-And-Eat-MicroServices`).
FM2	14 components 21 connectors	Variant of FM1 which uses the store service as an API composition and asynchronous interservice communication. Added Jaeger-based tracing per service.
FM3	13 components 15 connectors	Variant of FM1 which demonstrates a cyclic dependency case, uses the store service as an API composition and asynchronous inter-service communication
HM1	13 components 25 connectors	Hipster shop application using GRPC interservice connection and OpenCensus monitoring & tracing for all but one services as well as on the gateway. (from `https://github.com/GoogleCloudPlatform/microservices-demo`).
HM2	14 components 26 connectors	Variant of HM1 that uses publish/subscribe interaction with event sourcing, except for one service, and realizes the tracing on all services.
RM1	11 components 18 connectors	Restaurant order management application based on SAGA messaging and domain event interactions. Rudimentary tracing support (from `https://github.com/microservices-patterns/ftgo-application`).
RM2	14 components 14 connectors	Variant of RM1 which contains transitively shared services, API Gateway for client services communication, database per service and direct communication between service.
RM3	14 components 15 connectors	Variant of RM1 which demonstrates a cyclic dependency case, API Gateway for client services communication, database per service and direct communication between service.
RS	18 components 29 connectors	Robot shop application with various kinds of service interconnections, data stores, and Instana tracing on most services (from `https://github.com/instana/robot-shop`).
TH1	14 components 16 connectors	Taxi hailing application with multiple frontends and databases per services from (`https://www.nginx.com/blog/introduction-to-microservices/`).
TH2	15 components 18 connectors	Variant of TH1 that uses publish/subscribe interaction with event sourcing for all but one service interactions.

Table 2. Ground truth assessment results

	BM1	BM2	BM3	CO1	CO2	CO3	CI1	CI2	CI3	CI4	EC1	EC2	EC3	ES1	ES2	ES3	FM1	FM2	FM3	HM1	HM2	RM1	RM2	RM3	RS	TH1	TH2
Database-based inter-service coupling																											
Database per Service	N	S	S	S	S	P	S	S	S	S	S	S	N	N	N	P	S	S	S	S	S	N	S	S	N	S	S
Shared Database	P	N	N	N	P	P	N	N	N	N	N	N	S	S	S	P	N	N	N	N	N	S	N	N	S	N	N
Data Shared via Shared DB	N	N	N	N	N	P	N	N	N	N	N	N	S	N	N	N	N	N	N	N	N	N	N	N	N	N	N
Assessments	+	++	++	++	++	-	++	++	++	++	++	++	-	++	o	+	++	++	++	++	++	o	++	++	o	++	++
Inter-service coupling through synchronous invocations																											
Asynchronous Direct Interconnections	N	N	N	N	N	N	N	N	N	N	N	N	N	N	N	N	N	S	S	P	P	N	N	N	P	N	N
PubSub/Event Sourcing Interconnections	S	N	N	N	N	N	N	N	N	N	N	S	N	P	N	N	N	N	N	N	S	P	N	N	N	N	P
Asynch Inter-communication via API GW	N	N	S	N	N	N	N	N	N	N	N	N	N	N	N	N	N	N	N	N	N	N	N	N	N	N	N
Shared Database Interconnections	N	N	N	N	P	P	N	N	N	N	N	N	S	N	N	N	N	N	N	N	N	N	N	N	N	N	N
Messaging Interconnections	N	N	N	S	N	N	N	N	N	N	N	N	N	N	N	N	N	N	N	N	N	P	N	P	P	N	N
Assessments	++	-	-	++	++	-	-	-	-	-	-	o	o	+	-	-	-	+	+	-	++	+	-	-	o	-	+
Inter-service coupling through shared services																											
Direct Service Sharing	N	N	N	N	N	N	P	P	N	N	N	N	N	P	P	P	P	P	P	P	N	N	N	N	P	P	N
Transitively Shared Services	N	N	N	N	N	N	N	N	N	N	N	N	N	N	N	N	N	P	P	N	N	N	S	N	P	N	N
Cyclic Dependencies	N	N	N	N	N	N	N	N	N	N	N	N	N	N	N	N	N	S	S	N	N	N	N	S	N	N	N
Assessments	++	++	++	o	++	++	o	++	o	++	++	++	o	o	o	o	o	o	-	o	++	++	o	-	o	-	++

- **-:** None or some services communicate asynchronously, none or some communicate asynchronously via *Data Sharing*, some services communicate synchronously.
- **--:** All services communicate synchronously.

Finally, from the *Inter-Service Coupling through Shared Services* decision, we derive the following scoring scheme for our ground truth assessment:

- **++:** None of the services is a *Directly Shared Service* or *Transitively Shared Service* and no *Cyclic Dependencies* exist.
- **+:** Some of the services are *Transitively Shared Services*, but none are *Directly Shared Services* and no *Cyclic Dependencies* exist.
- **o:** Some or none of the services are *Transitively Shared Services* and some are *Directly Shared Services*, but no *Cyclic Dependencies* exist.
- **-:** Some of the services are *Transitively Shared Services* and all other services are *Directly Shared Services*, but no *Cyclic Dependencies* exist.
- **--:** There are *Cyclic Dependencies* or all the services are *Transitively Shared Components* and all the services are *Directly Shared Components*.

6 Metrics

In this section, we describe the metrics we have hypothesized for each of the decisions described in Sect. 3. All metrics, unless otherwise noted, are a continuous value with range from 0 to 1, with 1 representing the optimal case where a set of patterns is fully supported, and 0 the worst-case scenario where it is completely absent.

6.1 Metrics for Inter-Service Coupling Through Databases Decision

Database Type Utilization (DTU) Metric. This metric returns the number of the connectors from *Services* to *Individual Databases* in relation to the total number of *Service-to-Database* connectors. This way, we can measure how many services are using individual databases.

$$DTU = \frac{Database\,per\,Service\,Links}{Total\,Service\text{-}to\text{-}Database\,Links}$$

Shared Database Interactions (SDBI) Metric. Although a *Shared Database* is considered as an anti-pattern in microservices, there are many systems that make use of it either partially or completely. To measure its presence in a system, we count the number of interconnections via a *Shared Database* compared to the *total number of service interconnections*.

$$SDBI = \frac{Service\,Interconnections\,with\,Shared\,Database}{Total\,Service\,Interconnections}$$

6.2 Metrics for Inter-Service Coupling Through Synchronous Invocations Decision

Service Interaction via Intermediary Component (SIC) Metric. We defined this metric to measure the proportion of service interconnections via asynchronous relay architectures such as *Message Brokers*, *Publish/Subscribe*, or *Stream Processing*. These represent the best current practices, and are not exhaustive; should any new architectures emerge, these should be added to this list.

$$SIC = \frac{Service\ Interconnections\ via\ [Message\ Brokers\mid Pub/Sub\mid Stream]}{Total\ Service\ Interconnections}$$

Asynchronous Communication Utilization (ACU) Metric. This metric measures the proportion of the sum of asynchronous service interconnections (via *API Gateway/HTTP Polling/Direct calls/Shared Database*) to the total number of service interconnections.

$$ACU = \frac{Asynchronous\ Service\ Interconnections\ via\ [API\mid Polling\mid Direct\ Calls\mid Shared\ DB]}{Total\ Service\ Interconnections}$$

6.3 Metrics for Inter-Service Coupling Through Shared Services Decision

Direct Service Sharing (DSS) Metric. For measuring DSS we count all the directly shared services and set this number in relation to the total number of system services. To this add all the shared services connectors in relation to the total number of services interconnections. This gives us the proportion of the directly shared elements in the system.

$$DSS = \frac{\frac{Shared\ Services}{Total\ Services} + \frac{Shared\ Services\ Connectors}{Total\ Service\ Interconnections}}{2}$$

Transitively Shared Services (TSS) Metric. For measuring TSS we count all the transitively shared services and set this number in relation to the total number of system services. To this we add all the transitively shared service connectors in relation to the total number of service interconnections. This gives us the proportion of the transitively shared elements in the system.

$$TSS = \frac{\frac{Transitively\ Shared\ Services}{Total\ Services} + \frac{Transitively\ Shared\ Services\ Connectors}{Total\ Service\ Interconnections}}{2}$$

Cyclic Dependencies Detection (CDD) Metric. Let $SG = (S, C)$ be the service graph, S the set of service nodes, and C the set of connector edges in a microservice model. Based on the generic definition of closed paths, we define a *closed service path* in SG as a sequence of services $s_1, s_2, \ldots, s_n$ (each service $\in S$) such that $(s_n, s_n + 1) \in C$ is a directed connector between services for $i = 1, 2, \ldots, n$ and $s_1 = s_n$. A *service cycle* is a closed service path in which no service node is repeated except the first and last, and which contains at least two distinct service nodes. Let $ServiceCycles()$ return the set of all service cycles in a service graph. CDD returns 1 (True) if there is at least one cyclic dependency in the model:

$$CDD = \begin{cases} 1: & \text{if } |ServiceCycles(SG)| = 0 \\ 0: & otherwise \end{cases}$$

6.4   Metrics Calculation Results

We note that for the *Inter-Service Coupling through Shared Services* decision as well as *SDBI* metric, our metrics scale is reversed in comparison to the other two decisions, because here we detect the *presence of an anti-pattern*: the optimal result of our metrics is 0, and 1 is the worst-case result.

The metrics results for each model per decision metric are presented in Table 3.

7   Ordinal Regression Analysis Results

The dependent outcome variables are the ground truth assessments for each decision, as described in Sect. 5 and summarized in Table 2. The metrics defined in Sect. 6 and summarized in Table 3 are used as the independent predictor variables. The ground truth assessments are ordinal variables, while all the independent variables are measured on a scale from 0.0 to 1.0. The objective of the analysis is to predict the likelihood of the dependent outcome variable for each of the decisions by using the relevant metrics for each decision.

Each resulting regression model consists of a *baseline intercept* and the independent variables multiplied by *coefficients*. There are different intercepts for each of the value transitions of the dependent variable ($\geq Badly\ Supported$, $\geq Neutral$, $\geq Well\ Supported$, $\geq Very\ Well\ Supported$), while the coefficients reflect the impact of each independent variable on the outcome. For example, a positive coefficient, such as $+5$, indicates a corresponding five-fold increase in the dependent variable for each unit of increase in the independent variable; conversely, a coefficient of -30 would indicate a thirty-fold decrease.

The statistical significance of each regression model is assessed by the p-value; the smaller the p-value, the stronger the model. A p-value smaller than 0.05 is

Table 3. Metrics calculation results

Metrics	BM1	BM2	BM3	CO1	CO2	CO3	CI1	CI2	CI3	CI4	EC1	EC2	EC3	
Database-based inter-service coupling														
DTU	0.33	1.00	1.00	1.00	1.00	0.60	1.00	1.00	1.00	1.00	1.00	1.00	0.00	
SDBI	0.00	0.00	0.00	0.00	0.00	1.00	0.00	0.00	0.00	0.00	0.00	0.00	1.00	
Inter-service coupling through synchronous invocations														
SIC	1.00	0.00	0.00	0.00	1.00	0.00	0.00	0.00	0.00	0.00	0.00	1.00	0.00	
ACU	0.00	0.00	1.00	0.00	0.00	1.00	0.00	0.00	0.00	0.00	0.00	0.00	1.00	
Inter-service coupling through shared services														
DSS	0.00	0.00	0.00	0.00	0.00	0.00	0.20	0.00	0.38	0.00	0.00	0.00	0.00	
TSS	0.00	0.00	0.00	0.00	0.00	0.00	0.00	0.00	0.00	0.00	0.00	0.00	0.00	
CDD	0.00	0.00	0.00	0.00	0.00	0.00	0.00	0.00	0.00	0.00	0.00	0.00	0.00	
Metrics	ES1	ES2	ES3	FM1	FM2	FM3	HM1	HM2	RM1	RM2	RM3	RS	TH1	TH2
Database-based inter-service coupling														
DTU	1.00	0.00	0.33	1.00	1.00	1.00	1.00	1.00	0.00	1.00	1.00	0.66	1.00	1.00
SDBI	0.00	0.00	0.00	0.00	0.00	0.00	0.00	0.00	0.00	0.00	0.00	0.00	0.00	0.00
Inter-service coupling through synchronous invocations														
SIC	0.60	0.00	0.00	0.00	0.00	0.00	0.00	0.80	1.00	0.00	0.00	0.11	0.00	0.60
ACU	0.00	0.00	0.00	0.00	1.00	0.08	0.50	0.20	0.00	0.00	0.00	0.11	0.00	0.00
Inter-service coupling through shared services														
DSS	0.27	0.34	0.34	0.62	0.47	0.55	0.52	0.00	0.00	0.00	0.00	0.36	0.33	0.00
TSS	0.00	0.00	0.00	0.00	0.00	0.18	0.00	0.00	0.00	0.18	0.16	0.00	0.00	0.00
CDD	0.00	0.00	0.00	0.00	0.00	1.00	0.00	0.00	0.00	0.00	1.00	0.00	0.00	0.00

generally considered statistically significant. In Table 4, we report the p-values for the resulting models, which in all cases are very low, indicating that the sets of metrics we have defined are able to predict the ground truth assessment for each decision with a high level of accuracy.

Table 4. Regression analysis results

Intercepts/coefficients	Value	Model p-value
Database-based inter-service coupling		
Intercept (≥Badly Supported)	2.6572	1.706019e−06
Intercept (≥Neutral)	0.8789	
Intercept (≥ Well Supported)	−1.3820	
Intercept (≥ Very Well Supported)	−3.1260	
Metric Coefficient (DTU)	6.4406	
Metric Coefficient (SDBI)	−3.7048	

(*continued*)

Table 4. (*continued*)

Inter-service coupling through synchronous invocations		
Intercept (≥Badly Supported)	−2.6973	6.705525e−11
Intercept (≥Neutral)	−4.4087	
Intercept (≥Well Supported)	−5.8513	
Intercept (≥Very Well Supported)	−15.3677	
Metric Coefficient (SIC)	17.3520	
Metric Coefficient (ACU)	6.5520	
Inter-service coupling through shared services		
Intercept (≥Neutral)	59.4089	1.625730e−10
Intercept (≥Very Well Supported)	9.7177	
Metric Coefficient (DSS)	−82.4474	
Metric Coefficient (TSS)	−122.2583	
Metric Coefficient (CDD)	−57.4650	

8   Discussion

In this section, we first discuss what we have learned in our study that helps to answer the research questions and then discuss potential threats to validity.

8.1   Discussion of Research Questions

To answer **RQ1** and **RQ2**, we proposed a set of generic, technology-independent metrics for each coupling-related decision, and to each decision option corresponds at least one metric. We objectively assessed for each model how well patterns and/or practices are supported for establishing the ground truth, and extrapolated this to how well the broader decision is supported. We formulated metrics to numerically assess a pattern's implementation in each model, and performed an ordinal regression analysis using these metrics as independent variables to predict the ground truth assessment. Our results show that every set of decision-related metrics can predict our objectively evaluated assessment with high accuracy. This suggests that automatic metrics-based assessment of a system's conformance to the tenets embodied in each design decision is possible with a high degree of confidence.

Here, we make the assumption that the source code of a system can be mapped to the models used in our work. To enable this, we used rather simplistic modeling means, which can rather easily be mapped from a specific source code to the system models. However, it should be noted that full automation of this mapping is an additional effort that needs to be considered and is the subject of ongoing work on our part.

Regarding **RQ3**, we consider that existing modeling practices can be easily mapped to our microservice meta-model and there is no need for major extensions. More specifically, for completing the modeling of our evaluation system set, we needed to introduce 25 component types and 38 connector types, ranging from general notions such as the *Service* component type, to very technology-specific classes such as the *RESTful HTTP* connector, which is a subclass of *Service Connector*. Our study shows that for each pattern and practice embodied in each decision, and the proposed metrics, only a small subset of the meta-model is required.

The decisions *Inter-Service Coupling through Databases* and *Inter-Service Coupling through Shared Services* require to model at least the *Service* and the *Database* component types and the technology-related connector types (e.g. *Database Connector*, *RESTful HTTP* and *Asynchronous Connector*) and the read/write process which explicitly modeled in the *Database Connector* type. The *Inter-Service Coupling through Synchronous Invocations* decision requires a number of additional components (e.g. *Event Sourcing, Stream Processing, Messaging, PubSub*) and the respective connectors (e.g. *Publisher, Subscriber, Message Consumer, Messages Producer, RESTful HTTP* and *Asynchronous Connector*) to be modeled.

8.2 Threats to Validity

We deliberately relied on third-party systems as the basis for our study to increase internal validity, thus avoiding bias in system composition and structure. It is possible that our search procedures introduced some kind of unconscious exclusion of certain sources; we mitigated this by assembling an author team with many years of experience in the field (including substantial industry experiences), and performing very general and broad searches. Given that our search was not exhaustive, and that most of the systems we found were made for demonstration purposes, i.e. relatively modestly sized, this means that some potential architecture elements were not included in our meta-model. In addition, this raises a possible threat to external validity of generalization to other, and more complex, systems. We nevertheless feel confident that the systems documented are a representative cross-cut of current practices in the field, as the points of variance between them were limited and well attested in the literature. Another potential threat is the fact that the variant systems were derived by the author team. However, this was done according to best practices documented in literature. We carefully made sure only to change specific aspects in a variant and keep all other aspects stable. That is, while the variants do not represent actual systems, they are reasonable evolutions of the original designs.

The modeling process is also considered as source of internal validity threat. The models of the systems were repeatedly and independently cross-checked by the author team that has considerable experience in similar methods, but the possibility of some interpretative bias remains: other researchers might have coded or modeled differently, leading to different models. As a mitigation, we also offer the whole models and the code as open access artifacts for review. Since we aimed only to find one model that is able to specify all observed phenomena, and this was achieved, we consider this threat not to be a major issue for our study. The ground truth assessment might also be subject to different interpretations by different practitioners. For this purpose, we deliberately chose only a three-step ordinal scale, and given that the ground truth evaluation for each decision is fairly straightforward and based on best practices, we do not consider our interpretation controversial. Likewise, the individual metrics used to evaluate the presence of each pattern were deliberately kept as simple as possible, so as to avoid false positives and enable a technology-independent assessment. As stated previously, generalization to more complex systems might not be possible without modification. But we consider that the basic approach taken when defining the metrics is validated by the success of the regression models.

9   Conclusions and Future Work

Our approach considered that it is achievable to develop a method for automatically assessing coupling related tenets in microservice decisions based on a microservice system's component model. We have shown that this is possible for microservice decision models that contain patterns and practices as decision options. In this work, we first modeled the key aspects of the decision options using a minimal set of component model elements. These could be possibly automatically extracted from the source code. Then we derived at least one metric per decision option and used a small reference model set as a ground truth. We then used ordinal regression analysis for deriving a predictor model for the ordinal variable. The statistical analysis shows that each decision related metrics are quite close to the manual, pattern-based assessment.

There are many studies related on metrics for component model and other architectures so far, but specifically for microservice architectures and their coupling related tenets have not been studied. Based on our discussion in Sect. 2, assessing microservice architectures using general metrics it is not very helpful. Our approach is one of the first that studies a metrics-based assessment of coupling-related tenets in the microservices domain. We aim to a continuous assessment, i.e. we envision an impact on continuous delivery practices, in which the metrics are assessed with each delivery pipeline run, indicating improvement, stability, or deterioration in microservice architecture conformance. With small changes, our approach could also be applied, for instance, during early architecture assessment. As future work, we plan to study more decisions, tenets, and related metrics. We also plan to create a larger data set, thus better supporting tasks such as early architecture assessment in a project.

Acknowledgments. This work was supported by: FFG (Austrian Research Promotion Agency) project DECO, no. 846707; FWF (Austrian Science Fund) project API-ACE: I 4268.

References

1. Allen, E.B., Gottipati, S., Govindarajan, R.: Measuring size, complexity, and coupling of hypergraph abstractions of software: an information-theory approach. Softw. Qual. J. (2), 179–212. https://doi.org/10.1007/s11219-006-9010-3
2. Allen, E.B., Gottipati, S., Govindarajan, R.: Measuring size, complexity, and coupling of hypergraph abstractions of software: an information-theory approach. Softw. Qual. J. **15**, 179–212 (2006)
3. Bansiya, J., Davis, C.G.: A hierarchical model for object-oriented design quality assessment. IEEE Trans. Softw. Eng. **28**(1), 4–17 (2002)
4. Basili, V.R., Briand, L.C., Melo, W.L.: A validation of object-oriented design metrics as quality indicators. IEEE Trans. Softw. Eng. **22**(10), 751–761 (1996)
5. Bogner, J., Wagner, S., Zimmermann, A.: Towards a practical maintainability quality model for service-and microservice-based systems, pp. 195–198, September 2017
6. Chidamber, S.R., Kemerer, C.F.: A metrics suite for object oriented design. IEEE Trans. Softw. Eng. **20**(6), 476–493 (1994)
7. Corbin, J., Strauss, A.L.: Grounded theory research: procedures, canons, and evaluative criteria. Qual. Sociol. **13**, 3–20 (1990)
8. Frank, E., Harrell, J.: Regression Modeling Strategies: With Applications to Linear Models, Logistic and Ordinal Regression, and Survival Analysis, 2nd edn. Springer, Heidelberg (2013)
9. Garousi, V., Felderer, M., Mäntylä, M.V.: Guidelines for including the grey literature and conducting multivocal literature reviews in software engineering. CoRR
10. Goldstein, M., Moshkovich, D.: Improving software through automatic untangling of cyclic dependencies. In: Association for Computing Machinery, New York, NY, USA (2014)
11. Harrison, R., Counsell, S.J., Nithi, R.V.: An evaluation of the mood set of object-oriented software metrics. IEEE Trans. Softw. Eng. **24**(6), 491–496 (1998)
12. Haselböck, S., Weinreich, R., Buchgeher, G.: Decision models for microservices: design areas, stakeholders, use cases, and requirements. In: Lopes, A., de Lemos, R. (eds.) ECSA 2017. LNCS, vol. 10475, pp. 155–170. Springer, Cham (2017). https://doi.org/10.1007/978-3-319-65831-5_11
13. Hohpe, G., Woolf, B.: Enterprise Integration Patterns. Addison-Wesley, Boston (2003)
14. Lewis, J., Fowler, M.: Microservices: a definition of this new architectural term, March 2004. http://martinfowler.com/articles/microservices.html
15. Newman, S.: Building Microservices: Designing Fine-Grained Systems. O'Reilly, Sebastapol (2015)
16. Pahl, C., Jamshidi, P.: Microservices: a systematic mapping study. In: 6th International Conference on Cloud Computing and Services Science, pp. 137–146 (2016)
17. Pautasso, C., Wilde, E.: Why is the web loosely coupled?: a multi-faceted metric for service design. In: 18th International Conference on World Wide Web, pp. 911–920. ACM (2009)
18. Richardson, C.: A pattern language for microservices (2017). http://microservices.io/patterns/index.html
19. Skowronski, J.: Best practices for event-driven microservice architecture (2019). https://hackernoon.com/best-practices-for-event-driven-microservice-architecture-e034p21lk

20. Taibi, D., Lenarduzzi, V.: On the definition of microservice bad smells. IEEE Softw. **35**(3), 56–62 (2018)
21. Zdun, U., Navarro, E., Leymann, F.: Ensuring and assessing architecture conformance to microservice decomposition patterns. In: Maximilien, M., Vallecillo, A., Wang, J., Oriol, M. (eds.) ICSOC 2017. LNCS, vol. 10601, pp. 411–429. Springer, Cham (2017). https://doi.org/10.1007/978-3-319-69035-3_29
22. Zimmermann, O.: Microservices tenets. Comput. Sci. - Res. Dev., 301–310 (2016). https://doi.org/10.1007/s00450-016-0337-0
23. Zimmermann, O., Stocker, M., Zdun, U., Luebke, D., Pautasso, C.: Microservice API patterns (2019). https://microservice-api-patterns.org

Formal Software Architectural Migration Towards Emerging Architectural Styles

Nacha Chondamrongkul[✉], Jing Sun, and Ian Warren

School of Computer Science, University of Auckland, Auckland, New Zealand
ncho604@aucklanduni.ac.nz, {jing.sun,i.warren}@auckland.ac.nz

Abstract. Software systems are evolved over time to enhance various qualities of the software system by adopting new technologies and principles. The architecture design is usually required to be migrated from one architectural style to another to support this adoption, while the key functionalities still need to be preserved. This paper presents a formal approach that supports architectural migration. Our approach automates refactoring the architectural design to support the exploitation of emerging technologies such as microservices and blockchain. With our approach, the refactored architectural design can be verified to ensure that the essential functional requirements are still preserved, and the design has complied with the behavioural constraints of new architectural styles. We have evaluated the accuracy and performance of our approach. The results prove that it performs reasonably well.

Keywords: Software architecture · Architectural migration · Microservice · Blockchain

1 Introduction

Emerging technologies and principles have been applied to the software system to enhance the system qualities such as maintainability, scalability and security. Software engineers have been facing challenges to modernise the software system by migrating the existing legacy system to take advantage of new technologies and principles [1], such as continuous software engineering, microservices, containerisation and blockchain. Architectural patterns [13,15,19] have been proposed to give structures of how software architecture should be designed to support new technologies and principles. At the migration, software architecture usually needs to be refactored to convert from an architectural pattern to another [6], while the key functionalities need to be preserved [10].

This paper focuses on the architectural migration that modernises the software system to support emerging technologies [18]. As discussed in Sect. 5, some works [2,7,20] have been proposed to provide guidelines and patterns that support architectural migration. A number of tools [3,9,11,14,17] have been proposed to support this task. However, existing approaches focus either refactoring at the implementation level or supporting particular architectural styles.

© Springer Nature Switzerland AG 2020
A. Jansen et al. (Eds.): ECSA 2020, LNCS 12292, pp. 21–38, 2020.
https://doi.org/10.1007/978-3-030-58923-3_2

Moreover, most of the existing tools have not addressed how to ensure that the refactored design would preserve the system functionalities. There is still a lack of approaches that generally support the architectural migration by both refactoring and verifying the architectural design in an automatic manner.

This paper presents a formal approach that supports architectural migration by refactoring and verifying the architecture design before the actual system migration can be performed. Our approach applies ontology reasoning and model checking technique. The contribution of this work can be summarised as follows: 1) The formal modelling of software architecture design is proposed to describe the structural and behavioural aspect of architectural design based on architectural styles. 2) A set of generic rules is presented to automate the architectural design refactoring towards new architectural styles that support emerging technologies and principles. 3) The verification approach helps to ensure that key functional requirements are preserved in the refactored design, and the design has complied with the desired architectural styles. 4) We have evaluated the accuracy and performance of our approach with the architectural design of four real-world software systems.

The rest of this paper is organised in the following sections. Section 2 shows how to model and refactor software architecture design. Section 3 presents the verification approach and migration benefits. Section 4 presents the evaluation result and the discussion. Section 5 discusses the related approaches in comparison to our approach. This paper is concluded in Section 6.

2   Formal Architectural Migration

The overall process of our approach is shown in Fig. 1. Firstly, the model of current architecture is analysed to identify parts of the design that require changes according to the refactoring rules. The refactoring rules help to select design entities such as connector and component that need to be changed according to the desired architectural styles to be applied. Secondly, the refactoring steps in the rules are performed to create the model of target architecture design. Lastly, the verification has been performed on the model of target architecture design to ensure that the functional requirements are still preserved, and the target architecture design behaves according to the architectural styles.

2.1   Architecture Modelling

As this work focuses on refactoring logical architecture design for the architectural migration, our architecture model is based on Connector and Connector (C&C) view [8]. Both structure and behaviour of architecture design are significant to refactor and verify the architecture design to support desired architectural styles [20]. Therefore, we apply ontology representation in Ontology Web Language (OWL) to capture the structural aspect of architecture design, according to the modelling proposed in [4]. The ontology model is expressive to

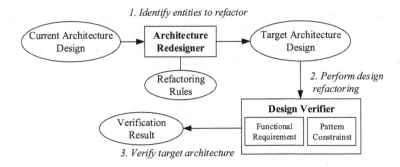

Fig. 1. Overall migration process

describe the concepts and their relationship in the knowledge domain. Architectural Description Language (ADL) is used to capture the behavioural aspect of architecture design according to Wright# language proposed in [5]. Wright# is expressive to describe the dynamic behaviour of components and connectors.

In the ontology model, the design entities in C&C view such as component, connector, role and port are defined as classes and their relationships are defined as object properties. The components have ports representing its interface. The connector have roles representing parties involved in the interaction. To form the connectivities, ports are attached to one or more roles. The architectural patterns are formally defined to support architectural styles based on this structure. The definition of architectural patterns describes specific structural and behavioural characteristics of different types of component and connector[1]. We have formally defined basic architectural patterns such as Client-Server (CS), Publish-Subscribe (PS), and Data Repository (RP). To support modern architectural styles, architectural patterns such as Event-Sourcing (ES) and Command Query Responsibility Segregation (CQRS - CR for command and QR for query) [13] are also defined for event-driven architecture that is commonly used in microservices. Oracle (OR) and Reverse-Oracle (RO) pattern are defined for the blockchain-based architecture [19]. The structure of these architectural patterns can be found in the refactoring rules presented in Sect. 2.2.

In this section, we use LifeNet as an illustrative example to present our approach. Figure 2 shows the current architecture design of LifeNet. The components are represented as rectangles and connectors are represented as rounded edged rectangles. LifeNet is a software system that assists patients with Alzheimer's disease and related dementia. The system allows patients to send an emergency request from his wristband (*Lifeband*) that notifies the mobile application for medical staff (*Lifeguard*) and caregiver (*Lifecare*) to help. These requests are verified and handled by *SOSGateway* and *RequestDispatcher* component. There are data storage components such as *EMCenter* and *PatientRecord*, represented by cylinder box, to allow other components to query and update data. This model

---

[1] The formal architectural patterns can be found at https://bit.ly/2vGv6qi.

applies three architectural patterns. Client-Server patterns are used for connectors such as *soswire* and *dispatchwire*. Publish-Subscribe patterns are used for *notiwire* connector. Data Repository patterns are used for connectors that query and update data such as *emwire* and *emupwire*.

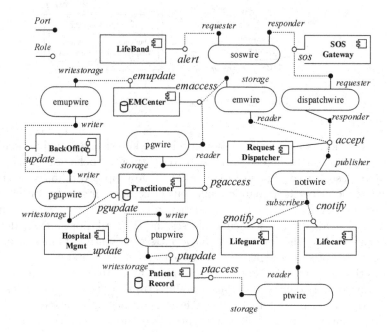

Fig. 2. LifeNet's current design

The structural model of a software system are semantically defined as ontology individuals based on the architectural pattern that are predefined as the ontology class. Due to the page limit, we present some part of the LifeNet model[2]. Listing 1.1 shows the definition of *Patient* component and its ports: *ptaccess* and *ptupdate*. *ptaccess* takes *readstorage* role of *ptwire* connector, which allows querying data. *ptupdate* takes *writestorage* role to allow updating data.

Listing 1.1. LifeNet's current structural model

```
Individual(ex: Patient
  value(ex: hasPort ex: ptaccess, ptupdate))
Individual(ex: ptaccess
  value(ex: hasAttachment ex: readstorage))
Individual(ex: ptupdate
  value(ex: hasAttachment ex: writestorage))
Individual(ex: ptwire
  value(ex: hasRole ex: reader,readstorage)
```

---

[2] The complete model in OWL of LifeNet can be found at https://bit.ly/3bhsCgO.

The behavioural model are defined to describe how the components are executed at runtime to serve the system functionalities. The description of different connector type are defined for the interactive behaviour of architectural patterns. Listing 1.2 shows some part of behavioural model of LifeNet[3]. The *CSConnector* is the definition of a connector type for Client-Server. The components and their port are defined such as *LifeBand* and *SOSGateway*. The *system* scope defines how component are interacting with each other. The connector such as *soswire* is declared, and used later in the *attach* statement to define what roles are attached to the component's port. The *execute* statement defines what ports are executed during runtime. More details about Wright# can be found in [5].

Listing 1.2. LifeNet's current behavioural model

```
connector CSConnector {
    role requester(j) = request -> req!j -> res?j -> process ->
        Skip;
    role responder() = req?j -> invoke -> process -> res!j ->
        responder(); }
component LifeBand {
    port alert() = onalert->alert();}
component SOSGateway {
    port sos() = acknowledge->alert->sos();}
system lifenet {
    declare soswire = CSConnector;
    attach LifeBand.alert() = soswire.requester(49);
    attach SOSGateway.sos() = soswire.responder() <*>
        dispatchwire.requester(19);
    execute LifeBand.alert() || SOSGateway.sos() ...
```

2.2 Refactoring Rules

To create the target architecture design, we defines a set of refactoring rules to automate revising the current design. Each refactoring rule consists of ontology definition and refactoring routine. The ontology definition captures the logic to find component or connector that needs to be changed. The refactoring routine is a sequence of steps that can programmatically change the design configuration to support architectural patterns of desired architectural styles. These refactoring rules are generic and can be applied to the architectural design of any software system. The rules presented in this paper focuses on the migration to event-based and blockchain-based architecture style. They represents the possible rules that cover most well-known cases and are frequently used for migrating basic architectural styles to modern styles. These refactoring rules are as follows:

Event Centre. The connector that helps to process events should be changed to Event-Sourcing pattern. The ontology definition aims to select the Publish-Subscribe connector (PSConnector) that has an inbound role subscribed to

---

[3] The complete model in ADL of LifeNet can be found at https://bit.ly/2zhLbnN.

events to process. *InboundRole* represents any role that waits to be triggered. Below is the ontology definition followed by the refactoring routine.

$$EventCentre \equiv PSConnector \sqcap \exists\, hasRole$$
$$(InboundRole \sqcap \exists\, isAttachOf(Port \sqcap EventProcessor))$$

a) Convert the type of connector to Event-Sourcing pattern (ESConnector) by roles mapping shown in Fig. 3; *publisher* is changed to *event publisher* and *subscriber* is changed to *event subscriber*.
b) Add an component of type *EventStore* to logs incoming events.
c) Connect the connector to the component in step b).

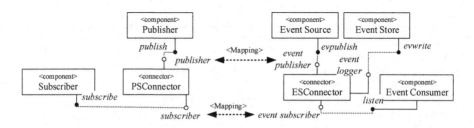

Fig. 3. Mapping of event centre

According to these steps, the LifeNet model can be refactored as shown in Fig. 4 a), the *notiwire* connector has been converted to Event-Sourcing connector and the *RequestLog* component is added as an event store component.

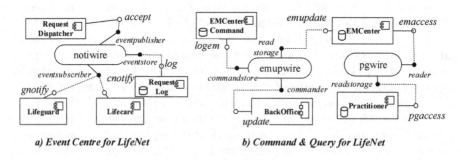

a) *Event Centre for LifeNet*   b) *Command & Query for LifeNet*

Fig. 4. LifeNet's refactoring for event-based patterns

Event-Based Command. The connector that transfers the event to persist on a data storage should be converted to a commander in CQRS pattern. The ontology definition selects the repository writing connector (WRConnector) that is attached to a component, where the events are created and written to the data storage.

$$EventCommand \equiv WRConnector \sqcap \exists hasRole$$
$$(Writer \sqcap \exists isAttachOf(Port \sqcap EventProcessor))$$

a) Convert the type of connector to CQRS's command (CRConnector) as shown in Fig. 5; *writer* and *storage* role is changed to *commander* and *command store*, respectively.
b) Add an component of type ViewDB to be a read-only data storage.
c) Connect the connector to the component in step b).

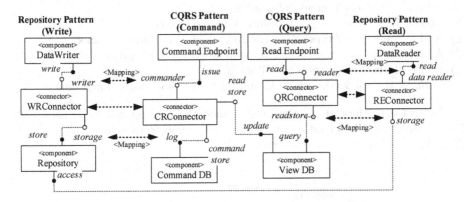

Fig. 5. Mapping of Event-based CQRS

The LifeNet model can be refactored as shown in Fig. 4 b). The *emupwire* has been converted to a command connector for CQRS pattern and *EMCenter-Command* has been added as an command store.

Event-Based Query. The connector that queries the events persisted on the data storage should be converted to a query processor of CQRS pattern. The ontology definition captures the connector that has an outbound role to query events on a data storage.

$$EventQuery \equiv REConnector \sqcap \exists hasRole$$
$$(Reader \sqcap \exists isAttachOf(Port \sqcap EventProcessor))$$

a) Convert the type of connector to CQRS's query (QRConnector) as shown in Fig. 5; *data reader* and *storage* role is changed to *reader* and *query* role of *QRConnector* respectively.
b) Reroute the connector to the *ViewDB* component that is a read-only data storage connected to the command connector.

According to these steps, the LifeNet model can be refactored as shown in Fig. 4 b). The *pgwire* connector has been converted to query connector for CQRS pattern. This connector links *EMCenter* as a *ViewDB* component.

Secure Data Writing. The repository component storing data that need to be tamper-proof can be converted to apply blockchain technology. The ontology definition selects the repository component (Repository) that its inbound port *InboundPort*) is data tampering-proof and write data to the storage. *InboundPort* represents any port that is attached to the inbound role.

$$SecureDataWriter \equiv Repository \sqcap \exists hasPort(InboundPort \sqcap$$
$$DataTamperingProofPort \sqcap \exists hasAttachment WriteStorage)$$

a) Add an oracle component (*Oracle*).
b) Attach *WriteStorage* role to a port of oracle in step a).
c) Add a connector of type *IOConnector*, which is an Oracle connector.
d) Attach *extsupplier* role of connector in step c) to the port added in step b).
e) Add a blockchain component (Blockchain).
f) Connect the connector added in step c) to the blockchain component.

According to these steps, the LifeNet model can be refactored as shown in Fig. 6. *MedRecord* is added as an oracle that connects to a blockchain called *MedChain* with *medupwire* connector.

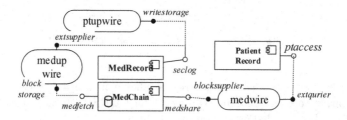

Fig. 6. LifeNet's refactoring to blockchain

Secure Data Reading. The blockchain should be applied at the component that allow data to be queries securely with tampering-proof control applied. The ontology definition selects the repository component (*Repository*) that its inbound port is data tampering-proof and allow data to be queried.

$$SecureDataReader \equiv Repository \sqcap \exists hasPort(InboundPort \sqcap$$
$$DataTamperingProofPort \sqcap \exists hasAttachmentReadStorage)$$

a) Convert the repository to a reverse oracle component (ReverseOracle) as shown in Fig. 7; *access* port is changed to *blockquery* port.

b) Add a connector of type ROConnector, which is a Reverse-Oracle connector.
c) Attach a port converted in step a) to the connector in step b).
d) Connect the connector added in step b) to the blockchain component.

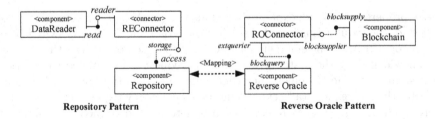

Repository Pattern   **Reverse Oracle Pattern**

Fig. 7. Mapping of secure data reading

As shown in Fig. 6 After these steps are applied, the PatientRecord is converted to a reverse oracle. The *medwire* is added to connect the *Medchain* that stores patient records on the blockchain.

3   Justification of Architectural Migration

After the architecture design has been refactored, it is verified to ensure that the functional requirements are preserved, and the target design is compiled according to the desired architectural patterns. The model checking technique has been applied to achieve this verification. We also address benefits to the system qualities that can be gained when new architectural styles are applied.

3.1   Verifying Functional Requirements

As the behavioural model has been expressed in ADL, we use Linear Temporal Logic (LTL) to define liveness properties that describe the key functional requirements of the software system. Liveness properties are generally used in the model checking technique to determine whether certain states occur. In this work, we use the liveness property to determine the sequence of events that occurred in the software system. The property $\Box(a \rightarrow \Diamond b)$ check whether every event a eventually leads to event b). According to the modelling proposed in [5], the events triggered from the ports are labelled as *[Comp.Prt.Evt]*, where *Comp* is name of a component, *Prt* is name of a port and *Evt* is name of event. The events triggered by the roles are labelled as *[Comp.Conn.Rle.Evt]*, where *Conn* is name of a connector, *Rle* is name of a role and *Evt* is name of event. The following shows the functional properties that are defined for LifeNet.

(1) $\Box(SOSGateway.sos.acknowledge \rightarrow \Diamond LifeBand.alert.onalert)$

(2) $\Box(RequestDispatcher.accept.dispatched \rightarrow \Diamond SOSGateway.sos.acknowledge)$

(3) $\Box(RequestDispatcher.accept.dispatched \rightarrow \Diamond EMCenter.emaccess.emaccessed)$

(4) $\Box(Lifeguard.gnotify.acknowledge \rightarrow \Diamond Patient.ptaccess.ptaccessed)$

(5) $\Box(Lifecare.cnotify.acknowledge \rightarrow \Diamond Patient.ptaccess.ptaccessed)$

These properties can be explained as follows: (1) When the emergency is requested, the request is acknowledged and the wristband's status is switched to alert mode, (2) After the emergency request is dispatched to process, the request is acknowledged by the system, (3) After the request is dispatched to process, the system must find the emergency center in the proximity of patient location, (4) After the emergency staff acknowledges the emergency request (through Lifeguard application), the patient record can be fetched and verified, (5) After the caregiver acknowledges the emergency request (through Lifecare application), the patient record can be fetched and verified.

These functional requirement properties describe how the system should respond to the emergency request. They are specific to the software system and have been proved valid on the model of current architecture design. The same set of properties are used to verify the model of target architecture design. If the verification results are proved valid, the key functional requirements are preserved. We used PAT [16] as a model checker to make a verification in this work. Below are some part of the verification results. All properties above are proved valid after we verified them against the behavioural model of the target architecture of LifeNet. In other words, the target architecture design is proved to support all key functionalities that the current design has.

****** Verification Result ********

The Assertion (lifenet() $\models$ $\Box$(SOSGateway_ sos_ ... is VALID.

The Assertion (lifenet() $\models$ $\Box$(RequestDispatcher_ accept_ ... is VALID.

3.2   Checking Architectural Pattern Constraints

The liveness properties are defined to describe the behavioural constraints of the architectural pattern. Each refactoring rules has a corresponding constraint defined as the following formulas.

(1) $\Box([EventPublisher].[Prt].[Event] \rightarrow \Diamond[EventStore].[EventCentre].eventstore.persist)$

(2) $\Box([EventCommander].[Prt].[Event]$
$\rightarrow \Diamond[CommandStore].[EventCommand].commandstore.process)$

(3) $\Box([EventReader].[Prt].[Event] \rightarrow \Diamond[ViewDB].[EventQuery].readstore.process)$

(4) $\Box([Oracle].[Prt].[Event] \rightarrow \Diamond[Blockchain].[Conn].blockstorage.stored)$

(5) $\Box([Blockchain].[Conn].blocksupplier.process \rightarrow \Diamond[ReverseOracle].[Prt].[Event])$

Formula (1) for the Event Centre rule checks the behaviour of an Event-Sourcing connector *EventCentre*. This constraint ensures that every event is logged in the event store. *EventPublisher* is a component that its port (*Prt*) is attached to the *event publisher* role. *EventStore* represent the component that connects to the *EventCentre* connector. The *eventstore.persist* are role and event predefined for the architectural pattern. Formula (2) is for the Event-based Command rule. It ensures that every incoming command logged in the command store. *EventCommander* is a component that its port (*Prt*) is attached to the *event commander* role. *CommandStore* represents a component that connects to the *EventCommand* connector. Formula (3) is for the Event-based Query rule. It checks if the event can be queried from the view storage. *EventReader* is a component that its port is attached to the *reader* role. ViewDB is read-only storage. Formula (4) is for the Secure Data Writing rule. It ensures that the data can be stored on the blockchain according to Oracle pattern. *Oracle* is an oracle component added to the system. *Blockchain* represents a blockchain component and *Conn* represents a Oracle connector. Formula (5) is for Secure Data Writing rule. *Blockchain* represents a blockchain component and *Conn* represent a Reverse-Oracle connector. *ReverseOracle* is a Reverse-Oracle component. To verify the target architecture design of LifeNet, below are properties that are defined according to the formulas, respectively. After we have verified these properties defined for the architectural constraints, the results are given as valid for all properties. These results prove that the target architecture design has complied with the desired architectural patterns.

(1) $\square(RequestDispatcher.accept.dispatched \rightarrow \Diamond RequestLog.reqwire.eventstore.persist)$

(2) $\square(BackOffice.updateprofile.updating$
$\rightarrow \Diamond EmCenterCommand.emupwire.commandstore.process)$

(3) $\square(EmCenter.emaccess.emaccessed \rightarrow \Diamond Practitioner.pgwire.readstore.process)$

(4) $\square(MedRecord.seclog.ptcommit \rightarrow \Diamond MedChain.medupwire.blockstorage.stored)$

(5) $\square(MedChain.medwire.blocksupplier.process \rightarrow \Diamond Patient.ptaccess.ptaccessed)$

3.3   Benefits of the Migration

After the architecture designs of subject systems have been migrated to support new architectural styles, the target architecture designs generally gain the following attributes.

Maintainability. The event-based architecture style has been applied to mitigate cohesive interdependencies among components that are in the current architecture. This style changes component's reliance on service of another to the events. In the target architecture designs, components can, therefore, be independently modified, deployed and restored. In LifeNet, after Event-Sourcing pattern has applied to *notiwire* connector as shown in Fig. 4 a), *RequestDispatcher* chronologically stores all requests on the *RequestLog*. If the *RequestDispatcher* failed or went off-line, the restoration of system state can always be done by restoring the component's execution based on the requests logged in the *Request-Log*.

Scalability. As the target design embrace the loosely-coupled principle, each component can be self-contained in the container that allows the component to be deployed and executed individually. A prominence implementation of containers is Docker. Docker container is supported by tools like Kubernetes that can automatically scale the containers. In LifeNet, after the design has been refactored according to CQRS pattern as shown in Fig. 4 b), the query and update operation performs on separate storages; *EMCenterCommand* for logging update operation and *EMCenter* for query only. This enables us to optimise the read operation on *EMCenter* by caching or clustering to support higher loads. This optimisation can be achieved with less computational resources than traditional data repository.

Availability. The data repositories become decentralised as the data are replicated dispersedly on blockchain nodes. The decentralisation enhances the availability of data access, as there is no single point of failure. When a node fails, the data can be accessible through other available nodes. The transactions on data are also transparent, as the users with provided authority can always view the transaction. In the refactored design of LifeNet shown in Fig. 6, as the patient records are stored on *MedChain*, the data are replicated on every nodes joining in the blockchain network. If a node managed by a hospital fails, the data can be fetched or recovered from other nodes. Also, the patient records can be fetched and traced by any hospital that joins this blockchain.

Data-Tampering Proof. In term of security, the data structure in the blockchain is append-only, so data cannot be deleted or altered. The consensus of all the ledger participants is required to record data in the blockchain. As the target architecture design applies the architectural patterns that support the interaction to the blockchain, sufficient security control is required to secure the components that have direct communication with the blockchain network. In the refactored design of LifeNet, updating data requires a consensus among hospitals in the networks, so data can only be updated through nodes in the blockchain network by *MedRecord* component. Therefore, *MedRecord* must apply security controls such as authorisation and firewall to prevent malicious traffic.

4   Evaluation

This evaluation aims to assess the accuracy and performance of our approach. As there is no benchmark set to evaluate our approach, the architectural design of four real-world software systems are selected to create the models used in this evaluation, namely AgriDigital (AD), Life Net (LN), Sock Shop (SS), Supply Chain (SC). The details of their current architecture design are shown in Table 1. The *Cur.Ptn.* Column denotes the architectural patterns that are applied in the current architecture designs. *Tgt. Ptn.* denotes the patterns that of the target architecture designs to apply. The *C&C* column shows the number of component and connector. The *Req* column shows the number of key functional requirements that have been used to verify the design. The current architecture design of these systems is based on the monolithic architecture that needs the migration to the event-based microservice architecture to embrace loosely-coupling principle. Also, some data are to be securely persisted on the blockchain.

Table 1. Subject systems

System	Cur. Ptn.	Tgt. Ptn.	C&C	Req
Agri Digital *Agriculture asset tracking system*	CS, PS, RP	OR, RO, ES	20	5
Life Net *Medical emergency system*	CS, PS, RP	OR, RO, ES, CR, QR	19	5
Sock Shop *E-Commerce System*	CS, RP	CR, QR	22	5
Supply Chain *Business process management*	CS, RP	OR, RO	18	6

4.1   Experiment Setup

This evaluation aims at assessing the completeness and soundness of the refactoring rules, and has been conducted according to the following process. Firstly, we defined the models of current architecture design and functional requirements using ArchModeller[4]. ArchModeller is a graphical user interface that allows users to seamlessly draw a graphical diagram for software architecture design and make a verification. The tool can automatically converts graphical diagrams into the models in OWL and ADL for the verification. Secondly, all five refactoring rules have been implemented in the tool to refactor the current architecture model and create the target architecture model[5]. Thirdly, the functional requirement properties have been used to verify the target architecture model. Fourthly, we defined the pattern constraint properties to verify the target architecture model. Lastly, we have gathered the verification results to determine the completeness and soundness of refactoring rules. Each rule is assessed by the combination of verification result of its pattern constraints property and all functional requirement properties. If the functional requirements properties have any invalid result, the refactoring routine alters the system in the way that it incorrectly performs functionalities. If the pattern-constraint property is proved invalid, the refactoring routine may consist of steps that incorrectly refactor the design, according to the architectural pattern. The properties that are proved valid are considered as true-positive (T_{pos}), and invalid properties are considered as false-positive

---

[4] Arch Modeller can be found at http://bit.ly/2m3LITT.

[5] The implementation of refactoring rules can be found at https://bit.ly/2WEHaTw.

(F_{pos}). We also manually verified the target architecture design to find the false-negative (F_{neg}) result that is any part of the design that requires refactoring but not covered by the refactoring rules. Below is how we calculated the measurements, namely precision and recall that were used to evaluate the soundness and completeness of our approach.

$$Precision = \frac{T_{pos}}{T_{pos} + F_{pos}} \quad Recall = \frac{T_{pos}}{T_{pos} + F_{neg}}$$

To assess the performance of our approach, we gathered the performance statistic of the properties verification against the models of target architecture design. The performance statistics include processing time in milliseconds and the number of visited states. This performance evaluation was carried out using an Intel Core i7-7500U CPU @ 2.7 GHz with 8.00 GB Ram computer.

4.2   Evaluation Result

The result of accuracy evaluation[6] has been summarised in Table 2. This table classifies the results according to the rules presented in Sect. 2.2. The *ptn* denotes the verification result of pattern constraint properties. The *fnc* denotes the verification result of functional requirement properties. The numbers that are shown in *ptn* and *fnc* column are the precision rate; - means that the rule is not used in that system, as not all patterns are applied to the design. The *msn* column indicates the false-negative result as the number of the entities that need refactoring but not yet refactored. Overall, all refactoring rules have the precision rate of 100%. The recall rates are also 100% as we have not found any false-negative result.

Table 2. Evaluation results

Rule	AD			LN			SS			SC		
	ptn	fnc	msn	ptn	fnc	msn	ptn	fnc	msn	ptn	fnc	msn
#1 Event Centre	1.0	1.0	0	1.0	1.0	0	–	–	–	–	–	–
#2 Event Command	–	–	–	1.0	1.0	0	1.0	1.0	0	–	–	–
#2 Event Query	–	–	–	1.0	1.0	0	1.0	1.0	0	–	–	–
#4 Secure Write	1.0	1.0	0	1.0	1.0	0	–	–	–	1.0	1.0	0
#5 Secure Read	1.0	1.0	0	1.0	1.0	0	–	–	–	1.0	1.0	0

The result of the performance evaluation is presented in Fig. 8. This graph illustrates the verification performance of LifeNet model, as it applies all five refactoring rules. The properties *prop1* to *prop5* are functional requirement properties, while *const1* to *const5* are the pattern constraint properties. The

---

[6] The models and evaluation results can be found at https://bit.ly/3ft3gQv.

verification generally took less than 0.3 s. The processing times for the verification of functional requirements have no significant difference. The *const2* that was used to verify the event command of CQRS pattern took the most processing time, while the *const5* that was used to verify the Reverse-Oracle pattern took the least processing time. We have found the same trend in the other models.

4.3   Discussion

According to the evaluation result, the refactoring rules have been proved to be soundness as they have been used to refactor the subject systems, while their key functional requirements are still preserved. As all design entities that require changes are refactored, our refactoring rules are proved to be complete. However, this evaluation focuses on the migration to only event-based microservice and blockchain-based architecture, so the migration to other architectural styles requires more refactoring rules to be defined by software architect. The verification performance is acceptable for the size of model used in this evaluation, however more comprehensive evaluation needs to be conducted to better understand how it performs with different sizes of model.

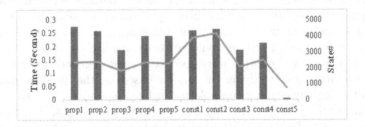

Fig. 8. Performance result

Other advantages of our approach are with the formal modelling of software architecture design. As the formal model facilitates the application of formal techniques, the ontology reasoning and model checking can be extended to support other aspects of verification. For example, the ontology definition can be defined to represent the security characteristics that measure and compare security between current and target architecture designs. Also, the model checking technique can be used to trace different execution scenarios to determine security vulnerability or design flaws.

5   Related Work

Fowler [7] presented a principle of how we can refactor the source code to eliminate design flaws. Most of these design flaws pose difficulties in maintaining the software system. Luca et al. [14] and Yun et al. [11] proposed automated approaches that suggest refactoring plans using search-based algorithm. However, these tools are performed on the source code and rely on the user feedback, unlike our approach that focuses at the architectural design level and rely on the formal logics. Tanhaei et al. [17] presented a framework for refactoring the architecture of software product lines (SPLs). Their approach aims to keep SPLs consistent with the feature model consisted of a set of similarities and differences. However, this approach requires a custom algorithm to reason and check the models, unlike our approach that is based on standard techniques such as ontology reasoning and model checking. Some guidelines such as Zimmermann [20], [2] have been proposed to support the migration to modern architecture style such as microservice and cloud-based software system. Holmes and Zdun [9] proposed an automated architectural refactoring approach for security and availability requirements. Their approach has applied formalised architectural knowledge in model verification and transformation. Their work focuses particularly on the infrastructure of cloud application, while our approach generally focuses on the logical view of architecture design with different architectural styles. Nunes et al. [12] proposed a complete workflow to support the migration to microservice architecture. Their approach applies the static analysis of the source code that is limited to a development framework. Bucchiarone et al. [3] proposed a model-driven approach for the automatic migration to microservice architecture. A meta-programming framework has been applied to transform the source code and generate the container configuration; however, it does not address how to ensure that the migrated system would correctly operate.

Overall, none of the existing works proposes a set of generic rules that support restructuring and verifying the design based on the architectural style. The architectural styles allow technologies to be exploited in the system implementation to take various advantages, as discussed in Sect. 3.3. Also, none has proposed to apply the formal technique to verify the target architecture design, so it is difficult to extend the verification to check other properties as the existing approaches rely on custom algorithms hard-coded in the tools. The verification in our approach can be extended by defining liveness property in LTL to describe other functional requirements or architectural pattern constraints.

6 Conclusion

In this paper, we introduce the formal approach to support architectural migration towards emerging architectural styles. A set of generic rules has been proposed to automate the refactoring and checking the architectural design according to the functional requirements and architectural styles. The verification ensures that the key functional requirements are still preserved after the design has been changed. Also, it ensures that the migrated system behaves according to the desired architectural styles. With the new architectural styles applied, new technologies can be exploited at the system implementation to enhance the system's qualities. The evaluation has proved that the refactoring rules are valid and practical to perform architectural migration for the subject systems.

As architectural migration is a part of system migration, we will extend this approach to automatically plan incremental migration steps that support system migration towards the target architecture.

References

1. Balalaie, A., Heydarnoori, A., Jamshidi, P.: Migrating to cloud-native architectures using microservices: an experience report. In: Celesti, A., Leitner, P. (eds.) ESOCC Workshops 2015. CCIS, vol. 567, pp. 201–215. Springer, Cham (2016). https://doi.org/10.1007/978-3-319-33313-7_15
2. Balalaie, A., Heydarnoori, A., Jamshidi, P., Tamburri, D., Lynn, T.: Microservices migration patterns. Softw.: Pract. Exp. **48**, 2019–2042 (2018)
3. Bucchiarone, A., Soysal, K., Guidi, C.: A model-driven approach towards automatic migration to microservices. In: Bruel, J.-M., Mazzara, M., Meyer, B. (eds.) DEVOPS 2019. LNCS, vol. 12055, pp. 15–36. Springer, Cham (2020). https://doi.org/10.1007/978-3-030-39306-9_2
4. Chondamrongkul, N., Sun, J., Warren, I.: Ontology-based software architectural pattern recognition and reasoning. In: 30th International Conference on Software Engineering and Knowledge Engineering (SEKE), pp. 25–34, June 2018
5. Chondamrongkul, N., Sun, J., Warren, I.: PAT approach to architecture behavioural verification. In: 31th International Conference on Software Engineering and Knowledge Engineering, pp. 187–192, July 2019
6. Ford, N., Parsons, R., Kua, P.: Building Evolutionary Architectures: Support Constant Change. O'Reilly Media Inc., Sebastopol (2017)
7. Fowler, M.: Refactoring: Improving the Design of Existing Code. A Martin Fowler Signature Book. Addison-Wesley, Boston (2019)
8. Garlan, D., et al.: Documenting Software Architectures: Views and Beyond, 2nd edn. Addison-Wesley Professional, Boston (2010)
9. Holmes, T., Zdun, U.: Refactoring architecture models for compliance with custom requirements. In: Proceedings of the 21th ACM/IEEE MODELS 2018, pp. 267–277. Association for Computing Machinery, New York (2018)
10. Klettke, M., Thalheim, B.: Evolution and migration of information systems. In: Embley, D., Thalheim, B. (eds.) Handbook of Conceptual Modeling, pp. 381–419. Springer, Heidelberg (2011). https://doi.org/10.1007/978-3-642-15865-0_12
11. Lin, Y., Peng, X., Cai, Y., Dig, D., Zheng, D., Zhao, W.: Interactive and guided architectural refactoring with search-based recommendation. In: Proceedings of the 2016 24th ACM SIGSOFT International Symposium on Foundations of Software Engineering FSE 2016, pp. 535–546. Association for Computing Machinery, New York (2016)
12. Nunes, L., Santos, N., Rito Silva, A.: From a monolith to a microservices architecture: an approach based on transactional contexts. In: Bures, T., Duchien, L., Inverardi, P. (eds.) ECSA 2019. LNCS, vol. 11681, pp. 37–52. Springer, Cham (2019). https://doi.org/10.1007/978-3-030-29983-5_3
13. Richards, M.: Software Architecture Patterns. O'Reilly Media Inc., Sebastopol (2015)
14. Rizzi, L., Fontana, F.A., Roveda, R.: Support for architectural smell refactoring. In: Proceedings of the 2nd International Workshop on Refactoring IWoR 2018, pp. 7–10. Association for Computing Machinery, New York (2018)
15. Stopford, B.: Designing Event-Driven Systems. O'Reilly, Sebastopol (2018)

16. Sun, J., Liu, Y., Dong, J.S., Chen, C.: Integrating specification and programs for system modeling and verification. In: Proceedings of the Third IEEE International Symposium on Theoretical Aspects of Software Engineering (TASE 2009), pp. 127–135. IEEE Computer Society (2009)
17. Tanhaei, M., Habibi, J., Mirian-Hosseinabadi, S.H.: A feature model based framework for refactoring software product line architecture. J. Comput. Sci. Technol. **31**, 951–986 (2016)
18. Ulrich, W.: Introduction to architecture-driven modernization. In: Ulrich, W.M., Newcomb, P.H. (eds.) Information Systems Transformation, pp. 3–34. The MK/OMG Press, Morgan Kaufmann, Boston (2010)
19. Xu, X., Pautasso, C., Zhu, L., Lu, Q., Weber, I.: A pattern collection for blockchain-based applications. In: Proceedings of the 23rd European Conference on Pattern Languages of Programs EuroPLoP 2018. Association for Computing Machinery, New York (2018)
20. Zimmermann, O.: Architectural refactoring for the cloud: a decision-centric view on cloud migration. Computing **99**, 129–145 (2017)

Monolith Migration Complexity Tuning Through the Application of Microservices Patterns

João Franscisco Almeida and António Rito Silva[✉][ID]

INESC-ID/Department of Computer Science and Engineering,
Instituto Superior Técnico, Av. Rovisco Pais 1, 1049-001 Lisbon, Portugal
{joao.santos.almeida,rito.silva}@tecnico.ulisboa.pt

Abstract. The microservices architecture has become mainstream for the development of business applications because it supports the adaptation of scalability to the type of demand, but, most importantly, because it fosters an agile development process based on small teams focused on the product. Therefore, there is the need to migrate the existing monolith systems to microservices. Current approaches to the identification of candidate microservices in a monolith neglect the cost of redesigning the monolith functionality due to the impact of the CAP theorem. In this paper we propose a redesign process, guided by a set of complexity metrics, that allows the software architect to analyse and redesign the monolith functionality given a candidate decomposition. Both, the redesign process and the metrics are evaluated in the context of candidate decompositions of two monolith systems.

Keywords: Microservices architecture · Monolith migration · Complexity metrics · Microservices patterns

1 Introduction

Microservices architecture emerged due to the need to have highly available and scalable systems that can be developed by multiple teams in an agile environment. This is achieved through the definition of independently deployable distributed systems, implemented around business capabilities. As the monolith application size increases, it imposes several drawbacks as the lack of agility, modifiability and deployablity. As a consequence there is the need to migrate monolith systems to a microservices architecture.

However, this transition imposes a cost because the application cannot preserve the behavior that existed in the monolith. This is due to the introduction of distributed transactions, as the monolith functionalities will be implemented through multiple independent microservices (transactions). Therefore, transaction management is more complex in a microservice architecture because transactions cannot be executed according to the ACID (Atomicity, Consistency, Isolation, Durability) properties, which introduces extra complexity for developers

© Springer Nature Switzerland AG 2020
A. Jansen et al. (Eds.): ECSA 2020, LNCS 12292, pp. 39–54, 2020.
https://doi.org/10.1007/978-3-030-58923-3_3

to handle. This extra complexity is explained by the CAP theorem [6], where the decision to maintain the same level of consistency as in a monolith can only be achieved through the application of a two-phase commit protocol, which does not scale with many local transactions. To solve this problem, the use of sagas [5] was suggested, in the context of the microservices architecture [11,13], as the main alternative to the two-phase commit protocol to handle distributed transactions. On the other hand, the *API Gateway* pattern has been proposed [11,13] to implement queries in a distributed system.

The *SAGA* pattern can be applied to functionalities that create or update data, and consist in dividing a transaction in multiple local transactions, where each local transaction is executed inside a single service following the ACID properties. A saga can have two different structures: (1) choreography where the decision and sequencing is distributed through the saga participants, or (2) orchestration, where the decision and sequencing is decided in one orchestractor class, inside a cluster. Independently of the structure, the usage of sagas can guarantee the properties atomicity, consistency, and durability but cannot ensure the isolation property [13].

The lack of isolation can generate anomalies such as: (1) lost updates - when a saga overwrites data without reading changes performed by others sagas, (2) dirty reads - when a saga reads data changed by others sagas that have not been committed, (3) nonrepeatable reads - a saga reads the same data twice and gets different results. To correct this anomalies there is a set of countermeasures that can be applied. One of them is the semantic lock that corrects these errors by creating intermediate states as application-level locks that indicate if an entity was written by one saga, alerting others concurrent sagas to these events. It can be integrated with the *SAGA* pattern typically indicating the current saga state. Because now all the functionalities must be aware of the semantic lock, this imposes extra complexity to the functionalities design and implementation. It also adds complexity to queries, that have to handle the possible combination of semantic locks of the data that they are integrating.

Due to the lack of isolation, the saga local transactions can be of three types: (1) pivot - a transaction that if succeeds then the saga is going to succeed; (2) retriable - transactions that occur after the pivot transactions, do not rollback; and (3) compensatable - the transactions that may have to rollback. In a saga there is at most one pivot transaction, and all transactions that are not retriable nor the pivot transaction, are compensatable.

In previous work [12,14], a tool was developed that collects information from monolith systems and, based on similarity measures, suggests a microservice candidate decomposition. Its level of complexity can be assessed through a complexity metric that determines the decomposition complexity based on the mean of its functionalities complexity. This metric calculates the impact that the relaxing of atomic transactional behaviour has on the redesign and implementation of the functionalities. In this paper we leverage on the previous work by, given a decomposition and a complexity value, support the redesign of the functionalities and queries, applying the *SAGA* and the *API Gateway* patterns, while the complexity value is tuned, because there is more precise information on the decomposition. With our approach we intend to answer the following questions:

- **RQ1.** What set of operations can be provided to the architect such that the functionalities can be redesigned by applying the *SAGA* pattern?
- **RQ2.** Is it possible to refine the complexity value associated with the monolith migration when there is additional information about the functionalities redesign?

This paper makes two contributions. First, we define a set of operations that the architect can apply to the initial execution flow of a monolith functionality, such that it can be transformed in a microservices execution flow based on the *SAGA* pattern. Second, we define new metrics that provide a more precise value on the cost of the migration, due to the inclusion of the information about the application of the *SAGA* pattern.

In the next section we present the set of operations used in the redesign. In Sect. 3 we present the new complexity metrics. In Sect. 4 we evaluate our work in the context of two monolith systems. Section 5 addresses the related work and Sect. 6 the conclusions.

2   Functionality Redesign

Definition: Monolith. A monolith is a pair (F, E), where F represents its set of functionalities, the functionalities are represented with lower case f, and E represents its set of domain entities, which are accessed by the functionalities, the domain entities are represented with lower case e.

The entities are accessed by the functionalities in two modes, read and write. Therefore, $M = \{r, w\}$ represents the access modes in a monolith, and an access is a pair domain entity access mode, represented by (e, m).

The accesses of a functionality f are represented as a sequence of accesses s, where S represents all the sequences of accesses done in the monolith by its functionalities to the domain entities, $f.sequence$ denotes the sequence of access of functionality f, $s.entities$ denotes the entities accessed in sequence s.

It is also defined the auxiliary function $entities(s : S, m : M) : 2^E$, as $entities(s, m) = \{e \in E : (e, m) \in s\}$, which returns the entities accessed in s in mode m.

When a monolith is decomposed into a set of candidate microservices, each candidate microservice is a cluster of domain entities.

Definition: Monolith Decomposition. A monolith decomposition into a set of candidate microservices is defined by a set of clusters C of the monolith domain entities, where each cluster c represents a candidate microservice and $c.entities$ denote the domain entities in cluster c, such that all domain entities are in a cluster, $\bigcup_{c \in C} c.entities = E$, and in a single one, $\forall_{c_i \neq c_j \in C} c_i.entities \cap c_j.entities = \emptyset$.

Given $e \in E$ and a decomposition C, $e.cluster$ denotes the entity's cluster, and given a set of entities $E' \subseteq E$, $E'.cluster = \{c \in C : \exists_{e \in E'} e \in c.entities\}$ denotes its set of entities clusters.

Given a monolith candidate decomposition, the monolith functionalities are decomposed into a set of local transactions, where each local transaction corresponds to the ACID execution of part of the functionality domain entity accesses in the context of a candidate microservice.

Definition: Functionality Decomposition. A monolith functionality f is decomposed, in the context of a candidate decomposition C, by a sequence of sequences of access to domain entities, denoted by $f.subsequences$, where all domain entities in a subsequence are in the same cluster, $\forall_{s \in f.subsequences} \exists_{c \in C}$: $s.entities \subseteq c.entities$, two consecutive subsequences occur in different clusters, $\forall_{0 \leq i < f.subsequences.size-1}$ $f.subsequences[i].entities.cluster \neq f.subsequences$ $[i+1].entities.cluster$. In order to have a consistent subsequence associated with a functionality f in a decomposition, the following condition must hold:

$$concat_{i=0..f.subsequences.size-1}(f.subsequences[i]) = prune(f.sequence)$$

Where the *prune* function removes, for each sequence of accesses inside each cluster $c \in C$, the accesses according to the following rules: (1) if a domain entity is read, all subsequent reads of that entity are removed, (2) if an domain entity is written, all subsequent accesses of that entity are removed. A sequence of domain entity accesses where these two rules hold is pruned, it only contains the read and write accesses that are visible outside the cluster, the ones that are relevant for the semantic lock countermeasure.

In the redesign of a functionality in the context of a decomposition we define the set of local transactions participating in the saga that implements the functionality.

Definition: Local Transaction. A local transaction lt of a functionality f, is a pair (s, t), where s is a pruned sequence of access domain entities, all its accesses are to domain entities of the same cluster, $\exists_{c \in C} : s.sequence.entities \subseteq c.entities$, and t is the transaction type, which can be *compensatable*, *pivot*, and *retriable*.

T denotes the set of transaction types, LT denotes the set of local transactions in a decomposition, lt denotes a local transaction, $lt.cluster$ denotes the cluster where the lt occurs, $lt.sequence$ denotes the sequence of accesses, and $lt.type$ denotes the type of the local transaction.

A local transaction sequence should be pruned, for each domain entity in the sequence there is 0..1 read accesses and 0..1 write accesses, and when there is a read and a write access to the same domain entity, the read access has to occur first. These are the accesses that have impact outside the local transaction atomic execution.

The redesign of a functionality in the context of a decomposition corresponds to the application of a set of operations to a graph which represents the functionality execution, where the nodes represent the functionalities' local transactions and the edges the remote invocations between transactions.

Definition: Functionality Execution Graph. A functionality f redesign in the context of a monolith decomposition is represented by a graph g, where the nodes are local transactions, denoted by $g.lt$, and the edges remote invocations between local transactions, denoted by $g.ri$:

- $g.lt$ is the set of local transactions, such that:
  1. $\bigcup_{lt \in g.lt} lt.sequence.entities = f.sequence.entities$
  2. $\#\{lt \in g.lt : lt.type = pivot)\} \leq 1$
- $g.ri$ is the set of local transactions pairs that represent the remote invocations:
  1. $\forall_{(lt_i, lt_j) \in g.ri}\{lt_i, lt_j\} \subseteq g.lt$
  2. $\forall_{(lt_i, lt_j) \in g.ri} \neg \exists_{lt_{k \neq i} \in g.lt}(lt_k, lt_j) \in g.ri$
  3. The remote invocations define a partial order between the local transactions, denoted by $<_g$, and build using the transitive closure of the following initial elements, $\forall_{(lt_i, lt_j) \in g.lt} lt_i <_g lt_j$. Therefore, given $lt_i, lt_j \in g.lt$ if $lt_i <_g lt_j$ then lt_i executes before lt_j.

The redesign of a functionality in the context of a decomposition starts with its initial graph, which is generated from the functionality decomposition.

Definition: Initial Graph. The initial graph g_I of a functionality f has as vertices the local transactions lt associated to each one of the subsequences of f, $g_I.lt = \{lt \in LT : lt.sequence \in f.subsequences \land lt.type$ is not defined$\}$, and has as edges the pairs of local transactions associated with consecutive subsequences, $(lt_j, lt_k) \in g_I.ri$ iff $\exists_{0 \leq i < f.subsequences.size-1} : lt_j.sequence = f.subsequences[i] \land lt_k.sequence = f.subsequences[i+1]$. It is trivial to observe that the initial graph g_I is a well-formed graph of f.

A semantic lock is an intermediate state set by a compensatable local transaction, a write access, that is visible by the other functionalities, and that may eventually be undone.

Definition: Local Transaction Semantic Lock. Given an execution graph g of a functionality f, and one of its local transactions lt, $lt.sl$ denotes the domain entities with a semantic lock in lt, such that $lt.sl = \bigcup_{(e,m) \in lt.sequence}(lt.type = compensatable \land m = w)$.

Definition: Functionality Semantic Lock. Given an execution graph g of a functionality f, $g.sl$ denotes the domain entities with a semantic lock in g, such that $g.sl = \bigcup_{lt \in g.lt} lt.sl$.

Definition: Final Graph. A final graph g_F of a functionality f is a graph of f where all transactions have a type, $\forall_{lt \in g_F.lt} lt.type$ *is defined*, and all the transactions that follow the pivot transaction are retriable, given $lt_i \in g_F.lt : lt_i.type = pivot \implies \forall_{j t_j : lt_i <_{g_F} lt_j} lt_j.type = retriable$. Additionally, it is not possible to have a remote invocation between local transactions belonging to the same cluster, $\forall_{(lt_i, lt_j) \in g_F.ri}\{lt_i.cluster \neq lt_j.cluster\}$. Given that a graph has at most one pivot transaction, and in a final graph all transactions have a defined type, it is trivial to observe that all the transactions that do not occur after the pivot transaction should be compensatable.

Definition: Redesign Process. The redesign of a functionality f is a process that starts with its initial graph g_I and through the application of graph operations produces a final graph g_F, where, in a first step, the software architect will perform operations over the execution graph to redesign the execution flow of f, and, finally the architect will characterize the type of local transactions, such that the $SAGA$ pattern is applied to the functionality f in the context of the monolith decomposition.

We propose three basic operations and a composed operation to support the redesign of a functionality. The basic operations are: *Sequence Change*, where the order by which the local transactions are invoked is changed; *Local Transaction Merge*, where two local transactions belonging to the same cluster are merged; and, *Add Compensating*, where a new local transaction is added when it is necessary to undo the changes done by local transactions. Additionally, we propose a composed operation, *Define Coarse-Grained Interactions*, where repetitive fine-grained interactions between two candidate microservices are synthesized into a single coarse-grained interaction.

By applying these operations, the software architect transforms the sequence of local transactions in the initial graph to a saga like interaction, either an orchestration or a choreography, where in the former case there is a cluster that coordinates the execution flow between the local transactions.

Definition: Sequence Change. Given a graph g of functionality f, three distinct local transactions, $lt_1, lt_2, lt_3 \in g.lt$ where $lt_1 \neq lt_2 \neq lt_3 \neq lt_1$, $lt_3 <_g lt_2$, and a remote invocation $ri = (lt_1, lt_2) \in g.ri$, it is possible to replace ri by $ri' = (lt_3, lt_2)$, such that g is transformed to $g' = (g.lt, g.ri \setminus \{ri\} \cup ri')$, a graph of f. It is trivial to observe that the transformed graph is a well-formed graph of f in the context of the decomposition, because lt_3 executes before lt_2 we can conclude that the resulting order continues to be a partial order and all local transactions are remotely invoked by at most one local transaction.

The *change sequence* operation is used to change the flow of execution of the functionality in the context of the decomposition and it is possible to apply when no local transaction in the invocation chain between lt_3 and lt_2 requires data produced by lt_2. For instance, to change the local transaction (hence the cluster) that is responsible to trigger the execution of another particular local transaction, which may be useful to centralize the control of execution in a microservice that coordinates the execution of other local transactions, and so reduce the transactional complexity behavior.

Definition: Local Transaction Merge. Given a graph g of functionality f and two local transaction $lt_1, lt_2 \in g.lt$, such that they belong to the same cluster, $lt_1.cluster = lt_2.cluster$, and they have adjacent executions, either (1) $(lt_1, lt_2) \in g.ri$ or (2) $\exists_{lt_i \in g.lt} : (lt_i, lt_1) \in g.ri \wedge (lt_i, lt_2) \in g.ri$, a new graph g' of f is produced, where, considering the two cases: (1) $g'.lt = g.lt \setminus \{lt_1, lt_2\} \cup lt_m$, where $lt_m.sequence = prune(concat(lt_1.sequence, lt_2.sequence))$ and $g'.ri = g.ri \setminus \{(lt_1, lt_2)\} \setminus \{(lt_o, lt_1) : (lt_o, lt_1) \in g.ri\} \setminus \{(lt_k, lt_l) \in g.ri : lt_k = lt_1 \vee lt_k = lt_2\} \cup \{(lt_o, lt_m) : (lt_o, lt_1) \in g.ri\} \cup \{(lt_m, lt_i) : (lt_1, lt_i) \in g.ri \vee (lt_2, lt_i) \in g.ri\}$; (2) $g'.lt = g.lt \setminus \{lt_1, lt_2\} \cup lt_m$, where $lt_m.sequence =$

$prune(concat(lt_1.sequence, lt_2.sequence))$ or $lt_m.sequence = prune(concat(lt_2$
$.sequence, lt_1.sequence))$, and $g'.ri = g.ri \setminus \{(lt_i, lt_1), (lt_i, lt_2)\} \setminus \{(lt_k, lt_l) \in g.ri :$
$lt_k = lt_1 \vee lt_k = lt_2\} \cup \{(lt_i, lt_m)\} \cup \{(lt_m, lt_l) : (lt_1, tl_l) \in g.ri \vee (lt_2, tl_l) \in g.ri\}$.

The *local transaction merge* operation is used when, in the redesign process, two local transactions become adjacent in the execution graph, and can be included into a single local transaction. From the transactional perspective, it is necessary to integrate their execution sequences, what is achieved with the prune function, and in the second case, is the software architect that decide the order by which the sequences are integrated. As result of applying this operation, the number of intermediate states in result of the distributed execution of the functionality is reduced.

Definition: Add Compensating. Given a graph g of functionality f, a new graph $g' = (g.lt \cup \{lt_c\}, g.ri \cup \{ri_c\})$ of f is produced, where $lt_c \notin g.lt$, $lt_c.sequence.entities = \bigcup_{lt_i \in g.lt}\{e \in entities(lt_i.sequence, w) : lt_i.cluster = lt_c.cluster \wedge lt_i.type = compensatable \wedge lt_i <_g ri_c[1]\}, \forall_{(e,m) \in lt_c.sequence} m = w$, $ri_c \notin g.ri$ and $ri_c = (lt_j, lt_c)$, where $lt_j.cluster \neq lt_c.cluster \wedge lt_j \in g.lt$.

This operation is used to create new local transactions that access some of the domain entities changed by other local transactions. It can be used to create the compensating transactions that are necessary for each compensatable transaction.

Definition: Define Coarse-Grained Interactions: Given a graph g of functionality f, two candidate microservices, represented by the clusters $c_1 \neq c_2$, two remote invocations $\{(lt_{11}, lt_{21}), (lt_{12}, lt_{22})\} \in g.ri$, where the remote invocations are between the given microservices, $c_1 = lt_{11}.cluster = lt_{12}.cluster \wedge c_2 = lt_{21}.cluster = lt_{22}.cluster$, and lt_{11} executes before lt_{12}, $lt_{11} <_g lt_{12}$, a new graph g' of f is produced by applying the basic operations *change sequence* and *local transaction merge*. First, *change sequence* operation is applied for lt_{11} and (lt_i, lt_{12}), to produce a new graph with remote invocation (lt_{11}, lt_{12}). Note that is possible to apply the operation, because $lt_{11} <_g lt_{12}$ and so there exists the remote invocation (lt_i, lt_{12}). Then, *local transaction merge* operation is applied to lt_{11}, lt_{12} to produce a new local transaction lt_{1m} which has remote invocations to lt_{21} and lt_{22}. Finally, *local transaction merge* operation is applied to lt_{21} and lt_{22} which results in lt_{2m} local transaction and a coarser-grained remote invocation (lt_{1m}, lt_{2m}). Note that this operation can be applied to any number of remote invocations between two cluster, in the given conditions.

This operation is used to create two coarse-grained local transactions, one in c_1 and another in c_2, by joining local transactions that are executed in those clusters, in order to reduce the number of remote invocations. It must be used when, after the automatically generated decomposition, the software architect realizes that there are several recurring fine-grained interactions between two candidate microservices, due to an object-oriented programming style in the monolith, which promotes the use of fine-grained invocations between the domain entities.

After the operations have been applied to the initial graph g_I of functionality f, the last step of the redesign is to produce a final graph g_F through the characterization of each one of the local transactions. Therefore, the software architect must select one transaction in the graph to be the *pivot* transaction. Transactions that follow the pivot transaction are guaranteed to succeed are classified as *retriable*, and all other local transactions are classified as *compensatable*. The compensatable transactions that have semantic locks need to have at least one compensating transaction because some of the transactions that execute after it in the saga might fail.

3   Complexity Metrics

Given a monolith decomposition, the base metric [14] was defined in previous works, which measures the complexity associated with the migration of a monolith system to a microservices architecture. It considers the complexity of each functionality redesign for the overall complexity of redesigning the monolith system, due to relaxing the functionality execution isolation, because the redesign of a functionality has to consider the intermediate states introduced by the execution of other functionalities.

Definition: Functionality Complexity in a Decomposition. Given a candidate decomposition C of a monolith, the complexity associated with the migration of a monolith functionality f is given by

$$\sum_{s_i \in f.subsequences} \# \bigcup_{(e,m) \in s_i} \{f_i \in F \setminus \{f\} : (e, m^{-1}) \in prune(f_i.sequence)\}$$

Where f_i is a distributed transaction, it executes in more than one cluster, and m^{-1} represents the inverse access mode, $r^{-1} = w$ and $w^{-1} = r$.

The overall idea behind the metric is to count, for each subsequence of a functionality, executing inside a cluster, the impact domain entities accesses have. The impact of a write depends on other functionalities that read it, and, therefore, they may have to consider this new intermediate state, while the impact of a read depends on how many other functionalities write it, and, therefore, introduce new intermediate states to be considered by the functionality. This metric reflects how many other functionalities need to be considered in the redesign of a functionality, thus, how the functionality redesign is intertwined with others functionalities business logic redesign.

However, during the redesign process, while the functionalities are redesigned, the concepts of local transaction and remote invocation are introduced, which allows a refinement of the previous metrics, such that, during the redesign process, the software architect can have more precise values about the complexity.

Therefore, and because the metric will be used to inform the functionality redesign activity, we distinguish between the complexity of redesigning the functionality from the complexity that the functionality redesign adds to the redesign of other functionalities.

Definition: Functionality Redesign Complexity. The complexity of redesigning a functionality f, executed as a graph g, is the sum of the complexity of each one of its local transaction:

$$complexity(f) = \sum_{lt \in g.lt} complexity(lt)$$

The complexity of one local transaction depends on the number of semantic locks that are introduced, because each semantic lock corresponds to an intermediate state for which may be necessary to write a compensating transaction, and it also depends on the intermediate states set by other functionalities that the local transaction may have to consider in its reads. Note that, during the redesign of a functionality, some of the functionalities that f interacts with may not have been redesigned yet, and so, the metric should take into account both situations.

Definition: Local Transaction Redesign Complexity. The complexity of lt is given by the number of semantic locks implemented in entities of $lt.sequence$, plus the number of other functionalities that write in entities read in lt, or which have semantic locks in those entities:

$$complexity(lt) = \#lt.sl + \sum_{(e,r) \in lt.sequence} \#\{f_i \in F \setminus \{f\} : (e, w) \in writes(f_i)\}$$

where

$$writes(f_i) = \begin{cases} \{(e, w) : (e, w) \in prune(f_i.sequence)\} & \text{if } f_i \text{ not redesigned} \\ \{(e, w) : (e, w) \in g_i.sl\} & \text{if } f_i \text{ redesigned as } g_i \end{cases}$$

Note that when a functionality is redesigned some writes may not be considered, because if they belong to pivot or retriable local transactions, they will not introduce intermediate states, and so, the metric will provide a more precise value.

The redesign of a functionality impacts on other functionalities redesign complexity. For instance, if a semantic lock is created in one entity e due to the execution of a functionality f_i then every other functionality f_j (where $i \neq j$) that read the same entity e must have to be changed to accommodate the existence of the semantic lock. Hence, the cost of redesigning f_j depends on the amount of semantic locks created by f_i in entities that f_j access.

Definition: System Added Complexity. Given the redesign of a functionality f executed as a graph g, the system added complexity introduced by redesign g, is given by:

$$addedComplexity(f, g) = \sum_{lt \in g.lt} \sum_{f_i \in F \setminus \{f\}} \#(reads(f_i).entities \cap lt.sl.entities)$$

where

$$reads(f_i) = \begin{cases} \{(e, r) : (e, r) \in prune(f_i.sequence)\} & \text{if } f_i \text{ not redesigned} \\ \{(e, r) : \exists_{lt \in g_i.lt}(e, r) \in lt.sequence\} & \text{if } f_i \text{ redesigned as } g_i \end{cases}$$

The redesign of functionality f may introduce inconsistent states in the application when it has two or more semantic locks. However, this situation only occurs when the entities belong to different clusters, because inside one cluster the entities are updated simultaneously by ACID transactions. Hence, we consider that a functionality changes a cluster when it introduces a semantic lock in one of its entities. If we consider that a functionality f writes in more than one cluster, this behaviour may introduce inconsistency views for any other functionality f_i that reads two or more of the changed clusters. Therefore, any functionality f_i that reads domain entities in different clusters, previously changed by f, might encounter inconsistent states.

From a redesign point of view, the inconsistency state complexity is particular relevant for functionalities that only read and have a single local transaction for each cluster they access. We call queries to this type of functionalities.

Definition: Query. A query q is functionality which graph g has the following properties: (1) its local transactions are read only, $\forall_{lt \in g.lt} lt.sequence.mode = \{r\}$; and (2) they only access a cluster at most once, $\forall_{lt_i \neq lt_j \in g.lt} lt_i.cluster \neq lt_j.cluster$.

Note that, if there is a functionality that only has read accesses, it is possible, by applying the redesign operations, to generate an execution graph that is a query. We define the cost of implementing a query as the inconsistency state it has to handle.

Definition: Query Inconsistency Complexity. Given a query q, its inconsistency complexity is the sum of all the other functionalities that write in at least two clusters that q also reads:

$$queryInconsistencyComplexity(q) =$$

$$\#\{f_i \in F \setminus \{q\} : \#clusters(entities(prune(q.sequence)) \cap writes(f_i).entities) > 1\}$$

where $writes(f_i)$ is defined as in the local transaction complexity metric.

4   Evaluation

To evaluate the operations and metrics presented we analyzed two systems, LdoD[1] (122 controllers, 67 domain entities) and Blended Workflow[2] (98 controllers, 49 domain entities)[3]. Since the operations and metrics are applied in the context of a candidate decomposition, we used the expert decompositions of these systems. As the main goal of this work is to refine the existing complexity metric we start by showing that the base metric and the new metrics are correlated, when applied for the initial graph where every local transaction is typed

---

as compensatable. In Fig. 1 we can observe the correlation graphs, for the monolith functionalities, where each point represent for one functionality its values according to the base metric and to the sum of the refined metrics, complexity and added complexity. It can be observed that the metrics are correlated.

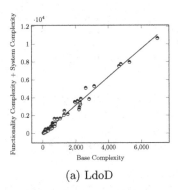

(a) LdoD

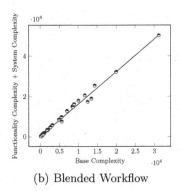

(b) Blended Workflow

Fig. 1. Correlation between the base metric and the sum of Functionality complexity and System complexity

4.1   Operations Evaluation

Firstly, the set of redesign operations were defined, and formalized, after an extensive experimentation by the expert that identified which changes have to be applied to the decomposition of a functionality to create a suitable SAGA implementation, while preserving its semantics.

To validate the proposed operations we started by filtering the functionalities in each system. The goal is to have two sets of functionalities, one with the functionalities that perform some create, update or delete operation (CUD operations), i.e, functionalities that write domain entities and that will be implemented using the *SAGA* pattern, and another with the functionalities that only read entities, i.e, functionalities that are queries and which implementation is done using other type of patterns, e.g. *API Gateway* pattern. Then, for each system, we performed a quartile analysis over the complexities in the CUD set where we got 4 distinct groups of functionalities, grouped by their complexity. We randomly picked a functionality from each group and after careful analysis of the source code we applied the operations to redesign the functionality for the given decomposition. The redesign goal was done to achieve a saga orchestration style as recommended in [13], to minimise the remote invocations between services and reduce the network latency effect.

In Table 1 are, for each of the selected functionalities, the number of operations performed to the initial execution graph of each functionality in the systems LdoD and Blended Workflow, and, for the final execution graph, the number of transactions of each type, the total number of local transactions and the total

Table 1. Operations performed and local transactions types in the functionalities of LdoD and Blended Workflow. C - Compensatable; P - Pivot; R - Retriable; # Clusters - number of accessed clusters; SC - Sequence Change; AD - Add compensating; DCGI - Define Coarse-Grained Interactions.

Functionality	Operations			Local transactions					Metrics	
	SC	AC	DCGI	C	P	R	Total	#Clusters	Sum for g_I	Sum for g_F
LdoD										
Q1: removeTweets	–	–	2	0	0	4	4	4	442	88
Q2: getTaxonomy	2	–	1	0	1	4	5	3	529	208
Q3: associateCategory	5	4	8	8	1	5	14	4	3470	783
Q4: signUp	–	–	4	0	1	5	6	4	3861	413
Blended workflow										
Q1: updateView	2	1	1	2	1	1	4	3	415	97
Q2: removeSequence ConditionToActivity	–	–	3	2	1	3	6	2	1110	301
Q3: addActivity	1	1	4	6	1	1	8	3	3343	1402
Q4: extractActivity	–	4	19	25	1	3	29	4	20628	5992

number of accessed clusters. Additionally, it presents the sum of the two complexity metrics, for the initial and final graph. We can observe that the number of operations performed to a functionality generally increases as the sum of the refined metrics increases, which seems to indicate that more complex functionalities have more room for improvement. We can also observe that, to preserve the data dependencies in the functionality, it is not possible to apply the operations until the number of local transactions is equal to the number of accessed clusters.

In what concerns the local transactions types, one clear and obvious conclusion, since the complexity depends on the number of local transactions, is that the sum of the refined metrics increases with the number of transactions. We can also observe that the number of compensatable transactions impacts on the complexity. This is due to the fact that the existence of compensatable transactions involves the creation of semantic locks (if the access mode is write) and also the creation of more transactions to implement the compensating transactions logic needed in case of a transaction abort.

4.2   Complexity Metrics Evaluation

Table 2 shows the complexities for each functionality analyzed in the systems LdoD e Blended Workflow. We can observe that for both systems the reduction in the functionality complexity surpasses, in average, 50%. This shows the advantage of the proposed redesign operations and the refined metrics. On the other hand, we also observe the relation between the functionality *associateCategory* and *signUp*. Before redesign the *associateCategory* has a lower complexity value than *signUp*. However after the redesigning, and the application of the *SAGA* pattern, that relation is reversed and the complexity value for the *associateCategory* is higher than for *signUp*. This shows that the impact of the redesign operations is not the same and depends on the functionality business logic. Additionally, it shows an advantage of allowing the software architect to redesign the model that results from the automatic decomposition of the monolith, in particular the verification of whether the most complex functionalities, according to the base metric, can or not be significantly reduced.

By analysing the system added complexity values, in both system we got a significant reduction in the complexity values after the redesign, which allows us to provide the architect with more precise values on the impact the functionalities redesign has in the system.

Since the refined metrics separate the base metric into two different concerns, functionality complexity and added complexity to the system, we can do a more rich and precise analysis. For instance, only the functionality *associateCategory* has a non zero value in the LdoD system, which indicates that only this functionality, of the four functionalities analyzed, introduces complexity in to others functionalities redesign despite that in g_I all functionalities had a non zero value. A strong example is the functionality *signUp*, which at the beginning was considered to have the most impact on the system, ended up having no impact on the system since it does not create any semantic locks.

Table 2. Functionality complexity and System complexity for the functionalities in the systems LdoD and Blended Workflow. FRC - Functionality Redesign Complexity; SAC - System Added Complexity.

Functionality	Initial FRC	Final FRC	% Reduction	Initial SAC	Final SAC	% Reduction
LdoD						
Q1: removeTweets	134	88	34%	308	0	100%
Q2: getTaxonomy	317	208	34%	212	0	100%
Q3: associateCategory	1803	677	62%	1667	106	94%
Q4: signUp	1490	413	72%	2371	0	100%
		Average:	50.4%			98.5%
Blended workflow						
Q1: updateView	204	51	75%	211	46	78%
Q2: removeSequence ConditionToActivity	861	301	65%	249	0	100%
Q3: addActivity	1775	712	60%	1548	690	55%
Q4: extractActivity	13849	3269	76%	6779	2723	60%
		Average:	69%			73.25%

When analyzing both tables, it is visible the relation between the existence of compensatable transaction and a positive value for the system complexity, where the only exception is the functionality *removeSequenceConditionToActivity* in the Blended Workflow system that contains 2 compensatable transactions and 0 system complexity. After analysing the final redesign graph we noted that the 2 compensatable transactions were read only transactions. They are considered compensatable because, by definition, all the local transaction that do not occur after the pivot transaction are compensatable, but in this case they do not need a compensating transaction in case of a transaction abort. However, as previously noted in the relation between the number of compensating transactions and complexity, we can conclude that most of the compensating transactions require semantic locks.

Due to space restrictions, the Query Inconsistency Complexity (QIC) analysis is omitted. However its evaluation on queries of both systems (LdoD and Blended Workflow) showed that, despite this new metric does not derive from the base metric, the complexity value from QIC increases as the base metric increases, they are correlated.

To answer the research questions: (1) we have defined a suitable set of operations that the architect can use in the design stage in order to design functionalities in a microservices architecture, (2) by separating the base metric in two distinct metrics we can target different affected areas during the functionalities design and implementation, and we obtained more precise values for the functionality migration cost.

4.3   Threats to Validity

In terms of internal validity, the use of the expert decomposition has no impact on the validation conclusions, actually, to evaluate the metrics refinement and the operations, any candidate decomposition could be used. The validation of the operations was done to a small subset of functionalities, but a systematic method to select them was chosen and functionalities with different levels of complexity were also chosen. Another threat to internal validity is that the redesign was done to follow an orchestration style for the functionalities sagas. However, considering that: (1) we are evaluating the applicability of the redesign operation; (2) evaluating whether the new metrics can provide a more precise value, this is not biased by following a orchestration style, though the complexity values reduction could be smaller, but precise anyway.

In terms of external validity, we believe that our conclusion can be generalized to the monolith systems that were implemented using a rich domain model, which is the case of the two analyzed systems, that were implemented using fine-grained object-oriented interactions.

5   Related Work

Previous work on the migration monolith systems to a microservices architecture [1, 7–9] and on the quality of microservices architectures [2–4], evaluate the candidate decompositions and the microservices architectures through metrics that focus on aspects like modifiability, cohesion, coupling, performance or even the size of clusters. However, they do not analyse the complexity associated with the effort of migrating the monolith, according to the candidate decomposition. Therefore, their focus is not in the complexity added to the functionalities business logic, as explained by the CAP theorem [6]. In this paper we address the effort required in the monolith functionalities redesign and the application of microservices design patterns.

Some research has been done on metrics and microservices patterns. In [15] a set of metrics is proposed to assess the architecture conformance to microservice patterns. Their metrics evaluate characteristics like independent deployability and shared dependencies between components. In [4] it is developed a system that evaluates microservices architectures conformance to a set of microservices design principles. For each principle a metric is defined. None of these research addresses the monolith functionality redesign cost using microservices patterns.

Although there are many proposals on how to decompose a monolith into a microservices architecture, as far as we know, only in [10] is proposed a tool that, besides providing visualisation of the decomposition, allows the creation of new microservices, move classes between microservices, and clone a class in several microservices, while recalculating a set of metrics on the decomposition quality. However, their modeling focus is not on functionality redesign.

The proposed redesign process, and metrics refinement, leverages on our previous work on the decomposition of monolith systems based on the identification of transactional contexts, to reduce the impact of transactional context changes on the functionalities behavior [12], and on a complexity metric for migration decomposition [14].

6   Conclusions

This paper proposes a set of operations for the redesign of monolith functionalities given a decomposition on a set of candidate microservices. The redesign is guided by a set of metrics which calculate the complexity associated with functionalities business logic rewriting, due to the lack of isolation. The *SAGA* pattern is applied to the functionalities and the number of semantic locks is used to calculate the complexity. On the other hand, by dividing the complexity into two distinct metrics, it becomes possible to distinguish between the complexity inherent to the each functionality redesign, and the complexity added in the redesign of other functionalities. As an extension of these two metrics, we also propose a query inconsistency metric that measures the cost of applying the *API Gateway* pattern. As result of the evaluation, we observed that through the application of the operations a suitable execution flow of the functionality, following the *SAGA* patterns, is obtained. As expected, more operations are required when the complexity of the functionality, before the redesign, is higher, but we also observed that the percentage of complexity reduction depends on the business logic functionality.

Acknowledgments. This work was supported by national funds through Fundação para a Ciência e Tecnologia (FCT) with reference UIDB/50021/2020.

References

1. Athanasopoulos, D., Zarras, A.V., Miskos, G., Issarny, V., Vassiliadis, P.: Cohesion-driven decomposition of service interfaces without access to source code. IEEE Trans. Serv. Comput. **8**(4), 550–562 (2015)

2. Bogner, J., Wagner, S., Zimmermann, A.: Automatically measuring the maintainability of service-and microservice-based systems: a literature review. In: Proceedings of the 27th International Workshop on Software Measurement and 12th International Conference on Software Process and Product Measurement, pp. 107–115. ACM (2017)

3. Cardarelli, M., Iovino, L., Di Francesco, P., Di Salle, A., Malavolta, I., Lago, P.: An extensible data-driven approach for evaluating the quality of microservice architectures. In: Proceedings of the 34th ACM/SIGAPP Symposium on Applied Computing, SAC 2019, pp. 1225–1234, New York, NY, USA. Association for Computing Machinery (2019)

4. Engel, T., Langermeier, M., Bauer, B., Hofmann, A.: Evaluation of microservice architectures: a metric and tool-based approach. In: Mendling, J., Mouratidis, H. (eds.) CAiSE 2018. LNBIP, vol. 317, pp. 74–89. Springer, Cham (2018). https://doi.org/10.1007/978-3-319-92901-9_8

5. Garcia-Molina, H., Salem, K.: Sagas. ACM Sigmod Rec. **16**(3), 249–259 (1987)

6. Gilbert, S., Lynch, N.: Perspectives on the CAP theorem. Computer **45**(2), 30–36 (2012)

7. Jin, W., Liu, T., Cai, Y., Kazman, R., Mo, R., Zheng, Q.: Service candidate identification from monolithic systems based on execution traces. IEEE Trans. Softw. Eng. (2019)

8. Klock, S., Van Der Werf, J.M.E., Guelen, J.P., Jansen, S.: Workload-based clustering of coherent feature sets in microservice architectures. In: 2017 IEEE International Conference on Software Architecture (ICSA), pp. 11–20 (2017)

9. Mazlami, G., Cito, J., Leitner, P.: Extraction of microservices from monolithic software architectures. In: 2017 IEEE International Conference on Web Services (ICWS), pp. 524–531 (2017)

10. Nakazawa, R., Ueda, T., Enoki, M., Horii, H.: Visualization tool for designing microservices with the Monolith-first approach. In: 2018 IEEE Working Conference on Software Visualization (VISSOFT), pp. 32–42, September 2018

11. Ntentos, E., Zdun, U., Plakidas, K., Schall, D., Li, F., Meixner, S.: Supporting architectural decision making on data management in microservice architectures. In: Bures, T., Duchien, L., Inverardi, P. (eds.) ECSA 2019. LNCS, vol. 11681, pp. 20–36. Springer, Cham (2019). https://doi.org/10.1007/978-3-030-29983-5_2

12. Nunes, L., Santos, N., Rito Silva, A.: From a Monolith to a microservices architecture: a approach based on transactional contexts. In: Bures, T., Duchien, L., Inverardi, P. (eds.) ECSA 2019. LNCS, vol. 11681, pp. 37–52. Springer, Cham (2019). https://doi.org/10.1007/978-3-030-29983-5_3

13. Richardson, C.: Microservices Patterns. Manning Publications Co. (2019)

14. Santos, N., Silva, A.R.: A complexity metric for microservices architecture migration. In: Proceedings of the IEEE 17th International Conference on Software Architecture (ICSA 2020), pp. 169–178. IEEE (2020)

15. Zdun, U., Navarro, E., Leymann, F.: Ensuring and assessing architecture conformance to microservice decomposition patterns. In: Maximilien, M., Vallecillo, A., Wang, J., Oriol, M. (eds.) ICSOC 2017. LNCS, vol. 10601, pp. 411–429. Springer, Cham (2017). https://doi.org/10.1007/978-3-319-69035-3_29

Uncertainty, Self-adaptive, and Open System

Decentralized Architecture for Energy-Aware Service Assembly

Mauro Caporuscio[1]([⊠]), Mirko D'Angelo[1], Vincenzo Grassi[2],
and Raffaela Mirandola[3]

[1] Linnaeus University, Växjö, Sweden
{mauro.caporuscio,mirko.dangelo}@lnu.se
[2] Università di Roma Tor Vergata, Rome, Italy
vincenzo.grassi@uniroma2.it
[3] Politecnico di Milano, Milan, Italy
raffaela.mirandola@polimi.it

Abstract. Contemporary application domains make more and more appealing the vision of applications built as a dynamic and opportunistic assembly of autonomous and independent resources. However, the adoption of such paradigm is challenged by: (*i*) the openness and scalability needs of the operating environment, which rule out approaches based on centralized architectures and, (*ii*) the increasing concern for sustainability issues, which makes particularly relevant, in addition to QoS constraints, the goal of reducing the application energy footprint. In this context, we contribute by proposing a decentralized architecture to build a fully functional assembly of distributed services, able to optimize its energy consumption, paying also attention to issues concerning the delivered quality of service. We suggest suitable indexes to measure from different perspectives the energy efficiency of the resulting assembly, and present the results of extensive simulation experiments to assess the effectiveness of our approach.

1 Introduction and Motivation

Contemporary systems (for domains including, for example, smart cities, intelligent transportation systems, augmented reality) more and more envision the definition of applications that dynamically emerge as an opportunistic aggregation of autonomous and independent resources available within the execution environment. Service-oriented architecture (SOA), in particular its microservice evolution, appears well suited as reference architectural model for this kind of applications, as it supports the vision of new services built as an assembly of independent services, where each service offers specific functionalities, and could require functionalities offered by others to carry out its own task.

However, to be successfully adopted in these emerging computing environments, the service assembly procedure should be able to tackle the following main issues: (*i*) *decentralization*: services are offered by autonomous and independent

A. Jansen et al. (Eds.): ECSA 2020, LNCS 12292, pp. 57–72, 2020.
https://doi.org/10.1007/978-3-030-58923-3_4

resources distributed in the environment, which makes hardly usable assembly procedures based on the presence of some centralized assembly manager; (*ii*) *dynamics*: the offered services are not statically defined but they appear and disappear or change their behavior; (*iii*) *quality-awareness*: the assembly should be able to guarantee quality of service (QoS) requirements (e.g., timeliness, availability, cost). Besides them, another major issue to be considered is: (*iv*) *energy-awareness*: the assembly should be able to take into account the energy consumption caused by its computation and communication activities. This latter issue is particularly important for several reasons: besides sustainability concerns that are more and more important in the contemporary world, systems often rely on battery-powered resources, where a parsimonious and effective use of available energy is mandatory to extend the system lifetime.

Considerable effort has been already devoted in the past to QoS-aware services assembly procedures [14]. On the other hand, energy efficiency of composite services has received less attention until recently, when the growing interest on sustainability themes has put this issue in the foreground [17, 19]. However, to the best of our knowledge, no available solution exists yet that is able to deal with all the issues (*i*)-(*iv*) mentioned above.

Paper Contribution. In this respect, we propose an initial solution of the following problem: *how to devise a decentralized architecture that supports the dynamic building of a fully resolved assembly of distributed services, collectively fulfilling functional requirements while minimizing the energy consumption, in an open and variable execution environment.* On answering to this question we also take into account the impact on the system's QoS.

Specifically, we propose a (fully) decentralized and dynamic service assembly framework whose main characteristics are: (*i*) a system architecture for service assembly management; (*ii*) explicit modelling of service energy consumption for both processing and communication activities; (*iii*) an energy-aware service selection and composition procedure; (*iv*) a set of "social welfare" indexes aimed at measuring the system effectiveness with respect to QoS and energy objectives.

Related Work. Our work lies within the general area of service selection and composition problem in a distributed environment. There is quite a large amount of literature on the topic (e.g., [2,4,14] and references therein); hereafter, we briefly review works closer to ours having a focus on energy-aware solutions. Recently, the software engineering community at large is paying increasing attention to energy efficiency solutions, a summary can be found in [6]. Also from a software architecture point of view, the need to consider the energy attribute at architectural level is gaining consensus [18]. However, to the best of our knowledge, only a limited amount of effort has been devoted up to now to the definition of architectural approaches for energy-aware decentralized service assemblies. Examples of existing solutions can be found in [15–17,19], where service assemblies are considered for cloud-based applications [17], in wireless-sensor-networks context/domain [16] and for cyber-physical systems [15,19]. However, the proposed solutions are based on the definition of single [16,19] or multi-objective optimization problems [15,17], which leverage on centralized approaches.

Structure of the Paper. Section 2 presents the system model we refer to Sect. 3 introduces the service assembly energy consumption model, and Sect. 4 the indexes derived from this model to measure the assembly energy and QoS effectiveness. Section 5 illustrates the decentralized architecture for the assembly construction and maintenance. Section 6 shows the results of our experiments, Sect. 7 discusses threats to validity, while Sect. 8 provides conclusions and hints for future work.

2 System Model

We consider a distributed system consisting of a set $\mathbf{N}$ of nodes (e.g., nodes of an edge cloud architecture), and a set $\mathbf{S}$ of (sw-implemented) services that must be deployed on these nodes. Each node provides basic computing and communication services, used by the other services hosted by the same node for their operations. For the sake of simplicity, we assume that each node offers only a single type of computing and communication service, and do not consider other basic service categories (e.g., storage). We leave to future work the extension of our model to these other categories, and to different types of services within each category (e.g., both specialized GPU and general purpose CPU as computing services). Each service $S \in \mathbf{S}$ must be bound to a computing and communication service. Besides this, S could require functionalities offered by other services in the set $\mathbf{S}$ to carry out its own task. We denote by $\mathbf{B}$ the set of all computing and communication services offered by nodes in $\mathbf{N}$, and by $node(S) \in \mathbf{N}$ the node hosting service $S \in \mathbf{S} \cup \mathbf{B}$. We assume that services in the set $\mathbf{B}$ are the only direct sources of energy consumption, while the energy consumption of services in $\mathbf{S}$ is related with the use they directly or indirectly make of services in $\mathbf{B}$.

For the purpose of the service assembly procedure we intend to devise, we now introduce a more detailed service model. A service $S \in \mathbf{S}$ is represented as a tuple $\langle \mathit{Type}, \mathit{Deps}, \mathit{Prov}, \mathit{Req} \rangle$, where:

- $S.\mathit{Type} \in \mathbf{T}$ denotes the type of the provided interface (we say that $S.\mathit{Type}$ is the type of S). We assume the existence of a function $match : \mathbf{T} \times \mathbf{T} \to [0,1]$ such that $match(T_1, T_2) = 0$ if type T_1 does not match type T_2 and $match(T_1, T_2) > 0$ if a matching exists according to some suitable matching criterion [1,9].
- $S.\mathit{Deps} \subseteq \mathbf{T} \bigcup \{comp, comm\}$ is the set of required dependencies for S. We assume that $S.\mathit{Deps}$ is fixed for each service and known in advance. Note that the dependency set $S.\mathit{Deps}$ does not contain duplicates, meaning that a service may depend at most once on any specific interface type. We assume that $S.\mathit{Deps}$ always includes two dependencies $d_1 = comp$ and $d_2 = comm$: in this way we model the fact that S needs at least to be bound to a computing and a communication service, for its internal operations and for its interactions with other services. For each $d \in S.\mathit{Deps}$ we assume that it is known (e.g., through a locally performed monitoring activity) a value $\mu_{S,d}$, which represents the average number of times service S requires dependency d to fulfill each request it has received.

- $S.Prov \subseteq \mathbf{S}$ is the set of *Providers* of S, i.e., the set of services to which S is bound to resolve its dependencies. We denote by $comp(S) \in \mathbf{B}$ and $comm(S) \in \mathbf{B}$ the computing and communication services used to resolve dependencies $comp \in S.Deps$ and $comm \in S.Deps$, respectively. It must obviously hold $node(comp(S)) = node(comm(S))$.
- $S.Req \subseteq \mathbf{S}$ is the set of *Requesters* of S, i.e., is the set of other services that are bound to S to resolve one of their dependencies.

A service is either *fully resolved* or *partially resolved*. Basic services in the set $\mathbf{B}$ are fully resolved by definition. A service $S \in \mathbf{S}$ is *fully resolved* if for all $d \in S.Deps$ there exists a fully resolved service $S' \in S.Prov$ such that $match(d, S'.Type) > 0$. On the other hand, a *partially resolved* service $S \in \mathbf{S}$ has at least one dependency that is either not matched, or is matched by a partially resolved service.

Finally, a *service assembly* $\mathbf{A}$ is a directed graph $\mathbf{A} = (\mathbf{S}, \mathbf{E})$, where $\mathbf{E} \subseteq \mathbf{S} \times \mathbf{S}$ is the set of resolved dependencies. Specifically, a directed edge $(S_i, S_j) \in \mathbf{E}$ denotes that S_i is using S_j to resolve one of its dependencies. In general, a given S_i has multiple simultaneous outgoing bindings (towards $S_i.Prov$), one for each dependency, and can have multiple simultaneous incoming bindings from other services (belonging to $S_i.Req$), using S_i to resolve one of their dependencies.

Figure 1 shows an example of a simple service assembly (including services S_1, S_2, S_3 and S_4) that illustrates the actual deployment of services on nodes N_1, N_2 and N_3. The figure highlights also the service dependencies and their binding to computation and communication services.

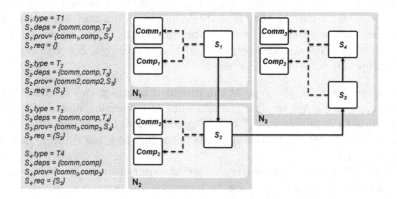

Fig. 1. Service assembly example

3   Energy Model

In this section we introduce the model we adopt to estimate the energy consumption of each service $S \in \mathbf{S}$, as a function of the bindings it establishes with other services to resolve its dependencies. As we are considering computing and communication services as the only "physical" resources causing energy consumption, the model consists of two parts: a *computing energy* model and a *communication energy* model.

3.1 Computation Energy

Let us consider a service $S \in \mathbf{S}$. When the flow of requests addressed to services in $S.Prov$ eventually reach a service of type $comp$, it will cause some computation energy consumption. This will happen in one step for the dependency of type $comp$ of S ("internal operations" of S). Otherwise, the flow of requests will go through a number of virtual services before reaching a service of type $comp$. To model this process, we introduce the following three indexes $S.I^{comp}$, $S.L^{comp}$ and $S.E^{comp}$ that model, respectively, the *individual, node level* and *system level* computation energy consumption caused by a single request addressed to S. They are defined as follows:

$$S.I^{comp} = h_{node(S)}(\mu_{S,comp}) \tag{1}$$

$$S.L^{comp} = S.I^{comp} + \sum_{\substack{S' \in S.Prov, \\ s.t. S'.Type \neq comp \\ \wedge node(S') = node(S)}} \mu_{S,S'.Type} \cdot S'.L^{comp} \tag{2}$$

$$S.E^{comp} = S.I^{comp} + \sum_{\substack{S' \in S.Prov, \\ s.t. S'.Type \neq comp}} \mu_{S,S'.Type} \cdot S'.E^{comp} \tag{3}$$

where $h_n(\mu)$ represents the energy consumption of the *comp* service hosted by a node n for the execution of μ operations[1]. As an example, $h_n(\mu)$ could be instantiated as $h_n(\mu) = a_n + e_n \cdot \mu$, with a *fixed* part a_n (energy consumed when the *comp* service is switched on, independently of its operations), and a *dynamic* part $e_n \cdot \mu$ linearly depending on the load addressed to the *comp* service (e_n represents the energy consumption for a single operation).

From the definitions given above, we see that $S.I^{comp}$ models only the energy consumption directly consumed by S for its internal operations. Besides the directly consumed energy, $S.L^{comp}$ includes also the computation energy indirectly consumed by S because of its use of services $S' \in S.Prov$, but limited to services co-located with S on the same node (their energy consumption is multiplied by the average number of times S uses S', given by $\mu_{S,S'.Type}$). Finally, $S.E^{comp}$ adopts a system-wide perspective and models the overall computation energy consumption caused by S on any node in the system.

We point out that $S.I^{comp}$, $S.L^{comp}$ and $S.E^{comp}$ refer to computing energy consumption caused by a single request addressed to S. To get measures of the

---

[1] By "operation" we mean a conventional average unit of computation. We make an analogous assumption for the communication model.

energy consumption per unit time (energy consumption rate), we introduce the concept of *load vector* $\mathbf{\Lambda}_S = [\lambda_S(n)]_{n \in \mathbf{N}}$ associated with any service $S \in \mathbf{S}$, where each vector entry $\lambda_S(n)$ denotes a flow of requests (expressed as requests per unit time) addressed to service S by services hosted by node $n \in \mathbf{N}$. $\mathbf{\Lambda}_S$ can be easily estimated by some local monitoring activity. Given a load vector $\mathbf{\Lambda_S}$, we can derive from $S.I^{comp}$, $S.L^{comp}$ and $S.E^{comp}$ corresponding measures of the computing energy consumption rate:

$$S.\rho_X^{comp} = \Big(\sum_{n \in \mathbf{N}} \lambda_S(n) \Big) \cdot S.X^{comp} \tag{4}$$

where X stands for any of: I, L, E.

3.2 Communication Energy

Let us consider a service $S \in \mathbf{S}$. As already stated in the previous subsection, S represents a "virtual" (software implemented) resource: the communication energy consumption caused by S depends on the interactions that S has both with services that use it to resolve their dependencies (services in the set $S.Req$) and services used by S itself to resolve its dependencies (services in the set $S.Prov$). In this respect, we assume that the energy spent by a communication service of a node for these interactions depends both on the data volume, and the latency and bandwidth of the links connecting it with other nodes [5].

To model this process, we introduce the three indexes $S.I_n^{comm}$, $S.L_n^{comm}$ and $S.E_n^{comm}$ that model, respectively, the *individual, node level* and *system level* communication energy consumption caused by a single request addressed to S by some other service hosted by a node $n \in \mathbf{N}$. They are defined as follows:

$$S.I_n^{comm} = \phi_{node(S)}^{req}(\delta_S^{rcv}, bw(n, node(S)), lt(n, node(S)))$$

$$+ \sum_{\substack{S' \in S.Prov, \\ s.t.node(S) \neq node(S')}} \mu_{S,S'.Type} \cdot \phi_{node(S)}^{prov}(\delta_{S,S'.Type}^{snd}, bw(node(S), node(S')), lt(node(S), node(S'))) \tag{5}$$

$$S.L_n^{comm} = S.I_n^{comm} + \sum_{\substack{S' \in S.Prov, \\ s.t.node(S')=node(S)}} \mu_{S,S'.Type} \cdot S'.L_{node(S)}^{comm} \tag{6}$$

$$S.E_n^{comm} = S.I_n^{comm} + \sum_{S' \in S.Prov} \mu_{S,S'.Type} \cdot S'.E_{node(S)}^{comm} \tag{7}$$

where:

- $bw(n_1, n_2)$ and $lt(n_1, n_2)$, with $n_1, n_2 \in \mathbf{N}$, denote, respectively, the bandwidth and latency of the link connecting nodes n_1 and n_2;
- δ_S^{rcv} and $\delta_{S,d}^{snd}$ denote, respectively, the average amount of data S receives for each service request addressed to it, and the average amount of data S sends for each invocation of its dependency d, to fulfill that request;

– $\phi_n^{req}(\delta, b, l)$ denotes the energy consumed by the *comm* service of node $n \in \mathbf{N}$ (in the following we denote it as *commserv(n)*), when it receives an amount δ^2 of data addressed to a service hosted by n over a link with bandwidth b and latency l;

– $\phi_n^{prov}(\delta, b, l)$ denote the energy consumed by *commserv(n)*, $n \in \mathbf{N}$, when it sends an amount δ of data to a service hosted by another node over a link with bandwidth b and latency l.

The first term in the r.h.s. of Eq. (5) represents the energy consumed by *commserv(node(S))* for the reception of a service request addressed to S, coming from an external node n. The second term in the r.h.s. of Eq. (5) represents the energy consumed by *commserv(node(S))* to send the requests S addresses to services solving its dependencies (i.e., services in *S.Prov*) and hosted by different nodes. Hence, $S.I_n^{comm}$ models the communication energy consumption of *commserv(node(S))* caused only by the direct interactions S has with other services hosted by different nodes.

On the other hand, $S.L_n^{comm}$ in Eq. (6) adds to the energy consumption measured by $S.I_n^{comm}$ also the communication energy consumption indirectly caused by S, corresponding to interactions that services in *S.Prov* have with other services to carry out their own task. As it can be seen from the r.h.s. of Eq. (6), $S.L_n^{comm}$ limits its scope to the energy consumption of *commserv(node(S))* only.

Finally, $S.E_n^{comm}$ in Eq. (7) adopts a system-wide perspective, measuring the communication energy consumption directly or indirectly caused by S on any node in the system, when S receives a single request from a service hosted by a node n.

Analogously to the computing energy case, we can derive from $S.E_n^{comm}$, $S.I_n^{comm}$ and $S.L_n^{comm}$ measures of the communication energy consumption rate, given a load vector $\mathbf{\Lambda}_S = [\lambda_S(n)]$:

$$S.\rho_X^{comm} = \sum_{n \in \mathbf{N}} \lambda_S(n) \cdot S.X_n^{comm} \qquad (8)$$

where X stands for any of: I, L, E.

4   Welfare Indexes

In this section we formally define the indexes, based on the model defined in the previous section, that we will use to measure the effectiveness of our approach with respect to its ability in achieving a good local and social welfare. By this we mean that our goal is to analyze our approach effectiveness from a two-fold perspective. On the one side, we measure the achievement of some average global system "quality", thanks to the contribution of all services. On the other side, we measure whether there is an unbalanced distribution among services of this global quality.

---

[2] δ is measured in terms of a conventional average communication unit.

Besides energy consumption, which is our main focus in this paper, we include in our notion of quality also the delivered QoS. For space reasons, we do not introduce an explicit QoS model of a service assembly. Several models of this kind have been already introduced (e.g., [4,19]). For notational purposes, we just assume that a QoS index $S.Q$ is associated with each service $S \in \mathbf{S}$, related with suitable QoS measures like response time or reliability, where the value of $S.Q$ is estimated at each node by some monitoring activity. We only point out that, for the sake of realism, we assume that the QoS delivered by a service is *load-dependent*, in the sense that it degrades with the increase of the load of requests addressed to it [10,12]. The welfare indexes we adopt are defined as follows.

Given a fully resolved assembly $\mathbf{A} = (\mathbf{S}, \mathbf{E})$, we first define the average *Global Energy Consumption* rate delivered by all services in $\mathbf{A}$:

$$GEC(\mathbf{A}) = \frac{1}{|\mathbf{N}|} \sum_{n \in \mathbf{N}} \left(\sum_{\substack{S \in \mathbf{S} \\ s.t.node(S)=n}} (S.\rho_I^{comp} + S.\rho_I^{comm}) \right) \tag{9}$$

We use $S.\rho_I^{comp}$ and $S.\rho_I^{comm}$, defined as in Eqs. (4) and (8), respectively, in the definition of $GEC(\mathbf{A})$ to avoid counting more than once the energy consumption caused by a service. Note that $GEC(\mathbf{A})$ is a "lower is better" index.

From the QoS perspective, we define as follows the average *Global QoS* delivered by all services in $\mathbf{A}$:

$$GQoS(\mathbf{A}) = \frac{1}{|\mathbf{S}|} \sum_{S \in \mathbf{S}} S.Q \tag{10}$$

However, both $GEC(\mathbf{A})$ and $GQoS(\mathbf{A})$ do not allow to capture to what extent all involved services and the nodes hosting them fairly contribute to the measured average quality.

To this end, we introduce the following *fairness* indexes based on the *Jain's fairness index* [7] as additional measures of the achieved social welfare, to measure how uniform is the quality achieved by all the participating services, from the energy consumption and QoS perspectives, respectively:

$$FEC(\mathbf{A}) = \frac{\left(\sum_{n \in \mathbf{N}} \left(\sum_{\substack{S \in \mathbf{S} \\ s.t.node(S)=n}} (S.\rho_I^{comp} + S.\rho_I^{comm}) \right) \right)^2}{|\mathbf{N}| \sum_{n \in \mathbf{N}} \left(\sum_{\substack{S \in \mathbf{S} \\ s.t.node(S)=n}} (S.\rho_I^{comp} + S.\rho_I^{comm}) \right)^2} \tag{11}$$

$$FQoS(\mathbf{A}) = \frac{\left(\sum_{S \in \mathbf{S}} S.Q \right)^2}{|\mathbf{S}| \sum_{S \in \mathbf{S}} S.Q^2} \tag{12}$$

The value of these fairness indexes ranges from $\frac{1}{|\mathbf{N}|}$ or $\frac{1}{|\mathbf{S}|}$, respectively (worst case), to 1 (best case), and it is maximum when all nodes experiment the same energy consumption rate or all services deliver the same QoS, respectively. In general, indexes of this type penalize situations where the quality achieved by different entities is highly unbalanced. Hence, by using $FEC(\mathbf{A})$ or $FQoS(\mathbf{A})$, we intend to reward assemblies that result in a fair share of the overall quality measured by $GEC(\mathbf{A})$ and $GQoS(\mathbf{A})$, respectively.

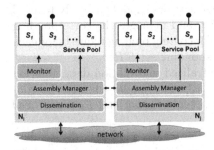

Fig. 2. Node architecture

```
1:  procedure ACTIVETHREAD
2:      loop
3:          Wait Δt
4:          for all Sⱼ ∈ GETPEERS() do
5:              Send ⟨S.Prov ∪ {S}⟩ to Sⱼ

6:  procedure PASSIVETHREAD
7:      loop
8:          Wait for message ⟨M⟩ from Sⱼ
9:          for all Sₖ ∈ M do
10:             if ∃d ∈ S.Deps − matches(d, Sₖ.Type) > 0 then
11:                 Best_{S,d} ← UPDATE(Best_{S,d}, Sₖ)
12:                 S.Prov ← SELECT(Best_{S,d}, S.Prov)
```

Fig. 3. Gossip based dissemination

Regarding energy-related indexes, we note that the relative importance of the indexes $GEC(\mathbf{A})$ and $FEC(\mathbf{A})$ could depend on the scenario where they are applied. In scenarios where all nodes have access to continuous power sources, the most relevant effectiveness index could be $GEC(\mathbf{A})$, for system sustainability reasons. On the other hand, in scenarios where system nodes are battery-powered, the most relevant effectiveness index could be $FEC(\mathbf{A})$, as a highly unbalanced energy consumption among nodes could lead to the premature "death" of some node, with possible negative consequences on the whole system lifetime.

5   System Architecture

In this section we present a fully decentralized architecture that drives a service-oriented system towards the construction of an energy-efficient fully resolved service assembly. The core idea underpinning this architecture is the use of a decentralized information dissemination procedure, based on a gossiping protocol [13], through which each service S advertises its functional ($S.Type$) and extra-functional (*energy* and *QoS*) characteristics. Thanks to this procedure, services at each node become eventually aware of other services in the system that can resolve their dependencies, thus providing the basis for the fulfillment of the goal of driving the system toward the construction of a fully resolved assembly. To fulfill the goal of energy-driven assembly, the advertised information is used to select, within a set of functionally equivalent candidates, the best suited service.

Figure 2 shows the main architecture components deployed at each node N_i: *Monitor*, *Assembly Manager* and *Dissemination*. Besides them, the figure shows also *Service Pool*, the set of services $S \in \mathbf{S}$ running on node N_i.

Monitor is in charge of monitoring the energy consumption (i.e., $S.X^{comp}$ and $S.X_n^{comm}$) for each service S in the Service Pool, and notifying detected changes to the *Assembly Manager*.

Assembly Manager receives information about the type, QoS and energy consumption of local and remote services from *Monitor* and *Dissemination*, respectively, which are used to build the assembly. In particular, it receives from *Dissemination* the set $S.Prov$ that specifies which services should currently be used to solve the dependencies of a local service S, and manages the corresponding bindings. Moreover, it receives notifications of incoming binding requests for each local service S, and keeps updated the corresponding set $S.Req$.

Finally, *Dissemination* implements decentralized information dissemination by exploiting a gossip communication model [13]. This model relies on the continuous execution of two concurrent threads, *Active Thread* and *Passive Thread* (see Algorithm in Fig. 3).

For each service S hosted by the node, *Active Thread* periodically sends a Gossip message to its *peer set*[3]. The message payload is a set of services, with the associated type, QoS and energy information, containing the list of currently bound dependencies $S.Prov$ plus S itself.

Passive Thread listens for messages coming from other peers. Upon receiving a message containing the set **M**, it checks all services $S_k \in$ **M** to see whether some of them can be used to resolve some dependency of S. If $S_k.Type$ is required as a dependency, then S_k is considered as a candidate to be added to $Best_{S,d}$ (line 10), where $Best_{S,d}$ collects the currently known "best" services according to the specific service selection criterion used to solve the dependency d (see Sect. 5.1). The decision whether to include S_k in $Best_{S,d}$ is taken by function UPDATE() (line 11), possibly dropping from $Best_{S,d}$ some other service whose utility is worse than S_k. The update of the sets $Best_{S,d}$ can lead to a substitution of the service currently used to solve dependency d (as specified in the set $S.Prov$) with a new "better" service taken from $Best_{S,d}$. The decision about this possible substitution is taken by function SELECT() (line 12), implemented following one of the selection criteria described in Sect. 5.1.

As it is typical with gossip-based protocols, a new instance of the algorithm in Fig. 3 is created at each node for each service S in the Service Pool.

5.1   Energy-Aware Service Selection

In this section we present possible energy-aware service selection criteria that could be used in the implementation of the SELECT() function in Fig. 3.

Given a service S and a set of candidates $Best_{S,d}$, we recall that SELECT() must select, within that set, a service that resolves a dependency $d \in S.Deps$.

Energy-Aware Overall. The *Energy-aware Overall* criterion aims at selecting the service that causes the minimal energy consumption on a system-wide basis

---

[3] The peer set is provided by the underlying gossip communication protocol [13].

(i.e., $GEC(\mathbf{A})$). In order to use this criterion, each service S is required to disseminate the values $S.E^{comp}$ and $S.E_n^{comm}$, $n \in \mathbf{N}$, defined by Eqs. (3) and (7), respectively. This criterion can be stated as:

Select $\overline{S} \in Best_{S,d}$ such that:

$$\overline{S} = \underset{S' \in Best_{S,d}}{\arg\min} \{S'.E^{comp} + \mu_{S,S'.Type} \cdot S'.E_{node(S)}^{comm}\} \tag{13}$$

Energy-Aware Local. The *Energy-aware Local* criterion is similar to the previous one, but it acts on the basis of a more limited scope, as it focuses on the minimization of the energy consumption involving $node(S)$ only (the definition of Eq. (14) is derived from the definition of the $S.L^{comp}$ and $S.L_n^{comm}$ indexes in Eqs. (2) and (6), respectively). For this reason, differently from the *Overall* criterion, it does not require the dissemination of any energy consumption value, as all the information needed for its application can be collected at each node by a local monitoring activity. This criterion can be stated as:

Select $\overline{S} \in Best_{S,d}$ such that:

$$\overline{S} = \underset{S' \in Best_{S,d}}{\arg\min} \{\mu_{S,S'.Type} \cdot S'.L^{comp} \cdot I_{\{node(S')=node(S)\}}$$
$$+ \mu_{S,S'.Type} \cdot \phi_{node(S)}^{prov}(\delta_{S,S'.Type}^{snd}, bw(node(S), node(S')), lt(node(S), node(S'))) \cdot I_{\{node(S')\neq node(S)\}}$$
$$+ \mu_{S,S'.Type} \cdot S'.L_{node(S)}^{comm} \cdot I_{\{node(S')=node(S)\}}\} \tag{14}$$

where $I_{\{cond\}}$ is the indicator function that holds 1 when condition *cond* is true, and 0 otherwise.

As pointed out in Sect. 4, focusing on the minimization of $GEC(\mathbf{A})$ could not be a good choice in contexts where one should instead aim at fairly balancing energy consumption among all nodes. We thus propose a third criterion, aimed at the maximization of the fairness index $FEC(\mathbf{A})$.

Energy-Aware Learning. The *Energy-aware Learning* criterion selects the service in $Best_{S,d}$ hosted by the node that currently results to have the lowest energy consumption rate. This criterion can be stated as:

Select $\overline{S} \in Best_{S,d}$ such that:

$$node(\overline{S}) = \underset{n \in node(Best_{S,d})}{\arg\min} \{ \sum_{\substack{S \in \mathbf{S} \\ s.t.node(S)=n}} (S.\rho_I^{comp} + S.\rho_I^{comm})\} \tag{15}$$

where, with a little abuse of notation, $node(Best_{S,d}) \subseteq \mathbf{N}$ denotes the set of all nodes hosting services that belongs to the set $Best_{S,d}$.

The actual application of this criterion deserves however more attention with respect to the former two criteria. Indeed, we can note that both Eqs. (13) and (14) used in the definition of *Energy-aware Overall* and *Energy-aware Local*, respectively, are based on load-independent indexes. They are thus well suited for the greedy approach underlying these two criteria. On the other hand, the indexes used in Eq. (15) are load-dependent, with consequent worsening of their value when the load of node n increases. The greedy approach underlying the definition of *Energy-aware Learning* given above can thus lead to well known problems of system instability. Indeed, what currently results to be the node with the smallest energy consumption rate could rapidly become overloaded, thus triggering the need of new selections, and so on. A more judicious definition of this criterion is thus necessary, more suited for the goal of achieving a fair energy consumption balance.

To this end, we implement this criterion according to the learning method proposed in [11], originally proposed for a scenario of decentralized load balancing in a distributed system with load-dependent QoS. In this method, resource selection by the participating services is based on a suitable balance between exploitation (what services have learnt from past observations about the current "best" resource, giving proper weight to the received information based on its age) and exploration (random selection of apparently "not best" resources). In our adaptation of this method, we assume that each node advertises the current value of $S.\rho_I^{comp}$ and $S.\rho_I^{comm}$, using the gossiping procedure we have described above. This information is then managed according to the method proposed in [11], to which we refer for details, omitted here for space reasons.

6   Experimental Evaluation

In this section we present a set of simulation experiments to assess the effectiveness of different service selection strategies on the social welfare of the system. To this end, we experiment with the three energy-aware service selection strategies introduced in Sect. 5.1. In addition, we consider a baseline *Random* strategy that randomly selects a functionally matching service; and a state-of-the-art *QoS-aware Learning*-based criterion [4], which serves as a benchmark to compare the impact on QoS of our energy-focused selection criteria.

We implemented a large-scale simulation model for the PeerSim simulator [8]. The replication package is publicly available to researchers interested in replicating and independently verifying the results presented in this paper[4].

6.1   Experimental Settings

Our experimentation mimics a wireless sensor network (WSN) deployment scenario of an edge computing application. We consider a system with N services and NUM_INT different interface types $\mathbf{T} = \{T_1, \ldots, T_{\text{NUM\_INT}}\}$. Without loss of generality we assume that each sensor node hosts a single service. We create $\lfloor N/\text{NUM\_INT} \rfloor$ services of each type and, for each service, we define a probabilistic attachment to interface types to generate $S.Deps$ with probability p.

We define the energy cost of a k-bits CPU operation equal to the average energy cost of sending k-bits. Moreover, the energy cost of sending k-bits is on

---

[4] https://github.com/mi-da/Energy-Aware-Service-Assembly.

average two times more costly than the energy cost of receiving k-bits [5]. We
deploy the services in a network area with a diameter of 200 m. The nodes are
randomly positioned in the area and are endowed with symmetric latency links.
Each node adopts a decentralized network coordinate system to estimate latency
values [3]. Without loss of generality, we assume that the packet loss in the network is null. We adopt the first order radio model, a commonly used communication energy consumption model for WSN [5], which leads to the instantiation
of $\phi_n^{req}(\delta, b, l)$ and $\phi_n^{prov}(\delta, b, l)$ (see Sect. 3.2). Finally, we assume that the load-
dependent QoS function of each service S is a randomly monotonic decreasing
function that returns values in the range $(0, 1]$ [4].

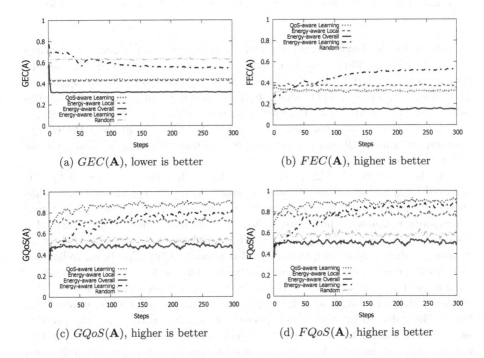

(a) $GEC(\mathbf{A})$, lower is better   (b) $FEC(\mathbf{A})$, higher is better

(c) $GQoS(\mathbf{A})$, higher is better   (d) $FQoS(\mathbf{A})$, higher is better

Fig. 4. Selection criteria effectiveness: $N = 500$, NUM_INT $= 10$, $p = 0.6$

6.2 Experimental Results

Each experiment shows the progress of our gossip-based decentralized architecture towards the construction of fully resolved assemblies[5].

Let us consider first the impact on the global indexes $GEC(\mathbf{A})$ and
$GQoS(\mathbf{A})$. Figure 4a shows that all strategies are better than the baseline *Random* with respect to the overall energy consumption. The greatest energy saving

---

[5] The gossip procedure eventually leads to the creation of fully resolved assemblies.

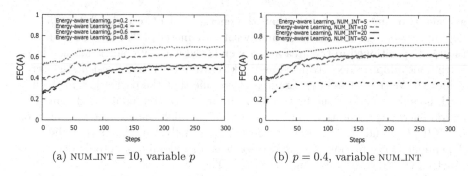

(a) NUM_INT = 10, variable p (b) $p = 0.4$, variable NUM_INT

Fig. 5. $FEC(\mathbf{A})$ of different classes of applications, higher is better, $N = 500$

is achieved by the *Energy-aware Overall* strategy, thus confirming the effectiveness of its system-wide perspective, which comes however at the cost of disseminating energy-related information. This cost is not incurred by the *Energy-aware Local* strategy, whose energy saving performance is slightly worse and comparable to the one achieved by the energy-unaware *QoS-aware Learning* strategy. The *Energy-aware Learning* shows instead that its goal of leveling the energy consumption rate of all nodes is not very compatible with the goal of minimizing the overall energy consumption.

On the other hand, Fig. 4c obviously shows that the best overall QoS is achieved by the *QoS-aware Learning* strategy, while *Energy-aware Overall* has the worst performance, even worse than *Random*. *Energy-aware Local* and *Energy-aware Learning*, notwithstanding their focus on energy, have instead a good impact on the overall QoS, quite close to the result achieved by *QoS-aware Learning*. Given our assumption of load-dependent QoS, this is an indication that both these strategies distribute better the load among the different nodes with respect to *Energy-aware Overall*: in case of *Energy-aware Learning*, this is likely due to its intrinsic balancing attitude; in case of *Energy-aware Local* this is likely due to its myopic perspective, which has in this case the positive side-effect of leading to the selection of services hosted by nearby nodes, as they make each node incur in less energy consumption (which is greatly influenced by the energy required to amplify the signal in WSN [5]). This behaviour causes a sort of geographical load-balancing effect, where clusters of nodes form service assemblies that run approximately in the same geographical area.

Let us consider now the fairness indexes $FEC(\mathbf{A})$ and $FQoS(\mathbf{A})$. In this case, Fig. 4b shows that *Energy-aware Learning* achieves the best result in balancing the energy consumption rate among all nodes, according to its primary goal, while *Energy-aware Overall* is the worst. This very bad performance is due to its energy information global sharing that leads every node to get the same energy-related knowledge. As a result, the most energy efficient services will be globally targeted by binding requests, with very good results on the overall energy consumption, but at the cost of an unfair energy allocation. All the other three strategies achieve instead quite similar and satisfactory results with respect to $FEC(\mathbf{A})$, with *Energy-aware Local* performing slightly better than the other two: for different reasons (the intrinsic randomness of *Random*, the energy-unawareness of *QoS-aware Learning*, the myopic perspective of *Energy-aware Local*), all these strategies have as a side effect a quite fair distribution of the energy load on the different nodes.

Figure 4d shows that also from a QoS perspective *Energy-aware Overall* performs very bad also in terms of fairness, thus confirming the negative impact that this strategy has on QoS because of the load unbalance it tends to favor. The balancing attitude of *Energy-aware Learning* leads instead to good results also in terms of QoS fairness (after a number of learning steps), quite close to the best result achieved by QoS-aware strategy.

Finally, we analyze the effectiveness of the *Energy-aware Learning* strategy on the $FEC(\mathbf{A})$ index for different classes of applications: they are simulated by varying independently the probabilistic attachment parameter (i.e., p) affecting the dependency set of a service, and the number of interface types (i.e., NUM_INT), affecting the maximum depth of a fully resolved assembly.

Our experiments (Figs. 5b-a) show that $FEC(\mathbf{A})$ decreases with increasing p and NUM_INT. These results highlight that architectures with many dependencies or many interface types impair the energy fairness of the system.

7 Threats to Validity

A threat to external validity concerns the approach evaluation. Indeed, we adopted an evaluation based on extensive simulations, instead of considering single case studies. However, to evaluate the practical implication of the adoption of our service assembly framework, we plan to select one of the existing service discovery platforms to support the actual implementation of our approach, so to validate it in a real-word settings.

A threat to internal validity is represented by the selection of the social welfare indexes. To smooth this threat we adopted two different indexes to complement measures of the overall energy consumption and overall QoS with fairness indexes. We are also planning to investigate the definition of other social welfare indexes to extend the validity of our approach.

8 Conclusion and Future Work

In this paper, we have proposed a decentralized architecture to build a fully functional assembly of distributed services, able to optimize its energy consumption in an open and heterogeneous execution environment, paying also attention to issues concerning the delivered quality of service. We also suggested suitable indexes to measure from different perspectives the energy efficiency of the resulting assembly, and presented the results of extensive simulation experiments to assess the effectiveness of our approach.

As future work we plan to analyse combined energy and QoS selection criteria, and to take into account also other sources of energy consumption. We also plan to investigate issues concerning the presence of finite sources of energy (e.g., batteries) and differentiate between green and brown energy sources.

References

1. Caporuscio, M., Ghezzi, C.: Engineering future Internet applications: the prime approach. J. Syst. Softw. **106**, 9–27 (2015)
2. Cardellini, V., Casalicchio, E., Grassi, V., Iannucci, S., Presti, F.L., Mirandola, R.: MOSES: a framework for QoS driven runtime adaptation of service-oriented systems. IEEE Trans. Softw. Eng. **38**(5), 1138–1159 (2012)
3. Dabek, F., Cox, R., Kaashoek, F., Morris, R.: Vivaldi: a decentralized network coordinate system. In: Proceedings of SIGCOMM 2004, pp. 15–26. ACM, New York (2004)
4. D'Angelo, M., Caporuscio, M., Grassi, V., Mirandola, R.: Decentralized learning for self-adaptive QoS-aware service assembly. Future Gener. Comput. Syst. **108**, 210–227 (2020)
5. Heinzelman, W.R., Chandrakasan, A., Balakrishnan, H.: Energy-efficient communication protocol for wireless microsensor networks. In: Proceedings of HICSS 2000, vol. 2, p. 10 (2000)
6. Horcas, J.M., Pinto, M., Fuentes, L.: Context-aware energy-efficient applications for cyber-physical systems. Ad Hoc Netw. **82**, 15–30 (2019)
7. Jain, R.K., Chiu, D.M.W., Hawe, W.R.: A quantitative measure of fairness and discrimination for resource allocation in shared computer systems. Technical report. DEC-TR-301, Digital Equipment Corporation (1984)
8. Montresor, A., Jelasity, M.: PeerSim: a scalable P2P simulator. In: 2009 IEEE Ninth International Conference on Peer-to-Peer Computing, pp. 99–100 (2009)
9. Paolucci, M., Kawamura, T., Payne, T., Sycara, K.: Semantic matching of web services capabilities. In: First International Semantic Web Conference (2002)
10. Paschalidis, I.C., Tsitsiklis, J.N.: Congestion-dependent pricing of network services. IEEE/ACM Trans. Netw. **8**(2), 171–184 (2000)
11. Schaerf, A., Shoham, Y., Tennenholtz, M.: Adaptive load balancing: a study in multi-agent learning. J. Artif. Int. Res. **2**(1), 475–500 (1995)
12. Schroeder, B., Gibson, G.A.: A large-scale study of failures in high-performance computing systems. In: Proceedings of DSN 2006, pp. 249–258 (2006)
13. Shah, D.: Gossip Algorithms. Foundations and Trends in Networking, Now Publishers (2009)
14. She, Q., Wei, X., Nie, G., Chen, D.: QoS-aware cloud service composition: a systematic mapping study from the perspective of computational intelligence. Expert Syst. Appl. **138**, 112804 (2019)
15. Sun, M., Zhou, Z., Duan, Y.: Energy-aware service composition of configurable IoT smart things. In: 2018 14th International Conference on Mobile Ad-Hoc and Sensor Networks (MSN), pp. 37–42. IEEE (2018)
16. Tong, E., Chen, L., Li, H.: Energy-aware service selection and adaptation in wireless sensor networks with QoS guarantee. IEEE Trans. Serv. Comput. (2017)
17. Wang, S., Zhou, A., Bao, R., Chou, W., Yau, S.S.: Towards green service composition approach in the cloud. IEEE Trans. Serv. Comput. (2018)
18. Woods, E., Fairbanks, G.: The pragmatic architect evolves. IEEE Softw. **35**(6), 12–15 (2018)
19. Zeng, D., Gu, L., Yao, H.: Towards energy efficient service composition in green energy powered cyber-physical fog systems. Future Gener. Comput. Syst. **105**, 757–765 (2020)

Continuous Experimentation for Automotive Software on the Example of a Heavy Commercial Vehicle in Daily Operation

Federico Giaimo[1]([✉])[ID] and Christian Berger[2]

[1] Chalmers University of Technology, Gothenburg, Sweden
giaimo@chalmers.se
[2] University of Gothenburg, Gothenburg, Sweden
christian.berger@gu.se

Abstract. As the automotive industry focuses its attention more and more towards the software functionality of vehicles, techniques to deliver new software value at a fast pace are needed. Continuous Experimentation, a practice coming from the web-based systems world, is one of such techniques. It enables researchers and developers to use real-world data to verify their hypothesis and steer the software evolution based on performances and user preferences, reducing the reliance on simulations and guesswork. Several challenges prevent the verbatim adoption of this practice on automotive cyber-physical systems, e.g., safety concerns and limitations from computational resources; nonetheless, the automotive field is starting to take interest in this technique. This work aims at demonstrating and evaluating a prototypical Continuous Experimentation infrastructure, implemented on a distributed computational system housed in a commercial truck tractor that is used in daily operations by a logistic company on public roads. The system comprises computing units and sensors, and software deployment and data retrieval are only possible remotely via a mobile data connection due to the commercial interests of the logistics company. This study shows that the proposed experimentation process resulted in the development team being able to base software development choices on the real-world data collected during the experimental procedure. Additionally, a set of previously identified design criteria to enable Continuous Experimentation on automotive systems was discussed and their validity confirmed in the light of the presented work.

Keywords: Software engineering · Software architecture · Continuous Experimentation · Cyber-physical systems · Automotive

1 Introduction

The automotive industry is currently investing considerable efforts and resources towards the achievement of an autonomous vehicle that would meet the specification of SAE level 3 [18]. Several companies have in fact already marketed

© Springer Nature Switzerland AG 2020
A. Jansen et al. (Eds.): ECSA 2020, LNCS 12292, pp. 73–88, 2020.
https://doi.org/10.1007/978-3-030-58923-3_5

vehicles exhibiting different semi-autonomous capabilities belonging to SAE level 2, ranging from adaptive lane keeping to self-parking features. The most relevant difference between level 2 and 3 in the SAE hierarchy is on who takes the responsibility of monitoring the driving environment: while in SAE level 2 the system assists the human driver in latitudinal and longitudinal adjustments, it is the driver who is expected to perform all the remaining tasks; instead, in SAE level 3 this is not required, meaning that the vehicle itself should be able to manage the *dynamic driving tasks* while the human driver is only expected to intervene upon request [17].

The software necessary to manage the diversity of situations that a vehicle can face is bound to be complex and computationally intensive, especially considering that the software present in modern vehicles already exceeds the Gigabyte in size [11]. Moreover, as all vehicles share the same basic capabilities but differ in the provided software functionality, it can be expected that the latter will constitute for the customers a relevant practical difference between automakers, thus fuelling a *functionality race* that will move the value concentration from the hardware, i.e., the vehicle itself, to its software capabilities.

1.1   Continuous Experimentation

When the software takes over the competitively distinguishing role from the hardware in the value-creation process, delivering new updates and functionality in a quick manner becomes necessary. This is very apparent in the software industry, especially for what concerns web-based software, where development techniques have been introduced to accelerate the process as much as possible by learning from how users and customers interact with such systems. Among them we find Continuous Integration (CI), Continuous Deployment (CD), and Continuous Experimentation (CE).

Continuous Integration proposes the integration of new software into the rest of the code base as soon as possible while Continuous Deployment involves the possibility of immediate deploying newly integrated software code into the target systems when all automated testing is successfully completed. There are many platforms that enable these two methodologies for software development teams, e.g., GitLab, Jenkins, and Zuul among many others. Continuous Experimentation builds upon the CI/CD pipeline and aims at enabling the developers to test new software performances by providing the possibility of deploying and running alongside the *official* software a number of *experiments*. These experiments could be either different versions of the official software or new functionality to be field-tested. While it adds computational overhead to the systems, Continuous Experimentation allows to confirm or reject hypotheses about the software suitability for a given task based on real-world data as opposed to simulations or speculations, making the software evolution process *data-driven*.

Continuous Experimentation has proven to be very effective on web-based software systems [10]. However, applying verbatim this way of working onto safety-critical cyber-physical systems such as vehicles would be an endeavour destined to face the specific challenges of the automotive context. One challenge is the added complexity given by the fact that the target systems in the case of vehicles are not virtual machines in server farms but highly mobile physical objects with limited computational performance. Moreover, there is a resource availability problem given by the Continuous Experimentation practice itself, which introduces a non-traditional approach when it comes to testing new functionality and needs additional computational power in order to manage the additional experiments and the data collection [9] on top of the system's nominal functions. This can pose issues to the automotive industry, which, being based on an economy of scale, has always built vehicles with hardware that is *just enough* powerful to fulfill its tasks in order to lower production costs. It also requires a rethinking of the classic system and software's architectures due to the new practice in which extra software is downloaded and run while its results are collected and uploaded back to the manufacturer. Nonetheless, new competitors seem to embrace this challenge as it can be seen from a manufacturer for luxury electric vehicles. In their quarterly financial reports, they mention already since 2015 the systematic gathering of driving and sensor data via "field data feedback loops" that are used to "enable the system to continually learn and improve its performance" [3]. While software experiments are not explicitly named, a company representative did mention the practice of installing "an 'inert' feature on vehicles" in order to "watch over tens of millions of miles how a feature performs" by logging its behavior in a real-world scenario [16].

A previous investigation in the automotive field by the authors shows that practitioners expect that they would benefit from the introduction of the Continuous Experimentation practice, even if it now faces these additional challenges [7]. Another recent study showed that literature was generally focusing increasing efforts in the study of this practice, but only a small portion of these studies were actually proposing practical experiments and none of them in the context of a Continuous Experimentation setting on an automotive or cyber-physical systems where the object of the experiment was not a visual change in a user interface [15]. Hence, the current work was devised to fill this research gap being the first study of this kind to propose and evaluate a system based on a proof-of-concept architecture for Continuous Experimentation built on previously identified design criteria [8], housed on a commercial truck tractor operated on a daily basis by a logistics company in Sweden (the truck is still in use throughout 2020).

1.2 Scope of this Work

While the aim of this work is to draw conclusions that are valid for the automotive field, it is worth mentioning the differences between the experimental work and a commercial automotive scenario. One such scenario would generally involve a fleet of vehicles, likely passengers cars, which are each controlled by a number of highly resource-constrained Electronic Control Units (ECUs). The experimental work for this study was instead performed on a single vehicle, i.e., a commercial truck tractor, equipped with a server-grade computing unit more powerful than a typical ECU, and the software was written using a high-level programming language. These differences are due to the fact that the aim of this study is *to provide and evaluate a proof-of-concept for the Continuous Experimentation process* rather than focusing on a particular automotive function. A key aspect is however preserved: in the real-world case and in this study the vehicle is physically inaccessible to the manufacturer, forcing all software deployment and data exchange to be performed via an Over-The-Air (OTA) connection while the vehicle is in operation. Finally, it should be noted that the scope of this study does not include autonomous driving tasks as the vehicle used in the experimental setting is manually driven by a driver from the logistics company.

1.3   Research Goal

Previous investigations clearly show that the literature lacks design science studies about Continuous Experimentation in realistic cyber-physical systems contexts, and especially in the automotive domain. This study aims to bridge this research gap. The Research Goal (RG) of this work can be expressed as:

RG: To provide and evaluate a proof-of-concept that shows the feasibility and benefit of a Continuous Experimentation decision cycle for an algorithmic choice in the context of an automotive system, based on previously identified design criteria.

The Research Goal of this article can be further divided in the following Research Questions (RQ):

RQ1: What software architecture can support a Continuous Experimentation decision process on a complex cyber-physical systems such as an automotive system?

RQ2: To what extent do previously identified design criteria for Continuous Experimentation in the context of automotive cyber-physical systems hold?

1.4   Contributions

To the best knowledge of the authors, this study presents for the first time a Continuous Experimentation decision cycle focused on an algorithmic experiment on a computational system housed in a commercial vehicle, where the deployment of experimental software to the system and the retrieval of gathered data are performed via a mobile data connection while the automotive system was operated by the owner company. The whole experimental setting aimed to be the least invasive for the company's operators and their commercial activities. Both the system and software architectures are reported and the experimental work offered the chance to discuss and validate a set of design criteria for Continuous Experimentation on automotive cyber-physical systems that were previously identified in a preceding study.

2   Related Works

A number of studies explore the Continuous Experimentation practice, in its native application field, i.e., web-based systems, and more recently in the context of cyber-physical systems. Gupta et al. [10] describe the First Practical Online Controlled Experiments Summit. During this summit, a number of experts in experimentation from several software and online-based companies convened to discuss the experimentation processes they have in place, the main challenges they are facing, and some relative solutions.

Fagerholm et al. [6] defined an organizational model for Continuous Experimentation in the context of web-based products, comprising the tasks and artefacts that different roles involved in planning and implementation of a software product should manage in order to enable the experimentation process.

Recent mapping studies on the Continuous Experimentation practice show that the majority of the works they encountered explore the statistical methods sub-topic and are often rooted in the web-based applications context, which is the originating field of this practice; only a minority of studies are addressing the Continuous Experimentation practice in the cyber-physical systems field [4,15].

A previous work led by the authors [8] explored the design characteristics that a cyber-physical systems should possess in order to enable a Continuous Experimentation process on an autonomous vehicle. These design criteria are evaluated in this study to discuss their validity in the light of the presented work and considering the difference between the scopes of the two studies.

Olsson and Bosch [14] published a study connecting post-deployment data and the cyber-physical and automotive field. They interviewed representatives from three companies, one of which is an automotive manufacturer. The study reports that while post-deployment data collection mechanisms are in place, the collected data is only partially used and the purpose of this feedback is troubleshooting, rather than supporting a product improvement process.

Mattos et al. [13] performed a literature review to identify a set of challenges for Continuous Experimentation in cyber-physical systems that was used a starting point for a case study where they tried to identify possible solutions with industrial representatives.

Cioroaica et al. [5] propose the analysis of Digital Twins to assess the trustworthiness of smart agents such as additional functionality or system component being downloaded to a smart vehicle. While the approach yields value especially to evaluate third-party functionality, it relies on simulating the new component's behavior in a partial simulation of the surrounding environment. While simulations should be part of the evaluation process for new software due to the safety they can guarantee, in the authors' view they cannot completely replace the value coming from a field evaluation since the very high complexity of the real world and the system's interaction with it cannot be perfectly simulated.

No relevant publicly available information was found about commercial companies' practices regarding internal software experiments to improve autonomous functionality, except from the aforementioned comments regarding inert features [3,16].

3   Methodology

A Design Science methodology, i.e., the design and investigation of artifacts in context [19], was adopted to achieve the Research Goal. A software architecture was devised to support a number of software modules that would run and interact on a system performing a Continuous Experimentation decision cycle, housed in a commercial heavy vehicle, shown in Fig. 3. The Continuous Experimentation practice was applied to answer in a data-driven fashion a software development question regarding an algorithmic choice, performed on a complex cyber-physical systems such as an automotive vehicle only accessible via a remote connection. While supporting a software experiment is the goal, the focus of this study is not on the experiment itself, i.e., what the production and experimental modules actually do, but instead on the experimentation process itself. In other words, even if an experiment has been set up, for the purpose of this study what matters is not the result of the experiment, but rather whether an experiment could be actually carried out according to the Continuous Experimentation practice. For this reason, the focus of the results and discussion is the architecture and infrastructure for the experiment and not its outcome.

The experiment consisted in running different Machine Learning-based object detectors connected to the live video feed in order to find an object detector module that would recognise, as accurately as possible, items and road users in the vehicle's field of view. The experiment was run in a series of time-wise short sessions and the resulting data were analysed manually. The machine learning software modules were based on publicly available detection models[1] pre-trained on the COCO dataset [12]. This dataset was chosen because of the breadth of its scope, which encompasses automotive items and more, making it a valuable choice for a general-purpose object detector.

4   Results

4.1   Research Question 1

The work here reported shows a system and software architecture for the application of a Continuous Experimentation methodology in order to answer a software development question regarding an algorithmic choice, on a system housed in a remotely accessible vehicle. The following paragraphs describe the details of the software architecture supporting the experimentation process, the system architecture enabling the software to gather data and communicate results, and the way that the software was packaged in order to ease the deployment process while following the Continuous Integration/Continuous Deployment practices.

---

[1] https://github.com/tensorflow/models/blob/master/research/object_detection/g3doc/detection_model_zoo.md.

Software Architecture. The experimentation process is based on the interaction of the three modules *Production Software*, *Experimental Software*, and *Supervisor*, as shown in Fig. 1. As the names suggests, Production Software simulates a production component, whose performance must not be influenced by any other components. Each instance of the Experimental Software module represents an experiment deployed to test a new software variant, which runs in a sandboxed way, i.e., they must not issue commands to the actual system (especially any actuators) but instead have their output logged for later analysis, similarly to what is done by an automotive manufacturer who revealed it uses "inert features" [16]. The Supervisor module poses as the experiment manager software, monitoring the other modules' performances and deciding at any time whether to continue or not with the experiment, depending on whether the Experimental Software modules abide to the experiment parameters. It is also the module that interacts with the team, represented by the "HQ" box in Fig. 1, that plans and conducts the deployment of both the software modules and the Experiment Protocol, which comprises the parameters of the experiment cycle. Finally, it reports the results observed during operation back to the team.

When an experiment is set up in the computing system, an *Experimentation Protocol* is provided, which is a file collecting relevant parameters for the experiment, e.g., CPU usage thresholds for the Experimental Software that should not be crossed. Upon starting, the Supervisor will wait for the other software modules to manage the experimentation process. If a performance drop in the Production Software or an increase in resources consumption by the Experimental Software modules is detected by the Supervisor, the change is compared to the thresholds as specified in the Experimentation Protocol. If necessary, the Supervisor has the capability to request the Experimental Software modules either a *performance degradation*, so that it consumes less resources thus leaving more for the Production Software, or a full stop of the experiment if the violations are deemed too severe. During the experiment, relevant data about the detection performances are collected. These results are transmitted back to the remote team at the end of each experiment, allowing them to analyze the experiment's performance and finally decide which software version fulfilled its functional objectives more effectively.

System Architecture. To provide a proof-of-concept for Continuous Experimentation in the automotive context and better understand the underlying challenges, a research project was initiated as a collaboration between Chalmers University of Technology's vehicular laboratory REVERE, Volvo, Trafikverket, GDL, Kerry Logistics, Speed Group, Borås Stad, Ellos, and Combitech to equip a modern Volvo tractor with a platform consisting of two computers, five cameras, three GPS sensors, and a GPS/IMU system for daily data logging during typical operations of a logistics company.

As depicted in Fig. 2, the system is designed in the following manner: The automotive platform, a commercial truck tractor, is equipped with a Linux-based, Docker-enabled computer as primary unit and an Accelerated Processing

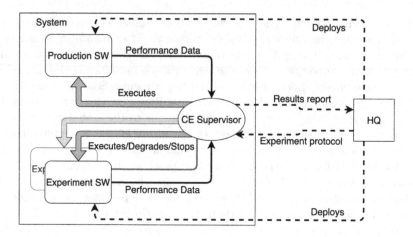

Fig. 1. View of the system and its components. The dashed lines represent Over-The-Air (OTA) communication.

Unit (APU) as secondary computing node. The main computer is equipped with an Intel Core i9-9900K CPU and an NVidia GP107 GPU. It is directly connected to two cameras, two GPS systems, and the vehicle's CAN network. The secondary unit has instead direct access to one camera, one GPS unit, and the vehicle's CAN network, since the computing systems are capable to access a subset of the CAN signals of the automotive platform, specifically the ones containing the vehicle's speed and the IMU data. The secondary unit has the purpose of providing a stable, low-energy demanding, highly available connection, enabling an additional point of access to the system for maintenance purposes.

Moreover, being directly connected to a number of input sensors, it can also act as a reliable fail-over system, although with degraded performances and a reduced amount of data, should the main unit malfunction during operations. Finally, the two mobile data connection routers acting as internal network nodes connect internally both computing units to the remaining two cameras and GPS units, and externally the whole system to the outside world. To provide a stable power supply to the hardware and not limit operations to only the time when the engine runs, the system is powered by a battery pack which is recharged by the engine when it is running.

The system is monitored live through a software dashboard, shown in Fig. 4, that allows to easily visualize important parameters such as system time, uptime, CPU temperature and consumption, system load, vehicle speed, GPS position and number of satellites, storage disk space utilization, battery level, and CAN connections data rates. As the vehicle is in daily operation by the logistics company, the software to test and the resulting data can only be extracted remotely hence making this project and platform well-suited for this study on Continuous Experimentation, as it represents the use-case of a single vehicle in

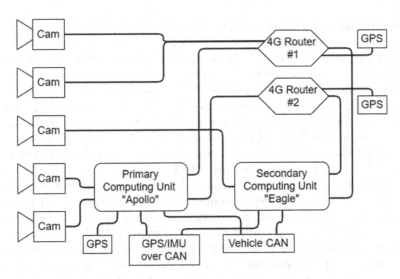

Fig. 2. Architecture of the system, named *Voyager*. The two computing units provide some redundancy should a fail occur while the system is in mission. A comprehensive set of cameras is available, as well as an IMU signal and several GPS sources.

a fleet that can run software experiments but cannot be physically accessed by the manufacturer.

Fig. 3. The vehicle housing the system is part of a project named Highly Automated Freight Transports (AutoFreight).

Fig. 4. Dashboard monitoring one of the computing systems on board the commercial truck tractor used in the experimental phase of this work.

Software Development and Deployment. To simplify the deployment phase, all software modules were developed and encapsulated using Docker[2]. Docker uses OS-level resource isolation to enable the execution of software in

---

[2] https://www.docker.com.

environments called containers, which are run on top of the host OS kernel, thus resulting in a more lightweight solution than a full-stack virtualization software. Each container is an instance of a Docker image, which acts similarly as a guest machine template and can be used to store and deliver applications.

The versioning, integration, and deployment operations were run in a GitLab-based environment. GitLab is a web-based DevOps lifecycle environment that provides a Git repository manager providing, among the other services, a Continuous Integration/Continuous Deployment pipeline. The resulting development cycle would follow these steps: firstly, a new change is introduced in the code-base via a Git repository commit; then, the Continuous Integration pipeline is automatically triggered and the new code is integrated and built within the code base; finally, the Continuous Deployment pipeline is executed triggering the build a Docker image, which is ready for distribution. If the new code was part of a software experiment, at the end of these three steps a Docker image with the experimental software is ready to be deployed and executed. These steps embody what we can expect an industrial Continuous Experimentation cycle to look like from development to deployment to execution and finally, by instrumenting the code, to data collection, analysis, and choice of a final software variant.

From what resulted during the development work, the average code base change would take around 4 min to be integrated while the Docker image building phase would last around 7 min. This means that a little more than ten minutes after new code was committed to the code base it was already available for deployment into the system. These phases took place at the team's end of the process and not on the automotive system itself, which had to download the software modules over the mobile connection. In the described setup, the resulting Docker image for an Experimental Software module amounted to approximately 5 GB in size due to the machine learning models and dependencies. While its size is significant, it is worth noting that no optimization nor compression was applied to the Docker image, which could have reduced significantly the amount of data to be deployed. The download of this image into the automotive system took approximately 14 min, which is comparable to the time needed to perform software updates in commercial vehicles. However, since Docker images are built as the aggregation of ID-marked layers based on their building process, most of the image downloads were only partial as several intermediate layers did not change between software builds and Docker allows to skip downloading duplicate layers. The experiment was run in a series of rounds while the vehicle was in operation in the Gothenburg area, as shown in Fig. 5. At the end of the experiment the resulting data were manually analyzed and it was concluded that the object detector used in one of the Experimental Software modules performed more accurately than the Production Software module. The results of the machine learning experiment are not reported nor discussed in detail as the focus of this work is not the object of the experiment in itself, but rather the architecture and infrastructure that made it possible. In the described experimental setup the process proved to be possible and feasible, and led to a successful experiment cycle that produced a data-based answer to a software development question.

4.2   Research Question 2

In a previous study on the subject a set of design properties was identified that would enable Continuous Experimentation on a complex cyber-physical system such as an autonomous vehicle [8]. These properties are here listed and discussed in the light of the work described so far.

Access to perception sensors and systems, this was of course needed to run the Production and Experimental Software and was used in this study; *access to full vehicle control*, in this work it was not needed since controlling the vehicle was not in the scope of the experimentation process nor the experiment itself. Had it been so, a system architecture capable of driving the vehicle would have been needed; *log internal activity and other relevant metrics*, a necessary step to allow the analysis of the experimental results; *enabling of data transmission from the developers to the deployed system* and *the feedback loop in the opposite direction*, also necessary to deploy software and retrieve the resulting data remotely; *reliability*, implemented through health checking techniques adopted to limit fault propagation and to enable remote troubleshooting and "graceful degradation" by having a secondary computing unit capable to restart the primary one and having access to own sensors and data streams; *testability*, as all changes in functionality were firstly tested on local machines fed with recordings of past camera streams to ensure that the new code to be deployed to the system would perform as expected; *safety*, in this case the software had no physical control over the actual vehicle, meaning that even in case of faults, the safety implications were limited. Nonetheless, safety constraints were implemented in the form of thresholds over the amount of computational power that the experiment modules could use in order to simulate how the system would respond to resource-hungry experiments endangering the execution of Production Software; *scalability*, an automotive system is naturally distributed across several computational units, in the present case the system adopted in this study is distributed over two computing nodes. While one was used to actually execute Production and Experimental Software modules, the other was still involved in the process as it was accessed to retrieve the camera feed used by the software. Would it have been possible or necessary, the modular nature of the software that was used would have allowed for even more spread-out distribution, since the communication between software modules was performed via UDP multicast message exchange, requiring simply a network connection among computing nodes; *separation of concerns*, meaning the establishment of abstraction layers between hardware and software and between data and exchanged messages, definitely a necessary part of any software running on complex cyber-physical systems; *simplicity to involve new developers*, a feature of the development process more than of the physical system itself, in this case provided mostly by the ease of use of the development tools, which automated the majority of the steps necessary to perform Continuous Integration/Deployment pipelines; *facilitation for operators*, meaning that the software should not be hard to operate for those who are not developers, in this study it was not possible to acquire an external perspective on this point, as the only tester and operator of the Continuous Experimentation cycle was also the developer. However it should be noted that the adoption of microservices allowed to run or stop the execution of Production or Experimental Software by using a very limited number of console commands; *short cycle from development to deployment*, which is necessary whenever possible in order to roll out changes and new features at a fast pace, was definitely present in this study due to the automated Continuous Integration/Deployment mechanisms.

5   Discussion

The presented Continuous Experimentation prototypical implementation shows that it is possible to achieve enough data feedback from candidate functionality in a vehicular system to get a better understanding about its performances. This allows researchers and developers to decide how to proceed with future software development efforts based on the data coming from the automotive system operating in real-life scenarios. As the goal was to verify the viability of the approach and qualitatively evaluate its architecture, the practical limits to the applicability or performances of the prototype, such as for example the minimum quality of service for the data connection or the base amount of experiments' results to be collected, were not in the direct focus of this study. Nonetheless it can be expected that certain parameters would be particularly relevant for the execution of the envisioned process, such as the remote connection quality, which has to be high enough to allow the exchange of software and the resulting data in the timeframe set for the experiment; and the computational capacity of the unit running the experiments, which has to support their execution so that the results of interest can be obtained.

Since this was a proof-of-concept implementation, some of the issues that are specific to commercial vehicles were not addressed in this study. One of them is connected to the computational limits of automotive ECUs, which were not used in the experimental setup but are envisioned to be the computational units of such a production system in the future. Since ECUs are less computationally powerful than the hardware that was used in this prototype, employing them as computational hardware could have provided additional insight on how much could the low resources of these units hinder the execution of experiments. It is however worth to mention that even with low hardware capabilities it could be possible to run additional software, although perhaps not by using an off-the-shelf solution like Docker as it requires support from the Linux kernel. However, if adding additional computing power to the system is not an option it may still be possible to find scheduling strategies for the experiments' execution that make use of computational resources not needed by the Production Software [9].

Another important difference between this prototype and commercial vehicles involves the safety constraints for the software. Automotive regulations demand strong safety standards for the software run in vehicles to which future experimental software may have to abide. In this prototype the only safety measures relied in the monitoring capabilities of the Supervisor module and its degradation/abort commands. Moreover, additional coding rules that apply to automotive software were not followed in this case, e.g., the prohibition to allocate dynamic memory. While sufficient for the aim of this test, it can be envisioned that more sophisticated coding standards and functional emergency stop mechanisms will be needed for future commercial implementations of this concept, unless perhaps it can be proved that the experiments cannot influence the vehicle's behavior in any way. Additional smaller challenges were posed by practical issues such as the size of software downloads to be undertaken by the automotive system, which was slowed by the bandwidth of the mobile data connection of the system. It should finally be mentioned that being this a prototype and not a system ready or close to commercial use, the company owner of the truck did not use the results of the study to change their strategy or operations at the present time.

Analyzing the design criteria identified in a previous study, it is the authors' conclusion that they do hold for a Continuous Experimentation process on an automotive system, with the only discrepancies explained by the lack of autonomous capabilities in the present study's vehicle and the presence of a single developer/tester instead of different team members covering different roles. The design criteria can thus be viewed as a form of checklist to validate the preparedness of a complex cyber-physical systems' architecture and development process to run Continuous Experimentation.

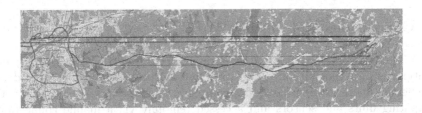

Fig. 5. Highlighted GPS traces of the vehicle in the first half of 2020 in the Gothenburg geographic area. The horizontal lines were artefacts of the overlay script in correspondence of GPS-denied areas.

5.1   Threats to Validity

A number of factors may threaten the validity of this work.

One threat is likely the fact that the experiment infrastructure and the software modules do not abide to current automotive standards like [1,2]. For example, one of the main differences between the software used in this work and the commercial automotive software is the use of dynamic memory allocation, which is currently forbidden in safety-critical systems due to the introduced vulnerability that could disrupt critical software capabilities when needed. This threatens the generalizability of the result since what was achieved in this study could be technically harder to obtain abiding to the strict automotive software standards. However, this threat is less impending considering that this work had the goal of providing a proof-of-concept showing that a working Continuous Experimentation-enabled vehicle is within the automotive industry's grasp, rather than provide one ready for commercial use.

Connected to the aforementioned threat, another potential issue is the fact that the software developed for this work had the capability to only run one or two Experimental Software modules at the same time. While this may seem an important limitation, it is worth noting that a higher number of experiments running concurrently would require a higher amount of spare computational power in a real-world scenario. Moreover, if a vehicle can only run a set amount of experiments at the same time this could play in favor of the development efforts necessary to tackle the previously mentioned threat to validity: the variables that would normally require an amount of memory dependent on the number of experiments could be in fact dimensioned *a priori* since the number is fixed.

Lastly, it should be noted that it is not necessarily possible to generalize the results obtained with Continuous Experimentation in the automotive field to the rest of the cyber-physical systems context. While the challenges lurking in the automotive field are increasingly recognized and faced, it is possible and not unlikely that several additional challenges peculiar to different cyber-physical systems sub-fields are still in the way and will prevent a rapid widespread adoption of this practice to non-automotive systems.

6   Conclusions and Future Work

The presented work demonstrated and evaluated the execution of a prototypical Continuous Experimentation cycle for an automotive system, which is in daily commercial operations by a logistics company. The system was equipped with computing units and sensors and accessed remotely via a mobile connection, which was the only communication channel used to deploy software and retrieve the data resulting from running a software experiment. A set of previously identified design criteria to enable Continuous Experimentation on autonomous vehicles was discussed in light of the (non-autonomous) system built for this work. This study could show for the first time that an algorithmic development question can be answered applying a Continuous Experimentation process, while also highlighting some relevant challenges still standing on the way towards a fully-functional experiment-enabled vehicle.

One direction for future studies could be for example the automation of those steps that were manually performed in this work, e.g., the deployment of software to the automotive system, or the analysis of the resulting experiment data. As previously mentioned, additional follow-up studies would be the replication of this proof-of-concept using software and hardware closer to those adopted for consumer vehicles. That would require the software to abide at least partly to existing automotive regulations, and to run experiments on hardware facing resource constraints closer to what is currently present in real-world vehicles.

Acknowledgment. This work was supported by the project *Highly Automated Freight Transports* (AutoFreight), funded by Vinnova FFI [2016-05413].

References

1. ISO 21448:2019: "Road vehicles - safety of the intended functionality". https://www.iso.org/standard/70939.html. Accessed 04 Nov 2019
2. ISO 26262-1:2011: "Road vehicles - functional safety". https://www.iso.org/standard/43464.html. Accessed 04 Nov 2019
3. Tesla financials & accounting information. https://ir.tesla.com/financial-information/quarterly-results. Accessed 31 Jan 2020
4. Auer, F., Felderer, M.: Current state of research on continuous experimentation: a systematic mapping study. In: 2018 44th Euromicro Conference on Software Engineering and Advanced Applications (SEAA), pp. 335–344. IEEE (2018)
5. Cioroaica, E., Kuhn, T., Buhnova, B.: (Do not) trust in ecosystems. In: 2019 IEEE/ACM 41st International Conference on Software Engineering: New Ideas and Emerging Results (ICSE-NIER), pp. 9–12 (2019)
6. Fagerholm, F., Guinea, A.S., Mäenpää, H., Münch, J.: The right model for continuous experimentation. J. Syst. Softw. **123**, 292–305 (2017)
7. Giaimo, F., Andrade, H., Berger, C.: The automotive take on continuous experimentation: a multiple case study. In: 2019 45th Euromicro Conference on Software Engineering and Advanced Applications (SEAA), pp. 126–130. IEEE (2019). https://doi.org/10.1109/SEAA.2019.00028
8. Giaimo, F., Berger, C.: Design criteria to architect continuous experimentation for self-driving vehicles. In: 2017 IEEE International Conference on Software Architecture (ICSA), pp. 203–210. IEEE (2017). https://doi.org/10.1109/ICSA.2017.36
9. Giaimo, F., Berger, C., Kirchner, C.: Considerations about continuous experimentation for resource-constrained platforms in self-driving vehicles. In: Lopes, A., de Lemos, R. (eds.) ECSA 2017. LNCS, vol. 10475, pp. 84–91. Springer, Cham (2017). https://doi.org/10.1007/978-3-319-65831-5_6
10. Gupta, S., et al.: Top challenges from the first practical online controlled experiments summit. ACM SIGKDD Explor. Newsl. **21**(1), 20–35 (2019)
11. Hiller, M.: Thoughts on the future of the automotive electronic architecture (2016). http://h24-files.s3.amazonaws.com/159726/874242-uLYqg.pdf. Accessed 22 Oct 2019
12. Lin, T.-Y., et al.: Microsoft COCO: common objects in context. In: Fleet, D., Pajdla, T., Schiele, B., Tuytelaars, T. (eds.) ECCV 2014. LNCS, vol. 8693, pp. 740–755. Springer, Cham (2014). https://doi.org/10.1007/978-3-319-10602-1_48
13. Mattos, D.I., Bosch, J., Olsson, H.H.: Challenges and strategies for undertaking continuous experimentation to embedded systems: industry and research perspectives. In: Garbajosa, J., Wang, X., Aguiar, A. (eds.) XP 2018. LNBIP, vol. 314, pp. 277–292. Springer, Cham (2018). https://doi.org/10.1007/978-3-319-91602-6_20

14. Holmström Olsson, H., Bosch, J.: Post-deployment data collection in software-intensive embedded products. In: Herzwurm, G., Margaria, T. (eds.) ICSOB 2013. LNBIP, vol. 150, pp. 79–89. Springer, Heidelberg (2013). https://doi.org/10.1007/978-3-642-39336-5_9

15. Ros, R., Runeson, P.: Continuous experimentation and a/b testing: a mapping study. In: Proceedings of the 4th International Workshop on Rapid Continuous Software Engineering, RCoSE 2018, pp. 35–41. ACM, New York (2018)

16. Ross, P.E.: Tesla reveals its crowdsourced autopilot data. http://spectrum.ieee.org/cars-that-think/transportation/self-driving/tesla-reveals-its-crowdsourced-autopilot-data. Accessed 31 Jan 2020

17. Smith, B.W.: SAE levels of driving automation (2013). http://cyberlaw.stanford.edu/blog/2013/12/sae-levels-driving-automation. Accessed 31 Jan 2020

18. SAE J3016: Taxonomy and definitions for terms related to on-road automated motor vehicles. Society of Automotive Engineers, Warrendale, PA (2014)

19. Wieringa, R.J.: Design Science Methodology for Information Systems and Software Engineering. Springer, Heidelberg (2014). https://doi.org/10.1007/978-3-662-43839-8

Towards Using Probabilistic Models to Design Software Systems with Inherent Uncertainty

Alex Serban[1,2(✉)], Erik Poll[1], and Joost Visser[3]

[1] Radboud University, Nijmegen, The Netherlands
`a.serban@cs.ru.nl`
[2] Software Improvement Group, Amsterdam, The Netherlands
[3] Leiden University, Leiden, The Netherlands

Abstract. The adoption of machine learning (ML) components in software systems raises new engineering challenges. In particular, the inherent uncertainty regarding functional suitability and the operation environment makes architecture evaluation and trade-off analysis difficult. We propose a software architecture evaluation method called Modeling Uncertainty During Design (MUDD) that explicitly models the uncertainty associated to ML components and evaluates how it propagates through a system. The method supports reasoning over how architectural patterns can mitigate uncertainty and enables comparison of different architectures focused on the interplay between ML and classical software components. While our approach is domain-agnostic and suitable for any system where uncertainty plays a central role, we demonstrate our approach using as example a perception system for autonomous driving.

Keywords: Software architecture · Machine learning · Uncertainty

1 Introduction

With the emergent adoption of ML components in software systems, there is an increased need to tackle and harness their *inherent* uncertainty. Methods to address uncertainty exist for design time [4, 7] and for run-time [3]. However, previous work focused primarily on uncertainty related to the parameters used to model a system or its context [3, 4, 7]. ML components add a new type of uncertainty that was only briefly explored previously; stemming from the fundamental impossibility to fully verify that they can satisfy their intended functionality and that they are able to cope with stochastic events during operation [11].

In this paper we introduce a method to evaluate architecture design alternatives for software using both traditional and ML components. The proposal, called Modeling Uncertainty During Design (MUDD), is based on two guiding principles. Firstly, the threats due to inherent uncertainty of ML components are evaluated both locally (for the specific components) and tracked as they

© Springer Nature Switzerland AG 2020
A. Jansen et al. (Eds.): ECSA 2020, LNCS 12292, pp. 89–97, 2020.
https://doi.org/10.1007/978-3-030-58923-3_6

propagate and influence other components in the system. Secondly, the prior information about uncertainty of ML components which is used at design time is considered incomplete and subject to continuous change.

The rest of the paper is organized as follows. Firstly, MUDD is introduced (Sect. 2), followed by a demonstration (Sect. 3), related work (Sect. 4) and conclusions (Sect. 5).

2   Modeling Uncertainty During Design (MUDD)

MUDD explicitly models two sources of uncertainty specific to "automated learning" [6]: (1) epistemic uncertainty, i.e., the uncertainty about the data generation process (used for training ML models), and (2) stochastic uncertainty, i.e., the uncertainty related to stochastic noise in the environment where a ML component operates. These uncertainty types have been studied in self-adaptive systems [8], where software architecture plays an important role. MUDD is distinct by modeling these uncertainties at *design* time, rather than at run time.

Notably, MUDD supports reasoning over which design alternatives are less sensitive to uncertainty and how design patterns can help mitigate it. Moreover, the method allows to evaluate hypothetical scenarios, in which the data about uncertainty used at design time is incomplete or assumed to take any value.

From a methodological perspective, MUDD only requires to annotate existing software architectures with the sources of uncertainty specific to ML components. Under the hood, MUDD uses Bayesian networks (BNs) to model a software system, propagate the uncertainties and obtain quantitative data about the architecture's sensitivity to uncertainty.

We emphasize that MUDD uses these two uncertainty types because they are application and context *independent*, i.e., they are valid for any ML model. The methods used to measure them can be different, depending on the ML algorithm employed. Therefore, they are parameters rather than fixed elements of MUDD. Nonetheless, MUDD is not limited to any type of uncertainty.

Throughout the paper we use an example from autonomous driving, inspired by [1,10] – the design of a perception system for scene understanding. The system performs three tasks: (1) object detection, which aims to identify the location of all objects in an image, (2) semantic segmentation, which assigns each pixel in an image to a predefined class, and (3) depth estimation, which determines the position of obstacles or the road surface.

The outcome of the example perception system is used in planning the next driving maneuvers. The functionality of all components is implemented using deep learning (DL) because no specification can be written for it, and other ML algorithms perform worse. We are interested to evaluate software architecture design alternatives and select the one which is the least sensitive to uncertainty.

In Fig. 1a and b we present two architecture candidates inspired by [10] and [1]. The relevant functional components are illustrated using circles while the input coming from the camera is depicted with a rectangle. The latter will not be later considered a node in the BN (therefore its shape).

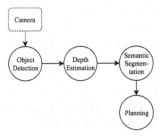

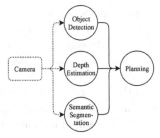

(a) End-to-end architecture.

(b) Component-based architecture.

Fig. 1. Functional architectures for a scene understanding system in autonomous vehicles.

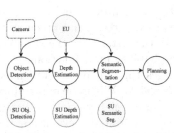

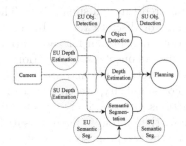

(a) End-to-end annotated architecture, as required by MUDD.

(b) Component-based annotated architecture, as required by MUDD.

Fig. 2. Uncertainty representation for the two architectures presented in Fig. 1, where EU stands for epistemic uncertainty and SU for stochastic uncertainty.

The first figure illustrates the end-to-end paradigm, where all components of the system are jointly trained to form a representation relevant to planning. This corresponds to the recommendation in [10]. The components share a base network for feature extraction and have independent layers to decode the features for each task. An alternative architecture is presented in the Fig. 1, where the system is organized into distinct ML components and integrated during planning. This corresponds to the architecture recommended in [1]. We have chosen these architectural styles as the only alternatives we could find in literature. However, MUDD is not limited to any architectural style.

For reasoning about uncertainties, we propose to annotate the two architectures with the sources of uncertainty specific to each component. An example is given in Fig. 2, which departs from the functional view presented in Fig. 1 by illustrating the uncertainty sources, for each component. In the first case, Fig. 2a, one base encoder is used for all tasks. Therefore, only one node representing epistemic uncertainty (EU) influences all components.

Different sources of stochastic uncertainty (SU) can impact the three tasks because one random event in the operational environment can influence segmentation, but not detection or depth estimation (and vice versa). Therefore, for each component there is a different variable for stochastic uncertainty. In the second scenario from Fig. 2b, the components process raw data from camera independently. Therefore, they are subject to distinct epistemic and stochastic uncertainties. We note that these decisions are not application and context specific. All ML components are subject to these types of uncertainty.

3   Quantitative Architecture Evaluation

Under the hood MUDD uses BNs to process quantitative data about uncertainties. The probabilities needed to populate the network can be defined by experts or inferred through simulations. The random variables in the BN can take continuous or discrete values. In the former case, the system designer chooses an a priori distribution for each variable, before seeing any data, and updates its parameters once new observations are available. In the latter case, the variables take discrete values and are described by their probability mass functions.

For simplicity, we choose to model all variables through probability mass functions with two discrete values: *low* or *high* uncertainty. When the uncertainty is low, the system is likely to satisfy its intended functionality and vice versa. Given the two proposed values for uncertainty, we are interested in evaluating the influence of different nodes in the network on planning and obtain quantitative results for the qualitative evaluation presented earlier. Both the probabilities and the thresholds can be decided by domain experts or by simulation.

For the running example we use a test data set to extract the uncertainty estimates from DL components, by averaging over samples in this data set. The thresholds between low and high represent the lowest uncertainty estimate from the incorrectly classified examples in the testing data set. The probability that a component has high (epistemic or stochastic) uncertainty will be the total number of test examples which have uncertainty higher than the threshold over the total number of testing examples. Note that the correctly classified examples with high uncertainty will contribute to the probability that a component has high uncertainty. This choice is deliberate because the system we study is safety-critical and uncertain decisions should be avoided altogether.

The conditional probabilities – i.e., the influence of components to the connected components – are evaluated in a similar manner. They represent the probabilities that a component has high uncertainty, given the uncertainty values of the parent variables. For example, $P(OD = \text{H}|EP = \text{H}, SU = \text{H})$ is the probability that the object detector is highly uncertain when the model has high epistemic and high stochastic uncertainty. We use the same method and data set as before, but average the results when the parent variables have the same value. The thresholds are also chosen as before.

Uncertainty Estimation. All experiments are carried out using the CityScape data set [2]. For the end-to-end architecture presented in Fig. 1a we train a variant of MultiNet [12] using an encoder based on the DenseNet architecture, pre-trained on the ImageNet data set with a dropout probability of $p = 0.2$. We use different loss functions in a multi-task learning setting for object detection, depth estimation and semantic segmentation. Epistemic uncertainty is approximated by casting a Bernoulli distribution over the model's weights and sample it at evaluation time using the dropout layers in the base encoder. The mean of the dropout samples is used for prediction and the variance to output the uncertainty for each class. Stochastic uncertainty is extracted from the final layer of each task. For the component-based architecture presented in Fig. 1b we use an independent encoder and decoder for each task. Training is performed by minimizing the task specific loss function used in the multi-task setting described above. The implementation of DL components was done in Pytorch[1] and the BNs in Pomegranate[2]. The uncertainty estimates are presented in Table 1 for the system in Fig. 1a and Table 2 for the system in Fig. 1b.

The heuristics applied to populate the tables represent the prior knowledge we embed in the network. Depending on the context, software designers may choose to embed more domain knowledge or rely on expert opinion.

Given the probability tables, we can use the inference rules of BNs to answer questions about the proposed architectures. We provide a working example: e.g., we wish to get quantitative evidence about the impact of high stochastic uncertainty in depth estimation on planning. Setting depth estimation stochastic uncertainty to "High" ($SU_{DE} = H$), we can compute the final impact on planning as follows. Let $\pi(x)$ represent the parent variables of node x (the nodes that have a directed edge to it). The probability that planning will have high uncertainty is:

$$P(Planning = \mathrm{H}) = P(SS|\ \pi(SS)) \cdot P(DE|\ \pi(DE)) \cdot P(OD|\ \pi(OD)) \cdot$$
$$P(SU_{SS}) \cdot P(SU_{DE} = \mathrm{H}) \cdot P(SU_{OD}) \cdot P(EU),$$

for the end-to-end architecture and:

$$P(Planning = \mathrm{H}) = P(SS|\ \pi(SS)) \cdot P(DE|\ \pi(DE)) \cdot P(OD|\ \pi(OD)) \cdot$$
$$P(SU_{SS}) \cdot P(SU_{DE} = \mathrm{H}) \cdot P(SU_{OD}) \cdot P(EU_{SS}) \cdot P(EU_{DE}) \cdot P(EU_{OD}),$$

for the component-based architecture, where the acronyms are as in Tables 1 or 2.

Running the computation we observe that the probability of uncertain planning is approximately 10% lower for the component-based architecture (Fig. 1b) than for the end-to-end architecture. Moreover, through the same model we can analyze how high stochastic uncertainty in depth estimation impacts planning within the minimum and maximum bounds. We plot the probability that planning is uncertain given that depth estimation stochastic uncertainty is high, by varying $P(DE = \mathrm{H}|SU = \mathrm{H}, \cdot\ )$ in Tables 1 and 2 between $[0, 1]$ with a step size of 0.01. The results are illustrated in Fig. 3a.

---

[1] https://pytorch.org/.
[2] https://github.com/jmschrei/pomegranate.

Table 1. Independent and conditional probabilities for the end-to-end architecture in Fig. 2a. The acronyms used are OD – object detection, DE – depth estimation, SS – semantic segmentation, EU – epistemic uncertainty and SU – stochastic uncertainty. The uncertainty values are L - low and H - high.

$P(\cdot)$	EU	SU_{OD}	SU_{DE}	SU_{SS}
H	0.18	0.16	0.11	0.19

$P(Planning \mid SS)$	
0.1	L
0.9	H

$P(OD \mid EU \mid SU_{OD})$		
0.0	L	L
0.64	L	H
0.61	H	L
1	H	H

$P(DE \mid EU \mid SU_{DE} \mid OD)$			
0.0	L	L	L
0.13	L	L	H
0.76	L	H	L
0.85	L	H	H
0.43	H	L	L
0.78	H	L	H
0.9	H	H	L
1	H	H	H

$P(SS \mid EU \mid SU_{SS} \mid DE)$			
0.0	L	L	L
0.28	L	L	H
0.64	L	H	L
0.72	L	H	H
0.66	H	L	L
0.58	H	L	H
0.61	H	H	L
1	H	H	H

The plot represents the influence of high stochastic uncertainty on depth estimation and the way it propagates on planning. We observe that in the component-based architecture stochastic uncertainty in depth estimation has a lower impact on planning than in the end-to-end architecture, for values up to ~0.7, after which the end-to-end architecture is more resilient to uncertainty. Depending on the operational environment, a software architect can choose the design that better fits the expected conditions. For example, if an autonomous vehicle operates in limited domains – e.g., inside a warehouse – where the probability of encountering stochastic events is low, the component-based architecture for the scene understanding system is more appropriate.

Table 2. Independent and conditional probabilities for the component-based architecture in Fig. 2b. The acronyms used are described in Table's 1 caption.

$P(\cdot)$	EU_{OD}	SU_{OD}	EU_{DE}	SU_{DE}	EU_{SS}	SU_{SS}
H	0.14	0.16	0.31	0.44	0.17	0.19

$P(OD \mid EU_{OD} \mid SU_{OD})$		
0.0	L	L
0.57	L	H
0.41	H	L
1.0	H	H

$P(DE \mid EU_{DE} \mid SU_{DE})$		
0.0	L	L
0.51	L	H
0.47	H	L
1	H	H

$P(SS \mid EU_{SS} \mid SU_{SS})$		
0.0	L	L
0.11	L	H
0.42	H	L
1.0	H	H

$P(Planning \mid SS \mid DE \mid OD)$			
0.0	L	L	L
0.34	L	L	H
0.34	L	H	L
0.66	L	H	H
0.34	H	L	L
0.66	H	L	H
0.66	H	H	L
1	H	H	H

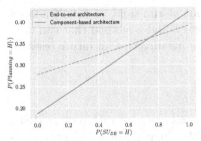
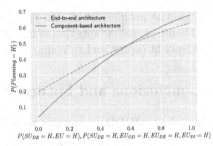

(a) Influence of high stochastic uncertainty in depth estimation on planning.

(b) Influence of high stochastic uncertainty for depth estimation and all epistemic uncertainties on planning.

Fig. 3. Quantitative evaluation of uncertainty in software architecture design.

Using the same model we can evaluate the influence of multiple sources of uncertainty on planning. We use the realistic assumption that the CityScape data set does not approximate all driving scenarios and thus may introduce high epistemic uncertainties. Therefore, we evaluate the influence of all epistemic uncertainty sources on planning in the scenario described above, where we assume high stochastic uncertainty in depth estimation. We use the same method as above to evaluate the probability that planning will have high uncertainty while we vary all epistemic uncertainty nodes simultaneously with the stochastic uncertainty in depth estimation. The uncertainties vary between $[0, 1]$, with a step size of 0.01. The results are plotted in Fig. 3b.

As in the previous case, the end-to-end architecture is more resilient to high uncertainties, for all the components mentioned above. Moreover, the threshold where the end-to-end architecture becomes more resilient than the component-based architecture is lower. However, epistemic uncertainty can be removed using more training data, so the scenario in which epistemic uncertainty is low is more realistic. In this case, the component-based architecture is more resilient to uncertainty than the end-to-end architecture.

4   Related Work

At design time, the uncertainty in the parameters used to model a software system has been taken into account for evaluating the reliability of software architectures using robust optimization [7], for comparing software architectures when the impact of architectural decisions can not be quantified, using fuzzy methods [4] and for evaluating trade-offs specific to quality attributes such as performance, using sensitivity analysis [5]. However, none of these methods take into account the uncertainty related to "automated learning", as indicated by [6].

At run-time, various sources of uncertainty can be mitigated through self-adaptation [3]. While several methods for self-adaptation use a related formalism, we tackle the problem at design time, and *not* at run-time, as in self adaptation. Therefore, self-adaptation is complementary, and a method that can unify uncertainty at design and run time is an interesting direction for future research.

5   Conclusions and Future Work

We introduce MUDD, a method to evaluate and compare architecture design alternatives for systems using ML components. In particular, we propose to explicitly model the inherent uncertainty specific to ML components at design time, and evaluate how it propagates and influences other components in a system. The proposed information needed to quantify the uncertainty for each ML component is well studied both in the software architecture and in the ML literature. For modeling software systems, MUDD uses Bayesian networks (BNs).

For future work we propose to further validate the sources of uncertainty with practitioners (e.g., through interviews), and to facilitate the use of MUDD by developing or integrating with appropriate tools. New scenarios, which can better exhibit the potential of MUDD and new uncertainty sources (e.g., [9]) are planned as well. Also, BNs are directed graphs and do not allow loops. Alternatives that can overcome this limitation are planned for future work.

References

1. Behere, S., Törngren, M.: A functional reference architecture for autonomous driving. Inf. Softw. Technol. **73**, 136–150 (2016)
2. Cordts, M., et al.: The cityscapes dataset for semantic urban scene understanding. In: IEEE CVPR, pp. 3213–3223 (2016)
3. Esfahani, N., Malek, S.: Uncertainty in self-adaptive software systems. In: de Lemos, R., Giese, H., Müller, H.A., Shaw, M. (eds.) Software Engineering for Self-Adaptive Systems II. LNCS, vol. 7475, pp. 214–238. Springer, Heidelberg (2013). https://doi.org/10.1007/978-3-642-35813-5_9
4. Esfahani, N., Malek, S., Razavi, K.: GuideArch: guiding the exploration of architectural solution space under uncertainty. In: ICSE, pp. 43–52. IEEE (2013)
5. Etxeberria, L., Trubiani, C., Cortellessa, V., Sagardui, G.: Performance-based selection of software and hardware features under parameter uncertainty. In: International Conference on Quality of Software Architectures, pp. 23–32 (2014)
6. Mahdavi-Hezavehi, S., Avgeriou, P., Weyns, D.: A classification framework of uncertainty in architecture-based self-adaptive systems with multiple quality requirements. In: Managing Trade-Offs in Adaptable Software Architectures, pp. 45–77. Elsevier (2017)
7. Meedeniya, I., Aleti, A., Grunske, L.: Architecture-driven reliability optimization with uncertain model parameters. JSS **85**(10), 2340–2355 (2012)
8. Perez-Palacin, D., Mirandola, R.: Uncertainties in the modeling of self-adaptive systems: a taxonomy and an example of availability evaluation. In: ACM/SPEC International Conference on Performance Engineering, pp. 3–14 (2014)
9. Serban, A., Poll, E., Visser, J.: Adversarial examples on object recognition: a comprehensive survey. ACM Comput. Surv. (CSUR) **53**, 1–38 (2020)

10. Serban, A., Poll, E., Visser, J.: A standard driven software architecture for fully autonomous vehicles. In: JASE, pp. 20–33. Atlantis Press (2020)
11. Serban, A.C.: Designing safety critical software systems to manage inherent uncertainty. In: IEEE ICSA-C, pp. 246–249. IEEE (2019)
12. Teichmann, M., Weber, M., Zoellner, M., Cipolla, R., Urtasun, R.: MultiNet: real-time joint semantic reasoning for autonomous driving. In: Intelligent Vehicles, pp. 1013–1020. IEEE (2018)

Model-Based Approaches

Empowering SysML-Based Software Architecture Description with Formal Verification: From SysADL to CSP

Fagner Dias[1], Marcel Oliveira[1(✉)], Thais Batista[1], Everton Cavalcante[1],
Jair Leite[1], Flavio Oquendo[2], and Camila Araújo[1,3]

[1] DIMAp, Federal University of Rio Grande do Norte, Natal, Brazil
fagnerdiasmorais@gmail.com, {marcel,thais,everton,jair}@dimap.ufrn.br,
cmlaraujo@gmail.com
[2] IRISA-UMR CNRS/Université Bretagne Sud, Vannes, France
flavio.oquendo@irisa.fr
[3] State University of Rio Grande do Norte, Natal, Brazil

Abstract. Software architecture description languages (ADLs) currently adopted by industry for software-intensive systems are largely semi-formal and essentially based on SysML and specialized profiles. Despite these ADLs allow describing both structure and behavior of the architecture, there is no guarantee regarding the satisfaction of correctness properties. Due to their nature, semi-formal ADLs do not support automated verification of the specified properties, in particular those related to safety and liveness of the specified behavior. This paper proposes a novel approach for empowering SysML-based ADLs with formal verification support founded on model checking. It presents (i) how the semantics of SysADL, a SysML-based ADL, can be formalized in terms of the CSP process calculus, (ii) how correctness properties can be formally specified in CSP, and (iii) how the FDR4 refinement checker allows verifying correctness properties through model checking. The automated model transformation from SysADL architecture descriptions to CSP composite processes has been implemented as a plug-in to the Eclipse-based SysADL Studio tool. This paper also describes an application of SysADL empowered with CSP to validate its usefulness in practice.

Keywords: Software architecture description · Formal verification · Correctness properties · CSP · SysML

1 Introduction

Software architecture descriptions play an essential role in the communication among stakeholders, e.g., architects, developers, etc. The precise communication of this artifact is quite important since a badly specified architectural model

---

This research was partially funded by INES 2.0, FACEPE grant APQ-0399-1.03/17, CAPES grant 88887.136410/2017-00, and CNPq grant 465614/2014-0.

A. Jansen et al. (Eds.): ECSA 2020, LNCS 12292, pp. 101–117, 2020.
https://doi.org/10.1007/978-3-030-58923-3_7

causes design and implementation flaws in a software system and can create misunderstandings [8]. Architecture description languages (ADLs) have been used as means of expressing software architectures and producing models that can be used at design time and/or runtime [3].

One of the major challenges in the design of software-intensive systems consists in verifying the correctness of their software architectures, i.e., if the envisioned architecture is able to fully meet the established requirements. Acknowledged as an important activity in software industry [10,14], the architectural analysis aims to verify system properties using architectural models at design time to detect incorrectness, inconsistencies, and other undesirable issues as soon as possible in the software development process. Due to the critical nature of many complex software systems, rigorous architectural models (such as formal architecture descriptions) are quite desirable as means of better supporting automated architectural analysis. The main advantage of adopting a formal approach is precisely determining if a software system satisfies properties of interest and constraints related to requirements and check the accuracy and correctness of architectural designs. The literature indeed reports studies that combine formal verification and software architecture descriptions as means of ensuring safety, correctness, and consistency in software systems [1,18].

Despite describing structure and behavior of a software architecture is possible, there is no guarantee on its correctness properties. Some ways of validating if a software architecture was correctly designed with respect to its functionalities are generating source code in a given target programming language or producing executable models able to be simulated. Nonetheless, simulating the architecture neither constitutes a proof of satisfaction of safety and liveness properties nor a guarantee that the execution respects the specified architecture behavior. Another important concern is that semi-formal languages such as SysML have well-defined syntax, but they lack complete formal semantics. This hampers the automated verification of the specified properties, in particular those related to safety and liveness of the architecture behavior.

This paper presents an approach for empowering SysML-based architecture descriptions with formal verification to support the model checking of correctness properties. Such an approach relies on the Communicating Sequential Process (CSP) [15], a process calculus applied in both academia and industry to formally specify and verify the behavior of concurrent processes/systems and how they interact with each other. More specifically, this paper proposes a CSP-based semantics for SysADL [13], a SysML-based ADL that combines typical constructs of ADLs with the use of the popular diagrammatic notation based on the SysML Standard for modeling software-intensive systems. SysADL is aligned with the ISO/IEC/IEEE 42010 International Standard [7] for architectural descriptions by providing multiple viewpoints and views in terms of requirements, structure, behavior, and execution of software architectures.

The automated transformation model from SysADL architecture descriptions to CSP composite processes has been implemented and integrated into SysADL Studio [9], a free, open-source support tool for SysADL. The formal verification itself is supported by FDR4 [5], a widely used refinement checker for CSP that allows verifying if the architectural model is free from deadlocks, livelocks, and miracles (i.e., specifications for which it is impossible to provide a valid implementation), as well as if the executable properties respect the behavioral specification. The application of SysADL formalized with CSP is herein illustrated with a room temperature control system (RTC).

The remainder of this paper is structured as follows. Section 2 briefly presents SysADL and CSP. Section 3 presents the CSP-based semantics for SysADL. Section 4 details the formal verification of properties regarding SysADL architecture descriptions with the FDR4 refinement checker. Section 5 presents the SysADL Studio extension to support the SysADL–CSP transformation. Section 6 discusses related work. Section 7 contains some concluding remarks.

2 Background

2.1 SysADL

SysADL defines three software architecture viewpoints for a system, namely (i) structural, (ii) behavioral, and (iii) *executable*. The structural viewpoint defines the architectural elements composing the structure of a system (*components, ports, connectors*) and relationships among them. Communication among components takes place through connectors that bind input and output ports. SysADL requires declaring all elements before creating their instances. The elements are declared by using *Block Definition Diagrams* (BDDs) whereas the *Internal Block Diagram* (IBD) is used to specify how instances of components and connectors form the configuration of architectures.

The behavioral viewpoint details the behavior of (i) components and connectors through *activities, actions, constraints* and (ii) ports through *protocols*. Activity instances are described in the *Activity Diagram* by instantiating actions and flows. Activities or actions may have validation constraints specified through expressions in the OMG Action Language for Foundational UML (ALF). Constraints can be also expressed using the *Parametric Diagram*.

The executable viewpoint represents the concretization of both structural and behavioral viewpoints by simulating the architecture behavior at runtime. The main purpose of the simulation is validating the behavior logic regarding the satisfaction of requirements and analysis of architecture functionalities. In the executable viewpoint, it is possible to specify details of each action by using ALF statements as well as define and instantiate elements. The executable instances should be interpreted by an ALF engine to execute the architecture.

2.2 CSP

CSP is a process algebra that can be used to describe systems composed of independent, self-contained processes with interfaces to interact with the environment [15]. Most CSP tools such as FDR4 [5] and ProBE [4] accept a machine-processable CSP called CSP_M. For the sake of presentation, this paper uses the CSP notation in theoretical definitions and CSP_M in FDR4 verification assertions.

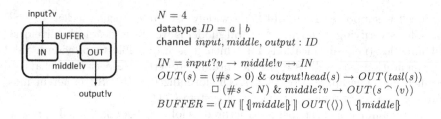

input?v

BUFFER

IN → OUT

middle!v

output!v

$N = 4$
datatype $ID = a \mid b$
channel $input, middle, output : ID$

$IN = input?v \rightarrow middle!v \rightarrow IN$
$OUT(s) = (\#s > 0) \ \& \ output!head(s) \rightarrow OUT(tail(s))$
$\qquad \Box \ (\#s < N) \ \& \ middle?v \rightarrow OUT(s \ ^\frown \langle v \rangle)$
$BUFFER = (IN \ [\![\{\!|middle|\!\}]\!] \ OUT(\langle\rangle) \setminus \{\!|middle|\!\}$

Fig. 1. CSP specification of a bounded buffer.

The two basic CSP processes are *Stop* and *Skip*: the former does nothing, i.e., deadlocks, and the latter does nothing but terminates. Prefixing $a \rightarrow P$ is initially able to perform only the event a, afterwards it behaves as process P. Prefixing may have input or output values. Process $c?x \rightarrow P(x)$ assigns the received value c to the implicitly declared variable x and behaves as process P with x in scope. Process $c!e \rightarrow P(x)$ outputs the value c of the expression e and behaves as process P. A Boolean guard may be associated with a process: $g \ \& \ P$ behaves as process P if the predicate g is true, otherwise it deadlocks. The operator $P_1 \ ; \ P_2$ combines processes P_1 and P_2 in sequence. The external choice $P_1 \ \Box \ P_2$ initially offers events of both processes P_1 and P_2. The environment has no control over the internal choice $P_1 \ \sqcap \ P_2$, which is internally resolved. The sharing parallel composition $P_1 \ [\![\ cs \ ]\!] \ P_2$ synchronizes processes P_1 and P_2 on events in the synchronization set cs, so that events that are not listed occur independently. Processes composed in interleaving $P_1 \ ||| \ P_2$ run independently. The event hiding operator $P \setminus cs$ encapsulates events in cs.

Figure 1 illustrates the CSP specification of a bounded buffer. There are two declarations: N is a constant with value 4 and ID is a datatype whose values are a and b. Process IN is the buffer component that receives a value through channel *input* and sends it to process OUT via channel *middle*. As process OUT can store N elements, it may receive new values via channel *middle* if the size of its sequence has not reached its capacity ($\#s < N$). The received value is stored at the tail of its sequence ($s \ ^\frown \langle v \rangle$). Process OUT may also provide an *output*, but only if its sequence is not empty ($\#s > 0$). In this case, it writes the head of the sequence ($head(s)$) and keeps only its tail ($tail(s)$). *BUFFER* is the parallel composition of process instances of IN and OUT starting with the empty sequence. Both processes IN and OUT synchronize on channel *middle*, which is hidden from the environment.

3   A CSP-Based Formal Semantics for SysADL

The translation from a SysADL architectural description to a CSP-based formal semantics allows verifying properties such as deadlock-freedom, livelock-freedom, and consistency among the structural, behavioral, and execution viewpoints of the model (see Sect. 4). The translation of types, those viewpoints, and the overall model are herein presented by using a room temperature control (RTC) system as running example[1]. The RTC system uses two temperature sensors to capture the current temperature. A user can set the desired temperature. A central controller receives the values from temperature sensors, compares them with the desired temperature, and turns the cooler/heater on/off. The system has a motion sensor to detect if there is someone in the room. In case of presence, the system operates to provide the desired temperature, otherwise it operates to keep the temperature at 22 °C.

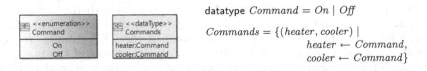

$$\text{datatype } Command = On \mid \textit{Off}$$

$$Commands = \{(heater, cooler) \mid$$
$$heater \leftarrow Command,$$
$$cooler \leftarrow Command\}$$

Fig. 2. Enumeration and composite datatypes in SysADL (left) and their translation to CSP (right).

Types. SysADL types are used in different viewpoints of the architecture description. These types can be basic types (*Integer*, *Boolean*, *String*, and *Real*), enumerated types, and composite types resulted from the composition of other types. *Integer* and *Boolean* are respectively mapped to *Int* and *Bool*. The *String* type is mapped to *String*, a set containing finite sequences of CSP characters (*Char*) with a maximum length. *Real* is translated to a pair of *Int* values. Enumerated types are mapped to CSP datatypes, which allow defining new types along with an enumeration of its values. Composite types are mapped to sets of tuples whose values come from the basic types.

Figure 2 shows the SysADL *Command* type and its mapping to a CSP datatype. A variable of the *Command* enumerated type may assume only values *On* or *Off*. The *Commands* type is a composition of two values of the *Command* type (*heater* and *cooler*). The *Commands* type is translated to a set definition that declares a set of pairs of values of the *Command* type.

3.1 Structural Viewpoint

Ports. SysADL ports are interaction points between a component and other architectural elements. They represent how data flow from a component (*out* ports) to another component (*in* ports). Composite ports are composed of other ports. Figure 3 presents an example of a port definition in SysADL. *CTemperatureITP* is an input port through which data of the *CelsiusTemperature* type flow.

Previously defined ports can be instantiated in component definitions, which can themselves be instantiated in configurations. In the CSP semantics for

---

[1] CSP files and the extended SysADL Studio are available at http://bit.ly/2PAqYiD.

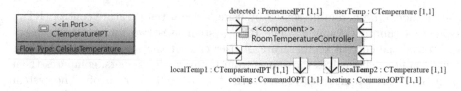

Fig. 3. Example of port (left) and composite component (right) in SysADL.

SysADL, a channel is declared for each port instantiated in component definitions or component instantiations. A simple port leads to the declaration of a CSP channel and a composite port leads to the declaration of one CSP channel for each port composing it. The names of the CSP channels related to ports attached to component definitions contain the name of the port and the name of its definition whereas the name of the channels related to component instantiations also includes the name of the instance. In Fig. 3, the instantiation *localTemp*1 of the port *CTemperatureITP* in the composite component *RoomTemperatureControllerCP* and the instantiation *rtc* of this component respectively yield the following CSP declarations:

channel *localTemp*1_*CTemperatureIPT* : *CelsiusTemperature*
channel *rtc_localTemp*1_*CTemperatureIPT* : *CelsiusTemperature*

Components. SysADL components can be defined as either (i) boundary components, i.e., they interface and exchange data with the physical environment or (ii) non-boundary components. These components repeatedly receive all input data through input ports, process them, and provide all their outputs in output ports. In Fig. 3, *RoomTemperatureControllerCP* is defined as a non-boundary component that receives four inputs and provides two outputs.

Figure 4 presents the architectural configuration of the RTC system in SysADL. This architecture is composed of seven component instances. $s1$, $s2$ and $s3$ are sensors that collect data about temperature and presence of people at the monitored environment. These data are processed by component *rtc*, which plays the role of the room temperature controller. Actuators $a1$ and $a2$ control cooling and heating according to decisions taken by *rtc*. *ui* is a user-interface component. In the translation of the definition and instantiation of these components, simple components yield processes whose behavior is the process that translates its activity, whilst composite components yield processes whose behavior is the process that translates its configuration. In Fig. 5, the simple component *PresenceCheckerCP* is translated to *PresenceCheckerCP* = *CheckPresenceToSetTemperatureAC* and the composite component *RoomTemperatureControllerCP* is translated to *RoomTemperatureControllerCP* = *RoomTemperatureControllerCP_Config*.

The semantics of boundary components such as *TemperatureSensorCP* (see Fig. 5) considers their non-deterministic behavior. For this reason, their semantics differs from that given for non-boundary components: the resulting process

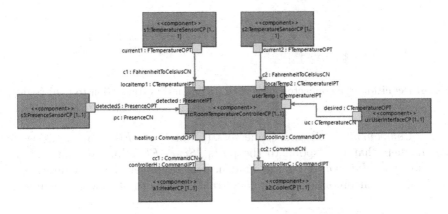

Fig. 4. Configuration of the RTC system in SysADL.

Fig. 5. Examples of SysADL boundary components.

randomly chooses a value to communicate in their output ports. As an example, the semantics of *TemperatureSensorCP* is a process that non-deterministically chooses a value from the type of the *FahrenheitTemperature* port.

Connectors. SysADL connectors bind ports of the connected components for exchanging data, possibly with some processing during transmission. In the CSP semantics for SysADL, connectors that do not process data are represented as CSP processes. Once connected to an output port and an input port, these processes repeatedly receive values from the output port and write them to the input ports. The behavior of a one-place buffer allows assynchronous communications among components, exactly corresponding to communications among components in SysADL. For example, the connector *CommandCN* (see Fig. 4) is translated to the following CSP process:

$$CommandCN = commandOut\_CommandOPT?out \rightarrow$$
$$commandIn\_CommandIPT!out \rightarrow CommandCN$$

Connectors that process data have their behavior defined by activities and their translation follows the same approach. For instance, *FahrenheitToCelsiusCN* is a connector that receives a Fahrenheit temperature and outputs the corresponding Celsius temperature. This conversion is defined by process *FahrenheitToCelsiusAC* as the behavior of the connector (see Fig. 6).

Configuration. In the SysADL structural viewpoint, the configuration defines how component instances are connected by connector instances. The behavior of a configuration *CFD* is the parallel composition of all its compo-

$FahrenheitToCelsiusCN =$
$FahrenheitToCelsiusAC$

Fig. 6. Definition of a connector in SysADL (left) and its translation to CSP (right).

nents ($Components_C FD$) and connectors ($Connectors_C FD$) synchronizing on the channels that correspond to the ports ($Sync_C FD$). Internal ports of the configuration ($Internal_C FD$) are hidden. For example, the configuration of the RTC system presented in Fig. 4 is translated to the following definitions:

$RTCSystemCFD\_config =$
$$\left(\begin{array}{c} Components\_RTCSystemCFD \\ [\![Sync\_RTCSystemCFD]\!] \\ Connectors\_RTCSystemCFD \end{array} \right) \setminus Internal\_RTCSystemCFD$$
$Sync\_RTCSystemCFD =$
$\{\!\!| \; current\_FTemperatureOPT, current\_FTemperatureOPT,$
$\quad detected\_PresenceOPT, desired\_CTemperatureOPT,$
$\quad controllerC\_CommandIPT, controllerH\_CommandIPT \; |\!\!\}$
$Internal\_RTCSystemCFD =$
$\{\!\!| \; detectedRTC\_PresenceIPT, heatingRTC\_CommmandOPT,$
$\quad coolingRTC\_CommandOPT, userTempRTC\_CTemperatureIPT,$
$\quad localTempP1\_CTemperatureIPT, localTempP2\_CTemperatureIPT \; |\!\!\}$

The processes corresponding to components and connectors of the configuration are defined as the interleaving of all components and connectors instances. The instantiation is achieved by using CSP renaming: every channel is renamed to a channel prefixed with the instance name and using the port instantiation name, rather than the port name. The resulting CSP specification[2] would be:

$Components\_RTCSystemCFD =$
$\quad |\!|\!| \; TemperatureSensorCP$
$\qquad [current\_FTemperatureOPT \leftarrow s1\_current1\_FTemperatureOPT]$
$\quad |\!|\!| \; TemperatureSensorCP$
$\qquad [current\_FTemperatureOPT \leftarrow s2\_current2\_FTemperatureOPT]$
$\quad |\!|\!| \; PresenceSensorCP[\ldots] \; |\!|\!| \; UserInterfaceCP[\ldots] \; |\!|\!| \; CoolerCP[\ldots]$
$\quad |\!|\!| \; HeaterCP[\ldots]$
$\quad |\!|\!| \; RoomTemperatureControllerCP[\ldots]$

$Connectors\_RTCSystemCFD =$
$\quad FahrenheitToCelsiusCN$
$\qquad \left[\begin{array}{l} Ct\_CTemperatureIPT \leftarrow rtc\_localtemp1\_CTemperatureIPT, \\ Ft\_FTemperatureOPT \leftarrow s1\_current1\_FTemperatureOP \end{array} \right]$
$\quad |\!|\!| \; FahrenheitToCelsiusCN[\ldots] \; |\!|\!| \; DetectedCN[\ldots]$
$\quad |\!|\!| \; CTemperatureCN[\ldots]$
$\quad |\!|\!| \; ControlCommandCN[\ldots] \; |\!|\!| \; ControlCommandCN[\ldots]$

---

[2] For the sake of conciseness, parts of the specification are omitted. The complete version can be found at http://bit.ly/2PAqYiD.

The proposed translation approach is indeed compositional. Therefore, the translation of simple and composite components follow the same rules. For instance, the configuration of the composite component *RoomTemperatureController CP* presented in Fig. 7 is translated like *RTCSystemCFD_config*, i.e., the parallel composition of its component and connector instances synchronizing on the channels that correspond to the ports with its internal events hidden from the environment. However, there is a minor increment in the definition of the process that represents connectors, *Connectors_RoomTemperatureControllerCP*: it also interleaves a process that translates the delegations, which are special connectors between proxy ports and ports in components as presented in Fig. 7:

$$Connectors\_RoomTemperatureControllerCP =$$
$$CTemperatureCN[\ldots] \;\|\|\; CTemperatureCN[\ldots] \;\|\|\; Delegation\_rtc$$
$$Delegation\_rtc = detectedRTC\_to\_detected \;\|\|\; userTempRTC\_to\_userTemp$$
$$\|\|\; localtemp1\_to\_s1 \;\|\|\; localTemp2\_to\_s2$$
$$\|\|\; heating\_to\_heatingRTC \;\|\|\; cooling\_to\_coolingRTC$$

For illustration purposes, the translation of delegation *detectedRTC_to_detected* is presented in the following. As for connectors, the behavior of a one-place buffer allows assynchronous communications among components, exactly corresponding to the behavior of SysADL delegations. The other translations follow the same approach.

$$detectedRTC\_to\_detected =$$
$$rtc\_detected\_PresenceIPT?PresenceIPT \rightarrow$$
$$pc\_detected\_PresenceIPT!PresenceIPT \rightarrow detectedRTC\_to\_detected$$

3.2   Behavioral Viewpoint

In SysADL, the behavioral viewpoint defines the behavior of components, connectors, and ports of the model. The behavior is described in terms of activities, actions, and constraints.

Constraints. Constraints are described as predicates that can be used to restrict the set of values of an activity. Once defined, constraints can be used in actions. As an example, Fig. 8 presents the constraint *FahrenheitToCelsiusEQ*, which verifies if the values given as arguments correctly correspond to the same temperatures in both Celsius and Fahrenheit units, and its translation to the CSP function $FahrenheitToCelsiusEQ(f, c)$.

Actions. SysADL actions process arguments given as inputs and provide an output that must respect its constraints. As many possible outputs may exist for the same input, the translation considers a non-deterministic choice of such possible output values. For example, the action *FahrenheitToCelsiusAN* returns the temperature value in the Celsius unit that corresponds to the temperature given in the Fahrenheit unit. In the translation, this corresponds to a communication on the channel that represents the output port. The translation of *FahrenheitToCelsiusAN* called by the connector named $s1$ is presented in Fig. 8.

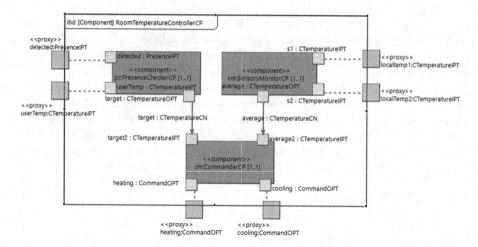

Fig. 7. Configuration of a composite component in SysADL.

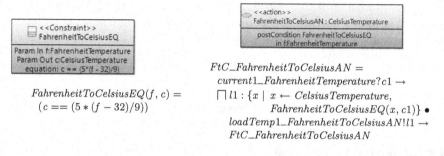

Fig. 8. Examples of constraint (left) and action (right) in SysADL.

Activities. SysADL activities are composed of one or more actions, which may communicate values between them. Figure 9 shows the *DecideCommandAC* activity as the composition of three actions that communicate values among them: actions *CommandHeaterAN* and *CommandCoolerAN* receive the output of the *CompareTemperatureAN* action.

The result of the translation of both constraints and actions is used in the translation of activities. Similarly to the translation of actions, the translation of activities also takes the name of the allocated component or connector. The activity is translated to a parallel composition of processes considering the activity entry and exit points (pins), i.e., the allocation of the activity on the associated component. For example, the activity *DecideCommandAC* is composed of actions *CompareTemperatureAN*, *CommandHeaterAN*, and *CommandCoolerAN*. The translation of this activity is:

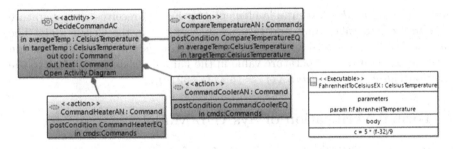

Fig. 9. Examples of activity (left) and executable elements (right) in SysADL.

$$DecideCommandAC = \begin{pmatrix} Pins\_DecideCommandAC \\ \|[Sync\_DecideCommandAC]\| \\ Actions\_DecideCommandAC \\ \setminus Internal\_DecideCommandAC \end{pmatrix}$$

Process $Pins\_DecideCommandAC$ is the parallel composition of the processes that represent all pins in the activity. The pin $average2_DecideCommandAC$ receives the value from the component port $average2$ and sends it to the $DecideCommandAC$ activity pin.

$Pins\_DecideCommandAC =$
$\quad \|[Sync\_DecideCommandAC]\| \; i : \{1 .. 4\} \bullet$
$\qquad Pins\_DecideCommandAC\_Func(i)$
$Pins\_DecideCommandAC\_Func(1) = average2\_DecideCommandAC$

$\ldots$

$Pins\_DecideCommandAC\_Func(4) = cooling\_DecideCommandAC$
$average2\_DecideCommandAC = average2\_CTemperatureIPT? average2 \rightarrow$
$\qquad\qquad\qquad\qquad average2\_CelsiusTemperature! average2 \rightarrow$
$\qquad\qquad\qquad\qquad average2\_DecideCommandAC$

$\ldots$

Similarly, process $Actions\_DecideCommandAC$ is the parallel composition of the processes that represent all actions in the activity:

$Actions\_DecideCommandAC =$
$\quad \|[Sync\_DecideCommandAC]\| \; i : \{1 .. 3\} \bullet$
$\qquad Actions\_DecideCommandAC\_Func(i)$
$Actions\_DecideCommandAC\_Func(1) = ct\_CompareTemperatureAN$

$\ldots$

3.3   Execution Viewpoint

The execution viewpoint must satisfy the conditions defined in the actions and related constraints within the behavioral viewpoint. The translation of executable elements translates their bodies to CSP functions. For example, the

FahrenheitToCelsiuEX executable element (see Fig. 9) receives a temperature value in the Fahrenheit unit and returns another one in the Celsius unit. The translation of the executable element *FahrenheitToCelsiuEX* is a CSP function parameterized on the temperature value in the Fahrenheit unit according to the equation $FahrenheitToCelsiuEX(f) = (5 * (f - 32)/9)$.

4 Formal Verification of SysADL Models

The translation of the SysADL models to CSP fosters their formal verification. This work uses FDR4 [5], a refinement model checker for CSP to automatically verify if the model satisfies (i) deadlock-freedom, (ii) livelock-freedom, (iii) absence of miracles, and (iv) the compliance of the execution model with the behavioral model. The translation of the model and the verification of these properties are fully automatic. The compliance with functional requirements can also be automatically verified. Nevertheless, the specification of the requirement currently needs to be expressed in CSP. The implementation of a user-friendly functional requirement description UI using SysADL diagrams is underway.

Deadlock-freedom and livelock-freedom are classical concurrency properties. A deadlock happens when a group of processes are permanently held on a situation in which each process waits for resources held by another process in the group. This makes the process to not progress. A livelock also has the same consequence, but for a different reason. In a livelock, processes are indefinitely progressing with internal events that cannot be seen by the external environment. This absence of external event leads the system to present no progress. It is possible to easily check the resulting CSP processes against these two properties by using FDR4 standard assertions for deadlock- and livelock-freedom. For example, the following assertions can be used in FDR4 to check if the running example (modeled as process *RTCSystemCFD*) is free of deadlock and livelock:

```
assert RTCSystemCFD:[deadlock free]
assert RTCSystemCFD:[divergence free]
```

Another property to be verified is that the behavioral model is not a miracle, i.e., the model has no possible executable model. Considering a SysADL constraint C defined in terms of inputs $i_1 \ldots i_n$ and outputs $o_1 \ldots o_m$, for every possible combination of input values that satisfy the pre-condition constraint *pre*, there must exist output values satisfying the post-condition constraint *post*. Formally, it is defined a CSP process that diverges if, and only if, the constraint is a miracle. For this verification, an auxiliary process $IS\_TRUE(c)$ is defined as successfully terminating only if predicate c is true, otherwise it diverges.

The process created for each constraint receives all input values and checks the pre-condition by using a guarded process *pre* & $IS\_TRUE(\ldots)$. If *pre* is false, then the process deadlocks avoiding a divergence, otherwise it checks if a set defined using the CSP set comprehension notation is not empty. This set contains all tuples $(o_1, \ldots, o_m)$ with values $o_1, \ldots, o_m$ respectively are of type $T_1, \ldots, T_n$ and satisfy the post-condition $post(i_1, \ldots, i_n, o_1, \ldots, o_m)$. Informally, this set is not empty if, and only if, the constraint is not a miracle. Therefore, it is possible to find output values satisfying the constraints when the input values satisfy the pre-condition.

```
C_check = C_i1?i1 -> ... C_in?in ->
            pre(i1,...,in) &
              let S = {(o1,...,om) | o1 <- T1, ..., om <- Tm,
                                    post(i1,...,in,o1,...,om)}
              within IS_TRUE(not(S == {}))
assert C_check:[livelock free]
```

In the running example, the constraint *FahrenheitToCelsiusEQ* is verified against miracles with the following assertion:

```
FahrenheitToCelsiusEQ_check =
  FahrenheitToCelsiusEQ_f?f ->
  true & let S = {c | c <- CelsiusTemperature, FahrenheitToCelsiusEQ(f,c)}
        within IS_TRUE(not(S == {}))
assert FahrenheitToCelsiusEQ_check:[livelock free]
```

The last verification is that the execution model is a refinement of the behavioral model. The only difference between these models regards the specification of actions, which are replaced by their executions. The former is composed of possibly constrained actions whereas the latter provides procedures that implement the behavior specified in the actions. This implementation must respect the constraints described in the activity. Theorem 1 states that an indexed internal choice over a set S is a failures-divergences refinement of an indexed internal choice over a set T if, and only if, S is a subset of T.

Theorem 1. $\sqcap x : T \bullet P(x) \sqsubseteq_{FD} \sqcap x : S \bullet P(x) \Leftrightarrow S \subseteq T$

The verification if the execution is a refinement of the behavior is done by simply checking subset containment: the set of pairs satisfying the executable *FahrenheitToCelsiusEX* must be a subset of the set of pairs satisfying *FahrenheitToCelsiusEQ*. Current work includes the integration with the CVC4 SAT solver [2] to optimize this verification.

$$FahrenheitToCelsiusEQ\_s = \{(f, c) \mid f \leftarrow FahrenheitTemperature,$$
$$c \leftarrow CelsiusTemperature,$$
$$FahrenheitToCelsiusEQ(f, c)\}$$
$$FahrenheitToCelsiusEX\_s = \{(f, c) \mid f \leftarrow FahrenheitTemperature,$$
$$c \leftarrow CelsiusTemperature,$$
$$c == FahrenheitToCelsiusEX(f)\}$$

```
assert IS_TRUE(subset(FahrenheitToCelsiusEX_s,
                      FahrenheitToCelsiusEQ_s)):[divergence free]
```

5   Tool Support and Validation

The translation from SysADL architectural models to CSP processes and the verification of the resulting processes has been implemented as a plug-in to the Eclipse-based SysADL Studio tool [9]. The main thrust behind implementing the plug-in is making both formalization and verification as much transparent as possible to end-users. The translation to CSP and further verification of SysADL models require a single action: the user selects the SysADL model and then the verification operation. This action opens a window at which the user can select the configuration of the SysADL model to be verified.

The tool translates[3] the SysADL model to CSP by using the rules presented in Sect. 3, interacts with FDR4, analyzes the verification results from this interaction, and presents them in a user-friendly way. For each verified property, the tool shows whether it has been satisfied or not. When the property has not been satisfied, a trace that exemplifies the violation of the property is textually displayed. Current work also includes visually displaying the indication of the problem source at the SysADL diagram itself.

The validation of the correctness and effectiveness of the proposed approach and tool support consisted in using the plug-in to verify the aforementioned properties in existing SysADL models publicly available at the literature[4]. These properties were also verified in variations of such models as means of intentionally inserting errors and confirming that the proposed approach indeed identify them. As an example, a miraculous specification was identified in the model presented in Sect. 3. The original authors used the same range of natural numbers for temperature values in Celsius and Fahrenheit units, thus making it impossible to find valid values in the Celsius unit to every valid value in the Fahrenheit unit while respecting the equation $celsius = (5 * (fahrenheit - 32)/9)$.

The errors intentionally inserted into the original models were also successfully identified. For instance, the implementation of $FahrenheitToCelsiusEX$ in the execution model was changed to $celsius = 5 * (fahrenheit + 32)/9$ and the plug-in identified that the execution model has not respected the specification of the behavioral model.

The implemented plug-in was also able to successfully verify the compliance of SysADL architectural models with functional requirements. A first requirement was that the cooler and the heater cannot be turned on at the same time (safety property). Another requirement was that if no presence is detected in the room, then its temperature is always adjusted to a predefined temperature (liveness property). These requirements are currently expressed as CSP processes. Future work will address the description of such requirements by using SysADL diagrams.

Ongoing work also includes computational experiments to demonstrate the scalability of the proposed approach. Preliminary results obtained with the run-

---

[3] The translation is implemented in Acceleo (http://www.eclipse.org/acceleo/).

[4] Available at http://sysadl.org.

ning example[5] showed a overall time of 774 ms when performing the verification on a computer with an Intel® Core™ i5 processor, 8 GM of RAM, and Microsoft® Windows 10 as operating system. These results demonstrated a linear increase of the verification time with the number of instances.

6   Related Work

The literature reports approaches with formal verification of software architectures based on model checking [1,18]. Some of them have formalized their architectural descriptions as one of the primary means of ensuring reliability, security, correctness, and consistency of their projects. However, as far as it is known, none of them targets improving a SysML-based ADL with formal verification founded on model checking and with tool support. This is specially interesting for industry, which largely adopts SysML-based modeling languages [10].

Mouraditis et al. [12] defined a set of structural, behavioral, and security primitives and conceptualized it with the Z specification language to capture a core architectural model to build secure architectures. The approach herein proposed does not rely on a restricted set of architectures, but rather on any software architecture modeled using SysADL, which is a general-purpose ADL. The Mokni et al.'s work [11] considered software architecture changes to be verified and validated as means of ensuring a valid, reliable evolution process. The authors proposed a set of rules defined as a B formal model of the Dedal ADL along with consistency properties, which were checked and validated by using the ProB animator and model checker. The approach proposed here also ensures consistency among different elements of a SysADL model, but it focuses on the consistency among different viewpoints and takes advantage of the use of a process algebra (CSP) rather than a model-based formalism (B or Z) to guarantee concurrency aspects of the model, such as the safe interaction among components (deadlock- and livelock-freedom). The Taoufik et al.'s work [17] proposed to open UML 2.0 on the Wright ADL to verify the behavioral consistency of architectures. The compatibility with the Wr2Fdr tool [16] motivated the use of Wright/CSP since the tool generates eleven standard properties related software architecture consistency. Moreover, the Wright/CSP target configuration can be automatically translated to an FDR specification acceptable by the FDR2 model-checker. Besides providing SysADL with the same verification possibilities, the proposed approach allows verifying concurrency properties and functional requirements. Furthermore, SysADL Studio was integrated with the translator to CSP and its communication with FDR4 in a transparent way to users.

7   Conclusion

This paper presented a CSP-based approach to support the automated formal verification of properties specified in SysADL, a semi-formal SysML-based ADL.

---

[5] A short demo is available at https://youtu.be/vlchTK3fk2Y.

The solution relies on empowering SysADL with model checking by combining the CSP process algebra and the FDR4 model checker, besides providing a semantics for SysADL diagrams. With the proposed approach, it was possible to verify properties related to deadlocks, livelocks, miracles, and consistency among the different viewpoints of the specified configuration-based behavior. The concretization of the approach in the Eclipse-based SysADL Studio tool allowed validating it in several scenarios, including the example presented throughout this paper. The same approach can be applied to other SysML-based ADLs to formally verify architectural properties. Future work includes providing a π-calculus based semantics for SysADL and the formalization of both translations and a cross-verification of the semantics by using the strategy presented in the Unifying Theories of Programming (UTP) [6].

References

1. Araujo, C., Cavalcante, E., Batista, T., Oliveira, M., Oquendo, F.: A research landscape on formal verification of software architecture description. IEEE Access **7**, 171752–171764 (2019)
2. Barrett, C., et al.: CVC4. In: Gopalakrishnan, G., Qadeer, S. (eds.) CAV 2011. LNCS, vol. 6806, pp. 171–177. Springer, Heidelberg (2011). https://doi.org/10.1007/978-3-642-22110-1_14
3. Clements, P., et al.: Documenting Software Architectures: Views and Beyond, 2nd edn. Addison-Wesley, Reading (2011)
4. Formal Systems (Europe) Ltd.: Process Behaviour Explorer - ProBE User Manual. FSEL, United Kingdom (2003)
5. Gibson-Robinson, T., Armstrong, P., Boulgakov, A., Roscoe, A.W.: FDR3: a parallel refinement checker for CSP. Int. J. Softw. Tools Technol. Transfer. **18**, 149–167 (2016)
6. Hayes, I.J., Meinicke, L.A.: Developing an algebra for rely/guarantee concurrency: design decisions and challenges. In: Ribeiro, P., Sampaio, A. (eds.) UTP 2019. LNCS, vol. 11885, pp. 176–197. Springer, Cham (2019). https://doi.org/10.1007/978-3-030-31038-7_9
7. ISO/IEC/IEEE 42010: Systems and Software Engineering - Architecture Description. ISO, Switzerland (2011)
8. Lago, P., Malavolta, I., Muccini, H., Pelliccione, P., Tang, A.: The role ahead for architectural languages. IEEE Softw. **32**(1), 98–105 (2015)
9. Leite, J., Batista, T., Oquendo, F., Silva, E., Santos, L., Cortez, V.: Designing and executing software architectures models using SysADL Studio. In: Proceedings of the 2018 IEEE International Conference on Software Architecture Companion, USA, pp. 81–84. IEEE (2018)
10. Malavolta, I., Lago, P., Muccini, H., Pelliccione, P., Tang, A.: What industry needs from architectural languages: a survey. IEEE Trans. Software Eng. **39**(6), 869–891 (2013)
11. Mokni, A., Huchard, M., Urtado, C., Vauttier, S., Zhang, H.Y.: Formal rules for reliable component-based architecture evolution. In: Lanese, I., Madelaine, E. (eds.) FACS 2014. LNCS, vol. 8997, pp. 127–142. Springer, Cham (2015). https://doi.org/10.1007/978-3-319-15317-9_8

12. Mouratidis, H., Kolp, M., Faulkner, S., Giorgini, P.: A secure architectural description language for agent systems. In: Proceedings of the Fourth International Joint Conference on Autonomous Agents and Multiagent Systems, pp. 578–585. ACM, New York (2005)

13. Oquendo, F., Leite, J., Batista, T.: Software Architecture in Action: Designing and Executing Architectural Models with SysADL Grounded on the OMG SysML Standard. Springer, Switzerland (2016). https://doi.org/10.1007/978-3-319-44339-310.1007/978-3-319-44339-3

14. Ozkaya, M.: Do the informal & formal software modeling notations satisfy practitioners for software architecture modeling? Inf. Softw. Technol. **95**, 15–33 (2018)

15. Roscoe, A.W.: Understanding Concurrent Systems. Springer, London (2010). https://doi.org/10.1007/978-1-84882-258-0

16. Rouis, T.S., et al.: Wr2Fdr tool maintenance for models checking. In: Fujita, H., Selamat, A., Omatu, S. (eds.) New Trends in Intelligent Software Methodologies, Tools and Techniques, Frontiers in Artificial Intelligence and Applications, vol. 297, pp. 425–440. IOS Press, Amsterdam (2017)

17. Taoufik, S.R., Tahar, B.M., Mourad, K.: Behavioral verification of UML2.0 software architecture. In: Proceedings of the 12th International Conference on Semantics, Knowledge and Grids, pp. 115–120 (2016)

18. Zhang, P., Muccini, H., Li, B.: A classification and comparison of model checking software architecture techniques. J. Syst. Softw. **83**(5), 723–744 (2010)

A Flexible Architecture for Key Performance Indicators Assessment in Smart Cities

Martina De Sanctis[1](✉), Ludovico Iovino[1], Maria Teresa Rossi[1],
and Manuel Wimmer[2]

[1] Gran Sasso Science Institute, L'Aquila, Italy
{martina.desanctis,ludovico.iovino,mariateresa.rossi}@gssi.it
[2] CDL-MINT, Johannes Kepler University, Linz, Austria
manuel.wimmer@jku.at

Abstract. The concept of smart and sustainable city has been on the agenda for the last decade. Smart governance is about the use of innovation for supporting enhanced *decision making* and planning to make a city smart, by leveraging on Key Performance Indicators (KPIs) as procedural tools. However, developing processes and instruments able to evaluate smart cities is still a challenging task, due to the rigidity showed by the existing frameworks in the definition of KPIs and modeling of the subjects to be evaluated. Web-based platforms, spreadsheets or even Cloud-based applications offer limited flexibility, if the stakeholder is interested not only in using but also in defining the pieces of the puzzle to be composed. In this paper we present *a flexible architecture supporting a model-driven approach for the KPIs assessment in smart cities*. It identifies both required and optional components and functionalities needed for realizing the automatic KPIs assessment, while showing *flexibility points* allowing for different specification of the architecture, thus of the overall methodology.

1 Introduction

In the domain of smart cities, the *smart governance* concerns the use of technology in processing information and decision making enabling open, transparent and participatory governments [1], by also supporting the knowledge sharing among the involved actors. The main instrument through which smart governance operates is represented by *Key Performance Indicators* (KPIs) [2] representing raw set of values that can provide information about relevant measures that are of interest for understanding the progress of a smart city. The European Commission released and promoted the *Sustainable Development Goals* (SDGs[1]) to be achieved in 2020 [3], on top of which the International Telecommunication Union (ITU) drafted a list of all the KPIs for Smart Sustainable Cities (SSCs), along with its collection methodology [4].

---

[1] https://sustainabledevelopment.un.org/sdgs.

© Springer Nature Switzerland AG 2020
A. Jansen et al. (Eds.): ECSA 2020, LNCS 12292, pp. 118–135, 2020.
https://doi.org/10.1007/978-3-030-58923-3_8

However, decision making for smart cities through KPIs assessment is a quite challenging task. This is also due to the complexity of smart cities that are, de facto, *systems of systems* involving different dimensions (e.g., mobility, environment, education), each managed by different stakeholders, from public administrations to private institutions, that not always communicate with each other. Moreover, despite the support provided by Information and Communications Technologies (ICT) in managing different aspects of complex systems, such as smart cities (e.g., [5]), the currently available frameworks for the KPIs assessment are too rigid, not easy to suit each specific smart city's peculiarity, and often not released as open frameworks. Examples are online spreadsheets or Excel programs[2] embedding the used models and KPIs calculation formulas, or web/cloud-based frameworks with pre-defined set of computable KPIs, without considering that smart cities may differ in several aspects, based on their stage of economic development, available services, geographical implications. Moreover, KPIs can vary depending on the spatial granularity (e.g., small, medium and metropolitan cities).

In this context, we argue that a systematic methodology allowing smart cities stakeholders to easily *define*, *model* and *measure* the KPIs of interest for their cities, efficiently supporting the decision making process, is necessary. The methodology should further support the KPIs *customization* and *evolution* to suit the unique features of different and heterogeneous smart cities. In this direction, we defined a model-based approach for the automatic KPIs assessment in smart cities as an effective instrument for smart governance enabling the stakeholders knowledge sharing, data interpretation and smart cities evaluation and comparison. The approach foresees the separate modeling of smart cities and KPIs by experts and stakeholders, leveraging Model-Driven Engineering (MDE) techniques [6]. The two models are then used by an evaluation engine that will provide the evaluated KPIs over the candidate smart cities.

To make the approach robust, a supportive software architecture is required, that needs to leverage the offered abstraction in order to keep deployment aspects outside of the box. In this paper, we present *a flexible architecture supporting the model-based approach for KPIs assessment in smart cities* that identifies both required and optional components and corresponding functionalities needed for realizing the automatic KPIs assessment approach, while showing two main *flexibility points* allowing for different specification of the architecture, thus of the overall methodology implementation. The flexibility is given by (*i*) *different deployment patterns* that can be followed for specifying the architecture (e.g., standalone, hybrid, online); (*ii*) the *technology-independent nature* of the shaped components, which enables the use of diverse technologies for implementing the designed architectural components, to also better suit the chosen deployment style (i.e., online modeling editors better suit in online deployment of the system). This last point also includes the tool-independent nature of the KPIs *evaluation engine*, which plays a central role in the overall methodology. The proposed architecture further benefits from all the positive aspects of the model-

---

[2] Key Performance Indicators in Power Pivot at https://bit.ly/37EFR9r.

based nature of the approach, i.e., support to software evolution, automation of software production with code generation, support to technological bridges, and so on. Moreover, our architecture may provide guidelines for the definition of MDE tools (i.e., for the development, interpretation, transformation of models) where quality evaluation is the main objective [7].

2   Related Work

Several architectures have been proposed in the smart cities domain. The minimal requirements that a robust smart cities architecture must meet, such as distributed sensing, integrated management and *flexibility* are given in [8]. In [9], the authors present an approach for designing smart city's ecosystems, by means of a reference architecture called *SmartCityRA*. It represents a way to create smart cities blueprint that can help the instantiation of smart cities projects. They exploit variability modeling and model-driven architecture techniques, to produce a Domain Specific Language (DSL) for modeling smart city systems (i.e., *SmartCityML*). The usability of the approach is further shown through a *Smart Parking* scenario. However, despite this approach provides features for smart cities modeling, like our, it does not support the KPIs modeling and assessment. In [10], a reference architecture for designing a smart city context through the use of Big Data adhering to the NIST (National Institute of Standards and Technology) standard is presented. Here, the focus is more on the design of Big Data processing in *smart environment* contexts. The aim is that of exploiting the proposed conceptual model to create a unified intellectual infrastructure for environmental monitoring. Thus, they do not consider other smart cities contexts, different than environment.

From the perspective of *using data for decision making* in smart cities, different architectures are also provided, as for instance in [11] where data is exploited to support administration processes. Another data-driven approach is presented in [12]. The authors propose a data-driven IoT Software Platform for realizing sustainable *Smart Utilities*, a.k.a. smart services, in order to further develop applications on top of them. Specifically, they provide a service-oriented architecture that makes use of Web standards and protocols. The proposed architecture is scalable over cities of different dimensions and is generalizable to different smart utility domains, other than smart water management. In [13] it is presented a reference architecture to support the development of smart cities platform in order to help stakeholders in making projects, investments and decisions about the cities they manage. In [14] a Distributed-to-Centralized Data Management (D2C-DM) architecture is proposed. It provides different software and services layers, which use distinct data types gathered from physical (e.g., sensors) and non-physical (e.g., simulated data) data sources in the smart city. The aim is to show the easy adaptation of the architecture in contexts with different software requirements.

Nevertheless, despite the availability of multiple architectures supporting smart cities modeling and analysis, either from a wide perspective or focusing on a few dimensions, to the best of our knowledge, none of them specifically targets the modeling and assessment of KPIs that are crucial in the performance evaluation of smart cities.

3   Approach and Proposed Flexible Architecture

In this section we give an overview of the approach for the automatic KPIs assessment in smart cities, which represents the background for this work. Basically the evaluation of a smart city can be summarized in 3 steps: Ⓐ Define the smart city in a way that is processable; Ⓑ Define/select the KPIs of interest; Ⓒ Evaluate the selected KPIs on the subject smart city. In order to support this process, we defined a model-based approach, by identifying smart cities' concepts and the relations among them. Furthermore, we investigated how KPIs can be represented and measured, i.e., what type of calculations and data they require. In MDE, metamodels are central assets that allow designers to formalize application domains and consequently to achieve superior automation [15] in the software life cycle. Indeed, this allowed us to design both a *Smart City metamodel* and a *KPIs metamodel*, on top of which appropriate modeling tools (i.e., graphical and textual concrete syntaxes and editors) can be defined. In particular, the KPIs metamodel reflects the KPIs list for SSCs released by the ITU [4] and conforming to the SDGs [3]. The modeling tools are devoted to smart cities stakeholders, supported by KPIs experts, and allow them to define in a uniform way the smart cities they manage (Ⓐ) together with the KPIs they are interested in (Ⓑ), without knowing technological aspects and abstracting from the target deployment platform. The generated models will be used as input for an *Evaluation Engine* that will interpret and calculate the modeled KPIs for the candidate cities, by giving as output an *evaluated KPIs model* (Ⓒ). We highlight here that the KPIs model can be easily *extended* or *customized* to accommodate specific smart cities requirements as well as the KPIs evolution over time.

Example. To better understand the approach, we report a basic but realistic example in Fig. 1. We show some simple portions of the models we used to evaluate the smart city of L'Aquila (Italy). We focus on a single KPI, *Bicycle Network* (BN), which is calculated as in Eq. (1). It measures the length of bicycle paths per 100.000 inhabitants as the ratio between the bicycle paths length and one 100.000th of the city population.

$$BN = \frac{Bicycle\ Path\ Length\ (km)}{\frac{1}{100000} \times City\ Population} \tag{1}$$

In the left side of Fig. 1 we show a portion of the graphical representation of the model for the city of L'Aquila (Ⓐ), where the concepts needed for the BN KPI calculation have been modeled, e.g., *PisteCiclabili.com* is the provider of the *BikePathLength* data. In the top-right side of Fig. 1, instead, there is the portion of the textual representation of the KPIs model (Ⓑ) that refers to the BN KPI and its formula, as in Eq. (1). Notice that, to be calculated, the BN KPI needs data coming from the smart city model (e.g., *BikePathLength*, *CityPop*).

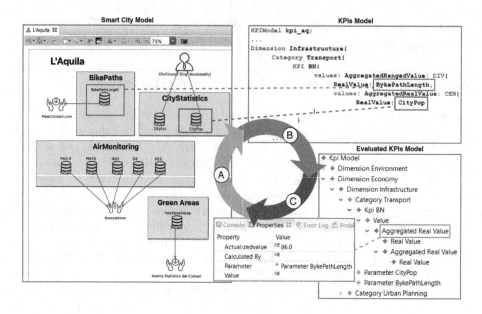

Fig. 1. Overview of the model-based KPIs assessment approach.

Once these two models have been processed by the evaluation engine, it will give as output the evaluated KPIs model (ⓒ), on the bottom-right side of Fig. 1, which corresponds to the actualized KPIs model. Note that for those cities with less than 100000 inhabitants, the denominator in Eq. (1) is evaluated to 1. Thus, for the city of L'Aquila with 69605 inhabitants and 86 km of bicycle paths, the BN KPI has a value of 86 *km per* 100000 *inhabitants*. What we want to highlight here is that (1) smart governance team can discover *weaknesses* of the assessed cities by interpreting the evaluated KPIs; (2) the approach enables *simulation* and *forecasting* of smart cities performances, by testing different settings in the models.

The Proposed Flexible Architecture. Figure 2 shows the proposed flexible architecture for KPIs assessment in smart cities supporting the process described above. It is made by six macro-components (also components from here on), representing the main required functionalities, and control- and data-flow between them. The architecture is devoted to several Stakeholders that can be divided in two main groups: *(i)* those designing or applying the architecture, i.e., the *Developers Team* (comprising also modelers, DSL engineers and software architects) and the *KPIs Experts*, which are responsible of the design and implementation of the main software components and modeling artifacts; *(ii)* the final users of the software solutions based on the architecture, i.e., *Municipalities, Smart Governance Team, Ranking Agencies, Researchers*, etc. They can be assigned different granting access, i.e., read, write, execute, depending on their profile.

For instance, municipalities can be interested in *modeling* the smart cities they manage and *evaluate* KPIs on top of them. On the contrary, ranking agencies might be interested only in the *analysis* and *interpretation* of (open) data about previously evaluated cities.

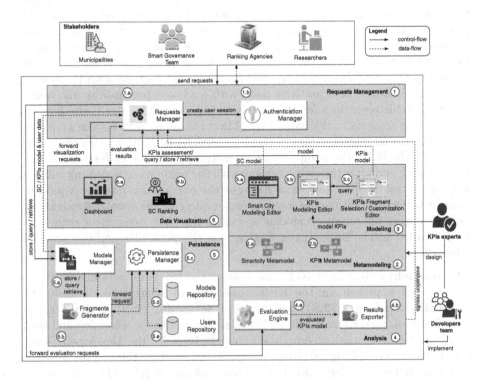

Fig. 2. The flexible architecture for the KPIs assessment in smart cities.

The six main components are Requests Management, Modeling, Metamodeling, Analysis, Persistence, and Data Visualization, labeled from **(1)** to **(6)**, respectively. In Fig. 2, solid arrows shape the control-flow among the components and dashed arrows shape the data-flow among them. It is worth noting that data-flow may involve entire models but also raw data may be exchanged, usually persisted via XML or customization of XMI. We now describe each component.

Requests Management. It behaves as the interface among the stakeholders and all the other components of our architecture. Indeed, it handles all the users requests through its two sub-components, the Requests Manager (1.a) and the Authentication Manager (1.b). The Authentication Manager handles the users registration, authentication and authorization. It supports the Requests Manager every time it needs to *create users sessions* to accomplish the requests they make, based on their access grants. It is an optional component, depending on the deployment style. E.g., it might be not required in standalone specifications of the architecture, while it is suggested for online ones. The `Requests Manager` handles several interactions. It receives and forwards the user's requests to the appropriate components and the requests among components. Three main requests can be handled at this stage, namely (1) the *model* request to the `Modeling` component, from those users (with proper permissions) who needs to model the smart cities they manage and to select/customize the KPIs they are interested in, through the available editors; (2) the *store/query/retrieve* request to the `Models Manager` in the `Persistence` component, from users that want to store/gather models relating to their previously interactions with the system (e.g., municipalities) or from those users with read only permissions who wants to get available open data for their analysis (e.g., researchers); (3) the *forward visualization requests* to the `Data Visualization` component for the graphical visualization and interpretation of the evaluated KPIs. Furthermore, the *model* request to the `Modeling` component can, in turn, give raise to further interactions: during and after the user interplay with the editors, the `Modeling` component can forward to the `Requests Manager` the *query/store/retrieve* request to interact with the `Persistence` component, for querying the `Models Repository` and for storing the produced models as well as the *KPIs assessment* request to be forwarded to the `Evaluation Engine`, via the *forward evaluation requests* interaction.

Metamodeling. It is responsible for hosting the two core metamodels of the model-based approach for the KPIs assessment in smart cities, namely the `Smartcity Metamodel (2.a)` and the `KPIs Metamodel (2.b)`, and the corresponding tools used to model them. It is also responsible for managing and keep trace of their evolution accomplished cooperatively by the Developers Team and KPIs Experts (*design* relation in Fig. 2), which adapt the two metamodels according to the evolving nature of both smart cities and KPIs. This component is developed at the beginning of the process and should be freezed and stable for enabling the modeling phase. In case evolution scenarios occur, coupled-evolution of the already modeled cities have to be performed in order to be compliant to the new metamodels [16].

Modeling. It is responsible for managing the generated editors required for allowing granted users to both model smart cities and model or select and customize KPIs. Modeling is the activity in which the designer creates/edits the contents of the application. Nowadays multiple modeling tools are available and they differ for various aspects, in which we distinguish textual or diagrammatic concrete syntax, or even more basic modeling editors, like tree view based. For this reason, the usability of the final product is strongly driven by the available modeling tools. Specifically, in this component we find the `Smart City Modeling Editor (3.a)` devoted both to experienced and non-expert MDE developers, such as the smart governance team' members that use the system to model the smart city they manage, to subsequently evaluate its performance. Graphical editors are recommended here, for usability reasons, such that to provide user-friendly editors. Differently, the `KPIs Modeling Editor (3.b)` is mainly devoted to KPIs Experts who are widely experienced in KPIs and up to date about the evolving KPIs documentation and collection methodology provided at European level. From one hand, they are in charge of modeling KPIs (*model KPIs* in Fig. 2) reflecting the official guidelines. From the other hand, different smart cities managers might be interested in diverse KPIs. For this reason, a certain degree of KPIs selection and customization must be provided. This is accomplished by the `KPIs Fragment Selection/Customization Editor` (**3.c**) that allows users to "*query*" the KPIs model in the `KPIs Modeling Editor` to select and possibly customize given KPIs and further generate the so-called *model fragments*. Borrowing the definition of interesting object structures [17], we define model fragments such KPIs model's internal selection. The main KPIs model includes all the KPIs defined by experts, while model fragments identify the selection made by the user. Eventually, the interaction of stakeholders with the modeling editors brings to the creation of the *Smart City model* (*SC model* from here on) and *KPIs model*, both conforming to the domain models in the `Metamodeling` component, indeed they can be managed by using its generated API.

Analysis. It is responsible for managing the automatic KPIs assessment over smart cities. It includes the `Evaluation Engine` (**4.a**) that is devoted to interpret and calculate the modeled KPIs for one or more candidate smart cities. In particular, it receives KPIs evaluation requests forwarded by the `Requests Manager` (*forward evaluation requests* in Fig. 2) together with the *SC model* and *KPIs model*. After the evaluation, it sends the *evaluated KPIs model* to the `Results Exporter` (**4.b**), which is in charge of exporting results in different formats (e.g., .csv, .xml or JSON files), depending also on the use that stakeholders intend to make of it (e.g., graphical visualization, textual interpretation, further elaborations) and from the tool which might be used for their visualization and interpretation. Eventually, the `Analysis` component forwards the *evaluation results* to the `Requests Manager` that sends them to the user who submitted the KPIs evaluation request and/or to the `Data Visualization` component.

Persistence. It manages the persistence of all the artifacts involved in the process of KPIs assessment, together with the stakeholders related data, such as their profiles, access grants and authentication data. In particular, it contains five components. The `Models Manager` (**5.a**) acts as the main interface of the `Persistence` component. It receives all the *store/query/retrieve* requests by the `Requests Manager`, together with the accompanying data, such as the *SC/KPIs models & user data*, and it sends the corresponding replies. Moreover, before forwarding the received requests to the `Persistence Manager` (**5.c**), the `Models Manager` interacts with the `Fragments Generator` (**5.b**) (*store/query/retrieve* in Fig. 2), to handle those cases in which the specific request deals with modeling artifacts and there might be the need of generating model fragments from them. The fragments generation does not apply for those requests addressed to the `Users Repository` and containing only user data, in which case the `Fragments Generator` does not execute any operation and only forward the request to the `Persistence Manager`. Once requests and relative data arrive to the `Persistence Manager`, it is responsible for storing, querying or retrieving data from the appropriate repository, such as `Models Repository` **(5.d)** and `Users Repository` **(5.e)**. In addition, artifacts stored in the `Models Repository` also contain metadata about the users holding their ownership, while the `Users Repository` stores information about users profiles and granting access.

Data Visualization. It is responsible for the *evaluated KPIs model* visualization and interpretation through the `Dashboard` **(6.a)** and `SC Ranking` **(6.b)** components. The former handles the graphical transformation of evaluated KPIs in appropriate and easy to understand charts. The latter shows the ranking among several smart cities whose models are made available and retrieved from the `Models Repository`, only for smart cities comparison purposes. To this aim, the `Data Visualization` receives *forward visualization requests* from the `Requests Manager` with the *evaluation results* from the `Analysis` component.

All the components and their functionalities, except for the `Data Visualization` component, are mandatory to allow architecture specifications to accomplish the task of KPIs assessment in smart cities. On the contrary, to implement its functionalities, a component might not always require all its sub-components as we will see.

4   Prototypical Implementation

The presented architecture can be specified by using a combination of various technologies and deployment patterns. In this section, we present implementation details about the prototype we developed, corresponding to a *standalone specification*[3], being the architecture entirely implemented as a standalone platform. Eclipse is the release platform we have chosen, which also provides pre-packaged bundles for specific development paradigms. Specifically, the target platform is represented by the *Eclipse Modeling Framework* (EMF)[4] that provides the modeling language to engineer DSLs [18]. The EMF core includes a metamodeling language, called *Ecore*, used for describing domain models, and runtime support for the models including change notification, persistence support with default serialization, and reflective APIs for manipulating objects in the models. On top of the EMF bundle, the `Metamodeling` component **(2)** has been defined and it hosts the two main domain models (**(2.a)** and **(2.b)**) from which the Java code, supporting model manipulation and editors composition, is generated.

On top of this layer, two editors are implemented (**(3.a)** and **(3.b)**) to better cope with the composition of the involved models, such as the editing of models with the possibility of filling them with model elements that can be composed. The editors implementation is supported by DSLs that, in general, can be *graphical* or *textual* [19]. From one side, graphical editors provide an intuitive GUI for modelers. On the other side, textual editors provide a support tool to

---

[3] Project available at: https://github.com/gssi/SmartCityModeling.git.
[4] https://www.eclipse.org/modeling/emf/.

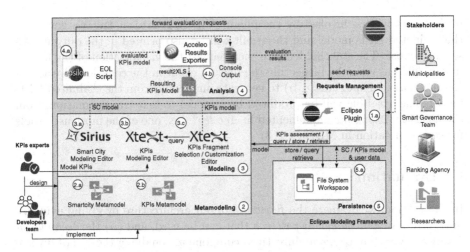

Fig. 3. Standalone specification of our architecture.

define models as textual specification, which is better transposed by developers. In order to enable the usage of the editors by both experienced and non-expert users (e.g., smart cities stakeholders), the component **(3)** is implemented with two different technologies. The `Smart City Modeling Editor` **(3.a)** is built on top of *Sirius* [20], a graphical concrete syntax generator creating the graphical modeling workbench for modeling smart cities. Smart city projects are quite large and involve different aspects and view points; since Sirius is based on a view points approach, it suits perfectly in this case. The `KPI Modeling Editor` **(3.b)**, instead, is devised for modelers supporting KPIs experts to specify KPIs and relative calculation formulas. For this reason it has been implemented with a textual concrete syntax by means of *Xtext* [21]. Xtext was chosen because it provides much more "expressiveness" and "agility" to the users, which can edit raw data in a very feasible way. The `KPI Modeling Editor` offers a way to declare how KPIs are calculated in detail, in the perspective of reuse, where the modelers can share their definitions. Lastly, the `KPIs Fragment Selection/Customization Editor` **(3.c)** is implemented by means of a custom reusable mechanism offered by Xtext. In particular, if the KPIs are declared as "reusable operations" in a library, the users can invoke the KPIs needed through this library. When the SC model and KPIs model have been defined, then the `Analysis` component **(4)** can be invoked, thus triggering the KPIs evaluation phase. This process is managed by the `Requests Manager` **(1.a)** that is implemented as an Eclipse plugin organized with the extension point mechanism. It can be activated by file saving operations or even directly by menu entries in the editors. By selecting a SC model and a KPIs model (with specific extensions), a menu entry is enabled and the *EOL script* implementing the `Evaluation Engine` **(4.a)** is triggered. The Epsilon Object Language (EOL) is an imperative programming language part of the Epsilon framework [22] for creating, querying and modifying models built on top of EMF. Basically, the EOL script is a file in the workspace of the project that will be invoked by the plugin. The `Evaluation Engine` generates the evaluated KPIs model and the result will be also printed in the output console of Eclipse. The stakeholders can then request the visualization of the results in two different ways: by inspecting the textual result in the console or by asking to the `Results Exporter (4.b)` to generate an .xls file from the evaluated KPIs model. The excel file will be produced by a model-to-text transformation, from the `Results Exporter` implemented in *Acceleo*[5], i.e., one of the most used tools for code generation in MDE (Fig. 3).

5   Evaluation

In this section, we evaluate the *flexibility* of our architecture by giving evidence of (*i*) alternative *deployment patterns* that can be used, and (*ii*) the *technology-independent nature* of the architectural components, enabling the use of diverse technologies, also w.r.t. the chosen deployment style. Moreover, we evaluate the *performance* of our architectural approach by running experiments based on the realized prototype.

5.1   Flexibility Evaluation

We now describe two additional specifications of our architecture, namely *hybrid* and *online*. They are currently under development, although they rely on a partial reuse of the implemented standalone specification, thus we focus on the differences w.r.t. it.

Hybrid Specification. In the hybrid specification, depicted in Fig. 4, part of the architectural components are deployed online and part of them reside locally on the user's machine. The Internet layer is in between them. Components (**2**) and (**3**) are the same as in the standalone specification. The `Requests Manager` (**1.a**) presents both a local and a remote instances. The local one is in charge of activating the editors and triggering the remote KPIs evaluation by sending a request, via the internet, to the remote one that will forward the request and the received models to the `Evaluation Engine` (**4.a**). This step is preceded by an authentication process started by the local `Requests Manager` that will authenticate the local user to the remote `Users Repository` (**5.e**) via the `Authentication Manager` (**1.b**). For the `Authentication Manager`'s implementation we plan to use the *J2EE framework* with the technologies it exploits for realizing the Model-View-Controller (MVC) architecture (e.g., Spring, Hibernate). The `Users Repository` and the `Models Repository` (**5.d**) are managed by the `Persistence Manager` (**5.c**). Models can be passed as parameters from the local Eclipse editors, if they are brand new models edited from scratch, or they can be requested to the `Persistence Manager` that will execute the query

---

[5] https://www.eclipse.org/acceleo/.

and retrieve operations on the `Models Repository`. The `Persistence` component **(5)** has different tasks that range over the usual repository operations, to the query management, in order to extract fragments of the models through the `Fragment Generator` **(5.b)**, which can be realized by means of a DSL similar to that used for the KPIs `Fragment Selection/Customization Editor` **(3.c)** allowing for querying models. Repositories operations are delegated to a repository manager called *MDEForge* [23] implementing the `Persistence Manager`. It consists of a set of core services that permit to store and manage typical modeling artifacts and tools, specifically conceived for models. It comes with APIs that can be used to interact with the repository functions without using the provided web interface. This allows MDEForge to be easily integrated in the infrastructure. Lastly, the `Models Manager` **(5.a)** will be interposed between the MDEForge and the `Requests Manager`, as an interface of the `Persistence` component. When the required models are available for the analysis phase, the `Evaluation Engine` **(4.a)** implemented with a Java model parser can be invoked. Through model interpretation also called compilation, the input models are directly used to run the system [24] or to invoke other actions during the interpretation at runtime. As before, the analysis phase will generate the evaluated KPIs model, however the console output in the hybrid specification is only used for testing purpose, being accessible only from the server-side. In this specification, the Acceleo `Results Exporter` can export results in other format than .xls file or it can expose itself an API for results visualization purposes, to be forwarded by the `Requests Manager`. We then plan to provide a local `Data Visualization` component **(6)** as an Eclipse plugin. It can read the evaluation results both by receiving the generated results file or by listening to the dedicated API, thus implying a sort of asynchronous call to the `Evaluation Engine`. The `Data Visualization` populates the charts shaping the results of the KPIs evaluation in an Eclipse view used by the stakeholders.

Online Specification. The online specification has the peculiarity of being completely deployed online. For lack of space, we do not show its deployment design[6] and we describe only its relevant differences w.r.t. the hybrid specification. Being everything online, the main instrument to use the platform is the browser, that provides access to a web application including the different components. More specifically, the `Modeling` component **(3)** will be implemented through *Eclipse Theia*[7] allowing to run Eclipse online, with all the benefits of having an in-browser extensible IDE. For the editors, the two candidate technologies allowing for running modeling editors in web browsers are *Eugenia Live* [25] for the `Smart City Modeling Editor` **(3.a)** and Xtext (from version 2.9 on) for the `KPIs Modeling Editor` **(3.b)**.

The advantage of an online environment supports one of the main problems that slows down the path of MDE towards a standard: the reluctance in installing different tools, most of them academic, with all the related issues linked to safety

---

[6] For the interested readers it can be found at https://bit.ly/3bqbqG2.

[7] https://theia-ide.org.

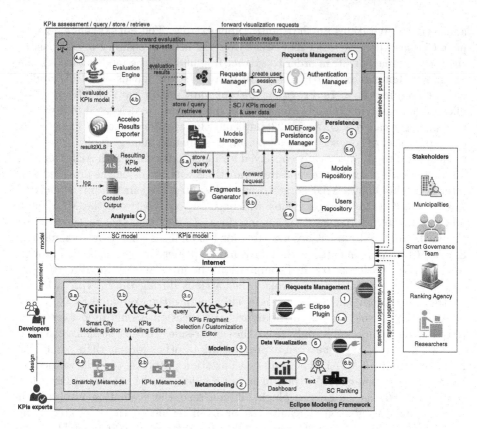

Fig. 4. Hybrid specification of our architecture.

and reliability. These aspects cannot be neglected in an industrial scenario. Moreover, collaborative repositories have been extensively proposed and investigated in MDE [26], highlighting multiple challenges. Among these, visibility of the repositories stored artifacts seem to be one of the hot topic in industry. Multiple resolutions have been proposed to tone down the reluctance in employing these tools, and extended visibility management seems to be needed [27] to assure that only artifacts intentionally shared will be visible to the community and not the models including intellectual property rights.

Alternative Candidate Technologies. We did an analysis about available languages and technologies and their suitability for implementing our architecture. Several valid alternatives exist to implement the different components of Fig. 2, as shown in Table 1. This list is not intended to be exhaustive, given the panorama of possible integrations, but we give an idea of available tools. In the second column of the table, ✓ denotes that the corresponding component is mandatory, independently of the used deployment style, while ≈ denotes that the component may be missing, e.g., because its offered functionality may be omitted without compromising the functioning of the approach (e.g., the `Data Visualization`) or because it is not required for the used deployment (e.g., the `Authentication Manager` in a standalone instance).

Table 1. Architecture flexibility in terms of required components and technologies.

Components	Mandatory	Candidate Technologies
Requests Manager	✓	Eclipse plugin, Java
Authentication Manager	≈	Java
Smartcity Metamodel	✓	Ecore, Kermeta [28], UML
KPIs Metamodel	✓	Ecore, Kermeta, UML
Smart City Modeling Editor	✓	Sirius, Eugenia Live, Eugenia
KPIs Modeling Editor	✓	Xtext, EMFText [29]
KPIs Fragment Editor	✓	Xtext, OCL[a], EMF-Fragments[b]
Evaluation Engine	✓	Java, EOL Script, ATL[c], ETL[d]
Results Exporter	≈	Acceleo, JET[e], EGL[f], Xtend[m]
Models Manager	≈	Java, MDEForge
Fragments Generator	≈	EMF + Java + OCL
Persistence Manager	✓	MDEForge, Neo4EMF[g], Relational DB, EMFJson[h]
Models Repository	✓	MDEForge, EMFStore[i]
Users Repository	≈	NoSql [30], Mysql[j], MSSql[k]
Dashboard	≈	Spring[l], other J2EE or JS-based frameworks
SC Ranking	≈	Spring, other J2EE or JS-based frameworks

[a] https://bit.ly/3cGvJAC
[b] https://bit.ly/2z6pF5A
[c] https://www.eclipse.org/atl/
[d] https://bit.ly/2WZcYl6
[e] https://bit.ly/3eQQef6
[f] https://bit.ly/2Z9bzuR
[g] https://github.com/neo4emf/Neo4EMF
[h] https://emfjson.github.io/
[i] https://www.eclipse.org/emfstore/
[j] https://www.mysql.com/
[k] https://bit.ly/353KD0P
[l] https://spring.io/
[m] https://www.eclipse.org/xtend/

5.2   Performance Evaluation

To evaluate the performance of our architecture, we performed a set of experiments by running the standalone specification, using a 6 core CPU running at 2.2 GHz, with 16 Gb memory. The goal of our experiments is that of checking the evaluation engine execution time w.r.t. the *size of the input models*, i.e., the number of elements in the models. Thus, we designed a smart city model, in which we instantiated every concept of the metamodel, and a KPIs model. In particular, according to the ITU, KPIs are hierarchically organized [4]. A KPIs model is composed by $1 \dots n$ dimensions, also containing sub-dimensions, each composed by $1 \dots n$ categories that, in turn, contain $1 \dots n$ KPIs. The used KPIs

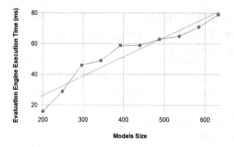

Fig. 5. *Exp*1: increasing the number of evaluated smart cities.

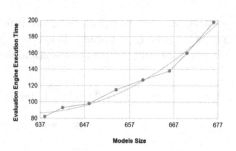

Fig. 6. *Exp*2: increasing the complexity in the calculation of each modeled KPI.

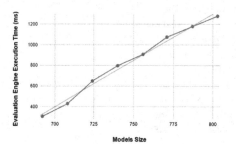

Fig. 7. *Exp*3: make each KPI of type *range*.

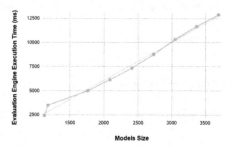

Fig. 8. *Exp*4: increasing the number of KPIs.

model is initially made by one dimension with one category of 8 KPIs, thus to cover all the calculations defined in the KPIs Metamodel.

In Fig. 5, we show the results of our first experiment *Exp*1. For each execution run of the evaluation engine, we increment the number of modeled smart cities in the SC model from 1 to 10 and we measure the 8 KPIs in the KPIs model for each of them. As shown in Fig. 5, the models size goes from 200 to 632 elements and the execution time goes from 16 milliseconds (ms) to 79 ms. Figure 6 reports the results of *Exp*2 for which we started by giving as input to the evaluation engine the SC model made by 10 smart cities, which remain fixed, and the KPIs model as in *Exp*1. Then, at every run we increase the complexity of the KPIs calculations, by adding new nested operations, one KPI at a time. This impacts on the time required to measure each KPIs. In Fig. 6 we can observe that the size of the models goes from 638 to 676 and the execution time goes from 82 ms to 198 ms. Interestingly, despite the models size does not increase significantly, the execution time particularly increases in the last run. This is due to the fact that this run involves a KPI whose calculation combines the *range* operation, i.e., the most time consuming one, with a basic operation (e.g., *AVG*). From this observation, we designed *Exp*3 (Fig. 7) such that, at every run, we add a *range* calculation in the definition of each KPI, one KPI at a time. In Fig. 7, we can observe that the size of models slightly increases from 692 to 803 elements (only

127 elements more than the last run in $Exp2$) while the execution time ranges from 306 ms to 1279 ms, by showing a considerable increase, thus confirming our prediction about the time consuming of calculations including the range operation. However, the overall execution time is still reasonable for the given models size. Eventually, in $Exp4$ (Fig. 8) at every run we increment by one the number of dimensions in the KPIs model, where each dimension includes 8 KPIs with complex calculations. Consequently, the number of evaluated KPIs goes from 16 in the first run to 80 in the last one, always assessed on top of the 10 smart cities in the SC model. This means that in the last execution we assessed 800 KPIs in the same run. Figure 8 depicts that the size of the models goes from 1124 to 3692 elements and the execution time ranges from 2426 ms to 12892 ms.

Summarizing, these experiments point out two main findings: (i) the efficiency in terms of the evaluation engine's execution time, since all the experiments show a linear or polynomial (of degree 2) increase of the execution time w.r.t. the increasing models size; (ii) promising scalability results showed by $Exp4$, indicating that the system takes 12.9 s for assessing 800 KPIs over 10 smart cities.

Threats to Validity. The settings of the input parameters in the evaluation might internally bias our experimentation. Both the SC model and the KPIs model lead to the execution of calculations of diverse complexity, depending on the size of the two models and the number of KPIs, but the overall evaluation procedure is not affected. For these reasons, we considered incrementally complex models in each run, to trigger more complex calculation and smooth biases in the output results. As external threats to validity, we are aware that we need to perform the KPIs evaluation by using SC models of real smart cities, but we leave this point as part of our future work, where we plan to evaluate the system by involving real stakeholders, also to evaluate the provided editors.

6   Conclusion and Future Work

In this paper we presented an architecture supporting a model-based approach for the KPIs assessment in smart cities. Its goal is to provide a robust and flexible platform for the performance evaluation of smart cities, to be easily used by smart cities stakeholders, during the decision making and planning process.

As future work we are finalizing the implementation of the *hybrid* and *online* specifications and designing an experiment to evaluate the *feasibility* and *usability* of the methodology with the involvement of real smart cities stakeholders who have to make use of the provided modeling and analysis tools and data visualization facilities. Finally, we consider the integration with legacy data formats such as CityGML.

Acknowledgment. This work was partially supported by the Centre for Urban Informatics and Modelling, National Project, GSSI as well as by the Austrian Federal Ministry for Digital and Economic Affairs and the National Foundation for Research, Technology and Development.

References

1. Mutiara, D., Yuniarti, S., Pratama, B.: Smart governance for smart city. IOP Conf. Ser. Earth Environ. Sci. **126**, 012–073 (2018)
2. Directorate-General for Environment (European Commission): Intrasoft International, University of the West of England (UWE). Science Communication Unit. Indicators for sustainable cities, April 2018
3. European Commission: Europe 2020 A European strategy for smart, sustainable and inclusive growth, March 2010
4. International Telecommunication Union (ITU): Collection Methodology for Key Performance Indicators for Smart Sustainable Cities (2017). https://bit.ly/2SkSZfi
5. Ferro, E., Caroleo, B., Leo, M., Osella M., Pautasso, E.: The role of ICT in smart city governance. In: International Conference for e-Democracy and Open Government (2013)
6. Brambilla, M., Cabot, J., Wimmer, M.: Model-Driven Software Engineering in Practice, 2nd edn. Morgan & Claypool Publishers, San Rafael (2017)
7. Mohagheghi, P., Aagedal, J.: Evaluating quality in model-driven engineering. In: International Workshop on Modeling in Software Engineering, p. 6. IEEE (2007)
8. da Silva, W.M., Alvaro, A., Tomas, G.H.R.P., Afonso, R.A., Dias, K.L., Garcia, V.C.: Smart cities software architectures: a survey. In: 28th Annual ACM Symposium on Applied Computing (SAC), pp. 1722–1727. ACM (2013)
9. Abu-Matar, M., Mizouni, R.: Variability modeling for smart city reference architectures. In: IEEE International Smart Cities Conference, pp. 1–8 (2018)
10. Voronin, D., Shevchenko, V., Chengar, O., Mashchenko, E.: Conceptual big data processing model for the tasks of smart cities environmental monitoring. In: Alexandrov, D.A., Boukhanovsky, A.V., Chugunov, A.V., Kabanov, Y., Koltsova, O., Musabirov, I. (eds.) DTGS 2019. CCIS, vol. 1038, pp. 212–222. Springer, Cham (2019). https://doi.org/10.1007/978-3-030-37858-5_17
11. Wenge, R., Zhang, X., Dave, C., Chao, L., Hao, S.: Smart city architecture: A technology guide for implementation and design challenges. China Commun. **11**(3), 56–69 (2014)
12. Simmhan, Y., Ravindra, P., Chaturvedi, S., Hegde, M., Ballamajalu, R.: Towards a data-driven IoT software architecture for smart city utilities. Softw. Pract. Exp. **48**(7), 1390–1416 (2018)
13. Santana, E.F.Z., Chaves, A.P., Gerosa, M.A., Kon, F., Milojicic, D.S.: Software platforms for smart cities: concepts, requirements, challenges, and a unified reference architecture. ACM Comput. Surv. **50**(6), 1–37 (2017)
14. Sinaeepourfard, A., Petersen, S.A., Ahlers, D.: D2C-SM: designing a distributed-to-centralized software management architecture for smart cities. In: Pappas, I.O., Mikalef, P., Dwivedi, Y.K., Jaccheri, L., Krogstie, J., Mäntymäki, M. (eds.) I3E 2019. LNCS, vol. 11701, pp. 329–341. Springer, Cham (2019). https://doi.org/10.1007/978-3-030-29374-1_27
15. Bettini, L., Di Ruscio, D., Iovino, L., Pierantonio, A.: Quality-driven detection and resolution of metamodel smells. IEEE Access **7**, 16364–16376 (2019)
16. Di Ruscio, D., Iovino, L., Pierantonio, A.: What is needed for managing co-evolution in MDE? In: International Workshop on Model Comparison in Practice, pp. 30–38. ACM (2011)
17. Brottier, E., Fleurey, F., Steel, J., Baudry B., Traon, Y.L.: Metamodel-based test generation for model transformations: an algorithm and a tool. In: International Symposium on Software Reliability Engineering, pp. 85–94 (2006)

18. Kolovos, D.S., Paige, R.F., Kelly, T., Polack, F.A.: Requirements for domain-specific languages. In: Workshop on Domain-Specific Program Development (2006)
19. Veisi, P., Stroulia, E.: AHL: model-driven engineering of android applications with BLE peripherals. In: Aïmeur, E., Ruhi, U., Weiss, M. (eds.) MCETECH 2017. LNBIP, vol. 289, pp. 56–74. Springer, Cham (2017). https://doi.org/10.1007/978-3-319-59041-7_4
20. Viyović, V., Maksimović, M., Perisić, B.: Sirius: a rapid development of DSM graphical editor. In: International Conference on Intelligent Engineering Systems (INES), pp. 233–238 (2014)
21. Bettini, L.: Implementing domain-specific languages with Xtext and Xtend. Packt Publishing, Birmingham (2016)
22. Kolovos, D.S., Paige, R.F., Polack, F.A.C.: The epsilon object language (EOL). In: Rensink, A., Warmer, J. (eds.) ECMDA-FA 2006. LNCS, vol. 4066, pp. 128–142. Springer, Heidelberg (2006). https://doi.org/10.1007/11787044_11
23. Basciani, F., Di Rocco, J., Di Ruscio, D., Di Salle, A., Iovino, L., Pierantonio, A.: MDEForge: an extensible web-based modeling platform. In: Cloud-MDE@MoDELS, pp. 66–75 (2014)
24. Mellor, S.J., Balcer, M.: Executable UML: A Foundation for Model-Driven Architectures. Addison-Wesley, Boston (2002)
25. Rose, L.M., Kolovos, D.S., Paige, R.F.: EuGENia live: a flexible graphical modelling tool. In: Extreme Modeling Workshop, pp. 15–20 (2012)
26. Di Rocco, J., Di Ruscio, D., Iovino, L., Pierantonio, A.: Collaborative repositories in model-driven engineering. IEEE Softw. **32**, 28–34 (2015)
27. Basciani, F., Rocco, J.D., Ruscio, D.D., Iovino, L., Pierantonio, A.: Model repositories: will they become reality? In: CloudMDE@MoDELS (2015)
28. Jézéquel, J.-M., Barais, O., Fleurey, F.: Model driven language engineering with Kermeta. In: Fernandes, J.M., Lämmel, R., Visser, J., Saraiva, J. (eds.) GTTSE 2009. LNCS, vol. 6491, pp. 201–221. Springer, Heidelberg (2011). https://doi.org/10.1007/978-3-642-18023-1_5
29. Heidenreich, F., Johannes, J., Karol, S., Seifert, M., Wende, C.: Model-based language engineering with EMFText. In: Lämmel, R., Saraiva, J., Visser, J. (eds.) GTTSE 2011. LNCS, vol. 7680, pp. 322–345. Springer, Heidelberg (2013). https://doi.org/10.1007/978-3-642-35992-7_9
30. Strauch, C., Sites, U.-L.S., Kriha, W.: NoSQL databases. Lect. Notes Stuttg. Media Univ. **20**, 24 (2011)

Performance and Security Engineering

A Multi-objective Performance Optimization Approach for Self-adaptive Architectures

Davide Arcelli$^{(\boxtimes)}$ (iD)

Università degli Studi dell'Aquila, via Vetoio 1, L'Aquila, Italy
davide.arcelli@univaq.it, davide.arcelli@gmail.com

Abstract. This paper presents an evolutionary approach for multi-objective performance optimization of Self-Adaptive Systems, represented by a specific family of Queuing Network models, namely SMAPEA QNs. The approach is based on NSGA-II genetic algorithm and it is aimed at suggesting near-optimal alternative architectures in terms of mean response times for the different available system operational modes. The evaluation is performed through a controlled experiment with respect to a realistic case study, with the aim of establishing whether meta-heuristics are worth to be investigated as a valid support to performance optimization of Self-Adaptive Systems.

Keywords: Self-adaptive systems · Software architecture · Software performance engineering · Search-based software engineering · Multi-objective optimization · Genetic algorithms · Queuing networks

1 Introduction

In the last 15 years, architecture engineering of Self-adaptive Systems (SaSs) has become a significant research topic, due to the fact that self-adaptation has emerged as a very suitable paradigm to represent modern system architectures.

A SaS is composed by a managing and a managed subsystem. The former implements system's adaptation logic and controls the latter, which provides system's functionalities for perceiving and affecting the environment through its sensors and actuators, respectively. Such control typically conforms to a MAPE-K feedback loop, i.e. a Knowledge-based architecture model that divides the adaptation process into four sequential activities, namely Monitor, Analyze, Plan and Execute [14], performed by controllers within the managing subsystem.

Approaches addressing architecture engineering of SaSs typically exploit Model-Driven Architecture (MDA) principles to abstract the system and its self-adaptation mechanisms. Besides, other kind of notations can be exploited to model and analyze non-functional SaS attributes [17]. In this context, additional

Supported by the Italian Ministry of Education, University and Research – MIUR, L. 297, art. 10.

A. Jansen et al. (Eds.): ECSA 2020, LNCS 12292, pp. 139–147, 2020.
https://doi.org/10.1007/978-3-030-58923-3_9

paradigms such as Control Theory (CT) [11] and Machine Learning (ML) [12] have been successfully used to devise efficient self-adaptation mechanisms for the managing subsystem, aimed at supporting performance optimization with a certain degree of automation [3,5,16].

In this paper we move towards ML, by exploiting evolutionary computation [1] for multi-objective performance optimization. In particular, we introduce an evolutionary approach for efficiently solving the so-called *Controller Selection Policy* (CSP) problem within SMAPEA QNs [4], i.e. a novel a family of QNs aimed at modeling and assessing the performance of SaSs, involving both their managing and managed subsystems. Job classes flowing into the QN represent MAPE tasks that have to be executed by controllers within the managing subsystem of a SaS, based on a predefined mode-adaptation strategy [15]). The CSP problem is thus defined as the problem of optimally choosing a destination controller for MAPE jobs. To this aim, we exploit the NSGA-II genetic algorithm [8] which explores the search space looking for (near-)optimal Pareto solutions. Ideally, our approach can be used for adapting the CSP both at run-time and design-time, introducing a further dimension for self-adaptation beside the mode-based one.

The paper is structured as follows: Sect. 2 discusses related work. Section 3 describes the approach and details how NSGA-II genetic algorithm can be tailored to the CSP problem. Section 4 illustrates a controlled experiment aimed at assessing if evolutionary meta-heuristics can provide a valid support to performance optimization of SaSs, by means of a realistic case study. Section 5 concludes the paper and devises the final goal for such research direction.

2   Related Work

A number of approaches aimed at optimizing SaS performance through ML have appeared in literature. Two of them have been included in the surveys by Becker et al. [5] and Arcelli [3]. In particular, Elkhodary et al. [9] have addressed run-time self-adaptation of system features, while supporting several learning algorithms to learn the impact of adaptation decisions on system's goals. Instead, Jung et al. [13] have enabled system reconfiguration taking place offline and directly on a (Layered) QN, by means of decision-tree learners.

More recently, Faniyi et al. [7] have presented a self-aware architecture style for SaSs, where adaptation was in terms of service selection. Models of sensed data are learnt by relying on learning mechanisms which are determined by a meta-self-aware component, based on trade-offs for goals, time, and interaction.

Borges et al. [10] has integrated formal verification and ML aimed at verifying properties from formal system specifications, coping with incomplete/incorrect information and providing effective error handling in the specification process through adaptation of system behavior for graceful performance degradation.

In his Ph.D. thesis, Araujo [2] has presented an approach that allows to inject learning techniques into (existing) software systems, enabling the latter to learn (sub-)optimal configurations of user-defined parameters and adapt to different contexts (i.e. workloads) at run-time, aimed at keeping the desired QoS.

Similarly to Faniyi et al. [7], SMAPEA QNs devise an architecture style for SaSs, including the managed subsystem rather than the managing subsystem only. However, Faniyi et al. [7] represent SaS architectures conforming to an agnostic notation, whilst SMAPEA QNs abstract SaSs in terms of performance models, similarly to Jung et al. [13].

The approach in this paper is aimed at finding (sub)optimal solutions to the CSP problem, i.e. system configurations, through NSGA-II. This opens to a comparison between the proposed approach and the above ones in the future. This shall imply dealing with actual SaS implementations and different modeling notations and, consequently, with different type of knobs for self-adaptation, thus requiring a significant effort to actually build up a common basis for comparison.

3 Evolutionary Approach for Performance Optimization

3.1 Approach Overview

Figure 1 illustrates the structure of the proposed multi-objective optimization approach, grounding on a customized version of the NSGA-II genetic algorithm [8]. The latter performs a search-space exploration taking as input a SMAPEA QN, which defines a performance-oriented architecture style for SaSs [4]. A SMAPEA QN is partitioned in three parts: S and A contain sensors and actuators, respectively; MAPE contains controllers which are in charge of executing MAPE tasks, based on a set of routing probabilities for $S \rightarrow M$ class-switch, i.e. the CSP.

The goal of the approach is to suggest near-optimal solutions to the CSP problem, i.e. $S \rightarrow M$ routing probabilities resulting into satisfactory mean response times for each system mode. The genetic algorithm explores the (potentially infinite) solution space by generating proper solutions.

Based on an initial population (i.e. solution set) of a certain size, at each iteration the best solutions are *selected* and combined by means of *Crossover* and *Mutation*, with probability $p(crossover)$ and $p(mutation)$, respectively. As a result, a new "generation" of solutions is produced, as basis for the next iteration. The total number of iterations is thus given by the ratio between the *number of evaluations* and the *population size*. The former represents the total number of (generated and then) evaluated models. The evaluation is in terms of mean response times modulo system modes (see $Mode_1$ and $Mode_2$), thus requiring the simulation of each SMAPEA QN model, by means of a *Performance Analyzer*.

3.2 NSGA-II Customization for the CSP Problem

In order to apply NSGA-II to the CSP problem, the genetic algorithm must be customized by specifying how to: (i) represent individuals (i.e. solutions); (ii) create new individuals using genetic operators (crossover and mutation) to explore the solution space; (iii) select the individuals to be supplied from one generation to another; (iv) evaluate individuals using a fitness function for each objective to optimize.

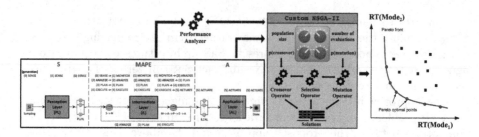

Fig. 1. Multi-objective performance optimization approach.

Solution Representation. In our approach, a (candidate) solution is represented as a $c \times 4m$ matrix, where c is the number of controllers within the IL and m is the number of system modes. Value rp_{ij} of the matrix represents the probability that a job of class j is routed from $S{\rightarrow}M$ to controller i, for each $1 \leqslant i \leqslant c$ and $1 \leqslant j \leqslant 4m$. Moreover, $\sum_{i=1}^{c} rp_{ij} = 1$, for each $1 \leqslant j \leq 4m$.

Figure 2 illustrates three solutions – namely *Chromosome 1.2, 2.1* and *1.1* – where each rp_{ij} is drawn as a knob for sake of illustration.

Genetic Operators. Crossover and mutation are illustrated in Fig. 2.

For the crossover operator, we use a single, random, cut-point crossover, which selects two parent solutions and creates two child solutions by halving those parents and properly mixing the resulting four halves.

Instead, the mutation operator picks one random column of a solution, e.g. *Monitor* for $Mode_m$, and replaces it with a randomly-generated brand-new one.

Notice that the solutions generated by crossover and mutation operations are correct by construction, i.e. $\sum_{i=1}^{c} rp_{ij} = 1$, for each $1 \leqslant j \leq 4m$. This is an advantage, as it avoids control procedures aimed at excluding invalid solutions.

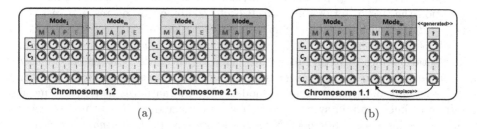

Fig. 2. Customized (a) crossover and (b) mutation operations.

Selection. NSGA-II sorts the population based on classification of individuals into different dominance levels and it exploits a crowding distance in order to select individuals for the next generation [8].

Fitness Function. At each iteration of the genetic algorithm, the solutions defining the current population must be evaluated with respect to the fitness function. For the CSP problem, the objective is to minimize the mean response times of the concurrent system modes.

In order to estimate mean response times, each solution must be applied to the reference SMAPEA QN model, which needs to be simulated by a performance analyzer. Simulation parameters may play a crucial role for putting the approach into practice; for example, letting the simulation running to infinite might determine disadvantageous conditions for the genetic algorithm.

4   Evaluation

Evaluation is aimed at investigating if evolutionary meta-heuristics can provide valid support to performance-based architectural optimization of SaSs. To this aim, we conduct a controlled experiment onto a realistic case study, i.e. an IoT system that evacuates people in a room in case of fire detection [4], represented in Fig. 3 as a SMAPEA QN.

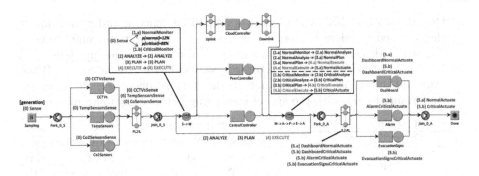

Fig. 3. SMAPEA QN for the considered case study [4].

A (shared) sampling rate (i.e. *Sampling*) is modeled by a workload source configured as a deterministic distribution, denoted by det(k), which describes a constant flow of samplings, arriving exactly every k time units [6]. Such sampling rate is shared among sensing components of the managed subsystem (at the LHS), i.e.: CCTV cameras to detect people position and movement, temperature and CO_2 sensors to detect possible fires.

Sensed data feed a MAPE loop run by control components (between the two class-switches), that decides about actuation based on the situation: (i) In *normal* mode, the system shows a 2D-representation of people position and movements on a dashboard; In *critical* mode – i.e. a fire is detected – additional information is shown on the dashboard, alarm actuators are activated and evacuation signs indicate the best evacuation routes.

The experimentation faces the (probability-based) CSP with respect to (i) three controllers – two are local and one is deployed at the cloud (i.e. *CloudController*), and (ii) two system modes, namely *normal* and *critical*.

4.1   Controlled Experiment

Assumptions. Two assumptions are introduced to control the experiment, i.e.:

A_1: Controllers own the same (exponential) distribution with the same mean value, modulo the job classes flowing through the QN.

A_2: Saturation is not allowed at all, with respect to the considered workload intensities (i.e. the mean values for the deterministic distribution), that are: 2.5, 2.25, 2, 1.75, 1.5, 1.25, 1, 0.75, 0.5.

Methodology. We start from a set of typical system configurations that a human could conceive, devised by considering controllers deployment: a `centralized` pattern routes all jobs to *CentralController*; a `collaborative` pattern exploits local controllers only, with equal probability (i.e. $\frac{1}{2}$); a `hybrid` pattern exploits all controllers with equal probability (i.e. $\frac{1}{3}$). Then, we run custom `NSGA-II` under disadvantageous conditions (i.e. small population and evaluations – 10 and 100, respectively – and potentially infinite simulation time), as follows:

a) One execution of NSGA-II for each workload intensity, in order to compare the returned solutions to the human-conceived configurations conforming to A_2, in the ideal situation that the system can reconfigure at <u>run-time</u>.

b) Each non-saturating solution returned for det(0.5) is simulated for all the workload intensities and compared to the human-conceived configurations conforming to A_2, with the aim of identifying better <u>design</u> alternatives.

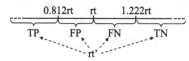

Fig. 4. True/False Positive/Negative classification.

A definition of *true positives* (TP), *false positives* (FP), *true negatives* (TN) and *false negatives* (FN), is needed, in order to classify `NSGA-II` solutions in terms of recall (R), precision (P) and f-measure (F_1), as: $R = \frac{TP}{TP+FN}$; $P = \frac{TP}{TP+FP}$; $F_1 = 2 \times \frac{P \times R}{P+R}$. Such definition is illustrated by Fig. 4, where rt' and rt denote response times of interest of, respectively, a returned solution and a reference configuration.[1]

Execution. All `NSGA-II` executions – and thus all the QN simulations as well – have been run onto a machine equipped with an Intel Core i7-3630QM CPU 2.40 GHz and 16 GB of DDR3 RAM at 1600 MHz. For sake of space, we do not provide simulation configuration parameters, as they can be found in the replication package available at https://github.com/davewilsonfbc/smapeaqn.moo.

Results. First, we remark that, among the human-conceived patterns, `centralized` and `collaborative` do not fulfill A_2, as they saturate with det(1) and det(0.5), respectively. Hence, `hybrid` is the reference pattern for comparison.

---

[1] The two factors 0.812 and 1.222 have been respectively obtained by solving the equations: $rt' + 0.1 \times rt' = rt - 0.1 \times rt$ and $rt' - 0.1 \times rt' = rt + 0.1 \times rt$, as the adopted simulation confidence interval is $\pm 10\%$ (0.1).

For **case a** – i.e. run-time (CSP) reconfiguration – we obtained 43 solutions across the considered workloads. Among those, 37 were distinct solutions.

Table 1 reports the resulting quantitative and qualitative metrics modulo system modes, based on the previously introduced classification mechanism.

Despite the relatively low precision for critical mode, having much more FPs than FNs is certainly encouraging, because FPs indicates non-pejorative solutions rather than non-ameliorative ones. Being able to very likely suggest ameliorative and non-pejorative solutions (94.6% on average, in the ideal case) might represent an added-value in non-controlled environment, i.e. when controllers have heterogeneous service demands.

Table 1. Obtained metrics vs. system modes.

	System mode	
	Normal	Critical
Quantitative metrics		
TP	32	22
FP	2	14
TN	1	0
FN	2	1
Qualitative metrics		
R	0.9411765	0.95652174
P	0.9411765	0.61111111
F_1	0.9411765	0.74576271

Unfortunately, run-time reconfiguration in terms of CSP is not currently supported by JMT [6], i.e. the reference performance modeling and analysis framework for **SMAPEA** QNs. For this reason, we have devised **case b** – i.e. identifying design alternatives. With this regard, the meta-heuristic returned one solution with det(0.5), namely S43. As can be noticed from Fig. 5, S43 tends to be non-ameliorative (i.e. FN). This is intuitive by looking at the actual routing probabilities of S43, as it can be seen as "a **hybrid** pattern slightly unbalanced towards *CloudController*" (see the replication package).

Being very close to **hybrid**, that is optimal due to A_1, demonstrates that the meta-heuristic can suggest near-optimal solutions to the CSP problem, resulting into valid design alternatives, even under disadvantageous conditions.

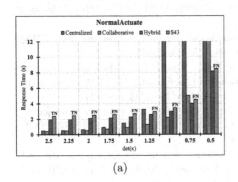

(a)

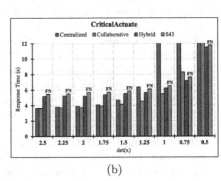

(b)

Fig. 5. Mean response times for (a) Normal and (b) Critical mode.

5 Conclusion

In this paper, we have presented a multi-objective performance optimization approach, based on custom **NSGA-II** genetic algorithm, aimed at identifying alternative self-adaptive architectures with enhanced performance. The approach is based on the SMAPEA Queuing Networks notation, which allows to represent such kind of systems and assess their performance by simulation.

We have preliminarily validated our approach through a controlled experiment onto a realistic case study, in order to understand if evolutionary meta-heuristics can provide valid support to performance optimization of self-adaptive systems. To this aim, NSGA-II has been run under disadvantageous conditions, i.e. small population size and number of evaluations, with potentially infinite simulations. Obtained results have shown that such an investigation is worth to be conducted. With this regard, we plan to enable simulation timeouts in order to run the meta-heuristic with greater population size and number of evaluations.

Our definitive goal is to release a tool supporting the performance-based architecture modeling, assessment and optimization of self-adaptive systems.

References

1. Al-Sahaf, H., et al.: A survey on evolutionary machine learning. J. R. Soc. N. Z. **49**(2), 205–228 (2019). https://doi.org/10.1080/03036758.2019.1609052
2. Araujo, R.: Enabling configuration self-adaptation using machine learning. Ph.D. thesis, University of British Columbia (2018). https://doi.org/10.14288/1.0379346
3. Arcelli, D.: Exploiting queuing networks to model and assess the performance of self-adaptive software systems: a survey. ANT. Procedia Comput. Sci. **170**, 498–505 (2020). https://doi.org/10.1016/j.procs.2020.03.108
4. Arcelli, D.: Towards a generalized queuing network model for self-adaptive software systems. In: MODELSWARD, pp. 457–464. SCITEPRESS (2020). https://doi.org/10.5220/0009180304570464
5. Becker, M., Luckey, M., Becker, S.: Model-driven performance engineering of self-adaptive systems: a survey. In: QoSA, pp. 117–122. ACM (2012). https://doi.org/10.1145/2304696.2304716
6. Bertoli, M., Casale, G., Serazzi, G.: Java modelling tools - user manual (2018). http://jmt.sourceforge.net/Papers/JMT_users_Manual.pdf
7. Borges, R.V., d'Avila Garcez, A., Lamb, L.C., Nuseibeh, B.: Learning to adapt requirements specifications of evolving systems (Nier track). In: ICSE, ICSE 2011, pp. 856–859. ACM (2011). https://doi.org/10.1145/1985793.1985924
8. Deb, K., Pratap, A., Agarwal, S., Meyarivan, T.: A fast and elitist multiobjective genetic algorithm: NSGA-II. IEEE Trans. Evol. Comput. **6**(2), 182–197 (2002). https://doi.org/10.1109/4235.996017
9. Elkhodary, A., Esfahani, N., Malek, S.: Fusion: a framework for engineering self-tuning self-adaptive software systems. In: FSE, FSE 2010, pp. 7–16. ACM SIG-SOFT (2010). https://doi.org/10.1145/1882291.1882296
10. Faniyi, F., Lewis, P.R., Bahsoon, R., Yao, X.: Architecting self-aware software systems. In: IEEE/IFIP WICSA, WICSA 2014, pp. 91–94. IEEE Computer Society (2014). https://doi.org/10.1109/WICSA.2014.18
11. Hellerstein, J.L., Diao, Y., Parekh, S., Tilbury, D.M.: Feedback Control of Computing Systems. Wiley, Hoboken (2004). https://doi.org/10.1002/047166880x
12. James, G., Witten, D., Hastie, T., Tibshirani, R.: An Introduction to Statistical Learning: With Applications in R, vol. 103. Springer, New York (2013). https://doi.org/10.1007/978-1-4614-7138-7

13. Jung, G., Joshi, K.R., Hiltunen, M.A., Schlichting, R.D., Pu, C.: Generating adaptation policies for multi-tier applications in consolidated server environments. In: ICAC, pp. 23–32. IEEE Computer Society (2008). https://doi.org/10.1109/ICAC. 2008.21

14. Kephart, J.O., Chess, D.M.: The vision of autonomic computing. Computer **36**(1), 41–50 (2003). https://doi.org/10.1109/MC.2003.1160055

15. Musa, J.D.: Operational profiles in software-reliability engineering. IEEE Softw. **10**(2), 14–32 (1993). https://doi.org/10.1109/52.199724

16. Shevtsov, S., Berekmeri, M., Weyns, D., Maggio, M.: Control-theoretical software adaptation: a systematic literature review. IEEE Trans. Softw. Eng. **44**(8), 784–810 (2018). https://doi.org/10.1109/TSE.2017.2704579

17. Weyns, D., Iftikhar, M.U., de la Iglesia, D.G., Ahmad, T.: A survey of formal methods in self-adaptive systems. In: C3S2E, pp. 67–79. ACM (2012). https://doi.org/10.1145/2347583.2347592

Data Stream Operations as First-Class Entities in Component-Based Performance Models

Dominik Werle$^{(\boxtimes)}$ ⓘ, Stephan Seifermann, and Anne Koziolek ⓘ

Karlsruhe Institute of Technology (KIT), 76131 Karlsruhe, Germany
{dominik.werle,stephan.seifermann,koziolek}@kit.edu

Abstract. Data streaming applications are an important class of data-intensive systems. Performance is an essential quality of such systems. It is, for example, expressed by the delay of analysis results or the utilization of system resources. Architecture-level decisions such as the configuration of sources, sinks and operations, their deployment or the choice of technology impact the performance. Current component-based performance prediction approaches cannot accurately predict the performance of those systems, because they do not support the metrics that are specific to data streaming applications and only approximate the behavior of data stream operations instead of expressing it explicitly. In particular, operations that group multiple data events and thus introduce timing dependencies between different calls to the system are not represented sufficiently. In this paper, we present an approach for modeling networks of data stream operations including their parameters with the goal of predicting the performance of the resulting composed data streaming application. The approach is based on a component-based performance model with queueing semantics for processing resources. Our evaluation shows that our model can more accurately express the behavior of the system, resulting in a more expressive performance model compared to a well-encapsulated component-based model without data stream operations.

Keywords: Data streaming · Performance modeling · Component-based software engineering · Complex event processing

1 Introduction

Systems that process large amounts of data from varied sources have become an important class of software systems in recent years. Reasons for this development are the vastly increasing amount of data sources from which data is gathered and improvements in methods for data analysis.

Partially funded by the German Research Foundation (DFG) as part of the Research Training Group GRK 2153: "Energy Status Data – Informatics Methods for its Collection, Analysis and Exploitation".

ⓒ Springer Nature Switzerland AG 2020
A. Jansen et al. (Eds.): ECSA 2020, LNCS 12292, pp. 148–164, 2020.
https://doi.org/10.1007/978-3-030-58923-3_10

From a software engineering viewpoint, building such software systems entails specific challenges in the different activities that are part of the software engineering process [8]: for example planning which types of processing hardware are required for the system and how the system will behave in future scenarios where the number of data sources or other data characteristics change.

In this paper, we address the problem that current component-based performance models to our knowledge cannot express stateful operations which are commonly used in data streaming applications. For example, when data is collected and emitted as a group when a data item with specific characteristics arrives or when a specified duration has passed introduce timing dependencies between calls. Expressing such state requires modeling workarounds that break the encapsulation and thus hinder the separate reusability and maintainability of components [21].

There are different paradigms for building systems that process large amounts of data. In the context of this paper, we will focus on applications that process continuously arriving streams of data (*streaming applications*), as opposed to applications that regularly process larger batches of data.

Overall, we present a new approach for modeling the performance of data streaming applications. More specifically, we provide a method for expressing the interaction between components that process data streams in performance models and a simulation approach for analysing these models. This article extends a previously presented sketch of the approach [21] with a more thorough discussion of the modeling approach and its relation to component-based performance models, as well as an implementation and initial evaluation of the approach.

The main stakeholders of the approach are the software engineers that have to make decisions about the configuration of the system, for example, suitable sizes for sliding windows. Furthermore, we target the operations engineers that have to predict how the system will scale with expected changes in the load or additional analyses on the data. We consider both groups by incorporating the decisions they have to make in the modeling language, thus allowing them to make what-if analyses using the presented approach.

Subsequently, the main goal of our approach is to support software engineers that build data streaming applications with suitable modeling and quality prediction tools. To this end, this article addresses the following two research questions.

RQ_1: What is a suitable way of representing data stream operations in component-based performance models while keeping components and data stream operations reusable and parameterizable?

RQ_2: How can the behavior of data stream operations be incorporated into simulations of otherwise stateless component-based performance models?

RQ_1 is targeted at the modeling language itself. It is focused on identifying the relevant operations and how they can be included in a modeling language in a composable way that can be used in combination with current component-based performance modeling tools. The second question, RQ_2, focuses on the way the models are then analysed. Particularly, the simulation of the system behavior that includes data stream operations needs to be able to interface with current simulation approaches. We present three contributions towards these questions:

C_1: An approach for representing operations in a composable, architecture level performance model,

C_2: A simulation approach for data stream operations,

C_3: An evaluation of the simulation for a case study system.

2   Running Example

To illustrate our approach, we use a running example that is an adaptation of the 2014 grand challenge of the conference on Distributed and Event-Based Systems (DEBS 2014) [10]. The example application processes meter readings that smart plugs send to a system to calculate an outlier score for houses.

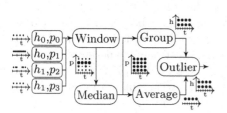

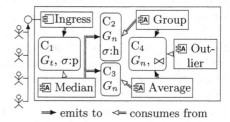

→ emits to   ⇐ consumes from

Fig. 1. Illustration of the running example (Source: [21]).

Fig. 2. Simplified illustration of the performance model (Source: [21]).

The example system is illustrated in Fig. 1. The following more detailed explanation is partially taken from [21, Sect. 3], where we initially introduced the example. Figure 2 shows an implementation of the system in our modeling approach and will be discussed in detail Subsect. 5.4. N smart plugs send data to the system. Each of the smart plugs belongs to one of H households. A plug with id j that belongs to household i is named h_i, p_j in the illustration. The rate at which plugs send data can differ for different plugs and can vary over time. *Window* creates data windows of time length S. The data is collected grouped by the plug id, i.e., *Window* emits a data window for each plug and each point of time that windows are created. The windows are created every Δ time units, at the points of time $T_i = \Delta \cdot i, i \in \mathbb{N}$, resulting in N newly created windows for each point in time T_i. Windows overlap if $\Delta < S$. Then, sensor readings are included in multiple windows. As a result, every window spans the S time units prior to its creation. *Median* creates a median for each window and plug, resulting in N (number of smart plugs) medians for each T_i. *Average* collects all medians for one T_i and calculates one overall average value of all medians for each T_i. *Group* collects all median values for one household for one T_i by collecting all median values of all plugs for the T_i and regrouping them by the household id. For each of the H households, *Outlier* calculates the ratio of readings of plugs inside the household that are greater than the overall average and emits this value as the outlier value of the household, resulting in H values for each T_i. The metric of interest for this system is the time between the creation of a date in the plug and its first appearance in the result of an outlier calculation, the *delay*.

Interesting questions that the architect of the system may want to answer are how well the system scales if the number of plugs increases, and which resources are needed for a particular load. Other questions can be more closely related to the actual functionality of the system: How does changing the shift and size of the windowing operation change the delay? How does the association between plugs and households change the quality of the system (i.e., small amount of households with many plugs each in comparison to large amount of households with little plugs each)?

3 Background

In this section, we present relevant foundations for our approach regarding the way component-based performance models are constructed and used.

3.1 Component-Based Performance Models

Component-based performance models allow a decomposition of systems into so-called components. An example for a modeling language that allows this is the Palladio Component Model (PCM) [17], which we have based our approach on. The model defines interfaces that describe a collection of services. A component can either require or provide interfaces and describes the observable effect regarding performance for each provided service. Particularly, components can call other components' services. A system model is composed of components that together provide services to the user of the system. Based on its modeling primitives, there are extensions to the model and its analysis that add capabilities for simulating additional behavior of the system that are relevant for its performance such as virtualization, network protocols or different types of hardware resources and operating system schedulers. A usual way of evaluating models is to map resources to queues and serving nodes that process items in those queues. This network of queues is then either statically analysed or simulated.

Performance models are used to evaluate different performance metrics, such as the response time of systems to requests of different types and the utilization of resources. It should be possible to model, calibrate and reuse the different parts of the model independent from each other. This allows simple reuse and extension of models. Additionally, the system should be described in a way that exposes all relevant design decisions to the architect.

Parametric dependencies additionally allow effect descriptions to be parametrized regarding characteristics of the environment of the call. An example for this environment are parameters that are passed into a method. The concrete values that these parameters take depend on the composition of the system from components and are usually resolved when the system is analysed or simulated. This approach enables both the reuse and exchange of components, as well as a change of the workload if parameters are also used at the system interface.

3.2 State in Performance Models

A basic idea for component-based architecture models is that they are *stateless*. This means that the *description* of the service effects cannot refer to the current state of the system, its resources, or other components, but the *analysis* will implicitly keep state and schedule or parametrize service effects accordingly. Therefore, the interaction between different calls to the system is clearly encapsulated in so-called resources. The PCM distinguishes two types of resources. *Active* resources represent for example CPUs or HDDs. They can be represented as queues and service places in queueing models. Incurring a resource demand in a process blocks and thus delays the process until the resource has satisfied the demand. If multiple processes request the same resource at the same time, there needs to be some form of queueing or scheduling. *Passive* resources behave similar to semaphores. They have a specified token count and tokens can either be acquired or released. If a process wants to acquire a token when there is none left, it is blocked until another process releases a token. To summarize, while the systems that are modeled have state at runtime, the model of the components themselves cannot refer to this state in an explicit way, for example by branching depending on the current load of the system. The only way to depend on the current state of the system is through resources.

3.3 Stochastic Expressions and Dependencies

Performance models use stochastic expressions to describe stochastic processes that occur in the system or in its usage. A common example for this is the behavior of users of the system. Furthermore, stochastic descriptions can be used for aspects of the system that are not modeled in detail, for example when garbage collection happens in the Java Virtual Machine. If stochastic expressions are used with parametric dependencies, they can be used to express *stochastic dependencies* regarding the performance of the system.

3.4 Challenges for Modeling Data Streaming Applications

In this section, we discuss the major challenge for modeling data streaming applications using component-based performance models: representing timing dependencies between calls to the system.

Data streaming applications usually describe the behavior of the system depending on incoming calls that deliver data at the system interface. In the following, we use the term *data events* for those calls. In our work, we consider data *stream* operations that are aligned with the well-established CQL continuous query language [2]. In contrast to business information systems that provide services that users can call, data stream operations are not described in terms of single requests that are handled independently. Instead, they operate on multiple requests. For example, data events may be grouped in windows and then processed further as a group instead of single elements, which introduces a delay for single data events that depends on other events or operation characteristics.

Secondly, stochastic descriptions of resource demands cannot be stochastically dependent at different points of the system for one data event, if system models do not operate on groups of data. For example, if a particularly hard to calculate data point arrives at the system, high resource demands might incur at different points of the system in succession, resulting in an outlier of the calculation time for this data event. However, if these stochastic dependencies are not made explicit across regrouping or joining of data, resource demand descriptions in the model are stochastically independently from each other and thus may lead to loss of accuracy of the model. The need for suitable state abstractions in component-based performance models has been previously identified and discussed in the context of messaging systems by Happe et al. [7].

In current modeling approaches, if architects desire to model a data streaming application, they have to use a model of the system that does not reflect the actual structure and behavior of the system, but an approximation that behaves similarly regarding the performance metric of interest. For example, data events that are grouped into sliding windows inside the system might have to be modeled by modeling the arrival of windows instead of single data events at the system boundary. As a consequence, the performance-related characteristics of windows, such as the number of contained elements, have to be modeled manually instead of being derived automatically by the model.

4 Approach

In this section we introduce the modeling concepts that are provided in our approach in detail. This section addresses RQ_1 (see Sect. 1): *What is a suitable way of representing data stream operations in component-based performance models while keeping components and data stream operations reusable and parameterizable?*

4.1 Modeling Concepts

In this section, we introduce the modeling concepts that are novel in our approach and their role in modeling data streaming applications. An overview of the concepts is illustrated in Fig. 3. The illustration is explained in detail in the following subsections.

We currently do not support the full set of operations for a streaming application (as for example in CQL [2] or in LINQ [15]). While our implementation focuses on operations that are required for our case study system, our simulation is implemented to be extensible for additional types of operations that change the stream of data that flows through the system.

Data Events. A *data event* describes the context of a call that is passed through the system in our approach. In our model, this context has an identity and can be passed between different calls.

Each data event is explicitly created by a process in the system. In addition to an implicit *date of birth*, the architect can also specify other characteristics that are relevant for the performance of the system or for the distribution inside data stream operations, for example because the characteristic influences how elements are grouped. Each characteristic is described via an expression and it is fixed when the data event is created. The expression can be stochastic, i.e., be described as a distribution function. Then, a value from this distribution is generated when the value is fixed. Additionally, the expression can depend on other parts of the current call context, such as parameters of the current call.

An example for a characteristic is the plug id of sensors that a data event is created from and then sent to the system. It is either specified as a distribution function in the workload that is applied to the system or is the result of different workload drivers (sensors) with fixed sensor types that send data to the system simultaneously. At some point in the system, the data events are then grouped by the type of sensor, resulting in different sizes of groups that have to be further communicated and processed in the system.

Note that a data event is separate from the notion of call flow through the system. While a workload might specify calls to system interfaces that pass data events to the system, this data event might then be picked up and further processed by other calls or recurring processes in the system. Thus, the data event carries an identity and fixed characteristics through the system. This identity and the attached date of birth of the data event can then be used for delay measurements in the system by specifying a point in the system where the current age of a data event is to be recorded. This information is then collected and presented to the performance analyst as a result of the analysis. Subsequently, our definition of data events addresses the challenge of parametric dependencies across calls (see Subsect. 3.4).

Data Channels. The main novelty in our approach are so called *data channels*. The concept is based on event channels as introduced by Rathfelder [16] which are, however, mapped to normal call semantics for a system. We extend the idea of event channels by additional state and active processing inside the channel. A data channel is a type of resource that encapsulates state regarding data events. When modeling a system, data can be either *emitted to* or *consumed from* a data channel.

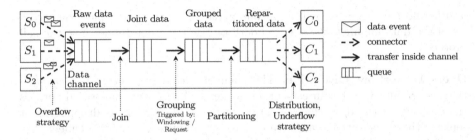

Fig. 3. Illustration of the model of a data channel. Data events that are emitted to the data channel by components pass through different queues.

Overall, a data channel can be seen as a series of queues that data events emitted to the channel are passed through, as illustrated in Fig. 3. The steps between queues have an associated *operation* and a *trigger*. When triggered, the step takes one or multiple elements from the previous queue and emits a new element to the next queue. For the first queue (*raw data events*, Fig. 3), elements are directly added by emitting components. For the last queue (*Repartitioned data*), consuming components can take data events. Our current implementation supports the following steps: *join, grouping* and *partitioning*. In principle, this can be extended to further steps, if required for different types of operations.

In the following we discuss how a data channel can be configured regarding the following aspects, in order of processing: 1) sinks, sources and connectors, 2) capacity, 3) over-/underflow discipline, 4) joining, 5) grouping, 6) partitioning, distribution strategy. Together, the configuration and the semantics contribute towards allowing timing dependencies in the model (see Subsect. 3.4).

Sinks, Sources and Connectors. A component can communicate with the data channel via a connector. A connector can be either a sink or a source connector, depending on whether it connects the channel to a source (i.e., a component that emits data to the channel), or a sink (i.e., a component that consumes data from the channel). Sink connectors can either be *pushing* or *polling*. If the connector is pushing then a process is immediately triggered when new data is available and starts a service that is associated with the given connector inside the component. The parameter to these service calls is the data event. If the connector is polling then data events can be actively consumed from any service inside the component.

Capacity. A data channel can define a capacity of data events it can keep at a point of time. If no capacity is defined, there is no limit to this number. The capacity is defined in terms of the number of data events, not their size; this would however be a possible extension to our concept, if required. Currently, our notion of capacity only considers total raw data events that are put into the data channel and have not been processed further yet; however, this can be extended to the total number of data elements currently residing in the channel, or other notions of capacity. If an incoming data event would surpass the capacity of the data channel, the over-/underflow discipline determines how the call proceeds.

Over-/Underflow Discipline. The channel specifies an *overflow discipline* that determines whether in case of an incoming data event that would surpass the capacity of the data channel, 1) an incoming data event is dropped, 2) it replaces the element that was last added to the channel, 3) the first element that would be emitted is dropped and the new element is added, or 4) the call that wants to emit an data event to the channel is blocked until the capacity is not reached anymore. In the latter case, the waiting calls are handled in the order they try to emit data to the channel, i.e., the first call that wants to emit data to the channel can do this first after data has been removed from the channel and there is free capacity again.

For consuming calls, the channel specifies an *underflow discipline* that determines how calls that want to consume data from the channel when there is none available should be handled. The available options are to either 1) return without data elements, or 2) block until data is available. In the latter case, similar to calls waiting to emit data to the channel, the calls are handled in the order they try to consume data from the channel.

The described disciplines focus on the capacity of the channel and do not address other reasons for not accepting data elements, such as elements that arrive too late at a channel, which we are planning to address in future work.

Joining. Joining regroups elements on a given join condition. In our implementation, joins are realized by tagging data with information about the incoming connectors. A joint data element is emitted to the *Joint data* queue, when a data event for each connector is available. The modeler specifies for each incoming connector whether a data event can contribute multiple times to joint data events or only once. If it can contribute multiple times, the last data event for each incoming connector is not removed but can be used multiple times; previous elements are removed if a new element arrives. If data events for a connector can only contribute once, they are removed from the data channel upon inclusion in a joint date.

Grouping. In general, a grouping operation retains elements until a trigger occurs. This trigger is either 1) based on the time in the system, 2) on characteristics of the data in the group, or 3) or on an external trigger. Our implementation currently provides three types of grouping, which are examples for the respective types of triggers: 1) sliding windows, 2) holdback grouping, and 3) consume-all grouping. We explain these types in the following in more detail to illustrate the principle of grouping channels.

Sliding windows are a concept where elements are grouped in windows at periodic points of time. Usually, a sliding window operation is configured with a *size* S and a *shift* Δ. Every Δ time units, the windowing operation emits all data events that have arrived in the last S time units as a grouped data event. This means that windows overlap if $\Delta < S$. Then, data events are included in multiple windows.

Holdback grouping is a type of grouping, where elements are grouped according to a key function. Elements with the same key are collected in a group and held back. The channel can keep a given number of groups at the same time (default is one). If an additional key is discovered in an arriving data event for whose calculated key function currently no group that is held back exists, a new one is created. If the number of groups then exceeds the specified maximum, the oldest group that is held back is emitted. Another example for grouping based on characteristics of the data in the group would be to emit a group of elements when a specified number of elements are reached.

Consume-all grouping describes the idea that elements are collected and emitted as a whole as soon as a trigger happens, such as a consume action.

Partitioning. *Partitioning* is an example for an operation that further operates on data that is already grouped. Particularly, it is regrouped according to a key function. This means that for every element in the input group of data events, the key function is calculated. Then, for each distinct value of the key function, a grouped data event is created that contains all elements that have mapped to this key. In our running example, this occurs when medians have been calculated for all plugs for a window and then are regrouped according to the household the plug belongs to. Note that for this to work, first all elements in the window, i.e., all calculated medians for all plugs in the sliding window, have to be collected and then regrouped according to the key function household id.

Distribution Strategy. Distribution strategy describes whether elements 1) are distributed to all target connectors, 2) are passed out to the connectors in succession (round-robin), or 3) the first connector to request data (for polling consumers) gets the next data event from the data channel.

5   Evaluation

In this section, we show how the presented approach can support software architects in predicting the performance of the system by explicitly representing its expected behavior in a performance model.

5.1   Evaluation Question

The evaluation presented in this section addresses RQ_2 (see Sect. 1): *How can the behavior of data stream operations be incorporated into simulations of otherwise stateless component-based performance models?* The derived evaluation question is: *Is it feasable to model and simulate the timing behavior of stateful data-stream operations using our approach?*

To answer this question we discuss how our modeling approach applies to the system introduced in Sect. 2. We first describe the workload and configuration of our system in our experiment (Subsect. 5.2). In Subsect. 5.3 we discuss the metric of interest and the expected behavior of the system regarding this metric. We subsequently show, how we can build a model that predicts its performance (Subsect. 5.4). We then discuss the results and benefits of the simulation. Our evaluation provides initial evidence that we can use the presented approach to model relevant data streaming applications. The evaluation of the accuracy of our modeling approach regarding measurements from a real system and the comparison with other modeling approaches is subject to future work and not addressed in this evaluation.

5.2   Experiment Setup: Workload and Configuration

We have created a workload that is based on the first ten minutes of the data from the house with house id 0 from the DEBS 2014 grand challenge data[1]. As a result, our workload represents 14 households with 107 plugs total. While our approach can handle larger experiments, we chose a small excerpt of the data to keep the following presentation easy to understand. To provide further evidence about the limits of the scalability of our approach, both for the simulation as well as for building the models, we need to model larger systems in future work and for more complicated workloads. On average, around 45.775 data points arrive at the system interface per second. For our chosen window size ($S = 25$ s), we can expect an average number of total data points per window of $R = 25 \cdot 45.775 = 1144.375$. The shift of windows is chosen as $\Delta = 50$ s.

5.3   Experiment Setup: Metric and Performance

We assume that in the case study system, the system architect is interested in the *delay* of data events when they appear in the ouput of the outlier detection for the first time. This delay of the system is formed as follows. Each data event has to be sent from the sensor to the system, resulting in a network delay. For each data event, windowing with size S and Δ leads to a delay that is uniformly distributed in $[0, S]$. The number of elements in the window is determined by the number of data events that arrive during this window, which depends on the usage scenario. Sensor readings that arrive just before a window is emitted are only negligibly delayed by the windowing, data points that arrive just after a window has been created are delayed by 25 s. Calculating the median takes a resource demand that depends linearly on the number of elements inside each window, or log-linear resource demand if implemented naively using sorting. This number of elements depends on the arrival patterns of data events. In our example, we chose every resource demand as $100 + 100 \cdot n$, where n is the number of elements in the grouped data element. Regrouping the elements results in a resource demand that depends on the number of elements to regroup. In this

---

[1] The data is available publicly via the website of the challenge [9].

example this is the number of plugs. The resource demand for calculating the average of all medians inside a time window depends linearly on the number of medians, i.e., the number of plugs. This number depends on the usage scenario. The calculation can only be triggered if the system determines that all relevant medians have arrived at the component. To do this, the system detects when a median for the next window has arrived. This leads to an additional delay of $\Delta = 50\,\text{s}$. The outlier detection has to wait for both the overall average and the household-wise regrouped elements. For each joint element, the calculation resource demand then depends on the number of plugs in the given household.

Additionally, communication delays between components occur and become relevant if the operations are distributed across resources. In our example, every operation is implemented as a single component. For each component there runs one process that takes all available input data, processes it and then waits for additional input data.

If we only consider the timing dependencies introduced by collective operations in the system, we can expect a delay inside $[50\,\text{s}, 75\,\text{s}]$: The sliding window contributes $0\,\text{s}$ to $25\,\text{s}$ to the delay, waiting for one window shift due to grouping contributes an additional delay of $50\,\text{s}$.

For a processing rate of $P = 10\,000$ resource demand units per second and no contention at active resources (i.e., resources can serve infinitely many requests in parallel), we assume about an additional delay of $2 \cdot (100 + 100 \cdot R)/P = 22.91\,\text{s}$ (R as defined in Subsect. 5.2): The creation of medians and the outlier calculation each have to pass over all data points in the window. As a result, we expect an overall delay in $[72.91\,\text{s}, 97.91\,\text{s}]$.

5.4   Experiment Setup: Model

In this section, we present how our approach can be applied to the example system. We have implemented the parts of the approach that are required to model this system and make on-going implementation publicly available [19]. All artefacts used in our evaluation and a guide on how to extract the relevant data from the DEBS data set and run the simulation are available online [20].

Figure 2 illustrates a realization of our running example in PCM. The following is an extended explanation based on previous work where we have introduced a sketch of this model [21, Sect. 4]. The component *Ingress* handles the sensor reading ingress and writes data to data channel C_1. There is a usage scenario for each sensor which calls *Ingress* with a characterization of its plug and household id. *Ingress* then creates a date with the specified characteristics (thus also implicitly creating a birth date) and emits it. The windowing of readings is specified in the data channel C_1. In our example setup, the data channel creates windows of size $25\,\text{s}$ every $50\,\text{s}$. This means that windows are created at points of time $T_i = 50\,\text{s}, 100\,\text{s}, 150\,\text{s}, \text{etc.}$ and span all data points that arrive during $[25\,\text{s}, 50\,\text{s}), [75\,\text{s}, 100\,\text{s}), [125\,\text{s}, 150\,\text{s}), \text{etc.}$ respectively. For every other component, there exists an additional usage scenario (and interface to trigger the component's processing) that repeatedly triggers the component after it has finished its current processing. Components for which such a scenario exists are depicted with the symbol ⚏. This means that for each of the components *Median*, *Group*, *Average* and *Outlier*, there is a process that tries to consume data from the respective data channel. If necessary, the process waits until data is available. Then it processes the data. The processes take an amount of time that depends on the number of elements that are processed. Each of the processes then emits data or, in case of *Outlier*, ends the processing and measures the *delay* of all data points in the currently processed group of elements.

For each plug and each T_i, *Median* consumes a window from C_1, possibly blocking until a window is available. It then emits to C_2 and C_3. C_2 groups depending on window start and end and partitions according to the household id. C_2 emits the group when it discovers that the window has changed, thus delaying the processing chain by one window size. *Group* consumes from C_2 and emits to C_4. C_3 again groups by the window start and end. *Average* consumes groups of medians for each time window from C_3 and emits to C_4. C_4 joins data from *Group* and *Average* based on the start/end of windows. Since the overall average of a window is only calculated once, it can contribute arbitrarily often to the join. As a result, C_4 contains a joint date for each *Outlier* consumes from C_4 and specifies an appropriate resource demand.

We have generated a usage model from the DEBS data set, which results in an additional usage scenario for each of the 107 plugs. Each of the users calls the system interface that is delegated to *Ingress* and provides its household id and plug id as parameters to the call. We create a distribution of times between readings for each plug and use this distribution as the time between readings in our model.

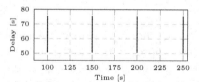

Fig. 4. Delay for data events that arrive in the analysis component in our evaluation system.

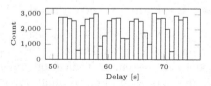

Fig. 5. Histogram of delays that are measured in the simulation for negligible processing times (cf. Fig. 4).

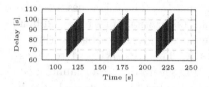

Fig. 6. Delay for data events that arrive in the analysis component in our evaluation system.

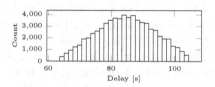

Fig. 7. Histogram of delays that are measured in the simulation for non-negligible processing times.

5.5 Results

Our simulation reproduces the expected number of arriving elements described in Subsect. 5.2 ($R = 1144.375$). Using the simulation we can derive the previously described metrics about the system. We first focus on the case where delay introduced by processing can be neglected and only consider temporal dependencies. Therefore, all data points and groups are processed as soon as they are available. The delay at the point of measuring (after the outlier calculation is finished) is depicted in Fig. 4. The distribution of delays across the simulation is displayed in Fig. 5. The results of the simulation with non-negligible processing times is depicted in Fig. 6 and Fig. 7. This shows a scenario, where processing of data groups uses resources and thus leads to additional delay.

5.6 Discussion

As can be seen from the results, our model can represent the expected number of arriving elements in the sliding window. Furthermore it predicts delays in $[51\,s, 75\,s]$ with an average of $63\,s$ and thus accurately reproduces the expected delay for negligible processing times in $[50\,s, 75\,s]$ (midpoint at $62.5\,s$). If processing times are not negligible, the resulting additional delay leads to a change of the distribution of the delay. The results of the simulation are in the interval $[63.67\,s, 105.85\,s]$ with an average of $84.66\,s$ as compared to the manually deducted estimate in $[72.91\,s, 97.91\,s]$ (midpoint at $85.41\,s$). Creating the estimate as discussed in Subsect. 5.3 requires manual effort for deriving how which part of the system influences the behavior and interacts with the type of data it receives instead of plugging the system together from components and simulating the actual behavior. This is particularly challenging, if the influence of different parts changes due to changes in the configuration of the system. For example, if the constant factors in the resource demands are relevant, the influence of the distribution of plugs to households can (unexpectedly) become more relevant than it is in the depicted case, because more groups with less elements have to be considered and delay the processing. Representing such effects is simplified if the model directly represents the behavior of the system.

If we want to use a state of the art modeling approach instead of a manual calculation of the performance, we have to approximate the behavior by deriving the points of time that windows are created, the distribution of their characteristics and partitions, and the delay incurred by grouping operations (i.e., waiting for the end of a window). While we have hinted at how this can be done for simple scenarios where data arrives in regular patterns and where processing does either not take additional time or the additional time can be estimated, it is unclear how this can be done in a systematic way for more complex scenarios.

6 Related Work

There have recently been considerable efforts in modeling the performance of Big Data applications. We identify two main groups of related work.

The first group is approaches that are used to model Big Data systems of different types. Kroß et al. [11,12] present an approach that utilizes the Palladio modeling language to extract performance models for Apache Spark and Hadoop. Their work is similar in the overall intent, predicting the performance of data-intensive applications. They do not represent stateful operations as model elements that are used in the analysis of the system natively but can represent streaming applications and the performance of streaming frameworks by modeling relevant impact factors, such as number of partitions for a data stream, directly. Other related work models the batch processing of large data sets. For example, Castiglione et al. [4] use an agent-based approach to analyse how highly concurrent big data applications behave in cloud infrastructures regarding the performance, number of used virtual machines and energy efficiency. Aliabadi et al. [1] present an approach that uses Stochastic Activity Networks for modeling different types of batch applications and how they perform when using different frameworks. In the context of the DICE project [3], methods for modeling Big Data systems have been developed. The models explicitly separate between platform, technology and concrete deployment [5] of a big data application. The authors also propose performance simulation methods for simulating their models by transforming models into Petri Nets [6]. Their approach allows modeling complex systems that combine different technologies, including Apache Storm topologies with different types of bolts. We are, however, not aware of an explicit modeling and simulation of stateful operations in their approach. Maddodi et al. [13] present an approach that uses Layered Queuing Networks (LQNs) to analyse the behavior of event-sourcing applications. While they support aggregation of multiple calls for event-sourcing, they do not generalize to other types of aggregation and interaction of calls, such as windows or joins.

The second group of related work addresses systems that process single events but, however, do not target the level of architecture and the abstractions required on this level. Sachs [18] presents an approach for the model-based evaluation of the performance of event-based systems. The work proposes patterns for Queueing Petri Nets that allow architects to model similar behavior as proposed in our approach (such as time windows). However, the work does not target the decomposition of systems on the architecture level. Wu et al. [22] describe a language for defining information needs as queries on event streams and a method for implementing the resulting queries in a high-performance manner. While approaches for specifying complex event processing networks provide similar concepts to the ones presented for our approach, they do not build abstractions that can be used in architecture-level performance models.

Overall, to our knowledge, the state of the art currently does not target the decomposition of data streaming applications in stateful data stream operations and a simulation of this composed system.

7   Conclusion

In this article, we have presented a novel approach for representing and simulating data stream operations in architecture-level component-based performance models. Our approach contributes towards two research questions: 1) how can we represent data stream operations in performance models and 2) how can we analyse the systems' behavior using these models? The representation of data stream operations is relevant, because they commonly appear in an important class of software systems: data-intensive streaming applications. Our evaluation shows that the models of our approach can be used to ease making quantitative statements about the performance of a streaming application because the models express the behavior of the system more accurately, particularly in comparison with a manually derived performance estimate. All of the code of our approach and the artefacts used for this article are publicly available.

Future work will extend our implementation and evaluation and consider the performance impact of employing specific technology realizations for data stream operations. We, furthermore, will investigate the applicability of our approach to other types of systems, particularly self-adaptive systems. Another interesting direction of research is how to extract the type of model presented in this article from code or other artifacts and how to integrate the prediction using these models in an agile software engineering process, as proposed by Mazkatli et al. [14].

References

1. Aliabadi, S.K., et al.: Analytical composite performance models for big data applications. J. Netw. Comput. Appl. **142**, 63–75 (2019)
2. Arasu, A., Babu, S., Widom, J.: The CQL continuous query language: semantic foundations and query execution. VLDB J. **15**(2), 121–142 (2006)
3. Casale, G., Li, C.: Enhancing big data application design with the DICE framework. In: Mann, Z.Á., Stolz, V. (eds.) ESOCC 2017. CCIS, vol. 824, pp. 164–168. Springer, Cham (2018). https://doi.org/10.1007/978-3-319-79090-9_13
4. Castiglione, A., et al.: Modeling performances of concurrent big data applications. Softw. Pract. Exper. **45**(8), 1127–1144 (2015)
5. DICE consortium: Deliverable 2.4 DICE Deployment Abstractions, European Union's Horizon 2020 programme (2017). http://www.dice-h2020.eu/deliverables/
6. DICE consortium: Deliverable 3.4 DICE simulation tools, European Union's Horizon 2020 programme (2017). http://www.dice-h2020.eu/deliverables/
7. Happe, L., Buhnova, B., Reussner, R.: Stateful component-based performance models. Softw. Syst. Model. **13**(4), 1319–1343 (2013). https://doi.org/10.1007/s10270-013-0336-6
8. Hummel, O., et al.: A collection of software engineering challenges for big data system development. In: Euromicro SEAA, pp. 362–369. IEEE (2018)
9. Jerzak, Z., Ziekow, H.: DEBS 2014 grand challenge: smart homes - DEBS.org. https://debs.org/grand-challenges/2014/
10. Jerzak, Z., Ziekow, H.: The DEBS 2014 grand challenge. In: DEBS 2014, pp. 266–269. ACM (2014)
11. Kroß, J., Krcmar, H.: Model-based performance evaluation of batch and stream applications for big data. In: MASCOTS, pp. 80–86. IEEE (2017)
12. Kroß, J., Krcmar, H.: PerTract: model extraction and specification of big data systems for performance prediction by the example of apache spark and hadoop. Big Data Cogn. Comput. **3**(3), 47 (2019)

13. Maddodi, G., Jansen, S., Overeem, M.: Aggregate architecture simulation in event-sourcing applications using layered queuing networks. In: ICPE 2020, pp. 238–245. ACM (2020)
14. Mazkatli, M., et al.: Incremental calibration of architectural performance models with parametric dependencies. In: ICSA 2020. IEEE (2020)
15. Meijer, E.: Your mouse is a database. ACM Queue **10**(3), 20 (2012)
16. Rathfelder, C.: Modelling event-based interactions in component-based architectures for quantitative system evaluation. In: The Karlsruhe Series on Software Design and Quality, KIT Scientific Publishing (2013)
17. Reussner, R.H., et al.: Modeling and Simulating Software Architectures - The Palladio Approach. MIT Press, Cambridge (2016)
18. Sachs, K.: Performance modeling and benchmarking of event-based systems. Ph.D. thesis, Darmstadt University of Technology (2011)
19. Werle, D.: GitHub repository of palladio indirections. https://github.com/PalladioSimulator/Palladio-Addons-Indirections
20. Werle, D.: Data Stream Operations as First-Class Entities in Component-Based Performance Models - Auxiliary Material (2020). https://doi.org/10.5281/zenodo.3937718
21. Werle, D., Seifermann, S., Koziolek, A.: Data stream operations as first-class entities in palladio. In: SSP 2019. Softwaretechnik Trends (2019)
22. Wu, E., Diao, Y., Rizvi, S.: High-performance complex event processing over streams. In: SIGMOD, pp. 407–418. ACM (2006)

Architecture-Centric Support for Integrating Security Tools in a Security Orchestration Platform

Chadni Islam[1,2(✉)], Muhammad Ali Babar[1], and Surya Nepal[2]

[1] CREST Centre, University of Adelaide, Adelaide, SA 5005, Australia
{chadni.islam,ali.babar}@adelaide.edu.au
[2] CSIRO's Data61, Sydney, NSW, Australia
{chadni.islam,surya.nepal}@data61.csiro.au

Abstract. Security Operation Centers (SOC) leverage a number of tools to detect, thwart and deal with security attacks. One of the key challenges of SOC is to quickly integrate security tools and operational activities. To address this challenge, an increasing number of organizations are using Security Orchestration, Automation and Response (SOAR) platforms, whose design needs suitable architectural support. This paper presents our work on architecture-centric support for designing a SOAR platform. Our approach consists of a conceptual map of SOAR platform and the key dimensions of an architecture design space. We have demonstrated the use of the approach in designing and implementing a Proof of Concept (PoC) SOAR platform for (i) automated integration of security tools and (ii) automated interpretation of activities to execute incident response processes. We also report a preliminary evaluation of the proposed architectural support for improving a SOAR's design.

Keywords: Security orchestration · Security automation · Software architecture · Security tool integration · Design space

1 Introduction

The adoption of Security Orchestration, Automation and Response (SOAR) platforms has recently gained major popularity among security analysts, Security Operation Centers (SOC) and incident response team [1–4]. SOAR platforms enable integration, orchestration and automation of the activities (e.g., block IP, scan endpoint and isolate host) performed by security tools and human experts [2].

Existing SOAR platforms lack proper abstractions for designing a platform at the architectural level [1–3, 5]. Most of the existing SOAR platforms are implemented in ad-hoc manners without much attention to the underlying infrastructure [2]. As a result, there can be several engineering challenges involved in embedding agility in a SOAR platform [2, 4, 7]. These challenges result in highly complex and monolithic design that is hard to evolve overtime. A SOAR' design complexity may also worsened by a lack of conceptual and practical guidelines for optimal architectural design decisions [2, 6].

© Springer Nature Switzerland AG 2020
A. Jansen et al. (Eds.): ECSA 2020, LNCS 12292, pp. 165–181, 2020.
https://doi.org/10.1007/978-3-030-58923-3_11

An architecture-centric approach [7–9] is expected to help in reducing the design complexity of a SOAR by modularizing the functionalities and non-functional requirements. The architectural design decision provides a foundation for analyzing and understanding the sub-optimal design choices [7], which can be improved by leveraging suitable architectural styles and patterns.

A design space is required to capture and characterize design decisions for integrating techniques and tools that underpin a SOAR platform [2]. Developing design spaces for different domains of software systems is a growing trend [7]. The design space of a SOAR platform involves many architectural design decisions and trade-offs that are impacted by security tools and applications integrated into these platforms. We propose a concept map considering the functionalities performed by a SOAR platform. It allows one to modularize the functions and separate the concerns of the components that provide the design space of a SOAR platform.

In this article, we present an architecture-centric approach to design and implement a SOAR platform. The proposed approach consists of three parts:

- *Abstraction to model SOAR platform design space*: We provide a concept map of a SOAR platform that defines and relates the key concepts of SOAR to support understanding of security tools integration and orchestration. The design space is useful for understanding and analyzing requirements of emerging SOAR platforms and integration technologies for faster response and efficiency.
- *Layered Architecture for SOAR platform*: We provide a layered architecture that modularizes the components into different layers based on two key functionalities – integration and orchestration. These two key requirements are to guide architects to design and deploy a SOAR platform to integrate security tools and orchestrate activities based on integrated security tools. We further consider the architecture style and pattern as a mean for delimiting the design space.
- *Proof of concept SOAR support*: We have developed a Proof of Concept (PoC) SOAR platform that has been designed to fulfill the quality requirements - *integrability*, *interpretability* and *interoperability* following the proposed architecture. We have used seven security tools with different capabilities. The evaluation results show the feasibility of the proposed architecture approach for (i) automated integration of security tools and (ii) automated interpretation of incident response activities.

This paper is organized as follows. Section 2 introduces a concept map of a SOAR platforms' design space. Section 3 presents the modularized architecture of a SOAR platform. Section 4 details the dimension of a SOAR platform's integration design space. Section 5 presents a case study. Section 6 demonstrates the evaluation of the PoC. Section 7 discusses related work and Sect. 8 concludes the paper.

2   Security Orchestration and Automation

The SOAR platforms are integrated solutions for an organization's SOC. The underlying technologies of SOAR platforms are designed to interweave people, process and technology. In a SOAR platform, people are responsible for intelligence-based decision making and technologies are used to streamline complex process. The key purpose of a SOAR platform is to power automation through orchestration. The functionalities of a SOAR are mainly categorized into integration, orchestration and automation [2].

The development of any SOAR platform first needs to focus on *integrating* the security tools in a single platform. Depending on the organizations, the security tools can be open source, commercial, proprietary, packaged or even legacy bunch of scripts. Security tools are generally integrated using plugins, scripts, APIs and modules. Mostly SOAR vendors provide plugins and APIs based support for 150–200 security tools [10, 11]. Security tools generate data in a variety of formats. Further, the data are unified to enable *interoperability* among security tools.

The second key task of a SOAR is *orchestration*. It allows organizations to deploy and operationalize their security process or Incident Response Process (IRP) using a piece of code or script, also known as a playbook. An IRP is a set of activities performed by security experts and security tools. Playbooks contain a set of instructions that makes security tools interoperate in a manner where the output of one tool is used as an input to other tools. An orchestration process improves the response to a security incident by reducing the manual and repetitive tasks done by human experts.

The third task of a SOAR is *automation* or *response*. An organization needs to identify what they need to orchestrate and what can be automated. Mostly validation, prioritization, reducing false alarms and checking for access control authorization are the different types of activities that are automated through orchestration processes. The SOAR community has not quite reached a consensus on any standard mechanism of automation of security activities.

2.1   Functional Requirements of Security Orchestration and Automation

SOAR as a Unifier or Hub. We adopt the functionality of a SOAR outlined in a recent multivocal review [2]. We consider a SOAR platform as a hub that unifies the activities of security tools and provides a single pane for supporting operations of a SOC. Security tool integration is one of the most important resource intensive and time-consuming activities in a SOC. Security tools can be integrated using several architectural integration styles [12]. Semantic technology can be leveraged for integrating security tools. A semantic integration mechanism ensures that a SOAR platform can *interpret* the data consumed and generated by security tools for *interoperability*. A SOAR platform first needs to integrate security tools and then based on integration mechanisms it interprets the IRPs. It can enable organizations to use playbooks from different vendors to model an orchestration process by unifying the semantics provided in playbooks. Most SOAR platforms filter incoming alerts based on their syntactic and semantics correctness before delivering them to analytics tools. A SOAR's architecture should support semantics integration among the artifacts produced and consumed by security tools.

SOAR as a Coordinator or Orchestrator. A SOAR platform orchestrates security tools activities and streamlines complex security processes into simplified processes. The orchestration processes can be considered as a sequence of actions, where the output of one tool needs to be the input of other tools. A simplified process is easy to follow and enables a SOC to differentiate between manual and automated processes. It also helps to keep track of the ongoing scans and activities that require immediate human involvement. It should be noted that a lot of SOAR literatures tend to use integration mechanisms or connecting tools as an umbrella term to cover all processes that happen under-the-hood of security orchestration. Whilst this abstraction is helpful to gain an initial understanding of security orchestration, we argue that architects would benefit from a more modularized model that clearly distinguishes the activities related to integration, orchestration and automation within SOAR platforms.

2.2 Quality Attribute Requirements

A SOAR should also satisfy certain quality attribute requirements. The essential quality attribute requirements or Non-Functional Requirements (NFRs) of a SOAR are categorized into design time and runtime requirements. To design an architecture of a SOAR platform, we focus on the following quality attributes.

- **Integrability**: Security tools integrated into a SOAR platform come from different vendors. An architecture of a SOAR platform is expected to seamlessly integrate security tools and quickly adapt modification of security tools' functionalities.
- **Interoperability**: A SOAR platform should support semantic integration of different types of artifacts generated by security tools and data sources. The integration mechanism needs to ensure that security tools can interoperate with each other.
- **Interpretability**: A SOAR platform should be able to semantically interpret the data generated and consumed by security tools.
- **Flexibility**: A SOAR platform's tasks depend on IRPs and emerging threat behavior which changes continuously. A SOAR architecture should be flexible to provide mapping support for security tools and IRPs to adapt the changes.
- **Usability**: A SOAR's architecture needs to be easily understandable so that a SOC can easily learn and operate a SOAR platform and interpret the input, output and activities of the components.

2.3 Abstraction for Security Orchestration and Automation

Organizations generically deploy and run a SOAR platform on top of existing security tools, information systems and organizational infrastructures to fulfill their security requirements and business needs. An architect must understand the core concepts of a SOAR platform to design and communicate about the orchestration process and required integration and automation technologies with stakeholders and developers of a SOAR platform. The lack of a comprehensive view might result in concept overlapping and ambiguity. To address this issue, we propose a conceptual map to capture the common terminologies of a SOAR. Figure 1 shows the conceptual map of a SOAR platform that provides the key elements and relationships among these elements.

A SOAR platform connects a wide variety of security tools that have different capabilities. By capability, we mean the features and characteristics of security tools, which can support different types of activities. Security tools are generally categorized as detection, analysis and response tools depending on their capabilities (Fig. 1). This categorization

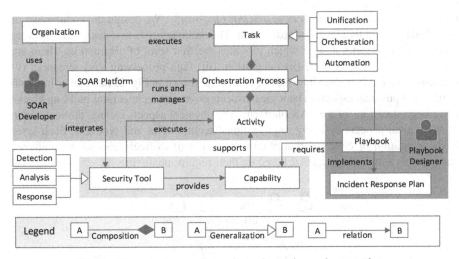

Fig. 1. Conceptual map of security orchestration and automation

is made based on the activities performed by security tools while responding to an incident. For example, monitoring tools can be considered under detection or analysis tools depending on their contribution to an IRP. A detailed description of security tools used for this research is out of the scope of this paper.

A SOAR platform is designed and deployed based on an organization's security requirements and the available security tools. A SOAR developer needs to design and develop different types of integration mechanisms (e.g., APIs, plugins or modules) to integrate security tools (Fig. 1). A SOAR platform performs a set of tasks that can be categorized in unification, orchestration and automation. It runs the orchestration process that invokes security tools to perform certain activities. An orchestration process is the composition of tasks performed by a SOAR and activities performed by security tools. It contains the invocation actions, scripts to invoke tools and the responses of security tools. Orchestration processes govern the integration, orchestration and automation task to respond to a security incident.

The orchestration process primarily is designed in the form of a set of playbooks, which are generally dedicated to a particular security incident and have a dedicated set of security tools that are deployed in an organization's environment. Most organizations also have dedicated Security Incident Response Team (CSIRT) who mainly design IRPs for security incidents based on an organization's preferred security requirements (i.e., confidentiality, integrity and availability), policies and quality requirements. SOAR developers or playbook designers design and develop playbooks based on the available security tools and well-known integration mechanisms.

3   SOAR Architecture

We propose an architecture to ensure the functional and non-functional requirements of a SOAR platform. The key research objective is *"how software architecture can play a role*

in improving the design practices of a SOAR platform?". We design the architecture of
SOAR platform at two levels of abstraction. The architecture is first designed following
the layered architectural style which provides the first level of abstraction. There are
six layers – (i) security tool, (ii) integration, (iii) data processing, (iv) semantic, (v)
orchestration and (vi) User Interface (UI) layer as shown in Fig. 2. Each layer has both
logical and physical aspects. The logical aspects cover the architectural building blocks
and design decisions of a SOAR platform. The physical aspects include the realization
of the logical aspects by using organizations' technologies and products. Each layer
has a separation of concerns that allows security staff to freely choose the preferred
components and deploy a SOAR based on their requirements (Fig. 2).

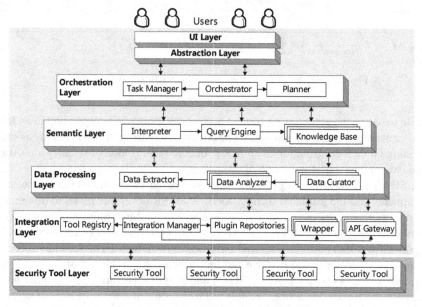

Fig. 2. High-level architecture for SOAR platform

Each layer is decomposed into components and sub-components. We consider the
components as the lower level of abstractions. Figure 2 shows the core components and
interactions among the components that are required to achieve the desire goals of a
SOAR platform. Different functionalities of a SOAR platform require different combinations of these components. We specify the components as a principle computation
element that implement different tasks of a SOAR to execute IRPs.

UI Layer: Security staff initiate existing IRPs or define new plans using a SOAR's User
Interfaces (UIs) such as interactive dashboards or Integrated Development Environment
(IDE) or Command Line Interface (CLI). The UI layer supports *flexibility* in designing
UIs that help define IRPs and integrate security tools. A SOC can easily learn and operate
a SOAR platform using the UI. An abstraction layer or API layer can be implemented as
part of the UI layers to maintain and encapsulate the interaction among a SOAR's user
and its components (Fig. 2).

Orchestration Layer: The *orchestrator* and *task manager* together form the coordinator of a SOAR platform (Fig. 2). The orchestrator is responsible for coordinating and forming configuration to achieve *interoperability* and automating the execution of IRPs. The *planner* in the orchestration layer has a set of '*playbooks*' to automate the execution of an IRP and keep track of the tasks being executed. Each playbook has a set of tasks that contains the details of the process about the input required to execute a task and also the output that is generated after task execution. The playbooks further contain the conditions that trigger the execution of a particular task. A playbook's tasks vary depending on the requirements of a SOC and the types of security tools available. The *orchestrator* monitors the successful or unsuccessful execution of tasks. The planner provides a set of APIs through which a user can update or modify the orchestration process. An orchestrator may use a set of APIs to govern the execution of an IRP.

Semantic Layer: The semantic layer is responsible for the semantic *interpretation* of data that flows across a SOAR platform. It consists of a *knowledge base*, *query engine* and *interpreter*. A knowledge base usually consists of an *ontology* of security tools, their capabilities and activities of an IRP, which enables the *interpreter* to semantically interpret security tools' capability and IRPs' activities. The details of the ontology can be found in [13]. The *query engine* is responsible for extracting data from a knowledge base. In our proposed architecture, we consider the semantic layer separate from other layers to give SOC the *flexibility* to define or modify an ontology.

Data Processing Layer: The information used by a SOAR ranges from business-critical data to usage systems logs, alerts logs and malicious activities that are processed by the data processing layer. *Data curator*, *data extractor* and *data analyzer* are the three main components of data processing layer. The *data curator* gathers the data produced by tools for analysis. This layer contributes toward *interoperability* and *interpretability* by processing the heterogeneous structured and unstructured data of different security tools and playbooks. It is responsible for sharing semantically structured data among different components of a SOAR throughout an IRP execution process. An architect can incorporate any automation algorithm or data analysis techniques as part of data analyzer without affecting other components of a SOAR.

Integration Layer: The integration layer has five components: *integration manager*, *wrapper*, *tool registry*, *plugin repository* and *API gateway*. This layer is designed to integrate security tools. The *integration manager* works as a description module through which security tools are integrated and information is provided to enable *interpretability* among them. A *tool registry* is responsible for discovering and registering available security tools to monitor their status and report any changes. Security tools are registered in terms of their capabilities (i.e., input, output and functions) and types. The *wrapper, API gateway* and *plugins* are intermediary components that provide interfaces to encapsulate security tools for data translation or imposing orchestration. An integration manager uses these components to initiate a request and become the ultimate recipient of orchestrator's commands. The difference between wrapper, plugins and API gateway lies in security tools integration and communication protocols.

Security Tool Layer: The security tools layer consists of multivendor heterogeneous security tools, which are typically a mix of open source, proprietary, custom and commercial-of-the shelf (COT) products. These tools are mainly characterized as unmodifiable components of a SOAR platform. Given most of the security tools are required to interact with each other, an in-depth understanding of the security tools' data structures and capabilities are necessary to integrate them into a SOAR platform.

Figure 3 shows an example UML sequence diagram for responding to a security incident that comprises of components from each layer.

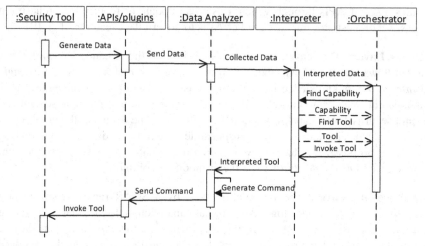

Fig. 3. An example sequence diagram showing the flow of data and interaction of components

4   Dimensions of the Design Space of SOAR

The design space of a SOAR reveals that the integrated security tools and orchestration process mainly govern the tasks of a SOAR platform. Hence, we have considered the architectural design decisions from the process and technology perspective for automatically integrating security tools and orchestrating IRPs.

Process Decision: Along with defining the orchestration process, it is important to define the process for integrating security tools and analyzing data. A SOAR's process varies depending on the mode of a task – automated, semi-automated or manual. The automation of the integration process relies on five design decisions for *integration process, interpretation process, security tools to capability mapping process, security tool discovery process* and *security tool invocation process*. A decomposition of the functions based on layers helps in selecting a suitable technology depending on required process. For example, the task to manually integrate security tools is separated from automatically interpreting the security tools' data. Security tools are first required to integrate into a SOAR platform, then processes are designed to interpret the security tools data and IRPs activities. Here, the modular architecture helps with defining different processes, which are mainly orchestration of security tools, SOAR's components and organizational information systems.

A SOAR platform can be centralized, distributed or hybrid depending on an organization's infrastructure [2]. For centralized or distributed applications, the communication protocols are different. In most cases, these communication protocols (i.e., REST API, RPC and event-driven) are hidden under the internal structures of security tools, which expose their functions through APIs. A communication process can be designed to manage distributed communication among different security tools.

Technology Decision: From a technology perspective, we mainly consider *the integration technologies, interpretation mechanisms* and *tools discovery mechanisms* that are required for integrating security tools, designing the orchestration process and powering automation. A SOAR's taxonomy has six automation strategies [2]. An underlying technology infrastructure consists of the assets of an organization depending on the type of the automation strategy. Example of assets includes various hardware and software infrastructures (i.e., computer systems, operating systems and applications) that an organization needs to protect from security attacks. Orchestrations can take place in different types of environments which can be open or restricted. We need to consider different architectural integration styles to ensure that the integration constraints related to different security tools and stakeholders (e.g., semantic, performance and component constraints) are addressed [12].

Following we provide a set of design decisions that need to be made by an architect.

- Building a generic block of a SOAR platform. An architect can choose to design a playbook and script for orchestration and automation.
- Disseminating tools that are integrated and participate in orchestration. Architects have to decide on how to map security tools to IRP and where to deploy them in an organization's environment so that orchestrator can invoke the tools when required.
- Setting up a mechanism for an orchestrator to discover security tools. An architect has to choose integration styles and define processes for discovery of security tools.
- Setting up and starting an orchestration process. An architect has to decide who has the right to modify the process and provide an interface to modify or add new IRPs.

Table 1 shows a summary of the architectural design decisions for achieving the desired functional and non-functional requirements of a SOAR platform. By architectural design decisions we mean the design decisions that would have system wide impact and/or impact on more than one non-functional requirements [8].

Table 1. Summary of architectural design decision

Design decisions	Expected benefits
Ontology for formalizing security tools and activities of IRPs	Make a SOAR architecture flexible to integrate different types of security tools with varied data formats
Use of ontology for semantic integration and information discovery	Support tools specific integration and automated execution of IRPs in dynamic environment
Layered architectural style	Easy evolution of SOAR's components and easy modularization of functionalities and components
Abstraction of SOAR's components task with a set of APIs	Make a SOAR platform easy to use, manage and learn for end-users
Automated integration and interpretation process	Enable reuse of existing components with changes in IRPs and security tools
Share ontology template in a centralized repository pattern	Provide access of the ontology to its end users and support flexibility in update

5   Case Study – Prototype Implementation

In this section, we present a Proof of Concept (PoC) SOAR platform that we have designed and implemented based on the proposed architectural approach [14]. The functional requirements of our PoC are to *automate the process of integrating security tools, automate the selection of security tools to execute an IRP* and *automate the execution of a set of IRPs*. We designed the PoC in a way so that it is easily evolvable for future changes. In this implementation, we considered two types of changes that are most common is SOARs execution environment – change in security tools and change in IRPs. Figure 4 presents the implementation architecture of the PoC. We analyzed the instruction of integration and orchestration to select the technologies and identify the design decisions. We designed automated integration processes and selected semantic technologies to enable semantic integration and interpretation of security tools data.

We selected seven open-source tools[1] with varied capabilities. The selected tools are *Snort, Splunk, LimaCharlie, MISP, Windows defender, Wireshark* and *WinPCap* which are IDS (Intrusion Detection System), SIEM (Security Information and Event Management Tool), EDR (Endpoint Detection and Response) tool, Open Source Threat Intelligence and Sharing Platform (OSINT), Firewall and packet monitoring and logging tools respectively. The security tools were selected based on the diversity in their capabilities because execution of an IRP would require multiple security tools. We used 24 different capabilities of the selected tools with MISP as a new tool to be integrated later. We have curated a set of IRPs from Demisto's (i.e., a SOAR platform provider)

---

[1] https://www.snort.org, https://www.splunk.com/, https://www.limacharlie.io/, https://www.misp-project.org.

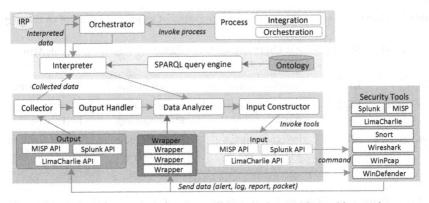

Fig. 4. Implementation architecture of the PoC for security tool integration

collaborative playbooks [15]. We have selected 21 IRPs and slightly modified them to fit the capabilities of the seven security tools used for our research. We designed another 48 IRPs as a new set of IRPs that PoC would require to execute without user intervention. The list of capabilities and IRPs are available at [14].

The implementation decision incorporated APIs based integration style as our primary mechanism to integrate security tools into a SOAR. The data from the security tools such as MISP and Splunk have been made accessible through their APIs. Besides, we have built wrappers for security tools that do not provide specific APIs such as Snort. Integrating a new tool required us to identify security tool's APIs or information sharing protocol and implement a suitable integration mechanism. The API and wrappers of Fig. 4 are part of the *integration layer* of the PoC.

We also designed an ontology to formalize security tools, their capabilities and IRP's activities to enable semantic interpretation of security tools data [13]. Each security tool can execute multiple activities and each activity can be executed by multiple security tools. We used Apache Jena Fuseki server to store the ontology. Security tools are formalized based on their capabilities and the activities of IRPs are mapped with security tool class of an ontology. Table 2 and Table 3 illustrate how security tools and IRPs have been mapped onto an ontology. We designed a SPARQL query engine to retrieve the required information from the ontology. The retrieve data are interpreted through an interpreter, which mainly deconstructs the data for further processing. The designed ontology along with the interpreter built the *semantic layer*.

We built a collector to gather security tools' data, which are sent to an orchestrator via the interpreter for actions, e.g., Splunks API is configured to receive system logs of various endpoints. This data is searched and processed to find programs, files or users that could be malicious. Further to formulate the commands, an input constructor is built.

The automation algorithms or processes have been mainly built as integration processes that are the parts of the orchestration layer (Fig. 4). We designed and implemented scripts to define the automated integration process, which includes selecting the security tools based on activity description, interpreting their capabilities, formulating the input commands and finally invoking the security tool by calling appropriate APIs [16]. An example is shown in Fig. 5 where the output of Splunk is sent to LimaCharlie. The

Table 2. Illustration of a selected set of object properties of security tool class of an ontology

Security tool	Security tool class	has Capability	Capability class	executeActivity
snort_s	IDS	intrusion_detection_s	IntrusionDetection	detectIncident
limaCharlie_l	EDR	intrusion_detection_l process_killing_l	IntrusionDetection ProcessKilling	detectIncident killProcess
splunk_s	SIEM	log_collection_s alert_analysis_a	LogCollection AlertAnalysis	collectAlertLog investigateAlert

Table 3. Illustration of a selected set of data properties of security tool class of an ontology

Security tool	Security tool class	isIntegrated	hasInputType	hasRule	hasConfigFile
snort_s	IDS	True	Network traffic	False	snorts.config
limaCharlie_l	EDR	True	Payloads	True	inputs.conf
splunk_s	SIEM	True	Logs	True	LCConf

orchestrator is required to collect the output of Splunk and then interpret it. All the data generated by Splunk might not be required by LimaCharlie; so, the orchestrator would require to construct the input of LimaCharlie from Splunk's output to invoke LimaCharlie. We developed and designed this process as part of the integration process to automate the interpretation of the security tools data, which enable seamless interoperability among security tools. Using the integration process, data sharing among the security tools of Fig. 5 happened seamlessly.

6   Evaluation

In this section, we report how the PoC has been evaluated to demonstrate the feasibility of the proposed architecture approach based on two scenarios.

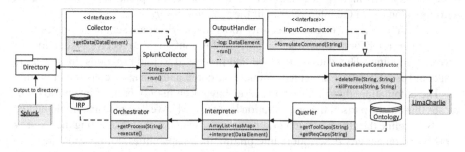

Fig. 5. Example of data transfer from Splunk to LimaCharlie

6.1 Automating the Process for Integration Security Tools

Let's assume that a user has expressed a goal of integrating security tools. We have decided to use the proposed architecture for automating security tools integration. In the current implementation, an ontology is available that works as a knowledge base of a set of existing security tools. To integrate the available security tools, the orchestrator provides a template of an ontology to users for specifying the tools' capabilities and map it with the available activities or activity it can execute. This process stores the security tools' information in an ontology that makes the information available to the orchestrator. If the security tools have different capabilities, the information is updated in the ontology. Further, the process for automating the integration of security tools is invoked which enables the collector to collect the security tools' output and orchestrator to formulate and send commands to the security tool for executing the desired activities.

Other integration approaches such as designing static APIs for communicating with security tools or plugin-based integration require to develop wrapper along with connection with the data curator and the orchestrator to collect the security tool data. The collector needs to be configured to access the data generated by security tools. Thus, integrating a single tool would require development of at least one component and connection of that component with the orchestrator. For a security tool with multiple capabilities, for instance, Splunk and Limacharlie have different sets of APIs to invoke different capabilities, a single API or wrapper would fail to invoke different capabilities. For example, for LimaCharlie with static API based integration, we have designed two sets of scripts to *kill a process* and *isolate a process*. For seven security tools with 24 capabilities at least 48 connections are required among the orchestrator and security tools while considering API and wrapper-based integration for taking the output and provide the commands to execute an activity. An increase in the connections and components increases the design space of a SOAR. With the inclusion of new security tools, a new connection emerges and a user would require to go through the existing APIs, wrapper and connection to integrate a security tool in a playbook to execute an IRP. An update in the existing security tool features, for example, addition of new capabilities or change in the existing API parameters also requires designing the connections and updating the playbook where the security tools have been used.

With the semantic-based integration approach, we only need to update security tools details in an ontology. The connections between the ontology and other components have already been designed and that do not require any changes. Thus, with the PoC, the number of components and connections remain constant with the integration of new security tools – that is MISP. Without considering the proposed architecture approach the number of components increased at least by 2 upon the integration of new security tools. We found that semantic-based integration is more suitable in this case. This demonstrates that the proposed architecture-based implementation keeps the components and connections lower by reusing the existing components.

Our observation from running the experiment reveals that building wrapper and APIs require more time than updating the security tool details in an ontology. Hence, ontology-based automated integration process free SOC's time.

6.2 Automating the Interpretation of the Activities to Execute an IRP

We assume a user has expressed his/her goal to identify and isolate suspicious endpoints. Using the current implementation, the orchestrator can identify the capabilities required to execute the activities and then select the security tools that can execute that capability. As the process for automatically identifying the capabilities required to execute an activity and selecting the security tools are already defined, a user would not require to manually identify the security tools. He/she just needs to request the orchestrator for security tools that can perform the required activities. The orchestrator runs the process and returns the available security tools. Then the user can also define which security tools would be used for each activity. Next, the orchestrator automatically generates the commands to invoke the security tools to execute a sequence of activities. In this whole process, the current architectural based implementation has reused the existing process, components and protocols.

With the non-modular and monolithic implementation of a SOAR platform, a playbook is required to design to fulfill a user's goal. Developing a playbook would require an understanding of a playbook's structure, knowledge of the available security tools, developing scripts to access the generated data of the security tools and their specific APIs to execute an activity. In the monolithic approach, each playbook is designed for a specific IRP which cannot be reused even if the new IRP is a subset of the existing IRPs. A user requires to modify the existing playbook to execute the new IRP.

Modularizing a SOAR's architecture provides a clear understanding of which part would require an update and which components can be reused without modification. Reusing the existing components provides the following benefits: a SOC spends less time in adapting the changes and the evolution of a system does not increase the complexity of architecture. Further, it has reduced the overhead for users in adopting the changes by providing the processes that can be reused. The evaluation shows that without separating the concerns, the number of changes would require more than our proposed architectural based implementation.

The PoC has accurately executed 45 IRPs among the new 48 IRPs. For three of the IRPs, the orchestrator could not find any security tools with the required capabilities to execute some of the activities, thus those were executed partially. The successful execution of the 45 IRPs demonstrates that the developed PoC has accurately interpreted the data generated by the used security tools without user intervention. The security tool MISP is also used by some of the new IRPs; thus, it has also been successfully integrated. From the evaluation, we also observe that incorporating the changes in the PoC is easier compared to other approaches.

This paper has demonstrated the feasibility of the proposed architecture for security tool integration and IRP interpretation based on three quality attributes - *integrability*, *interpretability* and *interoperability*. Other quality attributes of a SOAR can be evaluated by following different architectural evaluation techniques such as Scenario based Architecture Analysis Method (SAAM) and Architecture Tradeoff Analysis Method (ATAM) [8, 17].

7 Related Work

The leading security service providers aim to provide SOAR platforms to deliver end to end security services [10, 11, 18, 19]. For example, FireEye (i.e., a leading cybersecurity company) designs a SOAR platform to integrate its endpoint products and offer supports to its industry partners [10]. Whilst the start-ups mainly focus on developing APIs to integrate different third-party solutions and provide playbooks for automated and semi-automate IRPs [20]. The ad-hoc implementations of a SOAR platform increase the design complexity of such a platform as these platforms are built as a whole without separating the concerns of the deployed components. Further, a SOAR is a large-scale system that integrates an organization's information and security systems. Organizations are facing several challenges in managing these solutions while any changes occur in the underlying operating environment such as integrating new security tools and defining new IRPs [2, 13]. Our work addresses these kinds of challenges.

The current state-of-the-practices and state-of-the-arts of SOARs lack a shared understanding between the vendors and stakeholders of SOAR [1, 3, 4, 21, 22]. For example, there is no shared understanding of the key software components and technologies that are necessary to integrate and enable interoperability among various security tools and bring automation in IRPs execution. In these studies, a SOAR platform has mainly focused on security tools interactions, isolated processes and low-level infrastructures, while paying less attention to the problems of how different components of a SOAR and security tools coordinate.

A security team requires an understanding of the internal structure of a SOAR (i.e., libraries to integrate new security tools or requirements) to adopt the changes in a SOAR platforms execution environment. Adopting the changes remains a tedious and difficult undertaking for end-users. State-of-the-art approaches for security process modeling provide limited or no decomposition mechanisms, which easily results in monolithic processes that address multiple concerns in a single model [1, 3, 4, 22].

None of the existing works provides the architectural design space that could inform architects of the decisions to be made where multiple components are interconnected. Software architecture is composed of early design decisions, which can help to address some of the existing challenges to be addressed by SOAR platform designers [6–8]. An increased focus on architectural aspects of SOAR can also facilitate further research on the design decisions of the exiting SOAR platforms to form guidelines, rules and design techniques. The rise of security incidents has increased the demand for knowledge, processes and techniques for designing and deploying highly configurable and scalable SOAR platforms. As most organization prefer to utilize their available software and security tools, it would be helpful to consider architectural design decisions for trade-off analysis before deploying a SOAR platform to enhance a SOC' efficiency.

8 Conclusion

Exploring and understanding the architectural design decision before designing and implementing a SOAR platform is a valuable task. The captured design decision would help developers as well as a SOC staff of an organization to systemize their decision process and trade-off analysis. The architectural design decisions would serve as a standalone lexicon to describe and evaluate the existing and new SOAR platform. In this paper, we have designed a conceptual diagram of SOAR platform to support an architect's understanding of the design space of SOAR. We have further identified the requirement of a SOAR in terms of unification, orchestration and automation and proposed a layered architecture to modularize the functions and separate the concerns of the components of a SOAR platform. The architecture design decisions are chosen from the process and technology perspectives. We have used the proposed approach to design and implement a PoC SOAR platform for an ad-hoc SOC infrastructure and observe its impact on the automated integration and interpretation process. We have leveraged well-known architectural styles and patterns to implement the PoC. We have observed that the consideration of the principal dimension of the architecture design space has improved SOAR design practices.

The proposed approach has further laid a foundation for future research on the design space and deployment automation of SOAR platforms. In our future work, we plan to conduct a large-scale mapping of the existing SOAR platform and IRPs onto the architecture design decisions to generate patterns and hide interaction among the different components across multiple technology paradigm.

Acknowledgement. This work is partially supported by CSIRO's data61, Australia. We acknowledge the contribution of Faheem Ullah, Aufeef Chauhan and Triet Mihn Le for their feedbacks in improving the work.

References

1. Feitosa, E., Souto, E., Sadok, D.H.: An orchestration approach for unwanted internet traffic identification. Comput. Netw. **56**(12), 2805–2831 (2012)
2. Islam, C., Babar, M.A., Nepal, S.: A multi-vocal review of security orchestration. ACM Comput. Surv. (CSUR) **52**(2), 37 (2019)
3. Luo, S., Salem, M.B.: Orchestration of software-defined security services. In: 2016 IEEE International Conference on Communications Workshops (ICC 2016), Kuala Lumpur, Malaysia (2016)
4. Nadkarni, H.: Security orchestration framework. US Patent 9,807,118 (2017)
5. Koyama, T., Hu, B., Nagafuchi, Y., Shioji, E., Takahashi, K.: Security orchestration with a global threat intelligence platform. NTT Tech. Rev. **13**, 1–6 (2015)
6. Chauhan, M.A., Babar, M.A., Sheng, Q.Z.: A reference architecture for provisioning of tools as a service: meta-model, ontologies and design elements. Future Gener. Comput. Syst. **69**, 41–65 (2017)
7. Jansen, A., Bosch, J.: Software architecture as a set of architectural design decisions. In: Proceedings of the 5th Working IEEE/IFIP Conference on Software Architecture, USA (2005)
8. Bass, L., Clements, P., Kazman, R.: Software Architecture in Practice. Addison-Wesley Professional, Boston (2003)
9. Haesevoets, R., Weyns, D., Holvoet, T.: Architecture-centric support for adaptive service collaborations. ACM Trans. Softw. Eng. Methodol. **23**(1), 1–40 (2014)
10. FireEye.: Security orchestration in action: integrate – automate –manage. https://www2.fireeye.com/Webinar-FSO-EMEA.html?utm_source=fireeye&utm_medium=webinar-page. Accessed 20 Nov 2017

11. IBM.: Orchestrate incident response. https://www.ibm.com/security/solutions/orchestrate-incident-response. Accessed 1 Nov 2019
12. Andersson, J., Johnson, P.: Architectural integration styles for large-scale enterprise software systems. In: Proceedings Fifth IEEE International Enterprise Distributed Object Computing Conference, Seattle, WA, USA, pp. 224–236 (2001)
13. Islam, C., Babar, M.A., Nepal, S.: Automated interpretation and integration of security tools using semantic knowledge. In: Advanced Information Systems Engineering (CAiSE 2019), Rome, Italy (2019)
14. Islam, C.: Proof of concept SOAR (2020). https://github.com/Chadni-Islam/Security-Orchestration-PoC
15. Demisto.: Demisto platform content repository. https://github.com/demisto/content. Accessed 21 Jan 2020
16. Islam, C., Babar, M.A., Nepal, S.: An ontology-driven approach to automate the process of integration security software systems. In: IEEE/ACM International Conference on Software and System Processes (ICSSP 2019), Montreal, Canada, 25–26 June (2019)
17. Babar, M.A., Zhu, L., Jeffery, R.: A framework for classifying and comparing software architecture evaluation methods. In: Proceedings of 2004 Australian Software Engineering Conference, pp. 309–318 (2004)
18. Siemplify.: What is security orchestration and automation?. https://www.siemplify.co/resources/what-is-security-orchestration-automation/. Accessed 5 Dec 2019
19. Swimlane.: Security automation and orchestration. https://swimlane.com/use-cases/security-orchestration-for-automated-defense/. Accessed 20 Nov 2017
20. Demisto.: Security orchestration and automation. https://www.demisto.com/wp-content/uploads/2017/04/MH-Demisto-Security-Automation-WP.pdf. Accessed 5 Dec 2017
21. Digiambattista, E.: Enterprise level security orchestration. US Patent 2017/0017795 A1 (2017)
22. Poornachandran, R., Shahidzadeh, S., Das, S., Zimmer, V.J., Vashisth, S., Sharma, P.: Premises-aware security and policy orchestration. US Patent 14/560,141 (2016)

VisArch: Visualisation of Performance-based Architectural Refactorings

Catia Trubiani[1]([✉]) [iD], Aldeida Aleti[2] [iD], Sarah Goodwin[2] [iD],
Pooyan Jamshidi[3] [iD], Andre van Hoorn[4] [iD], and Samuel Gratzl[5] [iD]

[1] Gran Sasso Science Institute, L'Aquila, Italy
`catia.trubiani@gssi.it`
[2] Monash University, Melbourne, Australia
`{aldeida.aleti,sarah.goodwin}@monash.edu`
[3] University of South Carolina, Columbia, USA
`PJAMSHID@cse.sc.edu`
[4] University of Stuttgart, Stuttgart, Germany
`van.hoorn@informatik.uni-stuttgart.de`
[5] Johannes Kepler University, Linz, Austria
`samuel_gratzl@gmx.at`

Abstract. Evaluating the performance characteristics of software architectures is not trivial since many factors, such as workload fluctuations and service failures, contribute to large variations. To reduce the impact of these factors, architectures are refactored so that their design becomes more robust and less prone to performance violations. This paper proposes an approach for visualizing the impact, from a performance perspective, of different performance-based architectural refactorings that are inherited by the specification of performance antipatterns. A case study including 64 performance-based architectural refactorings is adopted to illustrate how the visual representation supports software architects in the evaluation of different architecture design alternatives.

Keywords: Software architecture · Performance · Visualisation

1 Introduction

Performance evaluation of software architectures is a complex activity, even more so when workload fluctuations and software/hardware failures contribute to distributions in requests and resources' availability [9,14]. These variabilities may be smoothed by equipping the architecture with a portfolio of refactoring actions to make it more robust [2,6], i.e., less prone to performance issues. Performance-based architectural refactorings are behaviour-preserving actions [10] that may

This work has been partially supported by the MIUR PRIN project SEDUCE 2017TWRCNB and the Baden-Württemberg Stiftung.

A. Jansen et al. (Eds.): ECSA 2020, LNCS 12292, pp. 182–190, 2020.
https://doi.org/10.1007/978-3-030-58923-3_12

span in multiple dimensions, such as design changes and/or redeployment, hardware settings, communication patterns among software components, etc. [16,17].

Understanding what are the most suitable performance-based architectural refactorings is indeed not trivial since there might be several trade-off decisions arising in the evaluation, and software architects are usually not supported in this task. To get system performance improvements, we make use of *software performance antipatterns* [22] since they have been applied in the context of software architectures and shown to be beneficial [24]. The main benefit of adopting antipatterns is that their specification includes reusable solutions that can be applied across different domains, e.g.., very recently performance antipatterns have been investigated for Cyber-Physical Systems [21]. Moreover, to deal with system uncertainties, *polynomial chaos expansion* has been applied [2] for computing the cumulative distributions related to performance metrics of interest that are known to be affected by uncertain parameters.

In the literature, the problem of optimizing the non-functional characteristics of software architectures, even under uncertainty, has been tackled by several approaches [1,4,5,7,9,18]. However, most of the developed methodologies focus on a specific modeling and/or analysis formalism (e.g., fuzzy logic [9]). As opposite, to the best of our knowledge, there is limited work in the field of visualising non-functional (e.g.., performance) data and its match with system architectural choices. The interest of the research community in software and performance visualisation is growing [3,19], and the state-of-the-art for performance visualisation techniques has been preliminary evaluated in [15].

This paper investigates the effectiveness of interactive visualisation techniques [12,13] in the selection of design alternatives. Our research question is:

How can visualisation help identify refactorings that improve performance?

To answer this question, we design a case study of 64 architectural refactorings by extending previous work [24] and investigate how visualisation supports the evaluation of the impact of these refactorings on performance metrics, such as system response time, service throughput, and resource utilization.

The main contribution of this paper is the VisArch visualisation approach, applied to a case study, that supports: (i) the evaluation of performance-based architectural refactorings (with a focus on performance antipatterns); (ii) the estimation of the uncertainty propagation by measuring the impact of an architectural change on system robustness (based on polynomial chaos expansion); (iii) the exploitation of the uncertainty and robustness estimates by software architects for their decision making in the selection of design alternatives.

The rest of the paper is organized as follows. Section 2 describes the details of our approach. Section 3 briefly discusses the case study and illustrates the visualisation results. Section 4 concludes the paper by outlining future research directions. All artifacts are publicly available [23].

2   VisArch: Visualising Architectural Refactorings

In this paper, we propose an approach to visualise the impact, from a performance-based perspective, of different architectural refactorings. The challenge is to keep track of the interweaving ways in which a refactoring action at the architectural level may impact the system performance. Our approach, called *VisArch*, aims to address this complexity, by leveraging the benefits of data visualisation to help with assessing the impact of refactoring techniques. Figure 1 provides an overview of the workflow we follow to apply the VisArch approach. Input/output artifacts and operational steps are described in the following.

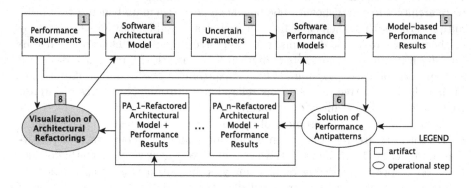

Fig. 1. Overview of VisArch.

Performance Requirements – see the box labeled as 1 in Fig. 1 – represent the required performance characteristics, e.g.., the system response time has to be less than 10 s. *Software Architectural Model* (2) represents the system in terms of software components, their interactions, and deployment settings. *Uncertain Parameters* (3) represent the system characteristics that are unknown, parameter values are expressed as distribution functions (e.g.., uniform, normal, discrete, triangular). For example, the workload can be specified as $[workload : Distribution = (UNIFORM, 100, 150)]$, meaning that number of users varies with a uniform distribution between 100 and 150. This allows a flexible specification of uncertain parameters and also captures their diverse nature. *Software Performance Models* (4) represent the abstractions of the system to derive its performance characteristics. Several performance models have been developed in the literature, and we use Layered Queuing Networks (LQNs) [8], since such models have been demonstrated to suitably approximate real-world scenarios [11]. *Model-based Performance Results* (5) represent the predictions of the performance characteristics of an application, such as system response time (RT), throughput (TH) of services, and hardware utilization (U), via analytical models. In our case, such results are obtained by adopting well-known solution techniques within the LQN solver [11]. *Solution of Performance Antipatterns* (6) takes as input performance requirements and model-based performance results that are compared. In case of requirements' violations, the generation of architectural refactorings is supported by the solution of performance antipatterns, since they have been demonstrated to be beneficial in the context of software architectures [24]. *PA_x-Refactored Architectural Model +*

Performance Results (□7) represent the set of architectural models that are generated after solving the performance antipatterns. Even if not reported in Fig. 1, all the generated architectural models are transformed into LQN models and analyzed. Performance results are then coupled with the corresponding architectural models, since they will be used for visualisation purposes.

Visualisation of Architectural Refactorings (□8) represents the main contribution of this paper. Performance results are presented using a new interactive visualisation technique for exploring heterogeneous multi-attribute rankings, i.e., LineUp [12][1]. This technique allows the large amount of performance data including the uncertainties to be presented as an intuitive visual overview. The technique can be described as an interactive table, consisting of visualisations in rows and columns that can be quickly filtered and reordered. It uses the concept of small-multiple visualisations [25] to provide first a overview, then analytical details on demand [20]. Performance results are loaded into LineUp, and a visualisation is built. Each row represents one possible refactoring combination that has been tested. Individual columns contain the results of the different samples (resulting from the specification of uncertain parameters), which are presented as boxplots to highlight the underlying distribution of each sample. Rows and columns can be sorted on the basis of whether a performance antipattern has been refactored or not (see Sect. 3). This presents a visual overview showing the refactoring impact on certain performance requirements. The visualisation provides an instrument to clearly recognize the most suitable architectural alternatives when analyzing the performance requirements of interest.

3   Visualisation Results

The visualisation approach is illustrated by means of a case study presented in [24], namely the Book and Movie online-Shop (B&M-S). Figure 2 depicts an excerpt of the software architectural model where the main software components and hardware machines are shown (legend at the top right). Table 1 briefly reports the performance-based architectural refactorings (AR), inherited from [24] and used for the visualisation. The complete description of the case study is reported in our supplementary material [23].

We applied the LineUp [12] technique to visualise the architectural refactorings. Figures 3, 4 depict the detailed outcomes. The first column indicates which refactoring action has been applied to the initial software architecture. The refactored solutions are associated to the following colours:

AR_1-CTH [Red] AR_2-CPS_{db} [Purple] AR_3-$BLOB$ [Brown] AR_4-EP [Pink] AR_5-EST [Olive] AR_6-CPS_{lib} [Teal]

The impact of the refactoring solution can be inspected visually via the performance metrics we consider, specifically the throughput (TH) and response time (RT) of these services: *Browse Catalogue* (BC), and *Purchase Product* (PP).

---

[1] https://lineup.js.org.

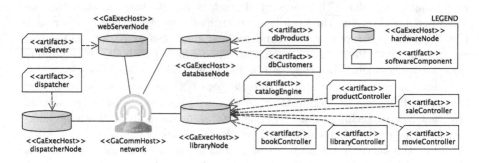

Fig. 2. B&M-S: excerpt of the Software Architectural Model.

Table 1. Performance-based architectural refactorings (AR) driven by the solution of performance antipatterns.

AR_1	Solving the CTH (Circuitous Treasure Hunt) performance antipattern. To better balance the load between the *saleController* and *dbCustomers* components, the latter is invoked twice. Its demand increases (i) to check user credentials from 0.03 to 0.09, (ii) to verify customer promotions from 0.03 to 0.06
AR_2	Solving the CPS_{db} (Concurrent Processing System detected on the database component) performance antipattern. To better balance the resources, the *dbCustomers* component is redeployed from *databaseNode* to the *dispatcherNode*
AR_3	Solving the $BLOB$ (God class/component) performance antipattern. To better balance the load between *libraryController* vs. *bookLibrary* and *movieLibrary* components, these latter components have been redesigned. The resource demand of *libraryController* decreases from 0.05 to 0.02, whereas the demands of *bookLibrary* and *movieLibrary* both increase from 0.03 to 0.045
AR_4	Solving the EP (Extensive Processing) performance antipattern. A newly added component, namely *catalogEngineMirror* handles generic and expensive catalogs, whereas book and movies catalogs are handled by the *catalogEngine* component
AR_5	Solving the EST (Empty Semi Trucks) performance antipattern. To better balance the load between the *saleController* and *productController* components, the computation is moved to this latter component that is invoked once to check the quality of products, and consequently its demand increases from 0.01 to 0.03
AR_6	Solving the CPS_{lib} (Concurrent Processing System detected on the library component) performance antipattern. To optimise the resources, the *libraryController* component is redeployed from *libraryNode* to the *dispatcherNode*

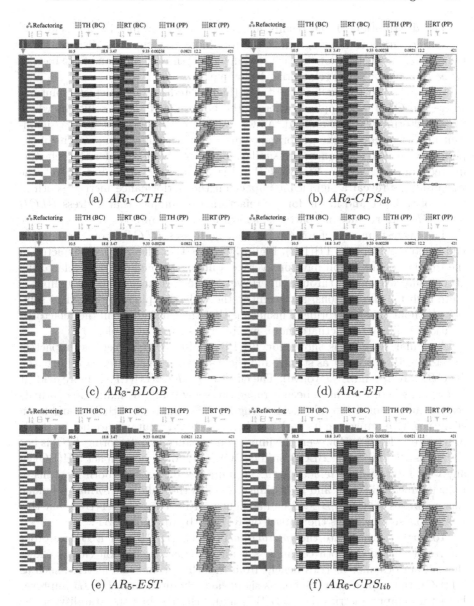

(a) AR_1-CTH

(b) AR_2-CPS_{db}

(c) AR_3-$BLOB$

(d) AR_4-EP

(e) AR_5-EST

(f) AR_6-CPS_{lib}

Fig. 3. Visualisations of performance-based architectural refactorings. Orange highlights reordering and the solutions where performance-based refactoring was applied. All figures include 64 rows representing the tested refactoring combinations.

TH(BC) (Blue), RT(BC) (Green), TH(PP) (Light Blue) and RT(PP) (Light Green)

The distribution of the results for each of the four metrics are shown in separate columns as a histogram at the top, indicating the total distribution of the results, and as boxplots in each row, depicting the distribution of the metrics for each combination of refactoring technique.

Figure 3a, the top half of the table (highlighted orange), depicts solutions where the CTH was applied, whereas the bottom half shows solutions where this refactoring was not applied. As we can see, CTH does not have a significant impact on any of the performance metrics, since the visual patterns of the performance metric columns are similar. The same holds true for the refactoring techniques: CPS_{db} in Fig. 3b, EP in Fig. 3d, and CPS_{lib} in Fig. 3f. Yet, the visualisations reveal a significant impact on the performance metrics, both in terms of variance and mean, for the refactoring techniques that address $BLOB$ and EST performance antipatterns, shown in Figs. 3c and 3e.

The biggest impact of refactoring that addresses $BLOB$ is on throughput, and is more evident on TH(BC). Figure 3c shows that the solutions depicted in the top half of the graph have on average a higher throughput, i.e., refactoring $BLOB$ improves mean throughput. However, the variance of the throughput is quite high for all solutions, as shown by the wider boxplots compared to solutions without this refactoring. This means that the throughput in the refactored solutions is likely to fluctuate more, making the system unstable.

A similar scenario is shown for TH(PP) in Fig. 3c, however the impact of refactoring BLOB is not as strong, and there seems to be an *interaction* between $BLOB$ (brown) and EST (olive). The effect of EST on TH(PP) is more evident in Fig. 3e, where rows have been arranged to show solutions fixing this antipattern at the top of the graph. Refactoring for EST improves TH(PP), and has a slight negative impact on its variance, i.e., refactored solutions are not as stable in terms of TH(PP). However, the impact on variance by refactoring EST is not as bad as the impact of BLOB on TH(BC). EST does not impact TH(BC) in any way. Interestingly, refactoring EST improves RT as well, both in terms of reducing mean RT(PP) and its variance. EST is the only refactoring technique that improves RT(PP). $BLOB$ had a slight positive effect on RT(BC), but this was not as significant as the impact on RT(PP) by applying EST.

To further investigate the *interaction* between $BLOB$ and EST, we order the results based on both columns, see Fig. 4. The visualisation clearly shows that all performance metrics benefit from it, although in some metrics, such as RT(BC), the improvement is not as significant. Summarising, $BLOB$ improves both throughput metrics, i.e., TH(BC) and TH(PP), but the stability of the system became worse. $BLOB$ also has a negligible impact on response time, by slightly improving RT(BC) and no impact on RT(PP). EST improves the distribution of TH(PP) and RT(PP), but has no impact on TH(BC) and RT(BC).

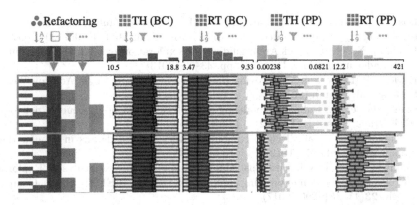

Fig. 4. Visualisation of $AR_{3.5}$-$BLOB$ and EST architectural refactorings. For sake of space, the first 32 rows are showed and represent a subset of tested refactorings.

4   Conclusion

In this paper we presented an approach to visualise performance-based architectural refactorings. Our experimentation mainly focused on the feasibility of applying visualisation techniques in the context of evaluating the performance of different architectural alternatives. As future work, we plan to quantify the gain for software architects through a user study to learn how do they perceive visualisation as support for the actual selection of design alternatives. Moreover, we plan to explore further visualisation techniques and apply the approach to more complex case studies, possibly from an industrial context.

References

1. Aleti, A., et al.: Software architecture optimization methods: a systematic literature review. IEEE Trans. Softw. Eng. **39**(5), 658–683 (2013)
2. Aleti, A., et al.: An efficient method for uncertainty propagation in robust software performance estimation. J. Syst. Softw. **138**, 222–235 (2018)
3. Beck, F., et al.: Visualizing systems and software performance - report on the GI-Dagstuhl seminar (2018). https://peerj.com/preprints/27253/
4. Berrevoets, R., Weyns, D.: A QoS-aware adaptive mobility handling approach for LoRa-based IoT systems. In: SASO, pp. 130–139 (2018)
5. Busch, A., Fuchß, D., Eckert, M., Koziolek, A.: Assessing the quality impact of features in component-based software architectures. In: Bures, T., Duchien, L., Inverardi, P. (eds.) ECSA 2019. LNCS, vol. 11681, pp. 211–219. Springer, Cham (2019). https://doi.org/10.1007/978-3-030-29983-5_14
6. Calinescu, R., et al.: Designing robust software systems through parametric Markov chain synthesis. In: ICSA, pp. 131–140 (2017)
7. Cámara, J., Garlan, D., Schmerl, B.: Synthesis and quantitative verification of tradeoff spaces for families of software systems. In: Lopes, A., de Lemos, R. (eds.) ECSA 2017. LNCS, vol. 10475, pp. 3–21. Springer, Cham (2017). https://doi.org/10.1007/978-3-319-65831-5_1

8. Das, O., Woodside, C.M.: Analyzing the effectiveness of fault-management architectures in layered distributed systems. Perform. Eval. **56**(1–4), 93–120 (2004)

9. Esfahani, N., et al.: GuideArch: guiding the exploration of architectural solution space under uncertainty. In: ICSE, pp. 43–52 (2013)

10. Fowler, M.: Refactoring: Improving the Design of Existing Code. Addison-Wesley Professional, Boston (2018)

11. Franks, G., et al.: Enhanced modeling and solution of layered queueing networks. IEEE Trans. Softw. Eng. **35**(2), 148–161 (2009)

12. Furmanova, K., et al.: Taggle: combining overview and details in tabular data visualizations. Inf. Vis. **19**(2), 114–136 (2020)

13. Goodwin, S., et al.: What do constraint programming users want to see? Exploring the role of visualisation in profiling of models and search. IEEE Trans. Vis. Comput. Graph. **23**(1), 281–290 (2017)

14. Incerto, E., et al.: Software performance self-adaptation through efficient model predictive control. In: ASE, pp. 485–496 (2017)

15. Isaacs, K.E., et al.: State of the art of performance visualization. In: EuroVis - STARs. The Eurographics Association (2014)

16. Jamshidi, P., et al.: Transfer learning for performance modeling of configurable systems: an exploratory analysis. In: ASE, pp. 497–508 (2017)

17. Jamshidi, P., Casale, G.: An uncertainty-aware approach to optimal configuration of stream processing systems. In: MASCOTS, pp. 39–48 (2016)

18. Mahdavi-Hezavehi, S., et al.: A systematic literature review on methods that handle multiple quality attributes in architecture-based self-adaptive systems. Inf. Softw. Technol. **90**, 1–26 (2017)

19. Okanovic, D., et al.: Concern-driven reporting of software performance analysis results. In: ICPE, pp. 1–4. ACM (2019)

20. Shneiderman, B.: The eyes have it: a task by data type taxonomy for information visualizations. In: Symposium on Visual Languages, pp. 336–343 (1996)

21. Smith, C.U.: Software performance antipatterns in cyber-physical systems. In: ICPE, pp. 173–180 (2020)

22. Smith, C.U., Williams, L.G.: Software performance antipatterns for identifying and correcting performance problems. In: CMG, pp. 717–725 (2012)

23. Trubiani, C., et al.: Artifacts. https://doi.org/10.5281/zenodo.3936656

24. Trubiani, C., et al.: Exploring synergies between bottleneck analysis and performance antipatterns. In: ICPE, pp. 75–86 (2014)

25. Tufte, E.: Envisioning Information. Graphics Press, Cheshire (1990)

Architectural Smells and Source Code Analysis

An Initial Study on the Association Between Architectural Smells and Degradation

Sebastian Herold[(✉)]

Department of Mathematics and Computer Science, Karlstad University,
651 88 Karlstad, Sweden
sebastian.herold@kau.se

Abstract. It is generally assumed that architectural smells are associated with software architectural degradation. Treating smells could hence help treating degradation. This article investigates the association between three types of architectural smells and the existence of architecture-violating dependencies as manifestation of architectural degradation in software.

We gathered data about architectural smells and violations from a single system with a validated prescriptive architecture. The data was analysed to identify and characterise associations between architectural smells and violations. Statistically relevant associations were identified for two of three smells, namely cyclic dependencies and unstable dependencies. Effect sizes were small for both though.

These results provide evidence for cyclic and unstable dependencies having a larger risk of including architectural violations. The small effect sizes indicate that the presence of architectural smells cannot explain architectural degradation alone. This shows that complementing methods and techniques are required for exhaustive treatment of both phenomena.

Keywords: Software architecture degradation · Architectural smells · Empirical study

1 Introduction

Software architecture degradation is the phenomenon of continuous divergence between the prescriptive and the descriptive software architecture of a system [15]. While the prescriptive software architecture manifests the intended principal design decisions made to achieve the desired quality attributes, the descriptive software architecture reflects the actual implemented design decisions. Several studies provide evidence that severe architectural degradation is prevalent in practice and may lead to expensive re-engineering efforts [1,4,9,10,16].

Another architectural phenomenon considered harmful to system quality is known as architectural smells [8]. It is frequently claimed that these smells lead

© Springer Nature Switzerland AG 2020
A. Jansen et al. (Eds.): ECSA 2020, LNCS 12292, pp. 193–201, 2020.
https://doi.org/10.1007/978-3-030-58923-3_13

to, or contribute to architectural degradation, or that avoiding architectural smells avoids degradation [5,7]. Empirical studies to support these claims are scarce though.

In this paper, we make a first step into a more detailed exploration of the association between architectural smells and architectural violations as symptoms of architectural degradation. This is motivated by the question whether mitigating smells would actually help mitigating degradation. If architectural smells that manifest in source code reliably indicated elements that very likely contributed to architecture degradation (if the prescriptive architecture was made explicit), the effort of recovering the prescriptive architecture for degradation detection could possibly be omitted.

We gathered data related to the presence of instances of three different types of architectural smells in a case study system and determined architectural violations through reflexion modelling [14]. We analysed the data to address the question whether or not dependencies contributing to those architectural smells are more likely to be architectural violations than other dependencies.

2   Foundations

2.1   Reflexion Modelling

Reflexion modelling-type approaches focus on the creation of graphical, box-and-lines models of prescriptive architectures in which boxes denote modules and arrows indicate desired, or allowed, dependencies. Reflexion modelling starts with manually constructing a model of the prescriptive architecture which consists of modules and allowed or expected architectural dependencies between them. In a second step, structural elements of the implementation, such as classes, packages, or source code files, are manually mapped to the modules in the model of the prescriptive architecture. In a third step, the source code is automatically analysed for dependencies. The relevant dependencies, such as method and function calls, field accesses, etc., are extracted from the source code and compared to the specified architectural dependencies.

The differences between the prescriptive architecture and dependencies as implemented are then visualized in the so-called reflexion model. *Divergences* are architectural dependencies that have manifested themselves as source code dependencies but have not been modelled in the prescriptive architecture. They might be indicators for architectural degradation in the modelled system. In the following, we will call a dependency between classes contributing to a divergence in the reflexion model of the system an *architectural violation*.

2.2   Architectural Smells

For this study, we focus on three types of smells that are described in, among others, the catalogue by Azadi et al. [2].

A *cyclic dependency* between two elements A and B exists if A depends on B, directly or indirectly, and B depends on A, directly or indirectly. In the following, we say a dependency contributes to a cyclic dependency iff it is part of cycle between A and B.

An element C, usually a class or interface, is said to be the centre of a *hub-like dependency* if it has a large number of both incoming and outgoing dependencies. We say a dependency d contributes to a hub-like dependency smell iff it is incident with the hub's centre C.

Unstable dependencies are dependencies from stable towards less stable elements, usually coarse-grained elements such as packages. Stability in this context refers to the amount of work required to implement a change in one element due to dependent elements in which the change might require consequent changes [13]. We say that a dependency contributes to an unstable dependency, iff the target of the dependency is contained in a less stable package/namespace/etc. than its source.

3   Study Setup

3.1   Research Question and Hypotheses

We formulate the research question of this study as follows: are the contribution to any of the three introduced types of smells and the classification as architectural violation dependent properties of dependencies, and if so, what is the effect size of this (statistical) dependency?

This leads us to the following three hypotheses:

- Hypothesis H^1: The contribution to circular dependencies and classification as architectural violation are dependent properties.
- Hypothesis H^2: The contribution to hub-like dependencies and classification as architectural violation are dependent properties.
- Hypothesis H^3: The contribution to unstable dependencies and classification as architectural violation are dependent properties.

The corresponding null hypotheses H_0^x state the independence of the respective properties.

3.2   System Under Study

For this preliminary and initial study our main requirements for candidate systems were the availability of a validated prescriptive architecture, access to the system code and non-trivial functional complexity and size (>50 KLOC).

We decided to use the open-source JabRef reference management software (version 3.5) as case study. JabRef is widely used in the academic community. It consists of over 80KLOC. In a previous study, we collaborated with the JabRef project team to recover the prescriptive software architecture and identify architecture degradation through reflexion modelling [12]. The developed model of the prescriptive architecture was discussed with and refined by the project team until they considered it an adequate representation of the prescriptive architecture.

3.3 Data Gathering

The data required to address the research question and test the hypotheses was gathered in three steps. In step one, we used the Arcan tool to detect and collect data about the architecture smells present in JabRef [6]. Arcan is cabable of identifying instances of the three types of smells of interest in Java bytecode. It stores the information extracted from the bytecode analysis as a graph in a neo4j graph database[1]. The database does not only contain data about smells but also about dependencies between types.

In order to model JabRef's prescriptive architecture and extract architectural violations, we used an adaptation of the reflexion modelling tool Jittac [3] for step two. JabRef's prescriptive architecture was modelled according to the specification in the replication package of the aforementioned study [12]. We added functionality to Jittac for exporting architectural violation information as .csv files that can be merged into the database created by Arcan. The resulting database contains all the data generated by Arcan complemented by edges labelled "violation" representing architectural violations detected by Jittac. After complementing the database with data from Jittac's analysis, we executed queries written in neo4j's built-in query language Cypher to retrieve the relevant data in step three.

3.4 Data Analysis

For each dependency we can define binary properties indicating whether or not the dependency represents an architectural violations and indicating whether a dependency contributes to any instances of a particular type of architectural smell. Based on the gathered data, we can determine the values of these properties for each dependency and type of smell.

For each type of smell, we performed a χ^2 test for independence between the corresponding property and the classification as architectural violation at a significance level of .01. In case of significance, i.e. rejection of the corresponding null hypothesis, we computed Φ, the risk factor, and confidence intervals to analyse the effect size.

4 Results

In total, JabRef consists of 1,486 classes, counting top-level level classes as well as nested/inner classes. Between these classes, there exist 6,111 dependencies of which 327 constitute architectural violation according to the model of the prescribed architecture.

Table 1 summarizes the results of the data analysis. The results for the originally tested hypothesis H^1 is shown in the left-most column. The χ^2 test for independence results in a p-value <.001, which lets us reject the null hypothesis and assume that contributing to cyclic dependencies and being a violation are dependent properties of dependencies. The value of φ indicates a small effect

---

[1] http://neo4j.com.

Table 1. Results for cyclic, unstable, and hub-like dependencies. Columns "NV" and "V" in the contingency tables stand for "No violations" and "Violations", respectively. Rows "NS" and "S" stand for "Not contributing to smells" and "Contributing to smells", respectively.

Smell Type	Cyclic Dependencies			Cyclic Dep. (> 5 classes)			Cyclic Dep. (> 15 classes)			Unstable Dependencies			Hub-like Dependencies		
Contin-gency Table	NV	V	Σ	NV	V	Σ	NV	V	Σ	NV	V	Σ	NV	V	Σ
NS	3755	136	3891	4200	136	4336	4721	160	4881	5218	266	5484	5357	299	5656
S	2029	191	2220	1584	191	1775	1063	167	1230	566	61	627	427	28	455
Σ	5784	327		5784	327		5784	327		5784	327		5784	327	
χ^2	72.83			144.54			205.76			105.5767			0.6256		
p	$< .001$			$< .001$			$< .001$			$< .001$			.4290		
φ	0.1092			0.1538			0.1835			0.1314			n/a		
Risk	NS	S		NS	S		NS	S		NS	S		NS	S	
	0.0350	0.0860		0.0314	0.1076		0.0339	0.1358		0.0485	0.0973		n/a	n/a	
Risk factor	2.46			3.43			4.64			2.01			n/a		
99% CI	$(-0.068, -0.034)$			$(-0.096, -0.056)$			$(-0.129, -0.077)$			$(-0.08, -0.017)$			n/a		

size. The risk factor and the confidence interval provide further evidence that there is an actual higher chance of having violations among smell-contributing dependencies than in other dependencies. The share of violations among dependencies contributing to cyclic dependencies is 8.6% and 2.46 times as large as in the set of dependencies not contributing.

During experimentation with Arcan, we noticed that dependencies, which only were part of small cyclic dependency instances involving five classes at most, were never architectural violations. We therefore tested also for the dependency between the property "contributes to cyclic dependencies involving more than n classes" and "representing an architectural violation" for $n \geq 5$. χ^2 peaked for $n = 15$ resulting in an effect size of $\varphi = 0.1835$ and a risk factor of 4.64 (equivalent to share of 13.58% of smell-contributing dependencies being violations).

The null hypothesis H_0^3 regarding unstable dependencies can be rejected based on the results as the p-value is $<.001$ and below the significance level. The value for φ indicates a small effect size. Almost 10% of dependencies contributing to unstable dependencies are architectural violations which is about twice as high as for non-contributing dependencies (risk factor 2.01).

Regarding hub-like dependencies, we fail to reject H_0^2 as the computed p-value of 0.4290 is well above the chosen significance level.

5 Discussion

5.1 Interpretation of the Results

The results of the statistical tests provide evidence that cyclic dependencies and architectural degradation are related phenomena. The higher relative frequency of violations contributing to cyclic dependencies compared to the relative frequency of violations in the non-cyclic parts of the investigated number is likely to be systematic and not caused by chance. The same holds for unstable dependencies.

This intuitively confirms that the validated prescriptive architecture of JabRef follows those design principles that the smells violate. The structure it defines is acyclic and from the description of its modules it seems to follow the stable dependency principle [12]. Hence, occurrences of those smells, as long as they cross module boundaries, are likely to cause architectural violations. We summarise this as *Finding 1: The results provide evidence for cyclic dependencies and unstable dependencies, respectively, being phenomena overlapping with architecture degradation. Architecture violations were roughly twice as common in these smells.*

It should be stressed that the phenomena only overlap partially. Cyclic dependencies involve 58.4%, unstable dependencies only 18.7% of the overall detected architectural violations. The effect sizes appear to be quite small (according to φ) and suggest that there might be other important factors than architectural smells hospitable to architectural degradation. This is supported by the observed absolute differences in the relative frequency of violations between smell-contributing and non-contributing dependencies which is about 5%. At this rate, it still seems far from trivial to identify those dependencies that are likely to violate the architectural intents. We conclude this as *Finding 2: The magnitude of the effect is too small to say that architectural violations could be explained by the presence of smells mainly; avoiding the right smells might reduce a fair share of degradation but is far from avoiding it.*

The results regarding cyclic dependencies seem also to suggest that the size of the cycles matter w.r.t. the degree of contributing architectural violations. A potential reason could be that small cycles are more often considered necessary structures between semantically cohesive units causing no significant harm. In JabRef, these smaller cycles mainly consist of bidirectional dependencies between classes and their inner classes or classes mapped to the same modules. We conclude this as *Finding 3: The results suggest that the risk for cyclic dependencies containing architectural violation increases with the cycle size up to a certain maximum; the smallest cycles might hardly contain any violations at all.*

Interestingly, the results provide no evidence that hub-like dependencies are related to architectural degradation. As a hub tends to aggregate too many responsibilities and dependencies, possibly due to poor design, it might also become crucial for parts of the system that are discouraged to use it. Over time, it could hence potentially aggregate more violations than non-hubs. This however, does not seem to be the case in JabRef in which the relative frequency of violations contributing to hubs is very similar to the overall relative frequency (6.1% vs. 5.3%). We summarise this observation as *Finding 4: There is no evidence that hub-like dependencies and architectural violations are related phenomena; hub-like classes are not necessarily hubs for architectural violations.*

5.2   Validity

Several factors of the presented study limit its external validity. First and foremost, its generalizability is limited by the fact that only a single system was examined Further studies with more systems of different sizes are planned to extend the external validity of the findings.

The limitation to three types of architectural smells can be considered another limitation to the study's external validity. Due to their focus on dependencies, the selected ones seem natural first candidates for a study like the presented one. We will, however, extend the study towards more smells in the near future.

Furthermore, we do not discuss the question which automatically detected architectural smells instances are actually critical. This could be considered impairing construct validity.

6 Related Work

To our best knowledge, the presented study is the first that explicitly explores the relationship between the presence of architectural smells and the presence of undesirable dependencies between source code entities violating the prescriptive architecture of a system. There are, however, a couple of studies on the relationship between smells and architectural issues.

Le et al. conducted a study to investigate the nature and impact of architectural decay in general [11]. The authors investigated whether source code units suffering from architectural smells are more likely to have associated issues reported and are more often modified over the course of the development and evolution of the system. While not directly related to architecture degradation, the addressed questions touch upon reduced maintainability and fault proneness which are also connected to architectural violation as discussed in the presented paper. It is not completely clear if Le et al.'s dataset could be used for that purpose as they do not require any prescriptive architectures.

A concept related to architectural smells are agglomerations of source code smells. Vidal et al. investigated different criteria to prioritize code smell agglomerations regarding their likelihood to be related to architectural problems [17]. One of the problems is called "architectural violation" by the authors and represents a situation in which an element is present in the descriptive but not in the prescriptive architecture or vice versa and is similar to the concept of violating dependencies used in our study. For one of the examined systems, the authors reported that 16 agglomerations were detected, 11 of which were related to architectural violations. This indicates that source code agglomerations might be useful indicators for architectural inconsistencies as well.

7 Conclusion

The results suggest that architectural smells and degradation overlap to a certain degree. In order to focus the treatment of smells on those which might also help remedying architectural degradation, the findings suggest to prioritize these two smells, in particular cyclic dependencies involving a larger number of classes.

However, many architectural violations appear to be unrelated to architectural smells. We plan to extend the presented study to a larger number of systems and intend to check the relevance of additional architectural smells both refining findings and extending their generalisability.

References

1. Ali, N., Baker, S., O'Crowley, R., Herold, S., Buckley, J.: Architecture consistency: state of the practice, challenges and requirements. Emp. Softw. Eng. **23**(1), 224–258 (2018)
2. Azadi, U., Fontana, F.A., Taibi, D.: Architectural smells detected by tools: a catalogue proposal. In: Proceedings of the 2nd International Conference on Technical Debt, pp. 88–97. IEEE (2019)
3. Buckley, J., Mooney, S., Rosik, J., Ali, N.: JITTAC: a just-in-time tool for architectural consistency. In: Proceedings of the 35th International Conference on Software Engineering (2013)
4. Buckley, J., Ali, N., English, M., Rosik, J., Herold, S.: Real-time reflexion modelling in architecture reconciliation: a multi case study. Inf. Softw. Technol. **61**, 107–123 (2015)
5. Díaz-Pace, J.A., Tommasel, A., Godoy, D.: Towards anticipation of architectural smells using link prediction techniques. In: 2018 IEEE 18th International Working Conference on Source Code Analysis and Manipulation (SCAM), pp. 62–71 (2018)
6. Fontana, F.A., Pigazzini, I., Roveda, R., Tamburri, D., Zanoni, M., Di Nitto, E.: Arcan: a tool for architectural smells detection. In: 2017 IEEE International Conference on Software Architecture Workshops (ICSAW), pp. 282–285 (2017)
7. Fontana, F.A., Pigazzini, I., Raibulet, C., Basciano, S., Roveda, R.: Pagerank and criticality of architectural smells. In: Proceedings of the 13th European Conference on Software Architecture, vol. 2, pp. 197–204. ACM (2019)
8. Garcia, J., Popescu, D., Edwards, G., Medvidovic, N.: Identifying architectural bad smells. In: 2009 13th European Conference on Software Maintenance and Reengineering, pp. 255–258 (2009)
9. van Gurp, J., Brinkkemper, S., Bosch, J.: Design preservation over subsequent releases of a software product: a case study of Baan ERP. J. Softw. Maint. Evol. Res. Pract. **17**(4), 277–306 (2005)
10. Herold, S., Rausch, A.: Complementing model-driven development for the detection of software architecture erosion. In: Proceedings of the 5th International Workshop on Modeling in Software Engineering, pp. 24–30. IEEE (2013)
11. Le, D.M., Link, D., Shahbazian, A., Medvidovic, N.: An empirical study of architectural decay in open-source software. In: 2018 IEEE International Conference on Software Architecture (ICSA) (2018)
12. Lenhard, J., Blom, M., Herold, S.: Exploring the suitability of source code metrics for indicating architectural inconsistencies. Softw. Qual. J. **27**(1), 241–274 (2018). https://doi.org/10.1007/s11219-018-9404-z
13. Martin, R.C.: Clean Architecture: A Craftsman's Guide to Software Structure and Design. Prentice Hall Press, Upper Saddle River (2017)
14. Murphy, G.C., Notkin, D., Sullivan, K.J.: Software reflexion models: bridging the gap between design and implementation. IEEE Trans. Softw. Eng. **27**(4), 364–380 (2001)

15. Perry, D.E., Wolf, A.L.: Foundations for the study of software architecture. ACM SIGSOFT Softw. Eng. Notes **17**(4), 40–52 (1992)
16. Sarkar, S., Ramachandran, S., Kumar, G.S., Iyengar, M.K., Rangarajan, K., Sivagnanam, S.: Modularization of a large-scale business application: a case study. IEEE Softw. **26**(2), 28–35 (2009)
17. Vidal, S., Oizumi, W., Garcia, A., Pace, A.D., Marcos, C.: Ranking architecturally critical agglomerations of code smells. Sci. Comput. Program. **182**, 64–85 (2019)

Architectural Technical Debt: A Grounded Theory

Roberto Verdecchia[1(✉)], Philippe Kruchten[2], and Patricia Lago[1]

[1] Vrije Universiteit Amsterdam, Amsterdam, The Netherlands
{r.verdecchia,p.lago}@vu.nl
[2] University of British Columbia, Vancouver, Canada
pbk@ece.ubc.ca

Abstract. Architectural technical debt in a software-intensive system is driven by design decisions about its structure, frameworks, technologies, languages, etc. Unlike code-level technical debt, which can be readily detected by static analysers, and can often be refactored with minimal efforts, architectural debt is hard to detect, and its remediation is wide-ranging, daunting, and often avoided. The objective of this study is to develop a better understanding of how software development organisations conceptualize their architectural debt, and how they deal with it, if at all. We used a grounded theory method, eliciting qualitative data from software architects and senior technical staff from a wide range of software development organizations. The result of the study, i.e., the theory emerging from the collected data, constitutes an encompassing conceptual theory of architectural debt, identifying and relating concepts such as symptoms, causes, consequences, and management strategies. By grounding the findings in empirical data, the theory provides researchers and practitioners with evidence of which crucial factors of architectural technical debt are experienced in industrial contexts.

Keywords: Software architecture · Technical debt · Grounded theory

1 Introduction

Quoting Avgeriou et al. [3], "In software-intensive systems, technical debt consists of design or implementation constructs that are expedient in the short term, but set up a technical context that can make a future change more costly or impossible. Technical debt is a contingent liability whose impact is limited to internal system qualities, primarily maintainability and evolvability".

Technical Debt (TD) can take many different forms in software development, and can be found in many different places [16]. While much of the literature and tooling available today address code-level TD, our focus is on Architectural Technical Debt (ATD). This is the technical debt incurred at the architectural level of software design, i.e., in the decisions related to structure (layering, decomposition in subsystems, interfaces), technologies (frameworks, packages, libraries,

© Springer Nature Switzerland AG 2020
A. Jansen et al. (Eds.): ECSA 2020, LNCS 12292, pp. 202–219, 2020.
https://doi.org/10.1007/978-3-030-58923-3_14

deployment approach), or even languages, development process, and platform. As software systems grow in size and their lifespan extends, many of these original design choices become constraints, limiting future evolution or even preventing it. To evolve the system, developers find workarounds, introducing quality issues and delays. Large and long-lived systems are suffering from architectural debt, while the small and short-lived ones die before ATD becomes a real problem.

To characterize ATD, find attributes of ATD, and develop an interpretation of ATD based on empirical evidence, we used a grounded theory approach [12] with experienced industry practitioners as subjects. The result of our study is an ATD "theory", providing empirical evidence of how software development practitioners conceptualize ATD and its management. Some of our theory results can also be applied to other forms of technical debt, such as code-level TD.

2   Research Method

For our study, we adopted the classic "Glaserian" Grounded Theory (GT) method [12], and we stayed with it throughout the whole study, from data collection, to data analysis and synthesis, with the exception of our adoption of a different "coding family" w.r.t. the ones suggested by Glaser [11], as explained in Sect. 2.2. This GT approach has given us a fresh and independent viewpoint on ATD, by letting concepts emerge from the personal experience of our participants, rather than the preconceived views of the researchers. In line with GT principles, we delayed the review of the literature until after our theory emerged, in order to avoid the influence of existing concepts on our theory [10]. Specifically, the first author was not too immersed in the TD world prior to this study, and refrained from conducting an extensive literature review on ATD before analyzing the data, minimizing possible confirmation biases, and improving his "theoretical sensitivity" [9]. In fact, as stated by Glaser et al., prior knowledge "violates the basic premise of GT - that the theory emerges from the data, not from extant theory" [13]. We also followed the recommendations of Stol et al. [27], on the application of GT to software engineering topics, and avoided the typical pitfalls they have identified. The investigation, including data collection, data analysis, and reporting, lasted approximately 6 months.

2.1   Data Collection

To collect data, we conducted semi-structured interviews with industrial practitioners. Initial participants were recruited by convenience and then subsequent ones driven by theoretical sampling [10], that is, tactically picking new subjects that would allow to confirm or disconfirm the findings so far, or to explore new areas. Specifically, the initial participants were contacted within our personal network. Subsequent participants were selected by following theoretical sampling, in order to fill the gaps identified in our emerging theory, and/or to explore unsaturated concepts [10]. Specifically, we identified via theoretical sampling [12] senior technical leaders as best fitted participants for data collection, given their hands-on experience on a vast range of ongoing (and concluded) long-lived software projects. We interviewed 18 experienced software practitioners, with a mean industrial experience of 17.5 years, from 14 distinct companies in different industrial domains. Table 1 presents an overview of the participant demographics. Interviews lasted approximately 1 h and were conducted face-to-face at the practitioners' workplaces or, when not possible, via video-calls.

Table 1. Participant demographics

ID	Role	Ex	Domain	OS	CC
P1	Senior Vice-President of SE	21	Banking	S	72
P2	Software Staff Engineer	17	Telecom	M	103
P3	Senior Director of SE	20	Enterprise Software	XL	130
P4	Chief Technology Officer	14	Financial Services	M	149
P5	Senior Software Engineer	22	Health	L	155
P6	Senior Software Engineer	8	Software Tooling	M	168
P7	Senior Software Engineer	18	Software Tooling	M	174
P8	Senior Software Engineer	23	Software Tooling	M	181
P9	Vice-President of Product	15	Data Analysis	M	188
P10	Senior Software Engineer	12	Software Tooling	M	191
P11	Senior Director of Technology	26	Data Technologies	M	198
P12	R&D Director	27	Enterprise Software	L	205
P13	Senior Software Engineer	14	Software Tooling	M	215
P14	Senior R&D Manager	16	Enterprise Software	L	220
P15	Chief Software Architect	11	Cloud Services	M	228
P16	Chief Technology Officer	12	Consultancy	S	231
P17	Co-Founder	33	Consultancy	XS	234
P18	Founder	22	Mobile Applications	XS	235

ID: participant identifier; Role: current participant role; Ex: industrial experience (years); OS: organization size (XS < 20; S < 100; M < 500; L < 5K; XL < 10K); CC: Cumulative number of codes per participant.

As the emerging theory should guide the sampling process, we solved the "bootstrap problem" [1] of GT by starting our first interview with the question: *"Which architectural design decision do you regret the most today?"*. Subsequently, and by following theoretical sampling [12], the other interview questions emerged iteratively. This strategy, following GT principles, is meant to let participants express their main concerns on ATD in their own words, and the researcher to explore unsaturated concepts. In addition, we also gathered data on the professional background of participants via a predefined set of demographic questions to collect the data summarized in Table 1.

Interviews were audio-recorded and transcribed manually by following the denaturalism approach, that is, grammar was corrected, interview noise (e.g., stutters) was removed, and nonstandard accents (i.e., non-majority) were standardized, while ensuring a full and faithful transcription [25].

The data collection terminated once we reached theoretical saturation, that is, when components of our theory are well supported and new data is no longer triggering theory revisions or reinterpretations [9]. The values reported in column "CC" of Table 1, display the slow increase of cumulative unique codes w.r.t. the number of participants, indicating that we achieved saturation around P16.

2.2   Data Analysis

We followed Glaser's grounded theory data analysis and synthesis processes to create our theory: open coding, selective coding, and theoretical coding [9,12]. Specifically we examined the whole body of text transcripts, subdivided them into separate "incidents" (sentences or paragraphs) [12], and labeled the incidents with codes to let the theory concepts emerge. When possible, codes are generated by directly quoting the incidents (e.g., see [S-Q1]). Otherwise, "synthetic" codes summarizing the semantic meaning and emerging concept of the incidents were created by the authors. Subsequently, concepts were clustered into core descriptive categories, which guided the future data collection. Finally, we established the conceptual relations between the different emerging core categories, leading to the formulation of our theory. We express the relationships between codes as hypotheses via a UML model to precisely describe the relations of different nature emerging between the categories of our theory (see Fig. 1).

Numerous concepts of our theory possess a multifaceted nature. For instance, the concept of "technical debt" itself can be both a *cause*, leading to the introduction of additional debt, and a *consequence*, e.g., of pre-existing debt. Following GT principles, concepts with multiple facets were coded according to the one deemed most important by participants. This ensured the emergence of concepts from the data, rather than from preconceived knowledge of the authors.

During the entirety of the coding procedures, we made use of *memoing* [12]. We created textual memos to elaborate concepts (i) related to single incidents, such as *"This incident exemplifies the impossibility to implement new functionality due to ATD"* and (ii) orthogonal to multiple incidents (e.g., relations between concepts, or categories, such as *"Developer's intuition can lead both to ATD identification and prioritization"*).

As described in Sect. 2.1, we analysed our data immediately and continuously, using simultaneous data collection and analysis, guided by theoretical sampling. Additionally, during data analysis, we constantly compared our data, memos, codes, and categories, in order to identify and keep track of common notions, topics, and patterns, as they emerged. Similarly, we continuously sorted our memos to evolve the emerging concepts and categories to best fit our codes, leading to the formulation of a substantive, cohesive theory. We performed continuous comparison until additional data being collected did not add new knowledge about the categories, i.e., until we reached the state of saturation (see Sect. 2.1).

Three researchers were involved in both the data collection and analysis phases, where the first author carried out the coding, memoing, and analysis processes, while the others collaboratively analysed and reviewed iteratively the results.

3   Results

An overview of our grounded theory on ATD is depicted in Fig. 1. In this section we describe the 6 core categories emerging from our data, which constitute the foundation of our grounded theory on ATD[1]. We also discuss the emerging relations between the different categories. In line with the grounded theory literature, this enables us to both present comprehensively the emerging theory, and offer explanations and predictions underlying ATD related phenomena [9].

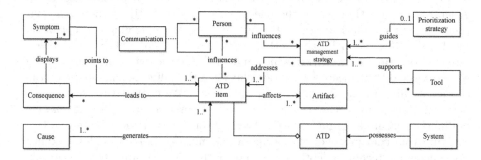

Fig. 1. Core categories of the ATD theory and their relations

At the core of our theory lies the **ATD item**, i.e., the category that embodies the instances of ATD residing in a software-intensive system (for an in-depth description of this category, see Sect. 3.1). The identification of the *ATD item* as the core category of our theory can be also observed from the numerous relations between this category and the other ones reported in Fig. 1.

At the root of each ATD item lies one or more **cause**. Each cause can *generate* one or more items (see Sect. 3.2). From our data time pressure and business drive are the main causes leading to the generation of ATD items: *"The plan is one thing, but the plan is not working now, we have to adapt quickly. Whether or not we meet the coding rules, I proceed. I don't care. Something is broken, nobody cares how nicely something fits the architecture, I care if it's gonna break our product. That is not a computer science issue, it's a business one."*-P8 [R-Q1]

As causes can generate one or more ATD items, so ATD items can lead to one or more **consequences**, e.g., reduced development velocity, higher maintenance

---

[1] Due to space limitations, in this paper we do not discuss in detail the categories with direct semantics in our theory (*ATD, Artifact, Tool,* and *System*), and the marginal categories related to human factors (*Person* and *Communication*).

cost, impossibility to implement new functionality (see Sect. 3.3). Additionally, in contrast to the relation between *Cause* and *ATD item*, ATD items can also be "dormant", i.e., the items are present in the system, but do not lead to any immediate consequence: *"There was a developer who wrote a component that nobody knows how it works, and so we are all afraid of touching it. It works well for now, but if something stops working, or we have to touch that, for example to implement some new functionality, we could have a problem."*-P12 [R-Q2]

Consequences can *display* one or more **symptoms**, e.g., recurrent customer, performance, and/or development issues. A consequence can also not display any symptom, either because an ATD item is "dormant", or because the observed symptoms are not sufficiently distinct to establish the relation: *"To be honest? I have a bit of a vibe. As a product manager, I'm pretty like face-to-face and hands on, and I kind of just gauge the winds on the face of developers"*-P9 [R-Q3]

Symptoms *point to* one or more ATD items, i.e., observing symptoms displayed by a *consequence* can lead to the identification of one or more *ATD items*. Often, multiple symptoms point to a single, widespread, ATD item: *"You do things like: "How are your bugs?", "How is your performance?". All of those things tell you something. They are indicators. Like code coverage, it tells you something, but does it really tell you anything? But it's just one big underlying problem!"*-P3 [R-Q4]

Nevertheless, as reported in quote [R-Q3], consequences of ATD items can also not display any clear symptom, making the discovery of related ATD items harder.

Each ATD item can *affect* one or more **artifacts**, e.g., software components, test suites, software development tools, and/or documentation: *"We reached the point where it [architecture] became quite brittle, and it was also quite difficult to change the test suite, because the architecture was so complex...so many connectors...and the variance of those connectors!"*-P7 [R-Q5]

Similarly, an ATD item can *reside* in one or more artifacts, i.e., it can be present simultaneously in various artifacts of different nature, or even occur in the relation established between two or more artifacts.

ATD items can be *addressed* via one or more **ATD management strategies**, e.g., via systematic time allocation, large-scale rewrites, and/or carry out opportunistic patching (see Sect. 3.5). Additionally, it is also possible to address multiple ATD items with a single management strategy (typically via rewrites): *"Usually, I just do a gut evaluation: if there is a large disconnect between what the system does and what it is supposed to achieve, usually it is a big indicator that there are many problems, and we need a rewrite."*-P1 [R-Q6]

ATD management strategies can be guided by a **prioritization strategy**, i.e., a strategy with which ATD management tasks are prioritized along with other development tasks, such as bug fixes, and implementation of new functionality [15] (see Sect. 3.6). Often, prioritization processes are not carried out systematically, and can consider one or multiple management strategies depending on the addressed ATD item(s): *"Given three weeks of development time, which architectural technical debt should we pay down? I would say, we're not doing it* *systematically, but we're probably not coming out with two very different answers. And if something was really painful, we would know."* -P9 [R-Q7]

ATD management strategies can also be supported by **tools**, e.g., static analyzers and linters. In some rare instances tools for detecting architectural problems, like component dependency anti-patterns, are used. Nevertheless, in most of the cases, ATD management strategies are not supported by any tools, potentially due to their perceived immaturity: *"The really expensive type of debt [ATD], I have not seen a tool which is able to detect that..."*-P10 [R-Q8]

Two marginal categories emerging in our theory are *person* and *communication*. Being related to *human factors* [5], the nature of these categories is different from the others. The relation between **person** and ATD items is of a multifaceted nature: among others, people's personal drive, skill set, and awareness can influence ATD from its establishment to its prioritization, and resolution. Further, ATD in a software system often leads to **communication** of ATD-related concepts among the people working on the system. ATD communication may regard the exposition of ATD items, the impediments related to discussing ATD, and even uneasy discussions on who is to blame.

As *person* and *communication* categories emerge as subsidiary categories in our theory, we focus the description of our theory on the categories related the closest to our core category (i.e. *ATD item*). Nevertheless, for the sake of completeness, a discussion of the *person* and *communication* categories is reported in the companion material of this study[2].

3.1   ATD Items

In this section we present the five most prominent types of ATD items residing in software-intensive systems which emerged from our results.

The Minimum Viable Product (MVP) that Stuck. Often ATD manifests itself in a software-intensive system as an MVP that, while intended as a temporary "bare-bones" solution, evolved into the architectural foundation of a system, without properly considering the architectural implications of adopting an immature artifact as architectural basis. This ATD item is often related to time pressure, lack of architectural awareness, and uncontrolled software evolution: *"It was an MVP solution that is still in place. And we were constantly broadening the scope of the problem. So for quite a long time, we just kept adding new functionality, and this problem was never solved."*-P6 [ATDI-Q1]

The Workaround that Stayed. ATD can be introduced in a software system as a temporary workaround to bypass some architectural constraints, which over time becomes deeply embedded into the architecture. As described by P8 in [R-Q1], such workarounds can be brought in deliberately, for the sake of development velocity, or triggered by unexpected context changes. Nevertheless, the awareness of the progressive consolidation of the workaround into the architecture can be inadvertent: *"... somehow we ended up with three pathways through*

---

[2] http://s2group.cs.vu.nl/files/ATD_GT_ECSA_companion_material.pdf.

the code, first we had one, then two, and so on ... there was duplication among the three, but also separate pieces to each one, that stuff was not isolated nicely ... "-P13 [ATDI-Q2]

Consolidated workarounds can become so embedded into an architecture that, while their consequences is evident, it is no more worthwhile fixing them: *"... at this point ... I think it's been deemed too expensive at best to change that [workaround], relative to the other business priorities we have."*-P7 [ATDI-Q3]

Re-inventing the Wheel. This type of ATD item refers to *ad-hoc* components developed in-house, which are chosen over already available components with similar functionalities (e.g., components available as open source software): *"We basically built our own thing ... why would we build our own persistence library? That doesn't make sense! It's just silly!"* P11 [ATDI-Q4]

In addition to the resources required to implement already available solutions, drawbacks include lower quality, additional maintenance, and lack of documentation: *"We built our own thing ... and now it's hard to maintain. And now that we have got to build on top of it, people are getting tired ... "*-P8 [ATDI-Q5]

Ad hoc components are often chosen due to the perceived velocity of developing a new component instead of getting accustomed to, and adapting, an existing one. Individual drive of developers can influence this decision: *"I thought to be smarter, but I was not ... in the long run, off-the-shelf solutions make people faster in ramping up, even if you [just] have to adapt them."*-P3 [ATDI-Q6]

Source Code ATD. These are technical debt items strictly related to the implementation of architectural components, and the relations between them. As described by P13: *"It was not really clear what was common and what was separated between the modules ... "*-P13 [ATDI-Q8]

This type of debt is often associated with poor separation of concerns, and/or tightly coupled architectural components, lowering the overall software quality, and directly affecting maintainability, modifiability, and adaptability: *"For example [consider] GDPR. They changed their policy, but our change was harder because our code was just one big clog. Either we built on top of it, making everything even harder, or we separated the pieces"*-P8 [ATDI-Q9]

As further discussed in Sect. 3.5, this type of debt can be very expensive to fix, and can even originate from systematic processes aimed at lowering ATD: *"We did a rewrite, and there the tight coupling started"*-P13 [ATDI-Q10]

Architectural Lock-in. Related to the previous debt item, ATD can arise in architectural components which, due to their deep embedment into a software architecture, become very costly or even impossible to replace. This debt item is often referenced as harmful if co-occurring with "dormant" ATD items [R-Q2], or if the lock-in is of technological nature and unreliable (e.g., a third party has complete ownership of a component and releases a breaking change). As described by P1: *"Sometimes you make something overly-specific, lock in completely into a specific library or technology. It's about how able your system is* *to change without crystallizing in design choices dictated by the need of adaptation."-P1* [ATDI-Q11]

New Context, Old Architecture. The last type of ATD item that emerged in our theory regards not paying continuous effort in order to keep the architecture of a software-intensive system aligned with its context, leading to an outdated architecture. This item is mostly incurred inadvertently. Nevertheless, this item can also be established deliberately, e.g., if driven by a business strategy: *"The business was to keep the costs down and make as much profit as possible, and after 8–10 years, the architecture was seriously showing its age ... "-P11* [ATDI-Q13]

3.2   Causes

In this section we discuss the four lead root causes of ATD items emerging from the data gathered for our theory.

Time Pressure. Sixteen of the eighteen participants acknowledged time pressure as the leading cause of ATD. P11 summarized: *"In a product you need to hit quarterly targets. Always on the treadmill, getting things done."-P11* [CA-Q1]

As [R-Q1] evinces, under time pressure, architectural quality is often sacrificed. This is a recurrent theme across participants. P2 noted: *"When time becomes tight, the first thing falling out is cleaning the architecture."-P2* [CA-Q3]

The rationale behind the sacrifice of architectural quality for the sake of velocity has to be attributed to the large amount of resources often involved in architectural changes. As P13 stated: *"One thing is always time, it's quicker to do feature development instead of doing architectural changes",-P13* [CA-Q4]

From our data emerges that developers often accumulate ATD when dealing with time pressure, under the (often incorrect) assumption that these shortcomings will be dealt with at a later stage, as further detailed in Sect. 3.6.

Lack of Architectural Knowledge and Documentation. In the presence of an unclear architecture, developers often introduce ATD (either inadvertently or deliberately), in order to save the time that should be invested in understanding comprehensively the architectural details.

This situation was described by many participants, including P12, who explained: *"When you are working on an older system, you have lots of constraints that you have to know about, and they are often not well documented, and so you don't know what things will come in your way, things that you have to work around. So you are constantly extinguishing this little fires to figure out what is going on, it takes a while ... "-P12* [CA-Q5]

In addition to the introduction of ATD, lack of architectural knowledge can also lead to the obfuscation of ATD items, hindering the awareness of the ATD present in a software system. P2 described: *"There was no documentation or tests. You never really understood if the code was intended like that, if it was intended that way, or if it was just "I will get to this later"."-P2* [CA-Q6]

Unsuitable Architectural Decision. ATD can arise by making inadvertently an inappropriate architectural decision. Often, inadvertent design decisions leading to ATD are associated to the lack of context awareness, resulting in approximate and/or ill-calibrated trade-off analyses. P14 described one of such instances: *"At the time there were reasons that supported our decision, but later on. . . when we think back at it, we see that we didn't evaluate all the options."*-P14 [CA-Q7]

The magnitude of the ATD associated to unfitted decisions varied greatly across participants, with some notable cases where the impact on a product was enormous: *"That decision didn't seem important at the time, but we should have considered the debt associated to it early on. For me, it was a lack in understanding properly the context. . . the project eventually got killed."*-P14 [CA-Q8]

Human Influence. Lastly, a recurrent concept of ATD cause regards the influence of human factors on ATD. Under this category fall aspects related to personal drive, such as the example reported in [ATDI-Q7], including lack of developer expertise and cognitive biases (notably the Dunning-Kruger effect [17]).

3.3 Consequences

In this section we document the 4 most prominent consequences of ATD which emerged from our data.

Carrying Cost. Often, the consequences of ATD are not immediate, but rather manifest themselves over time. Specifically, a recurrent consequence of ATD is an incremental amount of resources which have to be dedicated over time in maintaining and evolving software-intensive systems. As P1 described: *"We did not think hard enough of the [architectural] design, its cognitive overload, the associated carrying costs, how much will take us on a continuous basis to work on the system designed in this way."*-P1 [CO-Q1]

To mitigate the negative impact of the carrying on customer perception, some participants reported to actively invest resources to make refactoring efforts tangible to end-users: *"While doing the refactoring, we also enhanced the front-end, just to let the customer feel that the product is getting better."*-P4 [CO-Q3]

Implementing New Functionality Becomes Challenging. Associated to the carrying cost, ATD can also affect the ease with which new functionalities are implemented. This is often associated with "blurred" responsibilities among architectural components (cf. [ATDI-Q8]). In some cases, due to ATD, it can become necessary to completely discard functionality implementation. Especially telling are instances where such functionalities are characterized by a supposedly trivial implementation. P6 recalled: *"The new functionality, if you talked about it, was so reasonable to do. . . but in reality. . . it was so difficult to implement in the current architecture that we ended up scooping it out."*-P6 [CO-Q5]

In the most severe cases, architectures can become "crystallized", i.e., ATD hinders almost completely the implementation of new functionalities. One of this rare cases was described by P4: *"They [developers] could not even build new features, because of the architectural debt they were facing. They put workaround on workaround, and then they couldn't implement new features"*-P4 [CO-Q6]

Reduced Development Velocity. Related to the first two emerging consequences, most participants described one of the main consequences of ATD as a distinct loss of development velocity. This loss is in most cases associated to additional time required to understand the architecture, modify multiple components when carrying out small changes, and fixing bugs which, due to ATD, are hard to locate. P13 explained: *"Development takes much more time than expected, sometimes because you run into an unknown issue, and other times you just cannot properly size the thing that you are working on, because the architecture is much more complex then what you expected."*-P13 [CO-Q7]

Difficulties in Carrying Out Parallel Work. Due to poor separation of concerns and tight coupling among architectural components, ATD can impact also the ability to carry out parallel development. This is often occurring in the presence of overloaded components, i.e., components encapsulating a big portion of the business logic or data of a software intensive-system. P14 describes one of such incidents as follows: *"The module became very popular, we just kept building features on it ... and now it's a bottleneck, because we have many teams working on it at the same time, people are stepping on one another toes."*-P14 [CO-Q8]

3.4 Symptoms

Four types of symptoms, pointing to ATD items, emerged in our theory.

Recurrent Customer Issues. Among all symptoms of ATD, recurring customer issues is the most apparent. As P3 explains: *"The best indicator of all are customer issues: if you have an area with lots of recurring customer issues, either the team is garbage, or you have architectural issues."*-P3 [S-Q1].

With this symptom are often associated recurrent patches in the same area of the code, pointing to an architectural problem, P9 describes: *"There's this kind of hard to pin down feeling, when in order to meet some new need you are like"* *"okay, it feels weird but I'll patch it, and I'll patch it again, and again. And after a while, you realize that you're kind of like... you're playing whack-a-mole! It can't be that everything is an edge case!"*-P9 [S-Q2]

High Number of Defects. As reported by many participants, a high number of defects localized in a certain area of the code can indicate the presence of an ATD item. P10 explained: *"When you have a lot of bugs in an area of code, that means: either that area is complex by itself, or there is some unmanaged architectural complexity leading to that."*-S13 [S-Q3]

Performance Issues. Performance issues which are hard to address can also be a symptom of ATD. Commonly, performance issues caused by ATD are either *scalability issues*, representing the inability of systems to scale due to ATD, or *performance stalls*, i.e., performance bottleneck which cannot be solved without architectural refactoring. P3 described this symptom as follows: *"With performance, if you can really just move it around but not solve it, that is an indicator that you are doing something architecturally wrong."*-P3 [S-Q4]

"I Don't Want to Touch It". This symptom of our theory deals with human intuition and sensitivity. Rather than deriving from a systematic analysis, this symptom represents the instinctual refrain of software developers to modify a certain component in which ATD resides. R12 describes one of such instances, associated with a "dormant" ATD item: *"Developers will often tell you if something stinks, right? There is always something which is hard to work with, maybe it's a piece of code that no-one wants to touch, that's a symptom! It might do its job well, but no one wants to touch it!"*-P12 [S-Q6]

3.5 Management Strategies

Six managements strategies to cope with ATD emerged from our data. We identified three types of management strategies, namely *active*, *reactive*, and *passive*.

Active Management Strategies. Active strategies are based on the acknowledgment of the presence of ATD in a software system, and the development of a plan to actively manage it. In the following we present the 3 active management strategies emerging in our theory.

Boy Scout Rule. This management strategy borrows from the camping rule "Always leave the campground cleaner than you found it". Based on this metaphor, developers pay back the debt in small incremental steps while carrying out other development activities on a software component, such as new functionality implementation or bug fixes. P1 described: *"I generally advocate in "stealing time", when a component has bothered you enough, I would just say: fix it, and do not tell anyone. If you are already working on that area of code, just take some extra time to refactor it."*-P1 [MS-Q1]

   This strategy is rarely applied. In fact, unlike other forms of TD, ATD is in most cases hard, or even impossible, to be addressed in small increments.

Systematically Dedicate Time. This management strategy entails systematically allocating time in order to repay the accumulated ATD. Most participants described allocating a fixed percentage of development time per-sprint to refactor ATD items. The most recurrent percentage of time dedicated to ATD refactoring results to be between 20% and 30%, with the exception of P1 and P9, who reported 10% and 50% respectively. P12 jokingly described allocating an entire day per-sprint exclusively to ATD refactoring activities: *"We have a Lannister day, you know, because Lannisters always pay their debts. [laughs]."*-P12 [MS-Q2]

Technical Credit. This strategy regards the investment of resources to improve architectural maintainability and evolvability prior to the emergence of ATD. Specifically, this strategy aims at mitigating future ATD by proactively improving architectural elements which could slow down future development. Some participants described this strategy from a theoretical standpoint. Nevertheless, the common agreement is that, due to time pressure and uncertain pay-off, it is hardly ever adopted. P3 explained: *"You are spending time in trying to make something perfect. When do you have that time for that? You do not get paid by "I'll make it evolvable", you spend days or weeks in something that might not pay off, who can afford that?"*-P3 [MS-Q3]

Reactive Management Strategies. Reactive strategies entail that, while the presence of ATD is acknowledged, its management is postponed until the repayment becomes unavoidable (e.g., when ATD prevents the development of a new feature). Two prominent reactive strategies emerged in our data, namely *opportunistic patching* and *major refactoring*.

Opportunistic Patching. This strategy, rather than aiming at resolving ATD, deals with its occurrence by investing the minimum resources necessary to bypass the limitations imposed by the ATD. This often results in small patches, or temporary architectural workarounds, which build upon the existing ATD. As described in [S-Q2], opportunistic patching rarely resolves the root cause of an ATD item, but can nevertheless point to the underlying problem. P11 described a similar situation: *"It was architectural debt, but we were able to squeeze around it by doing little incremental changes here and there, which did not touch the architecture much... we were just kicking the can down the road... in retrospective we were just patching, patching all the way."*-P11 [MS-Q4]

Major Refactoring. Due to ATD severity, it can become necessary to methodically eradicate it, even at the cost of sacrificing other development activities. This constitutes a major undertaking, causing the loss of competitive advantage, and the investment of a conspicuous amount of resources. This strategy includes refactoring conducted by entire developer teams, or even complete rewrites of a products. Due to the resources required, and its uncertain outcome, timing this strategy is a complex problem. P11 explains: *"You always have to overcome this lump of "when is the right time?". There is never a right time. You have to decide when it is. It [ATD] has to reach a crest before you realize: "OK this is enough now", you bite the bullet, and try to do something about it."*-P11 [MS-Q5]

Passive Management Strategy. The passive management strategy, rather than aiming to actively or passively resolve ATD, attempts to cope with it by carrying out development activities by avoiding to address ATD items.

Neglect. Participants described strategies in which, while the negative impact of the ATD of a system is evident, the cost of fixing it is not worth addressing it. In such cases, development activities are carried out at a slower pace, embracing the ATD, and building upon existing debt. *"Sometimes you have a lot of edge cases but the cost of... you know it's bad, you know you don't want to do it, you know there's a better way, but the better way isn't worth it."*-P9 [MS-Q6]

3.6 Prioritization Strategies

In this section, we discuss our findings related to how the refactoring of ATD items is prioritized w.r.t. other development activities, such as feature development and bug fixes. Prioritization strategies guide management strategies of active nature, as reactive and passive strategies respectively manage ATD only when strictly necessary and not at all.

From our results emerged that often ATD is kept track of, e.g., by characterizing backlog items according to the classification of Kruchten [15], i.e., by making a distinction between functional features, bug fixes, architectural features, and technical debt. Nevertheless, while ATD items are often traced, prioritizing their refactoring w.r.t. to other development activities does not follow an established methodology. As P10 states: *"We fear we do not have a scientific method here... it is basically gut feeling. We do not have any research around what needs to have the highest priority."*-P10 [PR-Q1]

This "gut feeling" has been a recurrent theme among participants on how ATD is prioritized. Due to the difficulties associated with quantifying the impact of ATD, practitioners do not adopt systematic prioritization approaches; rather, they adopt informal ones, to balance their ATD refactoring activities with other development activities (cf. [R-Q7]). P3 further clarifies this concept: *"I would say, find your balance, do the minimum necessary. It is not a science, it's an art. Why do large companies fail? Because at some point that balance is tilted."*-P3 [PR-Q2]

4 Related Work

As recommended by Glaserian GT principles [12], to mitigate confirmation bias, we reviewed the related literature *after* building our theory. From the inspection of the ATD corpus, we identified four studies related the closest to ours.

Martini et al. [23] present a multi-case study adopting some GT techniques, while our investigation systematically applies the GT methodology. Accordingly, the two works use different techniques for data collection, incident coding, and results synthesis (cf. Sect. 2 of this study and Sect. 2 of [23]). Regarding the results, [23] presents a taxonomy of ATD items and a model of their effects: the specific *ATD items* are complementary to the ones emerging in our theory; the *effects* are categorized into *causes*, *phenomena*, and *extra activities* and the specific concepts resemble the categories *cause* and *ATD management strategy* emerging in our theory, which in turn resulted in a richer number of categories e.g., *tool*. Further, a previous work of the same authors [24] zooms into the evolutionary nature of ATD and its accumulation and refactoring over time, e.g., the causes specific to accumulation. Our work is complementary by emphasizing the theoretical structure underlying ATD instead. Overall, similarities and complementarities are promising for a future comparative analysis between the results of [23,24] and our substantive theory, with the ultimate goal of formulating a formal theory [29] of ATD.

Besker et al. [4] conducted a systematic literature review to define a descriptive model of ATD. By comparing the findings of such study with our theory, we can observe a noticeable gap between the results of the two studies. In fact, numerous aspects reported in the model of [4], such as *ATD detection*, *ATD identification*, *ATD measurement*, *ATD monitoring* and related concepts, did not emerge in our theory. Rather than attributing the absence of such concepts to unsaturation, we conjecture that such divergence in results is due to the research methodology followed. In fact, we can observe that the missing concepts are related to ATD aspects which, while actively discussed in academic settings (e.g. *ATD identification* [31]), did not yet get traction in industry (e.g., see [R-Q8]). From this finding we can conclude that more action research is needed to bridge the gap between studying ATD and dealing with it in practice.

Li et al. [19] present a set of architectural viewpoints and related metamodel for documenting ATD. The viewpoints were constructed via an iterative process driven by the stakeholder concerns on ATD. The viewpoint metamodel partially overlaps with some categories of our theory. However, by focusing on documenting ATD, it aims at the exhaustive characterization of ATD items. Differently, our theory shifts the focus from documentation of ATD items specifics, to the phenomena surrounding them, and as such, it is more encompassing, yet less detailed.

A broader review of the literature shows that the most studied type of technical debt is *source-code ATD* [18,31], such as ATD related to component dependency [26] or modularity [20]. This typology of ATD emerged in our theory as a specific concept of the *ATD Item* category, namely *source-code ATD*. This category is also mentioned in Brooks's popular book "The Mythical Man Month" [6], where a recurrent theme is to *plan to throw one away*, i.e., designing a system (and organization) by envisioning change, as it will eventually happen. Moreover, the "workaround that stayed" ATD item is extensively discussed in Fowler's book titled "Refactoring: improving the design of existing code" [7], again with a primary focus on TD at the source code level. The "re-inventing the wheel" ATD item is instead discussed in Szyperski's book [28], where design reuse is advocated as the practice of sharing certain aspects of an approach across various projects, thus avoiding to re-invent the wheel across projects and organizations. The book also presents various techniques for addressing this ATD item, e.g. using software libraries for sharing solution fragments, interaction and subsystem architectures. Other kinds of ATD items, such as "compliance violations" have been studied exclusively in narrower pockets of research [18,21,31], and are mapped to our category "new context, old architecture". In [22], Martini et al. identified the information required to prioritize ATD. By comparing their findings to our theory emerges again the current lack of awareness of research findings in industrial contexts, as in our theory prioritization emerged as a mere "gut feeling" (see Sect. 3.6). The literature further investigates other emerging categories, such as TD management strategies [2], and the impact of TD on morale [8], but does not systematically focus on the architectural level as we do.

Thanks to the adoption of the Glaserian GT method [12], our theory emerged independently from prior theories and, as such, either confirms or adds to them. This may pave the way for future works toward a joint formal theory [29].

5   Verifiability and Threats to Validity

We ensure the anonymity of our participants, their companies, and their collaborators. Hence, we keep confidential their identifying details, under the human ethics guidelines governing this study. Accordingly, as customary in grounded theory (e.g., [14]), the verifiability of our results should derive from the soundness of the research method followed. Therefore, we report in Sect. 2 an in-depth description of the method followed, and (within space constraints) we reference as much as possible to direct quotes from our participants (albeit excerpted).

Our report demonstrates how the emerging theory fulfills the grounded theory evaluation criteria [9], specifically: (i) our categories *fit* the underlying data, (ii) the theory is able to *work* (i.e., explain ATD related phenomena), (iii) the theory has *relevance* to the domain (i.e., development practices of large and long-lived systems), and (iv) the theory is *modifiable* as new data appears.

As any grounded theory study, our investigation establishes a mid-range substantive theory, i.e., a theory where elements belonging to the studied context can be transferred to other contexts with similar characteristics. We hence do not claim our theory to be absolute or final, and we highly welcome its extension, e.g., by refining its granularity and adding detail to emerging concepts, or even unveiling new concepts and categories that did not emerge in this investigation.

6   Conclusions

Our investigation presents structured insights into the challenges faced in industrial settings when dealing with ATD. From our study emerged a set of interrelated categories regarding ATD, leading to a cohesive theory of ATD that connects its causes, consequences, symptoms, management strategies, and other related phenomena. We made a deep-dive into each category, by grounding our findings in the experience of knowledgeable software practitioners. Our theory provides a solid empirical foundation which may benefit both (i) *practitioners* aiming at a better understanding of the ATD they experience, and (ii) *researchers* looking for a theoretical framework of how ATD is experienced in industrial settings. Notably, among other results, from our investigation emerge a set of symptoms, consequences, and management strategies on which future research, methodologies, and tooling, can be based. A research avenue we find particularly interesting exploring is the further study of ATD symptoms, with particular emphasis on quantifiable ones, in order to determine which symptoms are best suited as foundation for novel ATD identification and management techniques, e.g. by leveraging the method presented in [30].

References

1. Adolph, S., Hall, W., Kruchten, P.: Using grounded theory to study the experience of software development. Empirical Softw. Eng. **16**(4), 487–513 (2011)
2. Alves, N., Mendes, T.S., de Mendonça, M.G., Spínola, R.O., Shull, F., Seaman, C.: Identification and management of technical debt: a systematic mapping study. Inf. Softw. Technol. **70**, 100–121 (2016)
3. Avgeriou, P., Kruchten, P., Ozkaya, I., Seaman, C.: Managing Technical Debt in Software Engineering. Schloss Dagstuhl-Leibniz-Zentrum fuer Informatik (2016)
4. Besker, T., Martini, A., Bosch, J.: Managing architectural technical debt: a unified model and systematic literature review. J. Syst. Softw. **135**, 1–6 (2018)
5. Bourque, P., Fairley, R.E.: Guide to the Software Engineering Body of Knowledge. IEEE Computer Society (2014)
6. Brooks Jr, F.P.: The Mythical Man-Month, Anniversary edn. Addison-Wesley (1995)
7. Fowler, M.: Refactoring: Improving the Design of Existing Code. Addison-Wesley Professional (2018)
8. Ghanbari, H., Besker, T., Martini, A., Bosch, J.: Looking for peace of mind?: Manage your (technical) debt: an exploratory field study. In: ACM/IEEE EMSE Symposium (2017)
9. Glaser, B.: Theoretical Sensitivity. Sociology Press (1978)
10. Glaser, B.: Basics of Grounded Theory Analysis: Emergence vs Forcing. Sociology Press (1992)
11. Glaser, B.: The Grounded Theory Perspective III: Theoretical Coding. Sociology Press (2005)
12. Glaser, B., Strauss, A.: Discovery of Grounded Theory: Strategies for Qualitative Research. Aldine (1967)
13. Glaser, B.G., Holton, J.: Remodeling grounded theory. In: Forum Qualitative Sozialforschung/Forum: Qualitative Social Research, vol. 5 (2004)
14. Hoda, R., Noble, J.: Becoming Agile: A Grounded Theory of Agile Transitions in Practice. In: International Conference on Software Engineering. IEEE Press (2017)
15. Kruchten, P.: What colour is your backlog? (2008). https://tinyurl.com/y6f7vhpx. Accessed 10 May 2020
16. Kruchten, P., Nord, R., Ozkaya, I.: Technical debt: from metaphor to theory and practice. IEEE Softw. **29**(6), 18–21 (2012)
17. Kruger, J., Dunning, D.: Unskilled and unaware of it: how difficulties in recognizing one's own incompetence lead to inflated self-assessments. J. Pers. Soc. Psychol. **77**(6), 1121 (1999)
18. Li, Z., Avgeriou, P., Liang, P.: A systematic mapping study on technical debt and its management. J. Syst. Softw. **101**, 193–220 (2015)
19. Li, Z., Liang, P., Avgeriou, P.: Architecture viewpoints for documenting architectural technical debt. In: Software Quality Assurance, pp. 85–132. Elsevier (2016)

20. Li, Z., Liang, P., Avgeriou, P., Guelfi, N., Ampatzoglou, A.: An empirical investigation of modularity metrics for indicating architectural technical debt. In: International ACM Conference on Quality of Software Architectures (2014)
21. Martini, A., Bosch, J.: The danger of architectural technical debt: contagious debt and vicious circles. In: WICSA Conference. IEEE (2015)
22. Martini, A., Bosch, J.: Towards prioritizing architecture technical debt: information needs of architects and product owners. In: Euromicro Conference on Software Engineering and Advanced Applications, pp. 422–429. IEEE (2015)
23. Martini, A., Bosch, J.: On the interest of architectural technical debt: uncovering the contagious debt phenomenon. J. Softw.: Evol. Process 29, e1877 (2017)
24. Martini, A., Bosch, J., Chaudron, M.: Investigating architectural technical debt accumulation and refactoring over time: A multiple-case study. Inf. Softw. Technol. 67, 237–253 (2015)
25. Oliver, D., Serovich, J., Mason, T.: Constraints and opportunities with interview transcription: towards reflection in qualitative research. Soc. Forces 84, 1273 (2005)
26. Roveda, R., Fontana, F.A., Pigazzini, I., Zanoni, M.: Towards an architectural debt index. In: Euromicro Conference on Software Engineering and Advanced Applications. IEEE (2018)
27. Stol, K.J., Ralph, P., Fitzgerald, B.: Grounded theory in software engineering research: a critical review and guidelines. In: IEEE/ACM International Conference on Software Engineering (2016)
28. Szyperski, C., Gruntz, D., Murer, S.: Component Software: Beyond Object-Oriented Programming. Pearson Education (2002)
29. Urquhart, C., Lehmann, H., Myers, M.D.: Putting the 'theory' back into grounded theory: guidelines for grounded theory studies in information systems. Inf. Syst. J. 20(4), 357–381 (2010)
30. Verdecchia, R., Lago, P., Malavolta, I., Ozkaya, I.: ATDx: building an architectural technical debt index. In: ENASE Conference (2020)
31. Verdecchia, R., Malavolta, I., Lago, P.: Architectural technical debt identification: the research landscape. In: IEEE/ACM TechDebt Conference (2018)

Does BERT Understand Code? – An Exploratory Study on the Detection of Architectural Tactics in Code

Jan Keim[1]([⊠]) [iD], Angelika Kaplan[1], Anne Koziolek[1] [iD],
and Mehdi Mirakhorli[2] [iD]

[1] Karlsruhe Institute of Technology, Karlsruhe, Germany
{jan.keim,angelika.kaplan,koziolek}@kit.edu
[2] Rochester Institute of Technology, 134 Lomb Memorial Drive,
Rochester, NY 14623-5608, USA
mxmvse@rit.edu

Abstract. Quality-driven design decisions are often addressed by using architectural tactics that are re-usable solution options for certain quality concerns. Creating traceability links for these tactics is useful but costly. Automating the creation of these links can help reduce costs but is challenging as simple structural analyses only yield limited results. Transfer-learning approaches using language models like BERT are a recent trend in the field of natural language processing. These approaches yield state-of-the-art results for tasks like text classification. In this paper, we experiment with treating detection of architectural tactics in code as a text classification problem. We present an approach to detect architectural tactics in code by fine-tuning BERT. A 10-fold cross-validation shows promising results with an average F_1-Score of 90%, which is on a par with state-of-the-art approaches. We additionally apply our approach on a case study, where the results of our approach show promising potential but fall behind the state-of-the-art. Therefore, we discuss our approach and look at potential reasons as well as downsides and future work.

Keywords: Software architecture · Architectural tactics · Natural language processing · Transfer learning · Traceability · Language modeling · BERT

1 Introduction

Software traceability provides essential support for software engineering activities like coverage analysis, impact analysis, compliance verification, or testing. A problem of software traceability is the expensive creation and maintenance of traceability links [13]. Automation can reduce costs, but is challenging.

Although, the problem to detect architectural tactics is a special case of design pattern recognition, it turns out to be more challenging. Unlike design patterns that tend to be described in terms of classes and their associations [14],

© Springer Nature Switzerland AG 2020
A. Jansen et al. (Eds.): ECSA 2020, LNCS 12292, pp. 220–228, 2020.
https://doi.org/10.1007/978-3-030-58923-3_15

tactics are described in terms of roles and interactions [6]. Therefore, structural analyses only yield limited results.

Prior work by Mirakhorli et al. present an approach to detect architectural tactics in code, to trace them to requirements, and to visualize them to properly display the underlying design decision [23,24]. Their work is based on the premise that programmers use meaningful terms, e.g., for variables or methods. This is also a best practice [10] and used in other traceability approaches [3].

Recently, a lot of progress has been made in the domain of natural language processing (NLP), including text classification, by using (statistical) language models. Modern language models like the so-called *Bidirectional Encoder Representations from Transformers (BERT)* [11] can be fine-tuned on tasks such as text classification using so-called transfer learning. Hey et al. state in their introduction to BERT that fine-tuning (with BERT) for text classification is a good way to achieve good results with less training data [15]. For example, Ruder et al. [17] show that their transfer-learning approach could match performance with approaches that are trained on 100x the data. BERT and similar approaches are as of late replacing traditional discrete natural language processing pipelines [32]. However, Tenney et al. show that BERT also learns similar structures to traditional NLP pipelines.

In this work, we experiment with BERT and with the assumption that code is a special kind of text that can be used as input for BERT. Therefore, our research questions are: Do the available pretrained models of BERT understand code? Can we use language models like BERT and their transfer-learning capabilities to classify code for the detection of architectural tactics?

Thus, this paper has the following contributions: We present an approach that uses BERT to classify code that has, to the best of our knowledge, not been tried before. We evaluate our approach, compare it to others, and discuss results. Moreover, we discuss the lessons learned, especially benefits and downsides of using (natural) language models like BERT on code.

Additional details are given in our technical report [19].

2   Related Work

The most relevant related work regarding the detection of architectural tactics is by Mirakhorli et al. [23,24]. The authors use trained classifiers to detect the presence of architectural tactics like heartbeat, scheduling and authentication.

Besides that, there is other related work in the context of design pattern detection (cf. [4,9]). However, the detection of architectural tactics differs as these describe higher-level problems that can be solved using multiple different strategies.

Additional related work can be divided into three main areas: documenting design rationales, reconstructing architectural knowledge, and automated traceability. Documenting design rationales is important and different approaches try to help in this directions (cf. [5,8,25]). Unfortunately, knowledge about design decisions and architectures are mostly undocumented in many projects (cf. [16]). Therefore, researchers like Ducasse and Pollet [12] have developed techniques to reconstruct architectural knowledge. When documentation is present, approaches that create traceability links can be used. Our approach, where we want to trace architectural design patterns, is a special case of automated trace retrieval, similar to the work by Antoniol et al. [3] and further work.

Additionally, there is some related work about the application of language models like BERT to different problems like text classification using fine-tuning. Two examples for such work are Docbert for document classification by Adhikari et al. [1] and NoRBERT for the classification of requirements [15].

Finally, approaches that are also related to this work are about building language models for code. In context of code completion and suggestion, we can find approaches that apply statistical and neural language models such as recurrent neural networks (RNNs) and N-gram (cf. [21,29]). In addition to that, further approaches also use transfer learning with code by learning on one programming language and transfer to another language, e.g., in the context of detecting code smells (cf. [30]). However, these approaches are bound to a certain application, thus not as applicable here.

3   Our Approach

We use the BERT language model fine-tuned for multi-class classification to detect architectural tactics in code. This is based on two assumptions: programmers tend to program similar functionality similarly and we can treat code like text. These assumptions are also used in other approaches (cf. [3,10]).

We train the BERT model to classify given input code into architectural tactics, including a *Unrelated* class. The inputs are classes and code snippets that should be classified for architectural tactics. Inputs are pre-processed first to omit irrelevant or not processable parts, including removal of stop-words as well as separating compound words that are written in camel case or similar. Additionally, as BERT only supports a maximum input length of 512 tokens, we truncate the input. We employ two methods for truncation: The first method is to simply truncate after the first 512 tokens; the second method removes method bodies before truncating if there are still more than 512 tokens.

We use the pre-trained uncased base model of BERT and fine-tune it. We use the standard procedure (cf. [15]): We feed the pooled output of BERT into the classification head that consists of a single layers of linear neurons in a feedforward neural network. The softmax function gives us a probability distribution for the different outputs.

During training, we use the cross-entropy loss-function to assess the predicted distribution. Instead of a stochastic gradient descent, we use the so-called *AdamW*-optimizer [22]. AdamW usually gives better results in settings like ours.

We configure the parameters in the following way: We choose commonly used (default) parameters because of promising first empirical evidence. We use a weight decay of 0.01 and for the exponential decay rates we use a beta1 (first-moment estimates) of 0.9 for beta1 and a beta2 (second-moment estimates) of

0.999. Additionally we use a training rate of 2e−5 and a batch size of 2 to train the classification head for our fine-tuning, based on empirical selection as well as tested parameters for text classification [31]. We perform training for ten epochs.

Our approach currently uses a multi-class, but no multi-label classifier. Therefore, we can only attach one label for each input. We do not see this as a major drawback as the case study by Mirakhorli et al. [23] shows that less than 1% of classes contain more than one architectural tactic. In the future, we plan to extend our approach to support multiple labels as well.

After fine-tuning, the trained model can be used for classification. Here, we also propose the usage of a threshold to increase the precision of our approach: If the highest confidence value of a classification is below the given threshold, the class is classified as *unrelated*.

4 Evaluation

One goal of our evaluation is to compare our results with previous results, especially the results in [23]. We are using the common evaluation metrics precision, recall, and F_1-Score to enable comparisons to the other approaches. Additionally, we reuse the data set of Mirakhorli et al. [23]. As a results, we are aiming to detect the following five architectural tactics that are represented in the available data set (cf. [23]): *Audit trail, Authentication, Heartbeat, Resource Pooling,* and *Scheduling*. For each of these tactics, Mirakhorli et al. identified open-source projects that implement that tactic and collected tactic-related and non-tactic-related source files. The data set consists of 50 examples for related classes and 50 examples for unrelated classes for each architectural tactic. The data sets are publicly available [26].

We first look at multiple 10-fold cross-validation experiments. We performed multiple experiments to evaluate different characteristics, all results along with our code can be found on Zenodo [18].

For the different parameter settings we can conclude the following: Increasing the amount of epochs or the batch size as well as the threshold is likely to increase precision but decrease recall. A learning rate of 2e−05 performs best in our experiments, which confirms the empirical evidence by Sun et al. [31]. We can also confirm the observation of Keskar et al. [20] that larger batches result in an inferior ability of the model to generalize. The best configuration with an F_1-Score of 90% in our case is with a learning rate of 2e−05, a batch size of two, ten epochs of training and a threshold of 0.9 during classification.

Additionally, we also observe that more data, as expected, increases the performance. However, oversampling and undersampling both do not improve results. Lastly, the two truncation methods performed similarly, with the simple truncation (F_1: 90%) slightly outperforming the method body truncation (F_1: 89%) as the recall drops when truncating method bodies.

Table 1 presents the comparison of our results with the previously reported results for the approaches (cf. [23]). Overall, our approach performs similar to

Table 1. 10-fold cross-validation of our approach (BERT) and comparison to approaches by Mirakhorli et al. [23] using Precision (P), Recall (R), and F_1-Score. Reported F_1-Scores with asterisks do not fit to their values for precision and recall.

	SVM			Slipper			J48			Bagging			AdaBoost			Bayesian			Tactic Det.			BERT		
	P	R	F_1	P	R	F_1	P	R	F_1	P	R	F_1	P	R	F_1	P	R	F_1	P	R	F_1	P	R	F_1
Audit	.96	.46	.62	.85	.78	.81	.85	.85	.85	.88	.88	.88	.85	.85	.85	.94	.91	**.92**	.84	.92	.88	.89	.89	.89
Authentication	.91	.58	.71	.96	.94	.95	.98	.98	.92*	1.0	.92	.96	.98	.98	.94*	1.0	.80	.89	.96	.98	**.97**	.89	.87	.88
Heartbeat	.91	.62	.74	.84	.84	.84	.77	.88	.82	.89	.84	.87	.91	.86	**.89**	.92	.70	.80	.77	.92	.84	.92	.87	**.89**
Pooling	.97	.66	.79	.94	.96	.95	.94	.96	.95	.94	.94	.94	.98	.96	**.97**	.94	.96	.95	.92	.98	.95	.97	.93	.95
Scheduler	.98	.88	.93	.88	.92	.90	1.0	.98	**.99**	1.0	.98	**.99**	1.0	.98	**.99**	.96	.98	.97	.86	.88	.87	.94	.87	.90
Averages	.95	.64	.76	.89	.89	.89	.91	.93	.92	.94	.91	.93	.94	.93	.93	.95	.87	.91	.87	.94	.90	.92	.89	.90

others but yields relatively stable results between the different tactics, meaning the results do not vary as much between tactics compared to the other approaches.

A Friedman non-parametric statistical test indicates (disregarding the noncompetitive SVM) that the difference between the results is not statistically significant. Therefore, we conclude that these classifiers perform mostly equivalently for the task of tactic detection in our 10-fold cross-validation.

We further apply our trained classifier to a case study to evaluate the performance on a large-scale project and to test how well the approach generalizes. We replicate the case study of Mirakhorli et al. [23] and detect architectural tactics in the Hadoop Distributed File System (HDFS).

Table 2. Comparative evaluation of previous approaches (cf. [23]) and our approach (BERT) for detecting architectural tactics in Hadoop using Precision (P), Recall (R), and F_1-Score.

	SVM			Slipper			J48			Bagging			AdaBoost			Bayesian			Tactic Det.			BERT		
	P	R	F_1	P	R	F_1	P	R	F_1	P	R	F_1	P	R	F_1	P	R	F_1	P	R	F_1	P	R	F_1
Audit	.08	.29	.13	.02	.29	.04	.03	.29	.06	1.0	.29	.44	.03	.29	.06	.04	.50	.07	1.0	.71	**.83**	.50	.50	.50
Authentication	.14	.52	.22	.16	.61	.26	.57	.59	.58	.58	.56	.57	.17	1.0	.30	.15	.37	.21	.61	.70	**.66**	.29	.71	.41
Heartbeat	.07	.11	.09	.31	.59	.41	.22	1.0	.36	.50	1.0	.67	.35	.96	.51	.07	.04	.05	.66	1.0	**.79**	.45	.73	.56
Pooling	.71	.11	.19	.13	.44	.20	.89	.97	**.93**	.88	1.0	**.93**	.87	.87	.87	.16	.33	.22	.88	1.0	**.93**	.89	.39	.54
Scheduler	.36	.63	.46	.65	.20	.30	.64	.87	.74	.65	.89	.75	.66	.77	.71	.32	.78	.46	.65	.94	**.77**	.62	.69	.65
Averages	.27	.33	.22	.25	.43	.24	.47	.74	.53	.72	.75	.67	.42	.78	.49	.15	.40	.20	.76	.87	.80	.55	.60	.53

The results are displayed in Table 2 and compared against the results reported by Mirakhorli et al. [23]. The promising results in the 10-fold cross-validation do not transfer to this case study and the state-of-the-art outperforms our approach. However, compared to most other approaches within the paper by Mirakhorli et al., apart from Bagging and the Tactic Detection approach, our approach still performs similar or better. In this setting, we come to the conclusion that our approach is promising, but needs further work to compete with state-of-the-art.

Although unsuccessful, we think these results provide valuable information and lessons learned. However, we think that our approach is still a valuable contribution for the community and that it is important to publish our experiences, a view that we share with others (cf. [28]). The result demonstrates how important it is to also evaluate on different data and case studies as good cross-validation results not necessarily transfer to case studies.

5 Discussion

In this section, we want to briefly discuss our results, threats to validity, and potential future improvements to tackle the downsides of our approach.

We applied and copied commonly used experimental designs to be able to compare our approach to previous approaches as well as to mitigate potential risks to construct validity. For reproducibility, we used a randomly selected fixed (904727489) for the random number generators.

To overcome bias, we reused established data sets. This enables us comparability and increases the internal validity. However, this might affect the performance of our approach. Our data sets, both for training and for evaluation, come from the same source (cf. [23]), which causes and additional risks and is a threat to validity. The selection of training data is an important factor as well. Currently, there seems to be a problem in generalizing from the training data.

Potential issues of our approach are our assumptions that might be wrong. For example, we detect architectural tactics on a class level like previous approaches. Furthermore, we assume that we have Java code and developers use expressive, non-abbreviated variable names that are contained in BERT's dictionary.

Our approach also needs pre-processing for BERT that can influence the results (negatively). We tried to be conservative but the selection can still influence the results in various ways. However, there are some new ideas like the Longformer [7] approach that might remove input length limitations. We plan to look into them in future work.

Another risk is that BERT might look at other characteristics of the data set. Niven and Kao discovered that statistical cues in the (training) data can influence BERT's performance heavily [27]. Evaluating approaches on different case studies might help in such cases and we will look further into this.

We draw the conclusion that code is not quite the same as a common natural language text. BERT has proven to work well for text classification, but we showed that code cannot simply be treated like normal text Relations between the words in the input are different in normal text compared to code. However, BERT mainly focuses on these relations.

However, there are potential improvements to our idea of using BERT for code classification. One way is to try to transform code into a textual description in the pre-processing step with approaches like code2seq [2]. However, imprecise transformations might influence the outcome negatively (fault propagation). Another reasonable way is to adapt BERT more to our needs. We would need to train the language model on code instead of natural language texts. However, this is still an open research topic, because of differences in semantics.

We still think that transfer learning approaches are useful for tasks like the detection of architectural tactics. A clear benefit is the capability to train a task with a rather small data set. However, the underlying approach, e.g., the language model must be suitable for the kind of input.

6   Conclusion and Future Work

In this paper, we experimented with a transfer-learning approach using the natural language model BERT to classify if classes implement certain architectural tactics. We experimented with our hypothesis that BERT can understand code similarly to text after fine-tuning. We evaluated our approach using 10-fold cross-validation with promising results. However, the approach could not compete with state-of-the-are approaches in a case study using Hadoop. Therefore, we discussed our approach further as we see a lot of potential in transfer-learning approaches.

In future work, we plan to improve our approach to perform better, e.g., by adaptations to our architecture. Additionally, we want find proper ways to either train a new language model or fine-tune one using code, so that the language model is already trained on code, which might boost the performance. We also plan to experiment with different language models beside BERT. There are reports of new language models that show better results on standard NLP tasks as well as new language models that allow longer inputs like Longformer [7].

References

1. Adhikari, A., Ram, A., Tang, R., Lin, J.: Docbert: BERT for document classification. arXiv (2019). http://arxiv.org/abs/1904.08398
2. Alon, U., Brody, S., Levy, O., Yahav, E.: code2seq: generating sequences from structured representations of code. In: ICLR (2019)
3. Antoniol, G., Canfora, G., Casazza, G., De Lucia, A., Merlo, E.: Recovering traceability links between code and documentation. IEEE TSE 28(10), 970–983 (2002). https://doi.org/10.1109/TSE.2002.1041053
4. Antoniol, G., Casazza, G., Di Penta, M., Fiutem, R.: Object-oriented design patterns recovery. J. Syst. Softw. 59(2), 181–196 (2001)
5. Babar, M.A., Gorton, I.: A tool for managing software architecture knowledge. In: 2nd SHARK/ADI 2007 ICSE Workshops 2007, pp. 11–11. IEEE (2007)
6. Bass, L., Clements, P., Kazman, R.: Software Architecture in Practice. Addison-Wesley Professional (2003)
7. Beltagy, I., Peters, M.E., Cohan, A.: Longformer: The long-document transformer. arXiv (2020). http://arxiv.org/abs/1904.08398
8. Capilla, R., Nava, F., Pérez, S., Dueñas, J.C.: A web-based tool for managing architectural design decisions. ACM SIGSOFT 31(5), 4 (2006)
9. Chihada, A., Jalili, S., Hasheminejad, S.M.H., Zangooei, M.H.: Source code and design conformance, design pattern detection from source code by classification approach. Appl. Soft Comput. 26, 357–367 (2015)

10. Cleland-Huang, J., Berenbach, B., Clark, S., Settimi, R., Romanova, E.: Best practices for automated traceability. Computer **40**(6), 27–35 (2007). https://doi.org/10.1109/MC.2007.195

11. Devlin, J., Chang, M.W., Lee, K., Toutanova, K.: BERT: pre-training of Deep Bidirectional transformers for language understanding. In: NAACL-HLT (2019). https://doi.org/10.18653/v1/N19-1423

12. Ducasse, S., Pollet, D.: Software architecture reconstruction: a process-oriented taxonomy. IEEE TSE **35**(4), 573–591 (2009)

13. Egyed, A., Biffl, S., Heindl, M., Grünbacher, P.: Determining the cost-quality trade-off for automated software traceability. In: 20th IEEE/ACM ASE, pp. 360–363. ACM, New York (2005). https://doi.org/10.1145/1101908.1101970

14. Gamma, E., Helm, R., Johnson, R., Vlissides, J.: Elements of reusable object-oriented software. arXiv (1995)

15. Hey, T., Keim, J., Tichy, W.F., Koziolek, A.: NoRBERT: Transfer learning for requirements classification. In: 2020 IEEE 28th RE. IEEE (2020)

16. Hoorn, J.F., Farenhorst, R., Lago, P., Van Vliet, H.: The lonesome architect. J. Syst. Softw. **84**(9), 1424–1435 (2011)

17. Howard, J., Ruder, S.: Fine-tuned language models for text classification. arXiv (2018). http://arxiv.org/abs/1801.06146

18. Keim, J., Kaplan, A., Koziolek, A., Mirakhorli, M.: Gram21/BERT4DAT, July 2020. https://doi.org/10.5281/zenodo.3925165

19. Keim, J., Kaplan, A., Koziolek, A., Mirakhorli, M.: Using BERT for the detection of architectural tactics in code. Technical report 2, Karlsruhe Institute of Technology (KIT), Karlsruhe (2020). https://doi.org/10.5445/IR/1000121031

20. Keskar, N.S., Mudigere, D., Nocedal, J., Smelyanskiy, M., Tang, P.T.P.: On large-batch training for deep learning: generalization gap and sharp minima. arXiv (2016). http://arxiv.org/abs/1609.04836

21. Li, J., Wang, Y., Lyu, M.R., King, I.: Code completion with neural attention and pointer networks. 27th IJCAI, July 2018. https://doi.org/10.24963/ijcai.2018/578

22. Loshchilov, I., Hutter, F.: Fixing weight decay regularization in adam. arXiv (2017). http://arxiv.org/abs/1711.05101

23. Mirakhorli, M., Cleland-Huang, J.: Detecting, tracing, and monitoring architectural tactics in code. IEEE Trans. Softw. Eng. **42**(3), 205–220 (2016). https://doi.org/10.1109/TSE.2015.2479217

24. Mirakhorli, M., Shin, Y., Cleland-Huang, J., Cinar, M.: A tactic-centric approach for automating traceability of quality concerns. In: 34th ICSE, pp. 639–649, June 2012. https://doi.org/10.1109/ICSE.2012.6227153

25. Mirakhorli, M., Cleland-Huang, J.: Tracing architectural concerns in high assurance systems. In: 33rd ICSE, pp. 908–911. ACM (2011)

26. Mirakhorli, M., et al.: Archie. https://github.com/SoftwareDesignLab/Archie

27. Niven, T., Kao, H.Y.: Probing neural network comprehension of natural language arguments. In: 57th ACL (2019). https://doi.org/10.18653/v1/P19-1459

28. Prechelt, L.: Why we need an explicit forum for negative results. J. Univ. Comput. Sci. **3**(9), 1074–1083 (1997)

29. Raychev, V., Vechev, M., Yahav, E.: Code completion with statistical language models. In: 35th ACM SIGPLAN PLDI, pp. 419–428. New York, NY, USA (2014). https://doi.org/10.1145/2594291.2594321

30. Sharma, T., Efstathiou, V., Louridas, P., Spinellis, D.: On the feasibility of transfer-learning code smells using deep learning. arXiv (2019). http://arxiv.org/abs/1904.03031

31. Sun, C., Qiu, X., Xu, Y., Huang, X.: How to fine-tune bert for text classification? arXiv (2019). http://arxiv.org/abs/1905.05583
32. Tenney, I., Das, D., Pavlick, E.: BERT rediscovers the classical NLP pipeline. In: 57th ACL, pp. 4593–4601. ACL, Florence, Italy, July 2019. https://doi.org/10.18653/v1/P19-1452

Education and Training

Teaching Students Software Architecture Decision Making

Rafael Capilla[1]([⊠]) [iD], Olaf Zimmermann[2]([⊠]), Carlos Carrillo[3]([⊠]) [iD],
and Hernán Astudillo[4]([⊠]) [iD]

[1] Rey Juan Carlos University, Madrid, Spain
rafael.capilla@urjc.es
[2] HSR Hochschule für Technik, Rapperswil, Switzerland
olaf.zimmermann@hsr.ch
[3] Technical University of Madrid, Madrid, Spain
carlos.carrillo@upm.es
[4] Universidad Técnica Federico Santa María, Santiago de Chile, Chile
hernan@inf.utfsm.cl

Abstract. Making the right decisions is challenging for architects on all levels
of seniority. Less experienced architects in particular perceive the transition from
design problems to their solutions as hard; it is not always clear how to find suitable concepts and technologies, how to compare alternatives, and how to build
consensus. Lack of experience makes it difficult to train software engineering
students in the identification, selection, and collective evaluation of design alternatives. Moreover, human factors such as cognitive bias make "soft" topics like
architecture decisions rather hard to teach. To overcome these issues and let students gain the required experience, a Spanish University ran two experiments.
Undergraduate computer science students assumed different roles in collaborative
decision-making tasks and design activities. They used a novel decision-modeling
tool to capture and challenge the relevant design decisions. This paper describes
this new teaching setup and reports on lessons learned.

Keywords: Architectural knowledge · Collaborative decision making · Design
decision · Design thinking · Reflection · Teaching software architecture

1 Introduction

The creativity of software architects may lead to different designs or solution architectures serving for the same purpose. Diagrams illustrating proven designs may be worth a
thousand words [15]. Nevertheless, teaching novice architects and undergrad students in
the practice of software architecture is not easy because of the plethora of design alternatives and possibilities to compose them. Thus, it is challenging to select adequate design
solutions promoting well-known design principles; years of apprentice are required.
The ISO/IEC 42010 standard[1] considers a software architecture as the result of a set of

---

[1] ISO/IEC/IEEE 42010 – Systems and software engineering – architecture description. Available
at: https://www.iso.org/standard/50508.html.

© Springer Nature Switzerland AG 2020
A. Jansen et al. (Eds.): ECSA 2020, LNCS 12292, pp. 231–246, 2020.
https://doi.org/10.1007/978-3-030-58923-3_16

design decisions and first-class artifacts. An *Architecture Design Decision (ADD)* can be understood as a decision that addresses architecturally significant requirements and design problems. The tacit knowledge and expertise of software architects should be captured explicitly via their significant ADDs [35]; this is costly and challenging when adequate tools are missing [12]. Consequently, teaching novice designers on making and selecting the right decisions, evaluating the consequences of such selections and challenging the decisions made by others is still in its infancy.[2]

An additional challenge is that development teams tend to be decentralized and distributed more and more. This has raised new forms of collaboration, where several stakeholders take on different roles and often use collaborative modeling tools to arrive at adequate and accepted design solutions. This research explores behavior of software engineering students as novice software architects in different roles: how do they make, challenge and capture a set of ADDs and architectures in a collaborative way? The set of decisions captured serves as training material as reusable knowledge; the roles assumed by the students is supposed to enable and promote critical design thinking to produce decisions with better quality and architectures.

The remainder of the paper is structured as follows. Section 2 discusses related work and provides background information. Section 3 outlines the design of two experiments we run in a Spanish university to teach a collaborative decision-making practice. Section 4 outlines the results we obtained. Section 5 presents lessons learned and resulting insights for researchers, educators, and practitioners. Finally, Sect. 6 summarizes our conclusions and provides an outlook.

2 Background and Related Work

This section describes related background and similar studies used in our experience and around three different topics.

2.1 Teaching Design and Collaborative Decision-Making

Collaborative software engineering [18] gains more and more significant attention by software development teams, especially in cases of delocalization in distributed teams. One important task in the software development process is software modelling, essentially seen as a creative task used to yield the software architecture of a system. In any architecting process, the chief architect must discuss, evaluate and deliberate with solution architects, senior and junior designers about the resultant design.

This deliberative task, adapted to different project contexts (e.g. open source, global development, agile projects, etc.) should capture the significant architecture design decisions. Bang et al. [3] report the insights related to six different roles of software architects during collaborative software design tasks in a distributed environment. Some teaching experiences about software architecture [17, 24] reflect the importance of architecture

---

[2] The IBM e-business reference architecture taught about the importance of architectural decisions; decision capturing was a recommended practice at IBM since, at least, 1998.

design decisions as part as the architect's soft skills and how to explain the technical deci-sions to non-technical staff and also how students have to wrestle with the complexity of design decisions.

Collaborative approaches teaching software architecture [8] evaluate the effect of design decisions in a collaborative software architecture course in open source projects, or using ASQ, a collaborative web-based platform [36] which allows tracking and record-ing real-time students' interactions and thinking. Other experiences report about *Group Decision Making (GDM)* practices in software architecture [28] showing that brain-storming is a preferred activity for team members. The authors of [20] describe the DVIA approach to provide design verbal intervention analysis to capture GDM activi-ties; they also categorized the variety of decision topics. However, the lack of tool support is an important barrier to assist participants in the decision-making process [34].

2.2 Architectural Knowledge Research

The recent evolution in AKM tools has led to more collaborative approaches that let architects not only capture and share ADDs, but also discuss them collaboratively – supported by extended capabilities aimed to facilitate collaborative decision-making [5]. Research tools like RAT, AREL, SAW, and ADvISE (among others) offer sharing and voting mechanisms to deliberate around the design alternatives and facilitate the selection of the best design choices, many times complicated by the fact to achieve a consensus [35]. However, the dichotomy between AKM and software modeling tools still does not help to embed the design rationale and their decisions in software architecture modeling tasks [4]. ADMentor [39] helps novice architects to discriminate between the problem and solution spaces capturing the key design decisions and providing a design solution for the decisions chosen. A Markdown-based template and supporting tools are presented in [14].

2.3 Design Thinking, Reflection and Reasoning

Critical thinking can enhance problem-solving abilities, not only for learning program-ming concepts [13, 37], but also to acquire design skills and achieve a clear understand-ing of the problem and solution spaces. Producing to high quality decisions is not easy; sometimes reflective approaches [23] such as the Mind1-2 model are necessary [22] to challenge (Mind 2) the decisions made by others (Mind 1). This reflective thinking (i.e. reflection in action theory [24, 25]) and reasoning approach have also been highlighted in [28], considered a learning process to bring the tacit knowledge explicit [9]. As during the design activity design problems must be solved, designers must consider different options as design alternatives when they explore the solution space [2, 11] and reduce the cognitive bias.

Users can experience the reflective activity in different development context. Reflec-tion, as a conversation during the design thinking activity, can be integrated with agile practices [29] during software constructions, such as stated in [2]. In [19] the authors explore how students increase awareness and reflective practices during learning activi-ties. The study reports that the Critical Incident Technique (CIT) used in a software devel-opment course promotes critical reflection and communication skills. Other approaches describe how developers discuss rationale in open source software (OSS) projects [1] to understand how rationale is discussed using IRC channels. One recent experience [10] reports the results of teaching reflection in software engineering students as a computer-supported collaborative learning (CSCL) activity; software engineering teachers and students reflected during UML modeling sessions.

During the reflective modeling tasks, the participants increased their awareness on modeling assumptions and sharing knowledge to confront multiple perspectives using video-taped sessions. Moreover, as software design is recognized as an outcome of design reasoning, Tang et al. [33] argue that decisions made collectively are based on some rationale, but the reasoning and argumentation of such decisions may not be explicitly stated. They suggest an approach to identify the design issues [31] in an experiment with students and professionals using reminder cards to investigate the use of design reasoning explicitly. In an experiment with students and professionals reported in [32], the authors studied the differences in design reasoning between both groups and the effort spent in decision-making activities. Another study reports on decision making practices and the authors identify their gaps and mention a lack of improvement and no new practices [21].

Finally, one recent study investigates a rationale management case study in an agile context to uncover what matters to students when they need to integrate decision documentation into Scrum projects [27]. The authors run an experiment with 400 participants grouped in 82 teams to analyze the effects of a lightweight architectural decision capture and understand how students capture decision alternatives and their rationale and which types of decisions are more important when teaching agile methods. Part of the results show that the majority of the students do capture multiple design *alternatives*, but struggle to capture *rationale*. However, implementing continuous reflection in software tools is still challenging but feasible at least to a certain extent, such as described in the prototype discussed in [26].

3 Experimental Design

As there still not many students showing the impact in teaching architecture with the capture of design decisions and rationale and also how students reflect and think about different design choices, this study investigates the quality and effectiveness of teaching design thinking [30] in a software architecture course. We were interested in evaluation the positive impact of reflections in design thinking, were students challenge the design decisions made by others, and to what extent students acting as software modelers perceive value in having design decisions captured before the modeling tasks in order to ease the design activity.

The research questions that guided this study are:

RQ1: *How does consensus influence the decision-making process in collaborative environments?*
RQ2: *Do reflective practices like the Mind1-2 model [Razavian2016] have a positive influence on design thinking?*
RQ3: *Do the decisions captured have any positive effect on software architecture modeling tasks?*

3.1 Course Description

The learning objectives of the target course on software architecture (third year of under-graduate studies on Software Engineering) at the Rey Juan Carlos University of Madrid (Spain) encompasses common topics like design patterns, architecture styles, design principles and architecture evaluation methods like Architecture Trade-off Analysis Method (ATAM). Furthermore, we include a lecture on ADDs to train students on their importance of and the difficulty to capture the significant decisions and evaluate the design alternatives. Finally, we highlight the importance of reflection as a technique to challenge design alternatives when dealing with incomplete information and uncertainty (for instance, design patterns and/or technology selection). The teaching method follows a classical approach using slides to teach the lessons and minutes for discussion at the end of each lesson. The students need to pass two practical assignments and form groups of five to six persons, which is easy to achieve because the average number of students enrolled in the course is often more than 50.

3.2 Course Selection and Participants

From the course, we selected the following participants from two different years. We ran two experiments in 2016/17 and 2017/18, with 65 and 58 students respectively. The age of the participants enrolled in the course 2016/17 was between 19 and 29 years (plus one student over 30), while the age of the subjects in the course 2017/18 was between 19 and 29. However, most participants were between 19 and 24 years old. Only some of them have a few months of professional experience in software companies.

3.3 Training and Laboratory Activities

Before the experiment, students had around three weeks of software architecture lec-tures on concepts, design patterns and architectural design decisions; we used several examples to train them in modern software architecture practice and emphasized the importance of capturing the significant architecturally design decisions. The laboratory sessions for each of the two experiments took 4 weeks in sessions of 4 h per week. Additionally, the students spent additional time outside the laboratory to complete the weekly tasks. We established that each week students had to produce one iteration of the software architecture for the target system, including smaller sub-iterations according to the number and complexity of the software requirements and design problems.

3.4 Groups and Tasks

We organized the students in 10 teams composed by five to six participants each, with the following roles (see Fig. 1).

- *Two senior architects* are in charge of making architectural design decisions and capturing them, identify design problems, make and capture architecture design decisions;

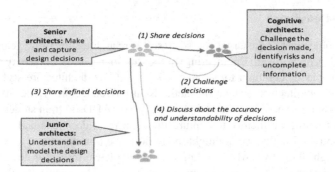

Fig. 1. Relationships between participants in collaborative decision making and design thinking

- *Two cognitive architects* challenge the decisions captured by senior architects and raise any concern when risks or incomplete information appear;
- *One or two junior architects* are in charge of understand and model the decisions captured providing a solution architecture.

Each team was composed of two senior architects, two cognitive architects, and one to two junior architects. We selected the most experienced students (i.e., those who had industry experience) as cognitive and senior architects while those students with no experience acted as junior architects. Because it was difficult to find enough cognitive and senior architects, we balanced the groups to have at least one senior and one cognitive architect. The students using the different roles interacted during $2 + 2$ laboratory hours weekly and via Skype to discuss and annotate the changes in the decisions and architecture documentation using Google drive docs.

In addition, we let the groups to use the ADMentor[3] tool [39] for modeling the problem space and solution space and we limited the granularity of the decisions up to UML classes to avoid an excessive number of small decisions. Finally, all groups captured the decisions using any of the three different templates provided: a minimalistic template including five attributes (i.e., useful for decisions captured in agile projects), a medium template comprising seven attributes and a longer template comprising eleven items.

4   Results

During the first experiment, we got responses from ten groups and we discarded one group because they did not provide significant results that could be used to evaluate the impact of design decisions in architecture modeling tasks. In the replica experiment, we received valid responses from ten groups, so in both experiments we had almost the same number of participants. The collaborative decision-making activities happened along four weeks, and we collected the following results.

---

[3] https://www.ifs.hsr.ch/ADMentor-Tool.13201.0.html?&L=4.

4.1 Collaborative Decision-Making

Once the senior architects made and captured the key design decisions during each iteration, they interacted collaboratively with the cognitive architects to produce better quality decisions. As we show in Fig. 2, cognitive architects from all groups challenged a number of 110 decisions during the deliberative tasks with senior architects. RQ1: *How does consensus influence the decision-making process in collaborative environments?*

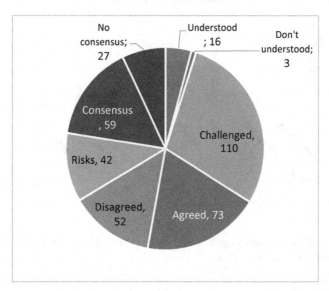

Fig. 2. Activity of senior and cognitive architects (Mind1-2 tasks) regarding the decision challenges, risks stated and consensus between decisions.

From the data obtained from the discussions between cognitive and senior architects, they agreed in 73 decisions and disagreed in 52 (please note that we included here decisions that were challenged and non-challenged). Finally, they achieved a consensus in 59 cases and no consensus in 27 times. In addition, the cognitive architects stated the appearance of risks in 42 decisions, as potentially critical decisions or caused by uncompleted information during the decision-making activity.

The distribution of the percentages during the interactions between senior and cognitive architects prove the utility of the Mind1-2 model and the importance for challenging the decisions made by others and the intention to arrive to a consensus during discussions and agree on as much decisions as possible in order to arrive to a solution architecture. Therefore, building a consensus in architecture decision-making seems to influence positively the speed to arrive to agreements, particularly for critical decisions.

RQ2: *Do reflective practices like the Mind1-2 model have a positive influence on design thinking?* Regarding the second research question, we can strongly affirm reflection has a positive impact in architecting practices and more specifically in design thinking activities. Figure 3 shows the results of the cognitive activity and discussions, which are quite similar in both experiments. In Fig. 3, the X axis represents the different states about the decisions as results of the discussion between senior and cognitive architects while in the Y axis we show how many decisions in both experiments where challenged, agreed, understood or needed a consensus.

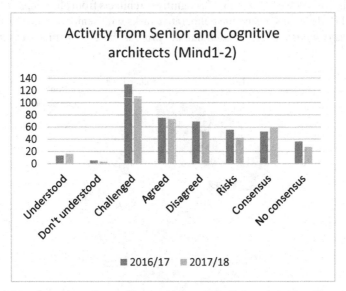

Fig. 3. Activity of senior and cognitive architects (Mind1-2 tasks) regarding the decision challenges, risks stated and consensus.

The results from the collaborative decision-making activity between both roles was very fruitful, and based on the number of decision challenged we can say that the Mind1-2 model [22] was proven better in yielding higher quality decisions than if senior architects make decisions alone without the criticism of the cognitive architects. In the replica experiment we got a bit better results in most cases than in the first experiment, maybe because we trained the students better in the second year, but the differences in general terms are small and the replica confirm our initial results.

4.2 Collaborative Analysis and Modelling Tasks

Figure 4 compares the activity of interactions between senior and junior architects in order to answer research question RQ3.

RQ3: *Do the decisions captured have any positive effect on software architecture modeling tasks?* One of the most interesting outcomes derived from both experiments is the satisfaction of junior architects as software modelers using the decisions made by others to depict the software architecture. During the interactions between them, junior architects widely used design patterns and the decisions shared by the senior architects were useful to model the software architecture. Figure 4 describes the activity of the interactions performed by junior architects. For instance, we can observe from the first experiment that junior architects believed decisions were useful to model the software

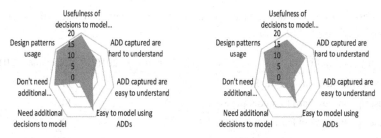

Fig. 4. Activities performed by junior architects in the experiment 2016/17 (left side) and in 2017/18 (right side).

architecture and, in most cases, they did not need an additional explanation. Also, in many cases junior architects didn't need additional decisions to model the solution. In addition, the subjects used design patterns and they experienced that software architectures were easier to model using ADD descriptions.

Similar results we obtained from the replica experiment run during 2017/18, as show in Fig. 4. In the replica, more junior architects than in the first experiment thought they did not need additional decisions to model the software architecture. In some cases, some of the subjects perceived the design were not so easy to model using the ADDs because some of the decisions had been not described or captured properly and hence were hard to use during the modeling tasks.

However, only two more subjects in the replica experiment thought decisions were hard to use (14 subjects in the replica versus twelve in the first experiment). Related to this, only three subjects in the first experiment thought more decisions were required, and four subjects in the replica thought the same. Although some decisions should be captured better, most of them were understood by the software modelers, and in only a few cases additional decisions were needed.

Moreover, during the sessions with the students we observed their activity and discussions but we did not participate in any form of action research as we only had minimal interventions about questions in order to avoid bias during the decision-making activity, as any kind of help could interfere in the decisions chosen by the senior architects. In addition, we run a questionnaire asking all participants from the three different roles a set of questions regarding about their activities performed, and with respect to the activity of junior architects and the interactions with senior architects. Table 1 shows the results from both experiments.

We got a maximum of 19 and 18 responses out from 20 and 19 junior architects belonging to the experiments 2016/17 and 2017/18 respectively. As we can see in Table 1, the results from the second experiment confirm the results from the initial one. Most subjects thought that decisions are useful to model the software architecture. However, 12–14 of junior architects thought also that the decisions descriptions provided by the senior architects were hard to understand for modeling an architectural solution, while only 4–7 thought the opposite. In general, most junior architects felt architectures are easier to model if they have design decisions, but the results of the replica show a higher disagreement at this point. In addition, in both experiments only three and four students respectively thought they would need additional decisions to model the solution

Table 1. Results from the questionnaire evaluating the activity and interactions of junior architects.

Activity of junior architects	Experiment 2016/17	Experiment 2017/18
Decisions are useful to model the SA	19	17
ADD descriptions are hard to model the SA	12	14
ADD descriptions are not hard to model the SA	7	4
Architecture is easy to model using ADDs	17	13
Need of additional decisions to model the solution architecture	3	4
Don't need additional decisions to model the architecture	17	12
Use of design patterns	19	18

architecture, while 17 subjects in 2016/17 thought they did not need additional decisions. Again, there are some differences with junior architects in the replica experiment as only twelve thought they do not need additional decisions. Finally, most students in both experiments agreed that using design patterns to define a solution architecture was quite useful.

4.3   Effort Spent in Cognitive and Modelling Tasks

In order to compare the effort spent in hours by the three different roles in the experiment, we illustrate in Fig. 5 the results (expressed in hours) from the replica. We observed that most groups with higher decision-making (including the capturing effort of the ADDs) and reflective activities required less modeling effort (i.e. groups G1, G2, G3, G6, G8, G9, G10) while only groups G4, G5 and G7 spent more time during modeling activities and maybe caused because the design thinking and reflective effort was low.

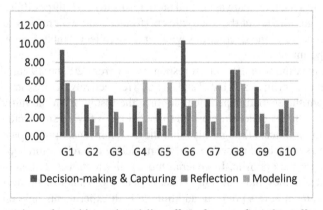

Fig. 5. Comparison of cognitive and modeling effort of groups from the replica experiment.

Some distorting results belong to group G6, which exhibits a high decision-making effort probably caused because they captured more design alternatives than the rest of the groups, and group G8, where team members spent the same time in decision-making and reflective activities. One reason for this (i.e. assuming they measured the effort correctly) might be that a significant number of discussions were devoted because unclear decisions, disagreements or high number of risks identified by the cognitive architects.

Finally, both experiments exhibited a similar pattern where junior architects classified more decisions as "hard to understand" easy to understand and model". Although junior architects perceived that having decisions eases the modeling tasks, the description of many decisions require further explanation, which added additional discussion cycles during the interactions with senior architects. As the subjects stated that in majority of the interactions, they did not need additional decisions to model the solution, it seems that it was just a matter of improving the descriptions captured in the templates.

Moreover, the interactions between the junior architects of each group to depict the architectural sketches [16] revealed that in many cases they performed short iterations until they model a bunch of design decisions. Fifteen groups out of 20 used Google drive to upload architectural sketches and documents with junior and senior architects annotating comments collaboratively to deliberate about the resultant architectures, whereas only five groups used a collaborative modeling tool.

4.4 Effort in Reflective Tasks

The importance of reflective effort compared to the time spent in decision-making and capturing the decisions is highly relevant to the quality of the decisions made and of the solution architecture as well. We compared this reflective effort in both experiments and we got the following results. Figure 6 (left) shows the effort (in hours) spent by the different teams in making and capturing decisions as well as the extra effort when they reflected about the decisions.

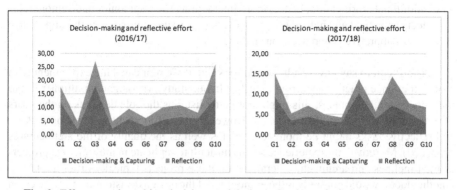

Fig. 6. Effort spent in making decisions and during reflective tasks in both experiments.

As shown in Fig. 6 (left), groups G2 and G4 spent little effort in making and capturing the decisions while G1, G3 and G10 spent much effort than the others. The rest of the groups spent similar time in this activity. The reflective activity indicates the extra effort required for producing better quality decisions. Apart from groups G3 and G10, which present distorting numbers, the rest of the groups employed a reasonable time in reflection compared to the previous decision-making activity. Only G2 and G4 groups required more time in reflection than making decisions but the differences are rather small.

As confirmation in the replica shown in Fig. 6 (right), reflective effort is an extra effort for all groups, not just in addition to making decisions but because the students were better trained in decision-making than in the first experiment, and they need significantly less effort for making and reflecting decisions (see effort the Y axis). In this case only groups G1, G6 and G8 required much more effort than the others and only G10 spent bit more effort in reflecting than in making decisions.

5 Discussion

The major results derived from both experiences are the following:

(i)   The groups using the ADMentor tool understood the distinction of the problem and solution space much better, while senior architects identified design problems and design alternatives more accurately.
(ii)   The quality of the architectures backed by high-quality design decisions led to an adequate solution architecture with the desired qualities.
(iii) Groups using ADMentor arrived at "better" architectures as they identified the design problems more clearly.
(iv)   The investment in reflective tasks paid off and produced "good" quality decisions as outcome of the discussions between senior and cognitive architects.
(v)   In most cases, the decisions were useful to model the design solutions; in some other cases, the description of the decisions was hard to understand by the junior architects.
(vi)   Sometimes a decision might not be fully clear to the junior architects and require additional clarification; hence, more interactions between junior and senior architects happened and helped to clarify the design issues; this stresses the importance of collaborative group decision-making.

It is difficult to say how results would look like if we replicated the experiment with more experience practitioners from industry: In our study, we assigned multiple roles to the subjects; in companies, this might not be realistic as the role depends on the years of experience and the project contexts. However, the effort spent in decision-making and reflective tasks might be more accurate (as well as the quality of the architectures produced). Moreover, the experience seems difficult to replicate in multiple real projects as the timelines and architecture iterations on these projects typically differ a lot [15]. Another factor we did not study is the granularity of the design decisions as we focused on the decision-making as well as reflective and collaborative tasks. Nevertheless, we limited the size of the decisions to the class level (i.e. in the sense of object-oriented classes) and dependencies between such classes in object-oriented programs; we did not capture smaller decisions such as the creation of an attribute or a method. In addition, we did not discuss the relevance of the decisions and the quality of the resulting architectures; the groups that spent more time in reflective tasks and discussions produced decisions with better quality (i.e. better described and argued). The quality of the final architectures was difficult to observe as we did not implement any system or evaluate quality properties to test how good the architecture is. However, we carried out interviews with the teams every week to mitigate the risk for having architectures not addressing the design problems. Our approach complements architecture design methods and techniques such as ADD [6] and the Architecture Tradeoff Analysis Method (ATAM) [7]. ADD in its latest version is also decision-centric but does not model these decisions explicitly; it rather collects related guidance informally. ATAM is an evaluation and review technique centered on desired quality attributes; it also can play a role in forward engineering. ATAM investigates architectural decisions made when exploring risks, sensitivity and tradeoff points. Hence, ATAM can also benefit from the explicit modeling capabilities of our approach and the ADMentor tool. In summary, one can view the concepts and their implementation presented in this paper as a sub-step or micro-methodology [38] for ADD and ATAM. Compared to previous related works and regarding the collaborative aspects, we investigated the interactions of the team members for the between different roles and for the same role. For instance, we studied how the students in the role as senior software architects reason to make decisions and how students acting as cognitive architects challenge and reflect on the decisions captured. However, we did not include such qualitative analysis in this paper due to space constraints. However, we did show the benefits of reflective practices in architecture decision-making using the Mind1-2 model. Nevertheless, a deeper analysis to examine the quality of the decisions after reflection is required. Moreover, we noticed that the students took some time until they learned how to reflect and challenge the decisions made; in the second and third iterations of the architecture development process, team members applied these reflective practices more commonly. We did not continue with the same experiment after 2018 as during 2019 and 2020 we moved and compared other architectural knowledge capturing approaches.

6 Conclusion

In this paper, we reported our experiences with teaching software architecture decision making, and we highlighted the importance of collaborative decision-making to produce more accurate and complete design decisions, by reducing the cognitive bias and anchoring through reflections using the Mind1-2 model. We summarize the main outcomes of our work as: (i) Adopting different roles when performing collaborative tasks such as challenging decisions improved the quality of the architectures. (ii) A significant number of decisions resulted from the agreement between the different stakeholders during the interactive decision-making process. (iii) The decisions captured using the Mind1-2 model exhibit better quality than those produced without reflection. To mitigate the threat to integrity that arises of not having test and control groups to evaluate the experimental design, we compared the resulting architectures with models produced in previous instances of the course, where subjects did not have access to captured decisions. Stating the risks of the decisions reduces the bias for making suboptimal decisions. In the future, we plan to explore voting systems to arrive to a faster consensus, and to explore cognitive activity in agile projects where the time for decision-making is limited and very lean documentation templates are applied. Furthermore, we will investigate a better form of representing decisions to avoid the problem that decisions are hard to understand or that additional decisions are required to model a design solution.

Acknowledgements. H. Astudillo's work was partially funded by grant ANID PIA/APOYO AFB180002. O. Zimmermann's work was partially funded by the Hasler Foundation (project number: 19083).

References

1. Alkadhi, R., Nonnenmacher, M., Guzman, E., Bruegge, B.: How do developers discuss rationale? In: International Conference on Software Analysis, Evolution and Reengineering (SANER 2018). IEEE DL (2018)
2. Babb, J., Hoda, R., Norbjerg, J.: Embedding Reflection and Learning into Agile Software Development (2014)
3. Bang, J.Y., Krka, I., Medvidovic, N., Kulkarni, N.N., Padmanabhuni, S.: How software architects collaborate: insights from collaborative software design in practice. In: 6th International Workshop on Cooperative and Human Aspects of Software Engineering, pp. 41–48. IEEE (2013)
4. Capilla, R.: Embedded design rationale in software architecture. In: Joint Working IEEE/IFIP Conference on Software Architecture and European Conference on Software Architecture, pp. 305–308. IEEE DL (2009)
5. Capilla, R., Jansen, A., Tang, A., Avgeriou, P., Ali Babar, M.: A 10 years of software architecture knowledge management: practice and future. J. Syst. Softw. **116**, 191–205 (2016)
6. Cervantes, H., Kazman, R.: Designing Software Architectures: A Practical Approach. SEI Series in Software Engineering. Addison-Wesley, Boston (2016)
7. Clements, P., Kazman, R., Klein, M.: Evaluating Software Architectures: Methods and Case Studies. SEI Series in Software Engineering. Addison-Wesley, Boston (2001)
8. van Deursen, A., et al.: A collaborative approach to teaching software architecture. In: ACM SIGCSE Technical Symposium on Computer Science Education SIGCSE, pp. 591–596. ACM (2017)
9. Dingsoyr, T., Lago, P., van Vliet, H.: Rationale promotes learning about architectural knowledge. In: 8th International Workshop on Learning Software Organizations (LSO), Rio de Janeiro, Brazil. ACM (2006)
10. Dittmar, A., Forbrig, P.: A case study on supporting teachers' collective reflection in higher education. In: 36th European Conference on Cognitive Ergonomics ECCE 2018, pp. 4:1–4:8. ACM DL (2018)
11. Dorst, K.: Design problems and design paradoxes. Des. Issues **22**, 4–17 (2006)
12. Hohpe, G., Ozkaya, I., Zdun, U., Zimmermann, O.: The software architect's role in the digital age. IEEE Softw. **33**(6), 30–39 (2016)
13. Hwang, W.-Y., Shadiev, R., Wang, C.-Y., Huang, Z.-H.: A pilot study of cooperative programming learning behavior and its relationship with students' learning performance. Comput. Educ. **58**(4), 1267–1281 (2012)
14. Kopp, O., Armbruster, A., Zimmermann, O.: Markdown architectural records: format and tool support. In: 10th Central European Workshop on Services and their Composition, pp. 55–62 (2018)

15. Larkin, J.H., Simon, H.A.: Why a diagram is (sometimes) worth ten thousand words. Cogn. Sci. **11**(1), 65–99 (1987)
16. Mangano, N., LaToza, T.D., Petre, M., van der Hoek, A.: How software designers interact with sketches at the whiteboard. IEEE Trans. Softw. Eng. **41**(2), 135–156 (2015)
17. Männistö, T., Savolainen, J., Myllärniemi, V.: Teaching software architecture design. In: Seventh Working IEEE/IFIP Conference on Software Architecture (WICSA 2008), pp. 117–124. IEEE DL (2008)
18. Mistrík, I., van der Hoek, A., Grundy, J., Whitehead, J.: Collaborative Software Engineering. Springer, Heidelberg (2010). https://doi.org/10.1007/978-3-642-10294-3
19. Nylén, A., Isomöttönen, V.: Exploring the critical incident technique to encourage reflection during project-based learning. In: Koli Calling, pp. 88–97. ACM DL (2017)
20. Pedraza-Garcia, G., Astudillo, H., Correal, D.: DVIA: understanding how software architects make decisions in design meetings. In: ECSA Workshops 2015, pp. 51:1–51:7. ACM DL (2015)
21. Razavian, M., Paech, V., Tang, A.: Empirical research for software architecture decision making. J. Syst. Softw. **149**(3), 360–381 (2018)
22. Razavian, M., Tang, A., Capilla, R., Lago, P.: In two minds: how reflections influence software design thinking. J. Softw. Evol. Process **28**(6), 394–426 (2016)
23. Razavian, M., Tang, A., Capilla, R., Lago, P.: Reflective approach for software design decision making. In: Qualitative Reasoning About Software Architectures, pp. 19–26. IEEE DL (2016)
24. Rupakheti, C.R., Chenoweth, S.V.: Teaching software architecture to undergraduate students: an experience report. In: 37th IEEE/ACM International Conference on Software Engineering, vol. 2, pp. 445–454. IEEE CS (2015)
25. Schön, D.A.: The Reflective Practitioner: How Professionals Think in Action. Basic Books, Nueva York (1983)
26. Schoormann, T., Hofer, J., Knackstedt, R.: Software tools for supporting reflection in design thinking projects. In: 53rd Hawaii International Conference on System Sciences (HICSS 2020), ScholarSpace, pp. 1–10 (2020)
27. Schubanz, M., Lewerentz, C.: What matters to students – a rationale management case study in agile software development. In: 17. Workshops "Software Engineering im Unterricht der Hochschulen (SEUH 2020)", CEUR Workshop Proceedings, pp. 17–26 (2020)
28. Smrithi Rekha, V., Muccini, H.: Group decision-making in software architecture: a study on industrial practices. Inf. Softw. Technol. **101**, 51–63 (2018)
29. Talby, D., Hazzan, O., Dubinsky, Y., Keren, A.: Reflections on reflection in agile software development. In: Agile Conference, pp. 11–112. IEEE (2006)
30. Tang, A., Aleti, A., Burge, J., van Vliet, H.: What makes software design effective? Des. Stud. **31**, 614–640 (2010)
31. Tang, A., Lau, M.F.: Software architecture review by association. J. Syst. Softw. **88**(2), 87–101 (2014)
32. Tang, A., van Vliet, H.: Software designers satisfice. In: Weyns, D., Mirandola, R., Crnkovic, I. (eds.) ECSA 2015. LNCS, vol. 9278, pp. 105–120. Springer, Cham (2015). https://doi.org/10.1007/978-3-319-23727-5_9
33. Tang, A., Bex, F., Schriek, C., van der Werf, J.M.E.M.: Improving software design reasoning - a reminder card approach. J. Syst. Softw. **144**, 22–40 (2018)
34. Tofan, D., Galster, M., Avgeriou, P., Schuitema, W.: Past and future of software architectural decisions - a systematic mapping study. Inf. Softw. Technol. **56**(8), 850–872 (2014)
35. Tofan, D., Galster, M., Lytra, I., Avgeriou, P., Zdun, U., Fouche, M.-A., de Boer, R.C., Solms, F.: Empirical evaluation of a process to increase consensus in group architectural decision making. Inf. Softw. Technol. **72**, 31–47 (2016)

36. Triglianos, V., Pautasso, C., Bozzon, A., Hauff, C.: Inferring student attention with ASQ. In: Verbert, K., Sharples, M., Klobučar, T. (eds.) EC-TEL 2016. LNCS, vol. 9891, pp. 306–320. Springer, Cham (2016). https://doi.org/10.1007/978-3-319-45153-4_23

37. Wachenchauzer, R.: Work in progress – promoting critical thinking while learning programming language concepts and paradigms. In: Proceedings of IEEE International Conference on Frontiers in Education, Savannah, GA, USA, pp. 13–14 (2004)

38. Zimmermann, O., Koehler, J., Leymann, F.: Architectural decision models as micro-methodology for service-oriented analysis and design. In: Lübke, D. (ed.) Proceedings of the Workshop on Software Engineering Methods for Service-oriented Architecture 2007 (SEMSOA 2007), Hannover, Germany, vol. 244. CEUR-WS.org (2007)

39. Zimmermann, O., Wegmann, L., Koziolek, H., Goldschmidt, T.: Architectural decision guidance across projects. In: Proceedings of IEEE/IFIP WICSA (2015)

The PDEng Program on Software Technology
Experience Report on a Doctorate Level Architecture Training Program

Ad T. M. Aerts[✉] and Yanja Dajsuren

Eindhoven University of Technology, 5600 MB Eindhoven, The Netherlands
{a.t.m.aerts,y.dajsuren}@tue.nl

Abstract. Attention for software architecture in higher education used to be limited to a few (or a single) courses in the later years of a Master program. In this paper we share our experience on a unique educational program in the Netherlands in which education and training on architecture is an integrated theme: the PDEng Software Technology program. The paper provides background information for the program focusing on its history and demand from industry. The program design adhering to the European Qualification Level (EQF) level 8 while satisfying industrial requirements is presented in some detail. The way we evaluate and monitor the quality of the program by Dutch government, industry partners, and alumni is discussed. In sharing the experience of the past 30 years of training architects and designers, the program has dealt with many changes and complexities on both academia and industry.

Keywords: Software architecture education · Software architecture training · PDEng program · Software technology

1 Introduction

Society in general and industry in particular are faced with rapid developments that pose tremendous challenges. From a technical point of view we observe that systems (e.g., consumer products) are becoming more and more complex. We also see that they are becoming increasingly more interconnected ([23] and references therein). From a business point of view, we are not only confronted with increasingly competitive markets, shorter time-to-market, and shrinking resources, but we are also more and more faced with multi-disciplinary products, international multi-site projects, and large-scale project teams with people from various national and professional cultures ([1]. The increase in complexity along several dimensions has the consequence that many products no longer are conceived and produced by a single person. Modern day products and services typically are realized by a (large) team of specialists under the leadership of one or a few high level professionals. Architects typically play a leading role in such a team on aspects such as connecting the problem and the solution space, keeping

© Springer Nature Switzerland AG 2020
A. Jansen et al. (Eds.): ECSA 2020, LNCS 12292, pp. 247–262, 2020.
https://doi.org/10.1007/978-3-030-58923-3_17

sight of the big picture, and guiding the team towards realization of a chosen solution ([16], Chap. 5).

Traditionally people develop themselves to the level of architect by being involved in a sequence of different projects in various roles and gaining the necessary experience under the mentoring and by the example of more experienced persons This is the Wellknown apprentice - journeyman - master approach. This educational model has been working fine for a long time, but in the current situation where innovations follow each other quickly and complexity rises accordingly, significantly more architects are needed to keep up the pace. The old one-on-one model no longer suffices: it takes ten to fifteen years of relevant projects in an industrial context to groom a fresh engineer to the level of architect. Moreover, once someone has become an architect, (s)he typically remains in that function for a limited number of years. This may be due, amongst other things to pressures on successful architects to join the company management, or to the fact that architects continue to evolve and at some point look for new challenges perhaps in a different organization or profession.

New educational approaches are needed to mature more technical talents more quickly to the level of architect. One approach is on-the-job architect training such as discussed in [12,20], where mature professionals (10 to 15 years of experience) are presented with background knowledge and skills and are stimulated to apply these in their current working situation. This provides them with a common frame of reference and a common language. But there is still a big gap with the level of fresh MSc graduates who may have followed Master courses on architecture and thus obtained a basic, useful awareness of architecture concepts and processes (see, e.g., [8,9], and [10] for illustrations in the case of Software Architecture).

In this paper we explain a different approach that is positioned between the two alternatives mentioned above and that is taken by the industry-oriented, doctorate level, technological designer programs [17] targeted at recent Master graduates. We will discuss in particular the technological designer program on Software Technology (ST) [21] that has been in existence for over 30 years.

The industrial landscape has changed quite a bit in the last 30 years. The role of software in products has changed from add-on to dominant. For example, new generation electric automobiles are sometimes referred to as "iPad on wheels". Neither existed as commercial products 30 years ago. Also the ST program has evolved during its existence to stay relevant. In this paper, we mostly focus on the characteristic features of later (post 2006) editions of the program.

2   General Background

In the early 1980's, the Dutch industry indicated a strong need for universities to educate and train motivated and talented people in such a way that they would have:

R1 knowledge of and experience with advanced, state-of-the-art methods and techniques for (software) engineering

R2 state-of-the-art (software) design and development project management competencies

R3 excellent social and communicative competencies

R4 a strong academic background like PhD's

R5 strong technical leadership competencies

Industry needed professionals who could immediately be deployed in the various companies (see also [18]).

Industry convinced the Dutch government of the urgency of their needs and the government invited the technology-oriented universities in the Netherlands to set up post-masters (i.e., EQF level 8 [5], NLQF level 8 [13]) education and training programs for motivated and talented university graduates who had already successfully completed their M.Sc. studies. Currently, there are nineteen of these two-year post-master (doctoral) technological designer programs, such as Data Science, Automotive Systems Design, Mechatronics Systems Design, Chemical Product Design, Design of Electrical Engineering Systems, and Software Technology (ST) operational in the Netherlands. These programs are, to our knowledge, unique in the world. They are organized in the 4TU.School for Technological Design, Stan Ackermans Institute [17]. The institute is a joint initiative of the universities of technology in the Netherlands. Recently, on Feb 13th, 2020 the 3000-th PDEng diploma was awarded. The educational models chosen by each of these designer programs differs according to the knowledge field of the program. In this paper we concentrate on the Computer Science field, addressed by the ST program.

The PDEng Software Technology program was founded in 1988 as the sixth technological designer program and started its first edition in 1990. Every year up to 20 trainees are appointed. By now it has almost delivered the impressive number of 500 graduates.

In contrast to the situation with regular B.Sc. and M.Sc. programs, and in line with the PhD programs, candidates cannot simply register or enroll in these programs, but they need to apply for admission (similar to PhD positions). Only after a strong selection process are a small number of candidates (trainees) actually allowed to participate in these programs. This procedure adds to the level of talent and motivation of our candidates. To emphasize the importance and relevance of these programs for Dutch industry, the trainees are salaried employees of the respective universities. Upon successfully completing the program, they are awarded a Professional Doctorate in Engineering (PDEng) degree, emphasizing the fact that they have outstanding qualifications after finishing their education and training program. Industry appreciates the high level of our graduates, none of whom are unwillingly without a fitting job upon graduation.

3   PDEng Program Design

The program is set up to supply a Bologna third cycle education [5] that is focused on an integral approach to building knowledge, and design and professional skills for a software architect profession. It aims at delivering young professionals who are well on their way to become Software Architects. As the program is to help reach that goal fully, it promotes a self-directing and learning attitude. The required elements of a software architect profession are illustrated in Fig. 1.

As illustrated in Fig. 1, the required elements of a Software Architect profession include among others Professional Societies such as Software Architecture scientific community, national and international associations, Code of ethics, Competence definitions adhering to comprehensive Body of Knowledge namely SWEBOK, PMBOK as well as Software Architecture Body of Knowledge (SABOK) [4] and Architecture Competency Framework (ACF) [3] defined by the ST management (currently proprietary). PDEng ST degree defines that individuals master defined competencies following the education and training offered by the ST program. As such a number of educational elements has been chosen that in an integrated fashion promote the growth of the trainees to the desired exit level. For instance, the curriculum contains a number of courses and workshops that focus on the explanation of a selected set of core concepts in a certain domain that are applied directly on representative problem instances to give the trainees not only insight into the abstract version of the concept but also into the practical application to solve a (particular type of) problem. The meta goals of this approach are to instill a methodical way of exploring new domains, which is the basis of a structured way of independent learning and promoting the ability of translating abstract concepts into practical solutions and reversely, abstracting from a practical, industrial problem (instance) to a more abstract formulation and relating this to (recent) research results.

Another characteristic feature of the program, in support of promoting the awareness and experience with technological leadership and management and control of software processes, follows from the fact that the development of industrial software is done in teams, many of the activities during courses and training and all activities during the projects are done in teams, small or large.

Since the time for learning is so short we do not have any pure elements in the program that only contribute knowledge or design of professional skills in isolation.

3.1   Engineer, Designer, or Architect?

In order to position the program more clearly, we briefly describe our nomenclature for the various functions in industry. The nomenclature is schematic and is only intended to delineate the path of growth we intend the trainees to follow. It reflects to some extent the function hierarchy in industry. The entry level for the program is that of Software Engineer. A software engineer can handle all phases of the software development life cycle, from problem description and requirements to deployment, as an independent professional. A software engineer typically will work on software projects with a complexity that one person can handle independently within a year or less. When he or she is a member of a team the software engineer typically is responsible for a well specified task or module. Because of the coverage of most of the phases of the software development

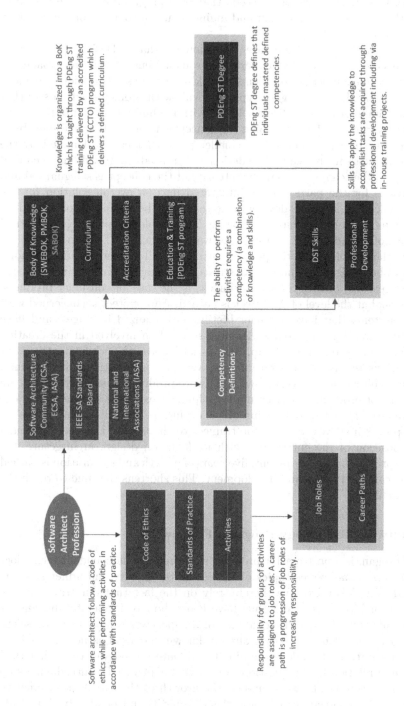

Fig. 1. Model of a software architect profession. Adapted from IEEE Model of Profession [14].

life cycle, this function clearly exceeds that of a programmer whose activities are mostly limited to the creation and maintenance of code, according to given specifications.

The next major level of software professional is that of Designer. A software designer exceeds the level of an experienced software engineer by the capacity to deal with more complicated problems. In addition to possessing more advanced problem solving skills, a designer typically deals with problems with a size that require a team in order to realize a solution within a limited amount of time. The designer is responsible for developing the concept for the solution of the problem and then refining this concept into smaller parts that can be handled by the software engineers in the team. The designer then needs to provide the technical leadership to the team such that the integrity of the concept is safeguarded and the solutions for the parts can be integrated into an overall solution for the initial problem. A software development team will be composed of specialists from various areas of software technology. The problem typically is concerned with a one-of-a-kind or first-of-a-kind software product (TRL levels 2–5 [7]).

When the complexity of the problem increases still further, because the solution has to be realized in a number of subsequent versions (for instance for time or budget reasons) or in several variations as is the case for consumer products, a professional at the level of Architect is needed. An architect is concerned with software systems that have a longer lifetime, are realized in stages, and have a strategic value for a company. Architects are often involved in the creation of the company product roadmap, and as such have to coordinate the work of the various teams working on different versions or variations of a product. Software architects are concerned with software products; system architects are responsible for products requiring multidisciplinary expertise and including also hardware (see [23] for an impression of the evolution of architects' activities).

The program strives to bring the trainees to the level of Designer. Through the composition of the curriculum with its focus on design, architecture and personal/professional development, five years of growth and maturation is packed into two years of training and development. This shortens the time to reach the level of architect.

3.2   Software Technology Program Framework

The ST progam is a post-master program that prepares independent technological designers. It addresses topics of increasing complexity and adheres to the EQF and NLQF Level 8. We thereby rely on the fact that our trainees have completed an MSc degree and thus have learnt how to formulate and answer scientific questions (under the guidance of a supervisor) and access the scientific literature to identify what is already known and what is not. They have developed a critical attitude to be able to evaluate the relevance of what they find there in relation to the question(s) they try to answer. By introducing step by step more complexity we stimulate the growth of their analytical, creative and critical skills so they can handle this complexity independently [R4]. PhD candidates experience a similar growth to become independent researchers who can create new theoretical knowledge independently.

As mentioned above, development of professional qualities, such as social and communicative competencies [R3], strong technical leadership competencies [R5], and strong project management competencies [R2], an important part of the program is done as a group. To facilitate this the program has only one starting date such that team processes can start from day one and be continued up to the graduation project. A group may be the entire group or a part of it. This way the trainees get insight into what is needed to make a good team and how to build one. In a team of 15–20 persons some structure may be introduced to provide sufficient roles (professional/technical, leading/supporting) to practice responsibility, communication, and action learning. For instance, a leadership role can be given to a trainee who has advanced technical knowledge in the problem domain, and therefore can look further ahead, which gives an advantage. If the problem domain is new to everybody, a trainee who has more advanced learning goals in communication and leadership (see below) is given the task.

The significant amount of time spent working in teams is productive for establishing a community of learners that will support inquiry learning [2]. In particular the first project, where everybody becomes visible to the others, in terms of what they know and can do is seminal in this. A safe environment emerges where knowledge is shared, complex problems are solved collaboratively and at the appropriate level, alternatives are generated and challenged, new insights are gained, communicated, criticized and provided with a sound rationale. This may take several iterations where new insights are used to create more complete solutions. Here a tight community of trusted peers is created that will endure as professional network long after graduation [R3, R4].

The trainees make a personal development plan in which they itemize which competency they want to strengthen at some point during the program and set a level they want to reach. Depending on the role they get assigned, they pick out appropriate learning goals to practice and realize, and reflect on the degree of success they reached after the project. They get feedback from their teachers and coaches before, during and after the project. In this way the trainees take control of their own development.

Industry is a dynamic environment, and so is academia. Importance of certain domains rises and wanes. One cannot teach all present and future subjects in two years time, and assume the acquired knowledge will be sufficient for an entire career. Insights progress. (A witness of this is that IEEE has made the SWEBOK guide as of version 3 a living document [19].) This means that in addition to teaching specific knowledge about some topic or training required skills, e.g., to be able to do particular project, meta skills such as the ability to quickly identify relevant/necessary knowledge and acquire it as well as the ability to master the corresponding skills to use it need to get sufficient attention. The graduate has to become a self-propelled, reflective learner who knows his/her level of ability and can organize the proper setting to acquire the required new knowledge or skill [R1]. To be able to do this we assume that most of the knowledge documented in SWEBOK is known by our trainees (and we test this in the application procedure) and we can build on this.

The training projects typically last a number of weeks, from 7–10 weeks. These are relatively short projects. The time typically is long enough to cover the requirements and design aspects of the problem and build a demonstrator that answers some important questions. After all, we do not need the trainees to practice their engineering skills: they are certified engineers to start with. This advantage makes it possible to introduce increasing complexity into the project, and cover a number of new knowledge domains from which they learn how to pick up new knowledge quickly. The duration of these projects is relatively short. This has the consequence that the pressure is high, tasks have to be performed in parallel and good communication is of the essence. This requires good organisation and a properly prepared starting point.

During the last ten months of our program our trainees are out-placed individually at a company to participate in a relevant project and get responsibility for a part of it. This way they get on-site experience and provide an added-value to that project in terms of a transfer of state-of-the-art methods and techniques, tools, best-practices, and other relevant competencies, as well as knowledge. These projects are paid for, adding to the responsibility of the trainee (and the supervisor). The trainees are daily supervised by a software/system architect from the host company as well as a TU/e scientific staff. The trainees are given ample opportunity to improve their competencies for a future career as a (senior) software designer or software architect.

Program Elements. In order to foster the abilities mentioned above, several ingredients have to be present in the program. Our training program consists of a number of strongly related courses (including training) and projects that focus on the various aspects related to

- technical and technology issues [R1]
- management and process issues [R2]
- professional, social, and communicative issues relevant for the project-based team-oriented design and development of software for resource-constrained software intensive systems and interconnected and intelligent software systems. [R3, R4, R5]

Element Details. In the context of the first category, our training program includes training primarily related to the early phases of design, such as usage modeling, requirements engineering, system thinking, software and hardware architecture, object-oriented analysis and modeling, artificial intelligence and some training related to relevant domain specific knowledge, such as language technology, system validation and concepts of distributed systems.

In the context of the second category, our training program includes short training's primarily related to controlling the design and development process, such as project management, agile software development, configuration management, quality assurance, and quality control.

In the context of the third category, our training program includes a personal/professional development program, including assessments, short awareness training's, and reflection sessions to develop a learning attitude, related to the relevant non-technical competencies necessary for effective and efficient communication and behavior, such as presentation techniques, meeting techniques, designer competencies, teamwork, discussion and negotiation techniques, decision making techniques, and leadership techniques.

The program covers sustainable competencies such as the various relevant aspects of systems architecting and software design, including technical aspects, business and management aspects, and professional development aspects. It also covers training/courses that add domain knowledge that is required for the projects (see below). This course and workshop-oriented training is supplemented with several other elements such as excursions to companies and seminars from industry partners and alumni. These activities help to acquaint the trainees with the role of software in the high tech industries and to give them a view on the state of the art in the industrial application of new software methods and technologies in practice. The training program provides the theoretical background, supported by small exercises, for end terms R1 through R5. The practical foundation for the end terms R1 through R5 is laid in the project part.

Our program therefore includes, as discussed above two kinds of projects, each with a different focus. The first kind of project is the in-house project. These projects are meant to provide an environment for the trainees to learn to work in a team and experience the different kinds of roles, structures, and communication needed to make a team successful. They also serve to let the trainees experience working with a real customer, dealing with real timing constraints, and other realistic projects, such as ill-defined problems, incomplete information, and multidisciplinary teams. For a recent example, see [15]. The multidisciplinary character arises naturally by the choice of industry problems from different problem domains in which the software problems are situated in a mechanical, electrical, physics or business context. At least one project is in the automotive or mechatronic domain, which allows our trainees to collaborate with trainees from the Automotive and Mechatronic System Design PDEng programs in a multidisciplinary team on a system engineering problem.

During the second kind of project, the trainees are out-placed for ten months to one of our industry partners to participate in an authentic, operational on-site project. During such a project the trainee has to start and manage a process to get from ill-defined wishes and needs to concrete results. These projects are usually related to a feasibility analysis, a proof-of-concept, or first-of-a-kind development (TRL levels 2–5 [7]). They may include an engineering sub-project that can be delegated to a group of third year Bachelor students. The trainee then acts as customer for this subproject and integrates the results into his own project. This ten month project is basically the concluding proof-of-ability.

The precise content of the program elements varies from year to year. Since we collaborate with industry and research partners to create win-win situations, projects are never repeated. Our partners propose projects from which they can learn about new methods or research results, and invest their time to define a suitable context in which these questions can be answered. In case of the in-house project we make sure that the trainees are supplied knowledge about the core concepts needed for the project. This can be done by rescheduling a short course or workshop by industrial experts or by inviting one of the research staff members to give an introduction. In this way, all trainees have a sufficient level of knowledge of the core concepts at the start of the project, which means the (rel-atively short) available time can be spent efficiently on identifying and resolving the problems particular to the project and translate theory into practice. During the project the teachers involved in the courses double as coaches, supporting the application of the theory in practice.

Since the introductions are meant to provide a solid foothold in the domain of the project, and the trainees all have good experience in doing research, work on the project can be done in parallel by the various trainees, with regular syn-chronisation of the knowledge at the team level. The trainees take ownership of the project and organize and execute it independently. Various roles are iden-tified and assigned to individuals such as project lead, product owner, team lead, system/software architect, designer, tester, developer, and integrator. The assignments rotate over the projects so that everybody gets to experience as many different roles as there are projects. This way of working produces much valued results.

Trainees come from all over the world. This implies that there is a large diversity in culture, knowledge, experience and skills in each group. These dif-ferences provide a rich source of knowledge as some trainees have more advanced knowledge on some topics than others. Such an advantage puts the trainee in a leading role, whereas he/she may be in a learning position on another topic or in another domain. Trainees thus learn quite a bit from each other and this peer teaching and learning is the best way to learn something fast. See also Ref. [2].

In varying the particular focus of the courses and training for a given gener-ation attention is paid to the coverage of the end terms, such that the balance of the program between the various learning targets is preserved.

4   Quality Evaluation

The quality of the program is monitored at several levels by the Dutch govern-ment, by the industry partners and by its alumni.

4.1   Certification of the Program

Since the program is an official university degree program (PDEng), it is certified by the government every five years, similar to the Bachelor, Master and Research programs. The certification procedure is carried out by the CCTO (Certification Committee for Technological Designer programs), an independent certification body, instituted by the Dutch government and hosted by the Dutch Engineering Association (KIVI).

Every five years, an overview is put together that demonstrates the quality of the program, in terms of the content of the program and the processes that are put in place to monitor the quality of the trainees and the teaching staff. This overview together with supporting documents is submitted for review by a committee appointed by the CCTO that is composed of representatives from industry and academia and is chaired by a professor from another university and supported by a secretary from the CCTO. This committee may request additional documentation, and visits the program to interview selected trainees, teaching staff and the program management. Based upon their findings they recommend the CCTO to certify the program, certify it conditionally or withdraw certification. The ST program has passed the certification procedure always unconditionally, the last time in 2018.

4.2 Industry Feedback

The program has instituted an Industrial Advisory Board (EAC) that convenes twice a year to review the performance and plans of the program. The board is composed of representatives of the industry from the Brainport area and industrial research institutes (TNO). The program management presents the achievements, concerns and any initiatives they want to take to the board for scrutiny, suggestions and possibly approval.

4.3 Alumni

The program is also rated every few years by the alumni association of the program in a survey in terms of value for the alumni career and possible program improvements or adaptations. This alumni association, called xOOTIc, was founded by the first generation. At that time the program was called OOTI, a Dutch abbreviation for Designers Program for Technological Informatics. The alumni association was called xOOTIc (pronounced as "exotic") for ex-OOTI community. The idea was to keep in touch with each other and the program by building a network of alumni.

The survey of the careers and professional experiences of the alumni gathers feedback for both the association, the EAC, and the ST program itself. In 2009 the questionnaire went online. From that point on, only the number of completed questionnaires are known. There was a survey in 2018, but the results of this one are not yet available for public. We see that the percentage returned in the last ten years is in the range of 30%–40%. For comparison, the number of alumni in 1993 was 22, that at the start of 2015 was 350.

Of the first three surveys only some summary information is available. The questionnaire's from 1998 to 2015 provide detailed information about a number of concerns. The questions asked change over time, in number, e.g., in 1998 53 questions needed to be answered, in 2012 57, and in 2015 59, but also in content. One of the consistently asked questions is the Job function. The answers are shown in Table 1.

Table 1. Job function percentage

Year	% SoftE	% SoftA	% SysE	% SysA	% Researcher	% Remainder
1998	26	14	7		17	36
2000	31	19	9	4	12	26
2002	30	26	4	4	9	27
2004	30	26	4	4	9	27
2006	26	17	5	17	12	23
2009	45	15	1	7	9	24
2012	25	11	9	14	20	21
2015	30	17	4	11	17	22

The abbreviations in Table 1 stand for Software Engineer (SoftE), Software Architect (SoftA), System Engineer (SysE), System Architect (SysA), Researcher (both academic and industrial), and Remainder that covers jobs such as Director or Business Owner, Department Head, Team Leader, and Project Manager. Note that we use anonymous survey results. We cannot make statements about individual careers, which would involve relating surveys from subsequent years. The survey's do include a question about the ambition of the graduates, which gives an indication of the desired career path.

One general conclusion is that a fair fraction of the graduates from the ST program reach architect functions at some point in their career. On average 18% of the graduates hold a software architect position in the various surveys, and 9% a system architect position, together more than 26% of the graduates who participate in the survey. (Note that in 1998, system engineers and system architects counted together for 7%.) These positions are not reached as a starting level. Many graduates start out as a software engineer or designer but reach the architect level sooner than, e.g., peers who start an industry career directly after getting their MSc degree and thus have a head start of two years. We used this observation in our hiring campaigns. Not all graduates go for architect functions; some choose are invited to a different career path. Note for instance the sizeable fraction (19%) of graduates holding research (academic or industrial) positions.

We see in Table 1 that the percentage of ST graduates reaching, e.g., the architect level is not monotonous. One reason for this is that the group of participants changes between surveys; some participants join, others leave the survey group. Also, after having been architect for a number of years, ST graduates move on to other functions, such as director or business owner, manager, researcher (PhD) or lecturer.

Starting in the 2006 survey, a section of questions were included on the topic "Relevance of PDEng in your career" that were meant to give feedback to the ST program and the Industrial Advisory Board. One question was: "Considering what you know now, would you still have done the PDEng program?" (Answer: yes or no). Another question was: "Do you feel that following the PDEng program has given you an advantage over other people with a similar background (age, studies, etc.) but who did not follow the PDEng program?". The answers included: "Yes, because I am more technically skilled" and "Yes, because I learn new things faster" (columns 3 and 4 respectively in Table 2). From column 2 in Table 2 it appears that 95% of the respondents consider enrolling into the program time well spent. We find a good deal of goodwill among our graduates for the program. Many of them keep in touch with program to offer, e.g., training of final projects or lectures about topics they are specialists on.

Table 2. Trainee satisfaction

Year	Do it again?	Tech skills	Fast learner (%)
2006	98	35	24
2009	97	58	43
2012	95	61	33
2015	98	46	51

The two aspects of the training they received in Table 2 consistently come out on top. They are statements about the fact that the program educates at a more advanced level than, e.g., MSc courses do. The first one may be an indication that the skills taught and practised in the training project are more relevant to their working situation than those of their colleagues. The second one may be an indication that the attention paid in the personal development courses to promoting a learning attitude is paying off as well. Both statements are supported by feedback on courses valued most and recommendations for new courses that also are part of the surveys. This is valuable input. In considering replacement of certain courses by others we keep in mind the coverage of the contribution of program elements to the end-terms.

5   Related Work and Discussion

The view that architects, to be successful, should not only be good at dealing with what and how to document architectures but also at sharing and explaining the architecture with a variety of stakeholders, and getting their support for finding the right balance between functional and non-functional requirements and the way to bridge the gap between the problem space and the solution space, became accepted around the beginning of this century (see [8,9] and references therein). The ensuing discussion, however, was constrained by the focus on how to teach this in an often single Bachelor or Master course setting. In [18] a professional Master program course is described based on SWEBOK2 engineering profile and includes a yearlong real life project, which is intended for students with at least one year of industry experience.

Since the architect role involves so many different aspects that have to get attention, and requires a certain readiness of the students to appreciate what is offered, only a (simplified) part will get across in an isolated course. It requires a multidisciplinary team of teachers and coaches to help with the various aspects to make the students aware of the learning opportunities and how they can handle them in an effective way. This takes time and can be done in a two year ST program. The students should try out roles and practice. Failing is an option, and a source of learning, as long as the same failures are not repeated, because that would constitute an inability to learn.

In [22] van Vliet reflects on teaching a Software Engineering course and formulates traps. Trap 1 reads: "A Software Engineering course needs an industrial project". Van Vliet speaks about a second year Bachelor SE course and he is right when he remarks that second year Computer Science students are not mature enough to appreciate ill-defined, inconsistent problem descriptions and assignments, inherent to industrial projects or the possibility of more than one "good" solution. These students need to focus on mastering the basic techniques in a more unambiguous setting. They need to learn to build a system correctly. In the Master phase they will be confronted with still mild forms of vagueness (see [9]). In contrast, in our case the trainees have all gone through the Master phase, where in the course of their thesis work they had to make a rather vague (open) question more precise and pick out one of the possibilities to answer. They are now mature enough to deal with authentic situations under real-life circumstances and corresponding uncertainties and challenges, which will be their future working situation. For this we need industry projects, and several of them. They need to learn to build the right system, i.e., they need to deliver the system that solves the customer's problem. It is remarkable to see how our industry partners can steer the projects by adding, changing or reducing the problem statement and thus ensure that a do-able project results and the trainees can savour a successful project. After all, this is a big motivator.

Muller lists the challenges mature professionals (10–15 years of experience) have to overcome during his course in systems architecting [11]. Galster and Angelov comment on the issues encountered in teaching architecture [6]. In the ST program the challenges occur as well (we mentioned among others the abstraction and integration issues). The time period, in which the modeling can be practiced with feedback from coaches, is advantageous in the ST case since it allows for multiple iterations. Also, most of our trainees are "fresh out of school" and their modeling education during the Masters is still there to apply. Some of it is reactivated by means of the modeling and architecting courses. In the projects it becomes practical and its consequences tangible. We introduce multidisciplinary aspects into the curriculum by collaborating with the Automotive and Mechatronics System Design PDEng programs in joint projects.

6   Conclusions and Future Work

In this paper we have presented the PDEng Technological Designer program on Software Technology (ST). As discussed above, the ST progam is unique in a sense that it is a doctorate level degree program to train software architects and designers for industry. It has been running for over 30 years now, with good results. One notable best practice in the last 25 years has been the collaboration with industry partners who have provided the program with innovative projects that were well suited to prepare the trainees for their future working environment.

Over the past 30 years many things have changed. As the program is positioned on the interface between academia and industry, two dynamic worlds, it has had to deal with changes and complexities on both sides and align. On the academic side, the program started after the change of the engineering education from a five to a four year program. Around 2000 a five year curriculum with a Bachelor-Master structure was introduced. Around this time the influx of trainees from abroad became more important than the influx from trainees with a Dutch educational background. On the industry side new methods and technologies developed that became mainstream and durable. These had to be incorporated into the program. This led to new courses, several of which were later adapted and incorporated in the Master program. Industry products became more complex. Automation claimed a bigger share and the corresponding training projects required appropriate teaching before the start to make them doable.

In view of the past evolution, it is quite certain that the program will continue to adapt in order to keep aligned with both academia and industry. The challenge is to stay abreast of developments and stay relevant by educating high level young professionals that can drive innovation in industry. We hope that similar programs can be implemented in other industrialized countries.

Acknowledgements. It is a pleasure to thank Harold Weffers, Dieter Hammer, Martin Rem, Johan Lukkien and Mark van den Brand for many interesting past and present discussions on the various topics in the paper.

References

1. Aerts, A.T.M., Goossenaerts, J.B.M., Hammer, D.K., Wortmann, J.C.: Architectures in context: on the evolution of business, application software, and ICT platform architectures. In: Information & Management, vol. 41, no. 6, pp. 781–794. North-Holland (2004)
2. de Boer, R.C., Farenhorst, R., van Vliet, H.: A community of learners approach to software architecture education. In: 22nd Conference on Software Engineering Education and Training, CSEET 2009, pp. 190–197 (2009)
3. Dajsuren, Y.: PDEng Software Technology - Architecture Competency Framework (proprietary) (2017)
4. Dajsuren, Y.: PDEng Software Technology - Software Architecture Body of Knowledge (SABOK) (proprietary) (2017)
5. EQF Advisory Group: EQF: Descriptors defining levels in the European Qualifications Framework (2020). https://ec.europa.eu/ploteus/content/descriptors-page
6. Galster, M., Angelov, S.: What makes teaching software architecture difficult? In: IEEE/ACM 38th International Conference on Software Engineering Companion, (ICSE-C), pp. 356–359 (2016)

7. Heder, M.: From NASA to EU: the evolution of the TRL scale in Public Sector Innovation. Innov. J. Public Sect. Innov. J. **22**(2), 1–23 (2017)
8. Jaccheri, M.: Tales from a Software Achitecture Course Project (2002). http://www.idi.ntnu.no/letizia/swarchi/eCourse.html
9. Lago, P., van Vliet, H.: Teaching a course on software architecture. In: Proceedings 18th Conference on Software Engineering Education and Training, CSEET 2005, pp. 35–42 (2005)
10. Mannisto, T., Savolainen, J., Myllarniemi, V.: Teaching software architecture design. In: Seventh Working IEEE/IFIP Conference on Software Architecture, (WICSA 2008), pp. 117–124 (2008)
11. Muller, G.: Challenges in teaching conceptual modeling for systems architecting. In: Jeusfeld, M.A., Karlapalem, K. (eds.) ER 2015. LNCS, vol. 9382, pp. 317–326. Springer, Cham (2015). https://doi.org/10.1007/978-3-319-25747-1_31
12. Muller, G.: Experiences of teaching systems architecting. In: Proceedings of the International Conference on Systems Engineering, no. 14. INCOSE, Wiley Online, Toulouse, June 2004
13. Nationaal Coördinatiepunt NLQF: The Dutch qualifications framework (NLQF) (2020). https://nlqf.nl/
14. PEAB-EIT: Model of a profession (2019). https://www.computer.org/volunteering/boards-and-committees/professional-educational-activities/model-of-a-profession
15. Roos, N.: Using AI to streamline remote communication in healthcare (2019). https://bits-chips.nl/artikel/using-ai-to-streamline-remote-communication-in-healthcare/
16. Rozanski, N., Woods, E.: Software Systems Architecture: Working With Stakeholders Using Viewpoints and Perspectives. Addison-Wesley, Boston (2005, 2012)
17. SAI: 4TU.School of Technological Design Stan Ackermans Institute (2020). https://www.4tu.nl/sai/en/
18. Shaw, M., Herbsleb, J., Ozkaya, I., Root, D.: Deciding what to design: closing a gap in software engineering education. In: Inverardi, P., Jazayeri, M. (eds.) ICSE 2005. LNCS, vol. 4309, pp. 28–58. Springer, Heidelberg (2006). https://doi.org/10.1007/11949374_3
19. SWEBOK-V3: Software Engineering Book of Knowledge, ISO/IEC TR 19759:2015 (2015). https://www.computer.org/education/bodies-of-knowledge/software-engineering
20. TNO-ESI, van den Aker, J.: Software Architecture (2020). https://www.esi.nl/innovation-support/competence-development/courses/software-architecture.dot
21. TU/e: PDEng Software Technology program (2020). https://www.tue.nl/softwaretechnology
22. van Vliet, H.: Reflections on software engineering education. IEEE Softw **2006**, 55–61 (2006)
23. Woods, E.: Software architecture in a changing world. IEEE Softw. **33**(6), 94–97 (2016)

**Experiences and Learnings
from Industrial Case Studies**

Architectural Concerns for Digital Twin of the Organization

Mauro Caporuscio[1]([✉]), Farid Edrisi[1], Margrethe Hallberg[2],
Anton Johannesson[3], Claudia Kopf[2], and Diego Perez-Palacin[1]

[1] Linnaeus University, Växjö, Sweden
{mauro.caporuscio,farid.edrisi,diego.perez}@lnu.se
[2] Scania AB, Oskarshamn, Sweden
{grethe.hallberg,claudia.kopf}@scania.se
[3] Virtual Manufacturing AB, Göteborg, Sweden
anton.johannessone@virtual.se

Abstract. Employing a Digital Twin of the Organization would help enterprises to change and innovate, thus enhancing their organization's sustainability. However, the lack of engineering best practices for developing and operating a Digital Twin of the Organization makes it difficult for enterprises to fully benefit from it. Many companies are currently investigating the potential use of it, but available solutions are often context-dependent or system-specific, and challenging to adapt, extend, and reuse. Therefore, digitalization is perceived as a slow, resource-demanding, and extremely expensive process whose outcome is uncertain. To this extent, enterprises seek solutions allowing them to gently introduce a Digital Twin of the Organization into their organization and to evolve it according to the changing needs and situations. This paper reports a first attempt on architecting a Digital Twin of an Organization, and discusses some architectural concerns to be addressed in order to facilitate its development and evolution.

1 Introduction

The digitalization of industry is a grand challenge. The advent of Cyber-Physical Systems (CPS) combined with Data-Driven (DD) technologies creates the necessary infrastructure for the 4th industrial revolution, where machines and humans are interconnected in sociotechnical systems, which are business or mission-critical [5]. Indeed, most sociotechnical systems are *organizational systems* which support enterprises to achieve their goals by explicitly including all those artifacts, processes and people needed to run the business. In this context, having an accurate digital representation of the organization would facilitate the decision-making processes in the value chain by providing (*i*) an aggregated view of the elements affecting a decision, and (*ii*) a prediction of the decision outcome: namely, a *Digital Twin of the Organization* (DTO) [11].

A Digital Twin of the Organization allows for representing all the elements and connections of a organizational system in virtual models, which can be

© Springer Nature Switzerland AG 2020
A. Jansen et al. (Eds.): ECSA 2020, LNCS 12292, pp. 265–280, 2020.
https://doi.org/10.1007/978-3-030-58923-3_18

perpetually simulated and analyzed to achieve *continuous assessment* and *optimization* of the organization. Employing a well-defined DTO is an important asset in positioning new developments within the context of existing processes and other assets of an organization, as it helps in identifying necessary and/or opportunistic changes. Indeed, good DTO practices can help organizations to change and innovate, thus enhancing the organizations *sustainability*.

However, the digitalization process is far from being fast, inexpensive, or effortless. The lack of engineering best practices for developing and operating DTOs makes it difficult for industry to fully benefit from them. Many companies are currently investigating the potential use of DTOs, but provided solutions are often context-dependent or system-specific, and challenging to adapt, extend and reuse. Indeed, making optimal business/design decisions and selecting the right technology (given the considerable number of DTO, CPS, and DD technologies and platforms available) able to satisfy both current and future needs is challenging. The following main question, raised by industry, should be addressed:

IQ: *"Digitalization can't happen overnight, but should be a long step-by-step journey into the future from where we start today. How to gently introduce a DTO satisfying current needs, and then evolve it according to changing situations?"*

In fact, the adoption of DTO is, as we describe above, not straightforward and the many challenges prevent organizations from deciding to move into and invest in DTOs and related technology. Some decisions, among others, are: (1) How to incorporate CPS, DD and DTO technologies into an existing organization? (2) How to benefit from incorporating DTO in products and/or production? (3) How to define and achieve a long-term strategy for adopting DTO? (4) How to access and analyze data in real-time and enact changes based on decision support mechanisms? (5) When the organization executes structural changes, how to systematically evolve the DTO to reflect these changes?

To this extent, engineering best practices suggest the exploitation of architectures (at different levels of abstraction) to capture different aspects of the system under development. Indeed, separation of concerns (e.g., structure from behavior) improves the design and eases the maintenance of the system.

In this paper, we report about a first attempt made in architecting and developing a DTO, and evolving it to accommodate changes occurred at the business level. Evolvability is investigated through development. Specifically, we first investigate how to employ a DTO in an already-in-place manufacturing process (representing only a small part of the whole production system), then we evolve it by developing and integrating, new features. The paper details the development process, and pinpoints a set of concerns to be confronted with when architecting a DTO that is expected to evolve overtime according to the organizations requirements. From the experience, it emerges the need for defining an architectural framework for facilitating DTO development and evolution.

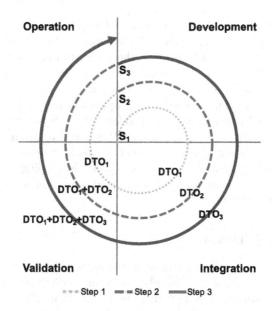

Fig. 1. Incremental approach

The paper is organized as follows. Section 2 reports our experience in implementing and evolving a DTO for a given industrial case study, whereas Sect. 3 pinpoints and discusses some architectural concerns to be addressed in order to facilitate the DTO evolution. Section 4 discusses related work, and Sect. 5 conclude the paper by addressing future research directions.

2 Industrial Case Study

This Section describes the first steps towards the digitalization of an existing production line. It provides details on the DTO development, and some examples about how the organization can benefit from the DTO.

2.1 Digitalization Journey

The digitalization journey in the organization requires the construction of the DTO focusing on its evolvability. *Evolvability* is a design principle that takes into account the future change and growth of the system. Within the incremental digitalization process, it serves as a measure of the ability to extend and modify DTO upon the introduction of new activities to be digitalized or new requirements to be fulfilled. We use the evolvability measure to assess the level of effort necessary to evolve the DTO and put it into operation.

As a key requirement for a DTO is to mimic the structure of the organization that produces it, we leverage on *Enterprise Architecture* [20] (EA) to describe the different aspects of a DTO. In fact, EA is by default positioned to play a key role in realizing a DTO, as it embeds all the *principles* and *models* used in the realization of an organization: (*i*) the *Organizational Architecture* (OA) and *Business architecture* (BA) provide the structural and behavioral models, respectively, whereas (*ii*) the *Information Architecture* (IA) provides the data representing the actual status of the organization.

We adopt the incremental development approach in Fig. 1, where each evolution step is divided into four phases: *development, integration, validation*, and *operation*. As illustrative example, consider that we start from a subsystem S_1 that has already been digitalized into DTO_1. We incrementally digitalize the organization by taking another subsystem S_2 and developing its DTO_2, implementing the necessary integration of digitalized subsystems and validating it, resulting in $DTO_1 + DTO_2$.

2.2   Organization Description

The organization is a supplier of articles in the automotive industry. It manufactures a product line with a large number of variants (≥ 1000). The automotive industry supply chain requires Just-In-Time production. This requirement prevents from, for instance, producing to a buffer. We focus only on one of the different activities, namely the manufacturing of a specific part P of the final product. To keep the appropriate synchronization among all parts of a product in the whole assembly line, there is an additional requirement for P: units must leave their production line in the same sequence as they were ordered.

Figure 2 illustrates the OA/BA representing the production line P according to the notation introduced in [20], which consists of two workstations: Workstation A (WA) manufactures the product and it is highly automated with two machines working in parallel (WA1 and WA2). An operator must supervise the machines and must change their configuration between orders of a different variant of P. Workstation D (WD) packages the product. It also has two machines working in parallel (WD1 and WD2), but it is less automatized and requires two operators continuously working on it, one on each machine. The business process is supported by a legacy in-house software for Enterprise Resource Planning (ERP), which constitutes the IA. Data about both the products and the production activities is collected by the operators, which are required to check the products (e.g., for identifying defects), to observe the process events (e.g., for identifying deviations in the production plan), and to report all their observations into the IA.

This section of the plant receives orders to produce P. Each order refers to a concrete variant v of P. An order specifies the number n of units to produce. The operator in WA will configure either WA1 or WA2 to produce n products P of variant v. When an order is received and both WA1 and WA2 are busy, it waits for its manufacturing turn in a queue. When the manufacturing in WA completes, P moves towards its packaging in WD. Operators in WD create packages containing up to 30 units. If both operators in WD are busy when P arrives for its packaging, then P joins a priority queue. The queue uses as

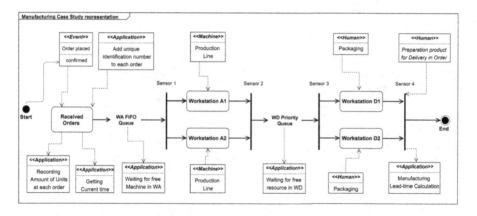

Fig. 2. OA/BA of the case study

priority the sequence number of the order. Older orders have more priority than newer orders, to help preserve the in-order delivery requirement.

The organization stakeholders (e.g., management and operators) want to digitalize this section of the plant. The reason is that they would like to know, in real time, the orders lead time, the utilization of resources, and the amount of work-in-progress in the line. They would also like to predict the near future of these three characteristics. These predictions will allow the sales department to give better estimations of the delivery time to the clients at the moment they are filling an order, and the production planning department can plan less disruptive maintenance of machinery.

2.3   DTO Development – Iteration 1

According to the IA, the monitorable data in the production line are: According to the IA, the monitorable data in the production line are:

- the moment when an order is placed, and its unique identifier ID;
- the type of variant v, and the number of units, n, to produce;
- the moment when an order ID enters WA;
- the moment when the units belonging to a given order ID are produced;
- the moment when the units enter WD;
- the moment when an order ID is packaged and ready to be delivered; and,
- the moment when an order ID is delivered.

Figure 3a shows the digitalization of the production line P based on the monitorable points. The model, developed using the Discrete Event System toolbox in Matlab/Simulink[1], shows the sequence of order arrival, waiting in queue for WA, execution in WA, waiting in queue for WD, execution in WD, and in order delivery. The last is modeled with a selection gate that controls the orders ID

---

[1] https://se.mathworks.com/solutions/discrete-event-simulation.html.

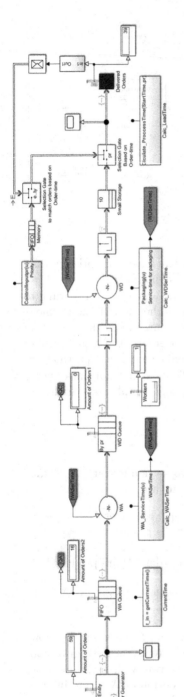

(a) Digital Twin of the Organization in the first iteration

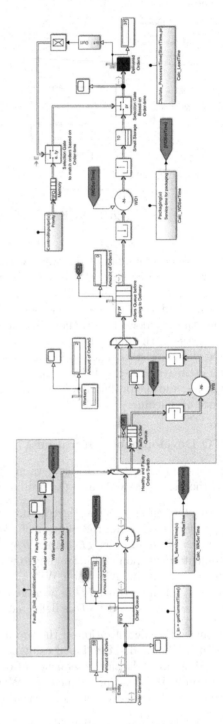

(b) Evolved Digital Twin of the Organization

Fig. 3. Digital twins of the organization (model for simulation) (Color figure online)

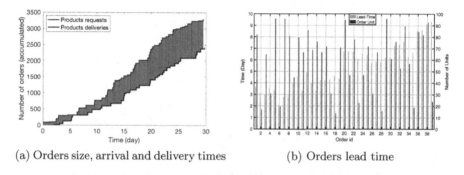

(a) Orders size, arrival and delivery times   (b) Orders lead time

Fig. 4. Observations from DTO (Color figure online)

and a small storage. The small storage stocks some orders if necessary until the order with the next ID to deliver is packaged in WD.

This DTO allows for observing the status of the plant –in terms of lead time of orders, utilization of workstations, amount of work-in-progress, products in queue waiting for an available workstation–, and simulating future scenarios.

Figure 4 shows this type of observations. The horizontal axis indicates the observation time, 30 days. Figure 4a shows the arrival (blue line) and delivery (black line) of orders along time, and the size of each order. In the last 30 days, 59 orders arrived to the production line, adding up 3303 units to produce. The blue area that is demarcated by these two lines exposes the work-in-progress in the line. The height of the blue area in each x value exposes the work-in-progress in the line in that moment.

Figure 4b illustrates the lead time of each order. The number of units to produce in a single order is variable in the interval [1]. Since the size of an order affects its lead time, Fig. 4b puts together a bar for the lead time of an order and a bar for the number of units n in the order.

2.4 DTO Development – Iteration 2 (Evolution)

The organization would like to predict more accurately the lead time and to estimate in real time what is the optimal task for an operator. To achieve these new goals, the organization needs to evolve its DTO.

The DTO evolution consists in providing a more realistic representation of what happens in the organization between the moment an unit leaves machines WA1 or WA2 and an order is ready for packaging. In the real production line, machines in WA do not always manufacture the units correctly. Sometimes they have defects and they need a subsequent rework before joining the queue for packaging. The rework is manually done, and requires one of the operators in WD. We refer to the new manual rework station as WB.

This evolved DTO will enable a more accurate estimation of the lead time of an order –coming from the explicit digitalization of WB– and a better understanding of the utilization of resources –coming from the more accurate repre-

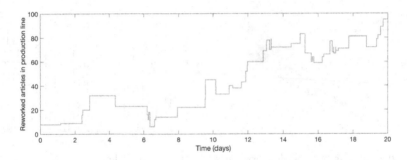

Fig. 5. Number of units in the production line that need rework

sentation of operators' tasks. In the first iteration in Sect. 2.3, the busy time of stations WD1 and WD2 also included the time that operators spent in the rework station. The separation of the operators' tasks into their actual work in WD and their work in WB enables a more accurate understanding of the busy time and service time of packaging activities in WD. Using this improved understanding, the DTO can assist the production planning in scheduling the optimal task for an operator in a given moment.

To gain this new information, it is necessary to first obtain new monitored data. This is achieved by connecting the quality sensors in the production line that inspect units for possible defects to their digitalized representation in the DTO. The operators gain awareness of defects at a glance since each quality sensor, upon the detection of a defect, sends a notification to a control panel and raises a short audible alarm. The DTO development in this phase includes that the notifications of each sensor are also sent to the DTO (the alarm is not). In case of defective unit, the DTO receives precise information of the necessary rework and, therefore, the expected lead time of its associated order is recalculated. This dynamic recalculation increases the accuracy of the lead time estimation. As soon as the quality sensors discover that an order will need a time-consuming "extra" activity (the number of defects from WA is relatively low), the information is sent to the DTO and integrated into the lead-time prediction calculations.

According to the incremental approach in Fig. 1, in this iteration we first need to develop the DTO of WB. After that, we need to integrate it with the previous DTO in Fig. 3a, considering the new data acquisition points and the sharing of human operators among WD and WB. Figure 3b illustrates the resulting model of the integration, where highlighted (yellow) areas represent the new parts that have been added to Fig. 3a to evolve the initial DTO.

The evolved DTO can be analyzed to estimate the most efficient allocation of operations in each moment, and to easily control the evolution of the number of units that require manual rework (Fig. 5 illustrates an example of this information) and the number of operators in WD and WB.

From the description in previous paragraphs, one can deem the DTO incremental evolution as a simple activity. However, it is not. The next section describes the difficulties and complications arose during the DTO integration and validation phases at iteration 2, and the lessons learned during the journey.

3   Architectural Concerns

As discussed in previous section, evolving the production line and the DTO accordingly is essential for the sustainability of the organization. To this end, we reported about the physical changes made in the production line (e.g., a new workstation WB, and new sensors in WA), as well as the changes made in the initial DTO to reflect the changes in the production line.

3.1   Architectural Concerns in the Case Study

By comparing the two DTOs depicted in Fig. 3a and Fig. 3b, it is clear that changes mainly occurred between WA and WD. We introduced in WA a set of different sensors, which are the quality sensors that identify defective units. As these quality sensors send different type of raw data (e.g., ASCII, Binary, Hex, and etc.) at different points in time, we added in the DTO a pre-processing entity (i.e., the Faulty_Unit_Identification in Fig. 3b), which is in charge of analyzing sensors data, tag defective articles, and aggregate data by number of defective articles in a concrete order. It is worth noticing that, due to the volume of raw data, this activity is complex and time consuming. After the analysis, the output of Faulty_Unit_Identification consists in: (i) the order ID, (ii) the number of defective articles in such an order (can be zero if none of the articles had any defect), and (iii) the predicted necessary time for reworking the defective articles (can be zero). Using this information, the DTO recalculates the estimation of the manufacturing lead time for the work-in-progress orders.

An order proceeds its way to either WD or WB according to the existence of defective articles. If the order is healthy (i.e., the number of defective units is 0) it is transferred to the priority queue that precedes WD, otherwise it is transferred to WB. When entering WB, the order is buffered into a FIFO queue and waits for an operator. Once the rework is finished the order proceeds to the priority queue before WD, while the operator can remain working in WB or go to WD. The DTO records the defective order ID, the number of defective units, and the actual rework time. The DTO uses this information to increase the accuracy of the future estimations of the necessary rework time and, in consequence, to increase its future lead time predictions accuracy.

Further, the evolved DTO also incorporates a policy that computes how to optimally allocate operators to WB and WD to minimize lead time. It uses the information about the status of the production line and the number of articles in each stage, including articles under rework and waiting for rework. In fact, while DTO_1 (see Fig. 3a) was not aligned with OA/BA because it naively assumed two human resources continuously working in WD, the evolved DTO can also suggest the calculated optimal allocation to the operators in each moment.

For example, suppose that the two operators are working in WD. When the quality sensors detect a defective article, one of the workers in WD may decide to attend the defective article and rework it. However, this decision can result in a sub-optimal allocation of resources. It is possible that the optimal allocation still assigns two operators to WD, maybe because the current bottleneck in the production line is still WD. The evolved DTO can continuously provide a suggestion about the optimal allocation operators.

From this discussion, it is clear that making an evolved DTO is challenging, as it requires to consider many different dimensions. Summarizing, the main issues emerge from:

– The OA, BA, and IA are misaligned, and it is difficult to understand the relationships between different resources, between resources and processes, and between resources, processes and the available data.
– Both OA, BA and IA are not flexible and they are hard to evolve. When introducing/changing resource/processes/data all of the architectures need be rearranged by introducing technical debts, which will lead to architecture erosion.
– DTO is not flexible and hard to evolve. When changes happen into either the OA or the BA or the IA, the whole DTO requires to be rearranged by still introducing technical debts, which will lead to architecture erosion.

3.2 Lessons Learned for Sustainable Digitalization

From the above discussion it emerges that, in order to facilitate a straightforward and sustainable digitalization of the structure, products, operations, and all relations tying these together, the OA/BA and IA must be fully *aligned*. In fact, once the OA/BA and IA are aligned, they can be straightforwardly mapped to the DTO and used for simulating and analyzing the organization: (i) OA/BA provides all the structural and behavioral models needed for the simulation and analysis of the organization, whereas (ii) IA provides both raw (from CPS) and aggregated (from DD) data representing the actual status of the organization.

Unfortunately, this is a necessary but not sufficient condition. In fact, as the sustainability of a DTO is largely determined by the sustainability of OA/BA and IA, it must be flexible and able to accommodate continuous and rapid change to OA/BA and IA. Indeed, if the OA/BA requires to be changed in response to new market forces (e.g., manufacturing a new product), the IA should change as well and fulfill the new requirements (e.g., a functionality for managing the new production process). Therefore, the DTO should *evolve* accordingly and reflect the changes made in both the OA/BA and IA. In fact, if the DTO does not evolve and align according to the enterprise, its benefits are drastically reduced. In other words, *rigid architectures restrain the sustainability and evolution of the DTO, and reduce its benefits*.

To this end, we need to define Architectural Frameworks, which provide principles and practices for jointly specifying, aligning, and evolving OA/BA, IA and DTO. In particular, the Architectural Framework shall include [4]: (1)

an *Architectural Pattern* describing architectural elements and connectors, with constraints on how they can be combined, achieving flexibility; (2) a *Reference Model* decomposing functionality into elements (and data between them) that cooperatively satisfy the organization needs; (3) a *Reference Architecture* mapping the Reference Model onto system elements and defining the data flows between them. Whereas a reference model splits functionalities, a reference architecture is the mapping of such functionalities onto a system decomposition. The Architectural Framework should explicitly address the following concerns:

Modularity – Software engineering defines abstraction as the process of identifying the important aspects of a phenomenon and ignoring the details that are not relevant. What must be considered as important and what should be considered as a detail to be ignored depends on the purpose of the abstraction. Modularity is the degree to which DTOs are decomposed and recombined in terms of abstractions. Specifically, a modular DTO should be structured into identifiable entities, which encapsulate the representation of abstractions, and are accessible through well-defined interfaces. A modular DTO can be then composed entirely from a set of constituent DTOs, where each of them takes care of a specific aspect (i.e., *single responsibility*), rather than having the aspect spread out over many parts of the DTO. Modularity and Single Responsibility are then important concerns, as they allow for separation of concerns, which can be applied in two phases: first, when dealing with each constituent DTO in isolation (bottom-up design) and second, when dealing with the overall characteristics of all constituent DTOs and their relationships as a whole DTO (top-down design).

Granularity – Granularity defines the level of detail of a single constituent DTO. Indeed, it refers to the extent to how small the constituent DTOs are. When a DTO is split into constituents, it is important to measure the degree of componentization. On the one hand, having small, fine-grained constituents provides greater flexibility when composing them into a DTO. On the other hand, small, fine-grained constituents are more difficult to govern. In fact, the larger and coarse-grained constituents are, the easier it is to manage and coordinate them in a whole DTO. Modularity and granularity are tightly coupled and affect each other. A DTO can have multiple possible levels of granularity. The granularity of the data that the physical system can transmit and that can feed the DTO is also a factor to consider during the decision of the most appropriate DTO granularity.

Decomposition/Composition Style – Understanding how to properly decompose/compose a DTO into/from constituents is relevant for defining the modularity and granularity of the different entities. A new DTO should be built by taking reusable constituents and combining them to form the required functionality. The capability of understanding each constituent DTO in isolation aids the adaptation and evolution of the whole DTO. To achieve modular decomposability/composability, and understanding, constituent DTOs must have two very important properties, namely *high cohesion* and *loose coupling*. A constituent has high cohesion if all its elements are strongly related, and they are together for a reasonable and well-defined specific purpose (i.e. single responsibility). Complementary, coupling is determined by the relationship of an individual constituent with other constituents in the same DTO. Coupling is a measure of the interdependence of two or more constituents in the form of interaction. If two constituents depend on each other heavily—i.e., they are tightly coupled—it will be difficult to observe, analyze, understand, and act them separately. In contrast, modular structures with high cohesion and low coupling allow for considering constituent DTOs as black boxes when the overall structure is described. Such constituents can be observed, analyzed and described separately.

Evolution – A DTO emerges from the interactions among the constituent DTOs. Despite the adoption of best engineering practices, the DTO must face inherently continuous evolution, as well as heterogeneous and inconsistent changing elements. Changes inside an organization are the cause of continuous DTO evolution. A DTO evolution occurs when any of the following three basic situations happen [8]: *self-evolution*, *joint evolution*, and *emergent evolution*.

In *self-evolution*, a change is introduced because of redesign, redevelopment or improvement of an existing DTO. Requirements include improved business-supporting functions, improved performance through using a new design and more advanced technologies, improved architecture for future development, and their combinations. Referring to the case study addressed in Sect. 2, an example could be an improvable production line WA able to accommodate newly designed robotic arms that best fit the product the machine is working on, or arms that are simply offering improved performance over the previous ones. Self-evolution targets a certain level of granularity of a DTO. In fact, self-evolution can occur at the highest level of granularity, or at lower levels. As the granularity of a DTO is strictly tied with its modularity, it is important to have a distinct vision of the constituents and the grains of a DTO to better locate where the evolution occurs.

In *joint evolution*, two or more DTOs are to be integrated for improved business support. Still referring to the case study in Sect. 2: the two communicating constituents, namely WA and WD, have to deal with possible multiple changes involving, interoperability, data sharing, improved functions and services, and workflow integration. Joint evolution targets two or more DTOs at the same or different levels of granularity. Furthermore, integration between DTOs could potentially change the connectors of the constituents involved.

Emergent evolution deals with the design and development of a new DTO based on existing DTOs. Requirements include new functions developed on a joint basis of existing constituents, and new DTOs supporting emerging business needs. An example could be the development of a DTO on the basis of the two constituents including WA and WD. The new DTO digitalizes the functionalities of the underlying smart manufacturing system. Emergent evolution targets two or more DTOs where the one emerging has a higher level of granularity.

The previously described evolution types could result in isolated changes. However, *Multiple evolutions* could also come out simultaneously, with self-evolution, joint evolution and emergent evolution directly affecting a large part of the DTO. If the evolution's complexity is not controlled the DTO will erode over time due to such changes. The laws of software evolution [13] state that uncontrolled evolution brings to

- *Increasing complexity:* as a large program is continuously changed, its complexity, which reflects deteriorating structure, increases unless work is done to maintain or reduce it.
- *Continuing grow:* the functional capability of E-type systems must be continually enhanced to maintain user satisfaction over system lifetime.
- *Declining quality:* unless rigorously adapted and evolved to take into account changes in the operational environment, the quality of an E-type system will appear to be declining.

Hence, an open and connected DTO requires that evolution dimensions are controlled to prevent costly reconstruction. Moreover, it is important to understand **why**, **how**, **when** and **where** this evolution occurs.

4   Related Work

Related work is manifold and spans over different topics, namely *Digital Twin Architectures*, *Architecture Alignment* and *Architecture Evolution*.

Digital Twin (DT) Architectures – Since the DT conception, more than a decade ago [21], pioneers have used it in the manufacturing domain in order to improve the production leveraging *Virtual Factory* [12]. In the Industry 4.0 domain, the simulation of different possible behaviors is a main enabler for construction of the desired intelligent systems [19]. Despite the efforts to systematize and guide the development and deployment of digital twins in companies [1,9], the systematic implementation of digitalization process in sociotechnical systems remains an open challenge. For instance, DT modeling is recognized as of paramount importance for its prosperous utilization, but there is not a general agreement in the community on a general approach to build the DT models [21]. The implementation of DT in domains such as the Cyber-physical fusion also remains an engineering challenge due to the lack of a generally accepted framework for acquiring the data, transmit the data, building operative knowledge from data through simulation or data mining, and controlling the CPS [14]. Only recently, researchers have started focusing on the architectural aspects of DT [16]. For example, in [2] authors propose a layered architecture reference model for cloud-based CPS, in [17] authors propose a four-layer architecture pattern to design DT incorporating various types of information sources. The pattern is designed to be extensible with respect to the number of sources, and flexible with respect to the type of information. However, in spite of the increasing interest in DT, little effort has been devoted to investigate architectural quality attributes, such as modifiability, scalability, evolvability, reusability.

Architecture Alignment – The need and importance for aligning the Organizational and IT architectures as been pinpointed over time by many research studies [7,22], and now many points of alignment are commonly recognized. Early studies focused on linking the business plan with the IT plan, and/or on ensuring the alignment of business and IT strategies. Other approaches instead examined the mapping between business needs and information system priorities. The implications of architecture alignment have been also demonstrated through many empirical case studies (e.g., [10,15]). The results demonstrate that the organizations that have their Organizational and IT strategies aligned outperform those organizations that do not. Indeed, alignment leads to more focused and strategic use of IT which, in turn, leads to increased performance [6].

Architecture Evolution – Sociotechnical systems obey the principle of *there is nothing permanent except change*. The Organizational/Business Architecture will evolve and the Information architecture needs to keep aligned. In consequence, the DTO of the sociotechnical system needs to evolve too. At present, evolving the software-based DT is possible, but doing it in a systematic way that does not boost the software engineering expenses resides in the research frontier. In [18], the authors propose a pattern-oriented development approach, where patterns are considered as the main building blocks of the architecture and changes are applied by means of patterns substitution, i.e., design evolution is identified in terms of replacement of patterns by other patterns. Another interesting approach is proposed in [3], where the authors present the Evolution Style, which defines a family of domain-specific architecture evolution paths that share common properties and satisfy a common set of constraints. The evolution style specifies the set of concepts needed to define and analyze the software architecture evolution: (*i*) the set of operators defining the evolution transitions, (*ii*) the set of evolution path constraints defining whether a path is allowed or not, and (*iii*) the set of evaluation functions used to compare different evolution paths with respect to quality metrics.

5   Conclusions and Future Work

A *Digital Twin of the Organization* is an accurate representation of an organization (including physical, software, and human elements), which aims at facilitating decision-making processes, and making informed decision in the value chain. However, the lack of engineering best practices for developing and operating DTOs makes industry difficult to fully benefit from this technology. Further, as current solutions are often context-dependent or system-specific, they result challenging to change, extend and reuse.

In this paper we reported an initial attempt made in architecting and developing a DTO from a manufacturing industry, and its further evolution. In particular, (*i*) we detailed a development process leveraging *Enterprise Architecture* to map the organization structure/behavior (i.e., Organizational/Business Architectures) and status (i.e., Information Architecture) into a DTO, (*ii*) we pinpointed a set of concerns to be confronted with when architecting a DTO, and (*iii*) we discussed the need for an Architectural Framework enabling the specification, alignment, and evolution of OA/BA, IA and DTO.

To this end, as a future work we mainly plan to address the aforementioned architectural concerns, by devising an architectural framework which specifically takes into account DTO's Modularity, Granularity, Decomposition/Composition, and Evolution.

References

1. Aitken, A.: Industry 4.0: demystifying digital twins. https://www.lanner.com/
2. Alam, K.M., El Saddik, A.: C2ps: a digital twin architecture reference model for the cloud-based cyber-physical systems. IEEE Access **5**, 2050–2062 (2017)
3. Barnes, J.M., Garlan, D., Schmerl, B.: Evolution styles: foundations and models for software architecture evolution. Softw. Syst. Model. **13**(2), 649–678 (2014). https://doi.org/10.1007/s10270-012-0301-9
4. Bass, L., Clements, P., Kazman, R.: Software Architecture in Practice. Addison-Wesley Professional, 3rd edn. (2012)
5. Baxter, G., Sommerville, I.: Socio-technical systems: from design methods to systems engineering. Interact. Comput. **23**(1), 4–17 (2011)
6. Chan, Y.E., Sabherwal, R., Thatcher, J.B.: Antecedents and outcomes of strategic is alignment: an empirical investigation. IEEE Trans. Eng. Manag. **53**(1), 27–47 (2006)
7. Chan, Y.E., Reich, B.H.: It alignment: what have we learned? J. Inf. Technol. **22**(4), 297–315 (2007)
8. Chen, P., Han, J.: Facilitating system-of-systems evolution with architecture support. In: Proceedings of the 4th International Workshop on Principles of Software Evolution IWPSE 2001, pp. 130–133. ACM, New York (2001)
9. Cognizant: Is your organization ready to embrace a digital twin?. https://www.cognizant.com/
10. de Leede, J., Looise, J., Alders, B., Alders, B.: Innovation, improvement and operations: an exploration of the management of alignment. Int. J. Technol. Manag. **23**(4), 353–368 (2002)
11. El Saddik, A.: Digital twins: the convergence of multimedia technologies. IEEE MultiMedia **25**(2), 87–92 (2018)
12. Grieves, M.: Digital twin: manufacturing excellence through virtual factory replication. White Pap. **1**, 1–7 (2014)
13. Herraiz, I., Rodriguez, D., Robles, G., Gonzalez-Barahona, J.M.: The evolution of the laws of software evolution: a discussion based on a systematic literature review. ACM Comput. Surv. **46**(2), 28:1–28:28 (2013)
14. Josifovska, K., Yigitbas, E., Engels, G.: Reference framework for digital twins within cyber-physical systems. In: Proceedings of the 5th International Workshop on Software Engineering for Smart Cyber-Physical Systems SEsCPS 2019, pp. 25–31. IEEE Press (2019)
15. Kearns, G.S., Lederer, A.L.: A resource-based view of strategic it alignment: how knowledge sharing creates competitive advantage. Decis. Sci. **34**, 1–29 (2003)
16. Malakuti, S., Grüner, S.: Architectural aspects of digital twins in IIoT systems. In: Proceedings of the 12th European Conference on Software Architecture: Companion Proceedings. ECSA 2018. Association for Computing Machinery (2018)

17. Malakuti, S., Schmitt, J., Platenius-Mohr, M., Grüner, S., Gitzel, R., Bihani, P.: A four-layer architecture pattern for constructing and managing digital twins. In: Bures, T., Duchien, L., Inverardi, P. (eds.) ECSA 2019. LNCS, vol. 11681, pp. 231–246. Springer, Cham (2019). https://doi.org/10.1007/978-3-030-29983-5_16

18. Ram, D.J., Rajasree, M.S.: Enabling design evolution in software through pattern oriented approach. In: Konstantas, D., Léonard, M., Pigneur, Y., Patel, S. (eds.) OOIS 2003. LNCS, vol. 2817, pp. 179–190. Springer, Heidelberg (2003). https://doi.org/10.1007/978-3-540-45242-3_17

19. Schluse, M., Priggemeyer, M., Atorf, L., Rossmann, J.: Experimentable digital twins-streamlining simulation-based systems engineering for industry 4.0. IEEE Trans. Ind. Inform. **14**(4), 1722–1731 (2018)

20. Sousa, P., Caetano, A., Vasconcelos, A., Pereira, C., Tribolet, J.: Enterprise architecture modeling with the unified modeling language. In: Rittgen, P. (ed.) Enterprise Modeling and Computing with UML, pp. 67–94. IGI Global (2007)

21. Tao, F., Zhang, H., Liu, A., Nee, A.Y.C.: Digital twin in industry: state-of-the-art. IEEE Trans. Ind. Inform. **15**(4), 2405–2415 (2019)

22. Ullah, A., Lai, R.: A systematic review of business and information technology alignment. ACM Trans. Manag. Inf. Syst. **4**(1), 4:1–4:30 (2013)

Quick Evaluation of a Software Architecture Using the Decision-Centric Architecture Review Method: An Experience Report

Pablo Cruz[1](✉), Luis Salinas[1,2], and Hernán Astudillo[1,2]

[1] Departamento de Informática, Universidad Técnica Federico Santa María,
Avenida España 1680, Valparaíso, Chile
{pcruz,lsalinas,hernan}@inf.utfsm.cl
[2] Centro Científico Tecnológico de Valparaíso (CCTVal),
Avenida España 1680, Valparaíso, Chile
https://www.cctval.cl/

Abstract. Software architecture evaluations allow systematic checking of software architecture fitness regarding the context and business. However, selecting and using an evaluation method always have some challenges and issues. This article reports an architecture review while developing an innovation projects support platform for a Chilean R&D and engineering institution. We chose DCAR (Decision-Centric Architecture Review) because it has lightweight requirements on documentation and resources, it can evaluate a project already running, and it did not impact a schedule where architecture reviews had not been considered from the start. We describe the review of three accepted and one rejected decisions. Lessons learned and benefits observed include recording decisions' rationale, visibilization of some technological issues, and rethinking of some previously made architectural decisions. Finally, we recommend making frequent mini-reviews of architecture decisions, to understand the architecture, formalize it with its resulting reports, and raise its visibility in the team itself.

Keywords: Architecture evaluation · Software architecture · Architecture decisions

1 Introduction

There is wide agreement that software architecture is key to reach the desired level of quality attributes in a software system. We can systematically approach the evaluation of those quality attributes supported by the software architecture by the use of software architecture evaluation methods.[1]

---

[1] The literature in the software architecture evaluation community use the phrases architecture evaluation and architecture review as synonyms. We will make use of this convention.

© Springer Nature Switzerland AG 2020
A. Jansen et al. (Eds.): ECSA 2020, LNCS 12292, pp. 281–295, 2020.
https://doi.org/10.1007/978-3-030-58923-3_19

This article describes our experience using the Decision-Centric Architecture Review (DCAR) method [18] for evaluating a research, innovation and technology transfer software system[2] developed by a local vendor for a Chilean R&D and engineering institution. With careful planning and allowing some activities to be executed in an offline fashion, we managed to perform a complete architecture review using DCAR requiring in-person participation in about two half days (four hours each day). Hereinafter, we will refer to the R&D institution for which the software was developed as "the organization" and to the software development company as "the vendor".

This article offers three main contributions. First, we describe how DCAR was enacted for our purposes, making the reader aware of the key elements to consider when using the method. Second, we explain how three decisions how were discussed and accepted, modified or rejected. Third, we present lessons learned from this case, which we believe interesting because we evaluated a software architecture while being developed by a third party.

The paper is structured as follows. Section 2 briefly surveys related work regarding architecture evaluation methods. Section 3 describes the evaluation context. Section 4 explains how we chose DCAR by using an evaluation method comparison and assessment framework. Section 5 presents an overview of DCAR and its steps. Section 6 describes the specific evaluation and presents three decisions worked on during the review. Section 7 presents lessons learned and some recommendations. Section 8 offers some considerations regarding the use of DCAR. Section 9 reviews validity threats and their mitigation. Finally, Sect. 10 summarizes and concludes.

2   Architecture Evaluation and Related Work

Software architecture evaluation is a systematic approach to assess how well the architecture of a software system meets its required quality attributes levels. Many methods have been developed, each serving a particular niche [6]. To mention just a few, the Software Architecture Analysis Method (SAAM) [10] was proposed for evaluating architectures in regard of maintainability quality attribute [6,10]. The Architecture Trade-off Analysis Method (ATAM) explicitly considered more quality attributes than SAAM, requiring the reviewer to deal with the trade-offs among quality attributes.

SAAM and ATAM are examples of scenario-based methods; while both have received wide attention, they require an almost complete architecture description (AD), something not always available at the time of the evaluation (or at any other, for the matter). To address this shortcoming, the Evaluation Method for Partial Architectures (ARID) [6] makes use of the well-known active design reviews [13]. More recently, the Pattern-Based Architecture Reviews (PBAR) [8] takes advantage of the relationship among patterns and quality attributes for

---

[2] In spanish: "Sistema de Gestión de Proyectos de Investigación, Innovación y Transferencia Tecnológica". As of this writing, the system is in production.

lightweight evaluation of agile projects. Finally, we mention DCAR (Decision-Centric Architecture Reviews) [18], whose usage we report in this article, a lightweight decision-centric method based on the concept of using decision forces to challenge the architectural decisions made.

Many issues arise when using an architecture evaluation method – making industrial applications of them worth being reported. While many of these issues are technical, many others are instead socio-political, managerial [3] or social [4]. A survey on the state of practice of architecture reviews [1] reports that most evaluations are informal; using external reviewers is recommended but not a common practice; there is a tendency to use practices or techniques from the methods rather than the complete method; most reviews take place in the early stages of the project life; and many architecture reviews occur on an ad-hoc way and not using the methods out-of-the-box. To address these issues, the well-known Software Architecture Review and Assessment report (SARA) [11] aims to provide concrete and experience-based advice for architecture evaluations.

In general, the reported perceived benefits of architectural evaluations include risks identification in the architecture, assessment of quality attributes, identification of reuse opportunities, promotion of good design, and rationale capture [1,7,14].

3   Evaluation Context

The client organization, located in Valparaíso, Chile, is in the midst of an improvement endeavor, called Organizational Improvement Project[3], funded by the Chilean government to enhance R&D and innovation activities. This project goals include building a software platform to manage the organization's internal projects of research, innovation and technology transfer.

Public bidding was won by a Chilean software company located in Viña del Mar[4], and software development started in the first days of March, 2018. Given the specific contractual aspects of the public bidding, a waterfall approach was proposed by the vendor and agreed-to by the organization, although we stipulated frequent reviews of working software. As expected, in the first two stages of the project (requirements elicitation and software architecture) there was little working software to review, and deliverables focused on reporting on the requirements elicitation tasks and the proposed software architecture. Some activities, especially requirements gathering, involved intensive in-person work by the vendor at the organization site; software development was done at the vendor site, and only the reviews were held at the organization site.

Following a high-level physical view, the vendor proposed a resource-based architecture [12] (see Fig. 1), with well-known technologies for front-end (Angular) and back-end (Spring and Java). After the last milestone related to the second stage (software architecture), the vendor formally started the software

---

[3] In spanish: "Proyecto de Mejora Institucional" (PMI) FSM 1402.
[4] Adjacent to Valparaíso.

implementation, with initially four-week iterations[5]; at the end of each iteration, we required a review of working software.

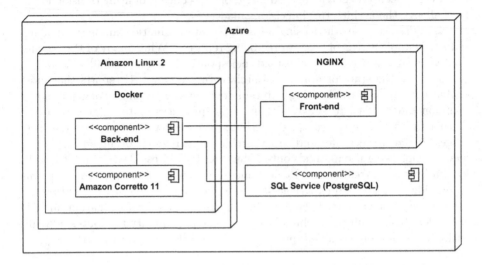

Fig. 1. Deployment view of the system front and back (as of this writing).

As the software development went on, we (as counterpart) decided to perform an architecture review with two clear goals: first, to assess the current architectural decisions made by the vendor; and second, to have visibility of the architecture.

Architecture reviews were not considered in the initial planning. Thus, although we had specific reasons to run an evaluation, we also wanted to minimize its impact on the project schedule. To this end, we ran some activities in an off-line fashion, choosing those whose input sources did not require our presence (see Sect. 6).

4   Choosing a Software Architecture Evaluation Method

As described in Sect. 2, several software architecture evaluation methods exist, and choosing one among them is not trivial. We adopted as basis an existing classification and comparison framework [2].

In the following items, we map DCAR characteristics to framework components, explaining the rationale behind the decision to use this method:

1. *Maturity stage*: according to the framework, DCAR is in the second maturity level, i.e. development: it has been validated (according to [18]) but still lacks validation in various domains, and to the best of our knowledge there are no published method refinements (a key requirement for the next maturity stage: refinement); the currently maturity level is enough for us.

---

[5] Later shortened to one-week.

2. *Definition of software architecture*: although DCAR does not offer a concrete and explicitly stated definition of software architecture, it does focus on architectural decisions, which allows to infer that its authors understand software architecture as a set of decisions [5,16]; since we are interested in checking the key architectural decisions, the focus method focus is suitable.

3. *Process support*: DCAR offers good process support with templates, concrete step descriptions, and many examples.

4. *Method's activities*: DCAR offers a manageable set of nine steps with an appropriate trade-off between complexity and granularity.

5. *Method's goals*: DCAR authors claim that its goal is to "determine the soundness of architectural decisions that were made"; As mentioned in item 2 above, checking architectural decisions is our main interest.

6. *Number of quality attributes*: there is no prescribed quality attributes list in DCAR; however, it explicitly states that achieving a desired property naturally requires combining some decisions; therefore, DCAR fits our purposes because it implicitly considers quality attributes and trade-offs, while providing enough freedom for the reviewers to focus on specific quality attributes.

7. *Applicable project stage*: DCAR is oriented to evaluate architectural decisions already made, and its input includes (informal) description of requirements, business drivers, and architectural design; therefore, DCAR is clearly applicable to a middle project stage, as was our case.

8. *Architectural description*: DCAR requires informal description of requirements, business drivers, and architectural design; these three artifacts were available at the time of evaluation, making DCAR feasible for us.

9. *Evaluation approaches*: in framework terms, DCAR has a questioning and experience-based approach. Questioning is carried out in step 8 (decision evaluation), where participants challenge the decisions already made. Its experience-based approach is somewhat more general than a scenario-based, as shown in the initial steps where stakeholders discuss forces and the architecture. In our opinion, questioning and experience-based analysis is appropriate for the kind of review we need.

10. *Stakeholder involvement*: DCAR defines a specific, though not short, set of roles that should participate in an evaluation; we had people for those roles.

11. *Support for non-technical issues*: DCAR does not offer explicit support for non-technical issues, and we feel that it is easier to use by teams knowledgeable in architecture evaluations; since we had previous evaluation experience, we decided to plan the evaluation of non-technical issues accordingly.

12. *Method validation*: the authors claim the method has been validated in the distributed control systems domain1, but this does not restrict its use to only that domain.

13. *Tool support*: DCAR does not require specific software tools to run an evaluation, and the provided templates where considered enough for our purposes.

14. *Experience repository*: DCAR does not explicitly incorporate reusable knowledge. However, we will be recording every issue deemed as important for reuse purposes¡ several of these recorded issues are reported in this article.

15. *Resources required*: DCAR is considered suitable for projects that do not have budget, schedule or stakeholders available for a full-fledged architecture evaluation; this was critical for us, because (as mentioned earlier) architecture evaluation was not considered in the initial project planning.

5 Decision-Centric Architecture Review (DCAR)

DCAR was proposed in [18] as a lightweight method (in terms of time and resources) to support a decision-by-decision software architecture evaluation. Unlike scenario-based methods, where reviewers expect to test the architecture against scenarios, DCAR favors working with a per-decision approach, putting decision rationale at the core of the method.

A key DCAR concept is "decision force," which is defined as any non-trivial influence on an architect making decisions to find a solution for an architectural problem [17,18]. Decision forces are discussed, and then used to challenge decisions, to see whether they are fit to purpose or must be modified.

DCAR has nine steps:

1. *Preparation*: the lead architect prepares a presentation of the architecture with a focus on patterns, styles and technology, and the customer representative prepares a presentation of the expected software product and its context (including driving business requirements); this step happens off-line.
2. *Introduction to DCAR*: the method is presented to all participants, explaining how DCAR works, its steps, review scope, potential outcomes, and participants and their roles.
3. *Management presentation*: someone from customer side or management gives a short (15–20 min) presentation to enable review participants eliciting business-related decision forces.
4. *Architecture presentation*: the lead architect presents the architecture to all participants; a highly interactive presentation (45–60 min) is recommended.
5. *Forces and decision completion*: the main goal of this step is to clarify decisions and relationships among them, and to complete and verify the forces relevant to these decisions.
6. *Decision prioritization*: stakeholders negotiate which decisions are more important to be reviewed in the following steps; although the prioritization is context-dependent, DCAR authors recommend considering decisions that are mission-critical, bear risks, or cause high costs.
7. *Decision documentation*: each participant selects two or three prioritized decisions, and start documenting them; ideally, each participant selects decisions that they are knowledgeable about.
8. *Decision evaluation*: using the previously assigned priority, decisions are presented and challenged by the team by identifying some forces against the proposed solution; and participants decide by voting on whether the decision is good enough, acceptable, or must be reconsidered.

9. *Retrospectives and reporting*: DCAR commands the review team to write an evaluation report within no more than two weeks of the session; reporting is also useful for *socializing* the decisions [16].

6   Evaluating the Architecture with DCAR

The evaluation was carried out in a mixed offline-online fashion. The online part of the evaluation took two half-days and had place at a meeting room of the organization site, with a whiteboard and a big screen for presentation purposes. In the first online evaluation session, five people were involved: two client's project engineers (one as review leader and the other as customer representative), one supporting quality engineer, and the vendor's project manager and lead architect. The second online evaluation session took place in the same location two weeks later, but without the supporting quality engineer; his absence forced us to reorganize some activities related to (1) challenging decisions and (2) writing down key insights gathered from the evaluation.

The offline activities were mainly devoted to completing decisions, decisions documentation, and retrospectives and reporting. Nevertheless, frequent emails and phone calls were required to assure alignment between both organizations.

Finally, when prioritizing decisions, we used consensus rather than voting.

6.1   Three Reviewed Decisions

We present three architectural decisions that were challenged and then validated or changed. Figure 2 shows the relationships among these decisions, as recommended by DCAR, using a published documentation framework for architecture decisions [9].

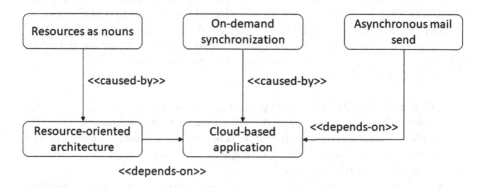

Fig. 2. Revised decisions and their relationships.

User Data Synchronization. The organization maintains a local Active Directory-based[6] repository for storing user data. Given that the new software will be running on Microsoft Azure[7], a synchronization between local and remote repositories is required. The vendor initially proposed frequent synchronization (once per hour). After discussing and challenging the decision, we finally agreed to decrease the frequency to once per day and to provide on-demand synchronization for urgent cases.

The final decision was:

- **Decision name:** On-demand urgent synchronization of user data between the platform and the main local repository.
- **Problem:** the main local repository (Active Directory) needs to be immediately synchronized with the remote user repository when a new required user for the software system has been created.
- **Considered alternative solutions:** More frequent (e.g.., one synchronization run every hour) cron-based synchronization.
- **Forces in favor of decision:**
  - Avoid unnecessary synchronizations.
  - Synchronization is enough if done once in a day for the general case.
- **Forces against decision:**
  - One person should run the synchronization procedure manually.
- **Outcome:** Accept.
- **Rationale for outcome:** We want to avoid unnecessary synchronizations that could end in failure, leaving the system in an unexpected state.

Asynchronous Project Profile Save. When a researcher wants to apply for public funding, the organization requires him or her to create a project profile and notify it to the organization's Office of Research and Innovation Projects. When sending the project profile, the system stores the data and then sends back a summary PDF file to the researcher. The initial implementation of this module considered synchronous mail sending (see Fig. 3). After discussing and challenging this decision, we agreed to decouple the mail sending with an asynchronous approach (see Fig. 4) to improve usability and performance.

The final decision was:

- **Decision name:** Asynchronous project profile saving.
- **Problem:** The researcher must receive an email with a summary.
- **Considered alternative solutions:** When saving a project profile, the system will require to wait for the email queue to send an email to researcher.
- **Forces in favor of decision:**
  - Usability improved as the system's response to storing a project profile is noticeably faster.
  - Mail sending will be decoupled from the main use case.

---

[6] Active Directory: https://azure.microsoft.com/en-us/services/active-directory/.

[7] Microsoft Azure: https://azure.microsoft.com/en-us/services/active-directory/.

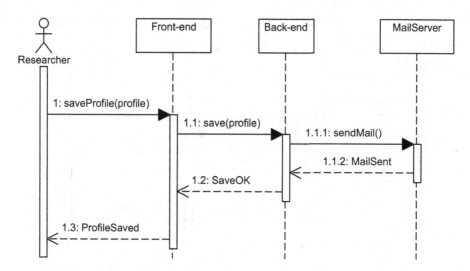

Fig. 3. Decision partial documentation, with synchronous project profile save.

- **Forces against decision:**
  - Harder to implement than the typical, natural synchronous way.
  - Asynchronous operations are harder to test and maintain.
- **Outcome:** Accept.
- **Rationale for outcome:** Current decision appears to be the simplest way to handle usability issues of storing a project profile.

6.2   Resources Naming

The initial vendor proposal was a resource-oriented architecture, in keeping with our own goals and preferences. However, in the evaluation we found many APIs incorrectly named (e.g., some were verbs indicating transactions rather than resources), so an explicit decision was made about resource naming.

- **Decision name:** Name representations of resources with nouns.
- **Problem:** Naming resources with verbs will indicate a transaction not adhering to the resource-oriented architecture.
- **Considered alternative solutions:** Use ad-hoc naming.
- **Forces in favor of decision:**
  - Resources will be easier to integrate with future developments.
  - Adherence to resource-oriented architecture.
- **Forces against decision:**
  - It implies some review and rework of already-implemented components.
- **Outcome:** Accept.
- **Rationale for outcome:** We want to avoid typical API naming-related integration problems with future architectures.

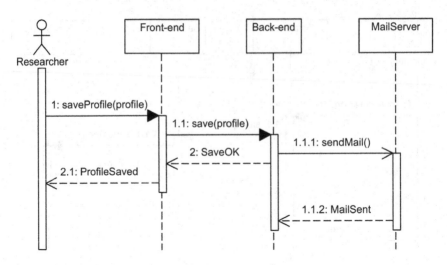

Fig. 4. Decision partial documentation, with asynchronous project profile save (thin arrowhead).

6.3 A Rejected Decision

Not all reviewed decisions were accepted. In particular, when we reviewed the proposed authentication solution, we immediately noticed some unusual elements. The system was required to use the organization's on-premise Active Directory, but the proposed system was to be tested and deployed in Microsoft Azure cloud solution (see sequence diagram in Fig. 1). The vendor proposed a non-standard hybrid approach that shared authentication elements between front- and back-end, which would have allowed some kinds of intrusion. We requested additional details on this proposed solution, and eventually rejected this decision (which had been already made) and decided to keep synchronized an Azure-deployed Active Directory instance with the on-premise Active Directory instance, for which a standard authentication method was in use (OAuth). Moreover, we requested the vendor to strictly follow Microsoft's documentation and guidance for authentication.

We made this decision in the meeting room itself, with the participants already mentioned. However, synchronizing both Active Directory servers was outside our domain. Therefore, this decision forced us to start a follow-up conversation with the organization's IT department personnel, which fortunately agreed to allow its account to synchronize with the cloud-deployed Active Directory.

An interesting issue is that when we rejected this decision, we made it almost intuitively and based on experience, not following any detailed guidance. DCAR does not define specific criteria for accepting or rejecting decisions (i.e., when a decision should be accepted with agreed improvements, and when just rejected). We did not find any workaround, so we believe this issue is still open and should be further developed in the future.

7 Lessons Learned and Recommendations

In this section we present the main lessons we learned and recommendations for DCAR adopters.

7.1 With Careful Planning Some Activities Can Be Done Offline

By considering the sources for inputs of some activities and weighting the risks of offline working, some DCAR activities can be left for offline execution. We note that, however, that this worked well in a case where development is carried out by a vendor, and would not necessarily be so for an in-house development.

7.2 Architecture Evaluation Should Be Continuous

Evaluating a proposed architecture allows the organization to make a snapshot of it (which can be confirmed, rejected or modified in the review), but development goes on after the evaluation, and architectural erosion may set in [15]. One way to avoid or minimize it is to continuously (re-)evaluate decisions. Of course, new decisions taken to address emerging high-priority issues must also be reviewed.

We kept on performing "mini-reviews" by meeting regularly with the lead architect, and using informally only three DCAR steps: for the already prioritized decisions we continued checking and updating decision forces and descriptions (step 5), updating documentation (step 7), and challenging decisions (step 8).

7.3 The Report Can Be Used to Formalize the Implemented Architecture

DCAR yields an evaluation report that includes all the reviewed decisions; this forced us to explicitly note the details of each architectural decision. When development finishes, we expect this report to contain a (final, updated) architecture description with minimal erosion (of course, it is our responsibility to maintain it up-to-date by discussing it with the vendor). In our case, we will also require the vendor to sign it off.

7.4 Some Decisions Imply Follow-Up Conversations

In one case, we made a decision (see Sect. 6.3) that implied technical issues outside our domain. We do not regard this situation as accidental: in fact, we expect that future quick reviews will experience similar issues given the natural trade-off between a quick evaluation and the time-consuming coordination to bring all related people into the review sessions.

Also, follow-up conversations should be carried out as soon as possible after a review session, to allow in the next session to reassess the decisions feasibility and rework them if necessary.

8   Reflections on the Use of DCAR

Some reflections regarding the use of DCAR in this project are in order.

8.1   Software Architecture Is Seen and Treated as a Set of Decisions

DCAR explicitly recognizes the key nature of architectural decisions, suggesting explicit writing of decision forces and decision relationships «depends on» and «caused by» from [9] in decisions diagrams. Besides making them visible to participants, these relationships also made evident to all a key characteristic of architectural decisions: they cannot be treated in isolation.

8.2   Quality Attributes Are Discussed Even If Not Explicitly Mentioned

While quality attributes are not directly addressed in the method, DCAR-using reviewers will find necessary to consider appropriate discussion about them when challenging decisions. We believe this characteristic makes DCAR a particularly appropriate method for experienced software architects and architecture reviewers, as they can be expected to be knowledgeable about quality attributes.

8.3   The Architecture Gains Visibility

The architecture review allowed us, buyers of the software and technical counterparts, to gain visibility over the implemented architecture. The vendor revealed many of the details of the architecture which allowed us to formalize the high-priority decisions for documentation. Even though some decisions like the second one presented as example in this paper appear to be simple, they become apparent only after discussing them as part of an architectural evaluation.

8.4   Architectural Decisions Rationale Is Discussed

This architectural review was the first formal occasion in which the rationale behind the architecture decisions in the project was actually discussed. This discussion also motivated writing down their rationale. Interestingly enough, at one point the project manager commented "we should have made this review earlier in the project".

9   Threats to Validity

Some concerns must be addressed regarding internal and external validity, especially for readers interested in leveraging this experience in future software architecture evaluations.

In terms of internal validity, i.e. correctness of results for this specific case, perhaps the most important threat to be mentioned here is cognitive bias, especially confirmation and anchoring biases [19]. Two members of the evaluation team had prior experience in architecture evaluations (specifically with ATAM); however, we believe this risk was mitigated by including members with no prior experience in architecture evaluation, as their stance was challenging enough to avoid experienced members to override other members proposals and opinions. In any case, these members with no architecture evaluation experience should have similar "level" to the experienced members, so they can fruitfully challenge decisions and engage in collaboration with them.

In terms of external validity, i.e.generalizability of results to other cases, the reader should note that the lessons we learned and the recommendations are to be considered for similar contexts. For example, one decision was made before consulting the IT department, but in some cases the relationship between development and IT department might not be as fluid, and the team should consider other mitigation approaches, e.g. incorporating in the evaluation sessions some IT department representative.

Another aspect here is the selection of the evaluation team members: all team members were related to software development and/or architecture, which might not always be the case.

10   Conclusions

Architecture evaluation is a systematic approach to assess a software architecture's fitness to software requirements, and especially quality attributes.

While running an innovation project support platform that was developed by a vendor, we considered necessary to evaluate its architecture. Among existing evaluation methods, we chose DCAR, a decision-analysis oriented method; we particularly appreciated that it is lightweight in terms of our resources, and that it would not impact the schedule of a project that had not included architecture evaluation to start with. We illustrated the method use in our project with three modified decisions and one rejected decision.

With careful planning, we managed to evaluate the architecture in a mixed online-offline fashion, with the online part taking just two half-days; since the software is being developed by a vendor, this allowed us to minimize in-person participation by their employees. Nevertheless, we are unclear whether this approach implied for us more or less effort than expected in a full online evaluation, and leave this comparison as invitation for future work.

Finally, we recommend our own experience of making frequent mini-reviews of architecture decisions, to understand the architecture, formalize it with its resulting reports, and raise its visibility in the team itself.

Acknowledgments. This work was partially supported by CCTVal (Centro Científico y Tecnológico de Valparaíso, ANID PIA/APOYO AFB180002), DGIIE-UTFSM, Project InES (PMI FSM 1402), and FONDECYT (grant 1150810). We also thank Rich Hilliard for his helpful comments on an earlier version of this article.

References

1. Babar, M.A., Gorton, I.: Software architecture review: the state of practice. Computer **42**(7), 26–32 (2009)
2. Babar, M.A., Zhu, L., Jeffery, R.: A framework for classifying and comparing software architecture evaluation methods. In: 2004 Australian Software Engineering Conference, Proceedings, pp. 309–318, April 2004
3. Ali Babar, M., Bass, L., Gorton, I.: Factors influencing industrial practices of software architecture evaluation: an empirical investigation. In: Overhage, S., Szyperski, C.A., Reussner, R., Stafford, J.A. (eds.) QoSA 2007. LNCS, vol. 4880, pp. 90–107. Springer, Heidelberg (2007). https://doi.org/10.1007/978-3-540-77619-2_6
4. Bass, L., Kazman, R.: Making architecture reviews work in the real world. IEEE Softw. **19**(01), 67–73 (2002)
5. Bosch, J.: Software architecture: the next step. In: Oquendo, F., Warboys, B.C., Morrison, R. (eds.) EWSA 2004. LNCS, vol. 3047, pp. 194–199. Springer, Heidelberg (2004). https://doi.org/10.1007/978-3-540-24769-2_14
6. Clements, P., Kazman, R., Klein, M.: Evaluating Software Architectures: Methods and Case Studies. Addison-Wesley Longman, Boston (2002)
7. Cruz, P., Astudillo, H., Hilliard, R., Collado, M.: Assessing migration of a 20-year-old system to a micro-service platform using ATAM. In: 2019 IEEE International Conference on Software Architecture Companion (ICSA-C), pp. 174–181 (2019)
8. Harrison, N., Avgeriou, P.: Pattern-based architecture reviews. IEEE Softw. **28**(6), 66–71 (2011)
9. van Heesch, U., Avgeriou, P., Hilliard, R.: A documentation framework for architecture decisions. J. Syst. Softw. **85**(4), 795–820 (2012)
10. Kazman, R., Bass, L., Abowd, G., Webb, M.: SAAM: a method for analyzing the properties of software architectures. In: 16th International Conference on Software Engineering, pp. 81–90. ICSE 1994, May 1994
11. Obbink, H., et al.: Report on Software Architecture Review and Assessment (SARA), Version 1.0, p. 58, June 2019. http://kruchten.com/philippe/architecture/SARAv1.pdf
12. Overdick, H.: The resource-oriented architecture. In: 2007 IEEE Congress on Services (Services 2007), pp. 340–347, July 2007
13. Parnas, D.L., Weiss, D.M.: Active design reviews: principles and practices. In: 8th International Conference on Software Engineering, pp. 132–136. ICSE 1885. IEEE Computer Society Press, Los Alamitos (1985)
14. Reijonen, V., Koskinen, J., Haikala, I.: Experiences from scenario-based architecture evaluations with ATAM. In: Babar, M.A., Gorton, I. (eds.) ECSA 2010. LNCS, vol. 6285, pp. 214–229. Springer, Heidelberg (2010). https://doi.org/10.1007/978-3-642-15114-9_17
15. de Silva, L., Balasubramaniam, D.: Controlling software architecture erosion: a survey. J. Syst. Softw. **85**(1), 132–151 (2012)
16. Tyree, J., Akerman, A.: Architecture decisions: demystifying architecture. IEEE Softw. **22**(2), 19–27 (2005)
17. van Heesch, U., Avgeriou, P., Hilliard, R.: Forces on architecture decisions - a viewpoint. In: 2012 Joint Working IEEE/IFIP Conference on Software Architecture and European Conference on Software Architecture, pp. 101–110, August 2012

18. van Heesch, U., Eloranta, V., Avgeriou, P., Koskimies, K., Harrison, N.: Decision-centric architecture reviews. IEEE Softw. **31**(1), 69–76 (2014)
19. Zalewski, A., Borowa, K., Ratkowski, A.: On cognitive biases in architecture decision making. In: Lopes, A., de Lemos, R. (eds.) ECSA 2017. LNCS, vol. 10475, pp. 123–137. Springer, Cham (2017). https://doi.org/10.1007/978-3-319-65831-5_9

The Quest for Introducing Technical Debt Management in a Large-Scale Industrial Company

Somayeh Malakuti[1(✉)] and Sergey Ostroumov[2]

[1] ABB Corporate Research Center, Ladenburg, Germany
somayeh.malakuti@de.abb.com
[2] Softability Group Oy, Helsinki, Finland
Sergey.Ostroumov@abo.fi

Abstract. The long lifetime and the evolving nature of industrial products make them subject to technical debt management at different levels such as architecture and code. Although the classical steps to perform technical debt management are known, in a study that we have been performing in a large-scale industrial company as our client, we realized that finding a starting point, which leads to the desired outcome, is in fact a major challenge. This paper elaborates on various causes that we have identified for this challenge, and discusses our stepwise approach to address them so that the software quality can be improved. We believe that our experiences can be beneficial for both practitioners and researchers to gain more insight into applying quality improvement in practice as well as indicating open areas for further research.

Keywords: Quality improvement · Technical debt management · Software architecture · Source code analysis

1 Introduction

Technical debt is defined as "design of implementation constructs that are expedient in short term but that set up a technical context that can make a future change more costly or impossible" [1]. Technical debt management can start by identifying technical debt, followed by measuring its impacts, prioritizing, documenting, repaying/preventing, and in parallel monitoring it [2]. Various proposals exist to implement each of these activities in practice [3,4].

The long lifetime and the evolving nature of industrial products (e.g., robots, controllers, sensors), as well as the usual time to market requirements of industrial companies, make the industrial products subject to technical debt at various levels. Since the field of software architecture has reached a level of maturity such that several commercial tools, methods and techniques exist to support practitioners, one might be tempted to start by adopting these in the companies. However, based on our experience, we realized that it is in fact a major

A. Jansen et al. (Eds.): ECSA 2020, LNCS 12292, pp. 296–311, 2020.
https://doi.org/10.1007/978-3-030-58923-3_20

challenge to find a starting point for technical debt management, which leads to the desired outcome.

We identified that there are various issues that contribute to this challenge. Examples are: a) The history of quality improvements in the company and its possible (negative) impacts on the perception of different people of the effectiveness of adopted methods, b) Lack of common understanding of software architecture and technical debt across the company, c) Adopting certain technical debt management approaches that would not necessarily lead to the desired outcomes, d) Necessary quality improvements beyond technical debt in software, for example, process debt, infrastructure, and hardware debt, and e) Unforeseen situations such as the impacts of COVID-19 on the availability of resources and on their priorities.

Using an illustrative case study that we have performed as consultancy for one of our clients, we explain that a stepwise method must be taken to address these issues and to introduce technical debt management in a company. Our case study is a project that has started in 2018, and so far consisted of three phases.

The first phase was focused on high-level identification of technical debt via assessing the modularity status of a pilot case. The second phase was about repaying technical debt via architecture and code refactoring. However, in the second phase we could not achieve our refactoring goal, because the adopted technical debt management approach was mainly based on gut feeling and domain experience rather than objective and systematic means. Nevertheless, this experience was important to raise awareness of systematic technical debt management approaches, as well as gaining more insights into possible causes of technical debt in the company. To perform systematic technical debt management in the third phase, we first identified various kinds of debt (e.g., technical, process, infrastructure) and their possible impacts on software quality improvement activities. Although it is not possible to address all debt at once, we explain our strategy to narrow down the scope to some feasible steps to be able to still proceed with technical debt management, while coping with the unforeseen changes in the company as well as the impacts of other debt on our activities.

Based on our previous experiences and this case study, we observe that most large-scale hardware-oriented industrial companies have more or less similar characteristics in terms of their time to market pressure, distribution of teams, software architecture competence, etc. Therefore, we believe that this paper can be beneficial for both practitioners and researchers to gain more insight into challenges in applying technical debt management in practice, as well as identifying open areas for further research.

This paper is organized as follows. Sect. 2 provides an overview of the project and its phases; Sect. 3 explains our experience in the phase 1 for identifying modularity issues; Sect. 4 summarizes our experiences in adopting a not very systematic technical debt management approach; Sect. 5 outlines our vision for a more comprehensive technical debt management methodology; Sect. 6 summarizes various challenges and lessons learned; Sect. 7 provides related work and our insight on open research areas; Sect. 8 outlines conclusion and future work.

2   Project Setting and Methodology

The illustrative case study is a project in the form of external consultancy that we have been offering to an industrial company as our client since 2018. The company naturally has stronger background in hardware design, but software has gained strong importance over the time as well.

Throughout the project, eight software developers/architects, one process manager and one technology manager closely participated in the case study. In addition, the project results were frequently presented to larger audience in the company. The software engineering competence differed among the participants.

Since the project team was geographically distributed, we have adopted different approaches such as frequent teleconferences, face to face workshops, field observation, interviews and surveys to reach the goals of the project.

Before the start of the project in 2018, there were several internal workshops in the company with the aim of achieving bug-free software. The result of those workshops was that insufficient modularity of the software is the main reason for the increasing number of bugs as well as long maintenance time. As a result, the project started in 2018 with the aim of validating this hypothesis and providing support for improving the modularity of the software in three phases.

Since we needed to gain deeper insight into the software and the way it was developed, the methodology that we adopted in the project was not fixed at the beginning; throughout the project we defined our next steps based on the learnings of the previous steps. Our activities can be summarized as follows:

Assessing the Modularity Status of the Software: The phase 1 of the project was about getting to know the software better and validating the hypothesis of our client regarding the low modularity of their software. As a result, we identified various kinds of technical debt that exist at the architectural and code levels.

Prioritizing and Repaying Technical Debt at the Architecture and Code Levels: Refactoring large-scale legacy software as a whole require significant amount of time and resources, which could not be offered by our client. Therefore, our client opted for an iterative approach of refactoring at architecture and code levels. Here, the key challenge was to identify architecturally-significant requirements for each iteration, and to improve their design and implementation. In the phase 2, a high-level sketch of new architecture was defined by our client, and we were requested to refactor two pilot modules based on the sketched high-level architecture.

However, this approach was not as effective as we expected, for example, because the actual time spent for refactoring was twice longer than the estimated time and still the code did not fully adhere to the envisioned architecture. Inadequate technical debt quantification and prioritization, as well as several other issues were among the reasons that we could not reach our refactoring goals.

Identifying the Root Causes of Software Quality Issues: Based on our field observation, we realized that there were multiple attempts in past to improve the quality of the software; however, the quality has eventually dropped over time. This observation besides our experience in the phase 2 motivated us to first identify various kinds of debt that exist (e.g., technical, process, infrastructure) and their root causes. Even if we could not resolve all the root causes at once, this study would help us be more aware of their impacts on technical debt management, and prioritize technical debt more effectively. Therefore, we gained more insight into these, in the phase 3 via field observation, interviews, workshops and a survey.

Adopting a More Systematic Technical Debt Identification and Prioritization Approach: As the result phase 2, we realized that the distance between the current architecture and the envisioned one is too large, and it is necessary to define intermediate architectures to reach to the envisioned one in an iterative manner. Each intermediate architecture must address certain technical debt, and must accept some other technical debt that will be addressed by future intermediate architectures. The phase 3 of the project focuses on defining such intermediate architectures, and adopting the state-of-the-art methods for identifying and prioritizing technical debt, while taking other kinds of debt and their impacts also into account.

The details of these phases and their results are explained in the subsequent sections.

3   Phase 1: Modularity Assessment

Since the company considered insufficient modularity as the main technical debt, we were requested to perform an initial study on modularity status of a pilot part to validate this hypothesis.

As the first step in this phase, via a requirement elicitation workshop with 15 participants, we collected the stakeholders' requirements regarding the modularity of the software. The requirements were assessed and classified from various perspectives, such as developers/architects, customers, and product owners. Examples of the collected requirements are: a) Reducing the required time for new developers to learn the software, b) Reducing the number of new bugs introduced during the maintenance phase, c) Flexibility in configuring the software for each customer, and d) Flexibility in deploying software modules on different processors.

Then a specific subsystem was nominated by the architects as the pilot case. The lines of code in the pilot case change over the time, as it is being actively developed and refactored. In 2018, it contained around 300K lines of code in C/C++. To understand the current architecture of the pilot case, we made use of the available documentation, which explained the modules and their responsibilities. The documents also described the data flow among the modules. Alongside the documents, we adopted various static code analysis tools such as Understand [5], TeamScale [6] and CppDepend [7] to recover the architecture of the software.

Various metrics such as afferent (incoming) coupling, efferent (outgoing) coupling, module size, and circular dependency were assessed using the aforementioned tools. Figure 1 shows a high-level call graph of the pilot case, which is generated using the Understand tool. Here, the anonymized boxes depict various subsystems, and the links among them show the dependencies.

Our analysis revealed several architectural and code smells, such as high number of circular dependencies, high number of fan-in and fan-out, high degree of code duplicate, excessive usage of global variables, God classes, etc. Moreover, it was clarified that no specific architecture pattern or principle was followed in the pilot software.

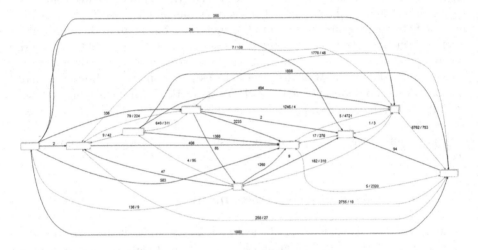

Fig. 1. The dependency graph of the pilot part

4   Phase 2: Modularity Improvement

As a result of the phase 1, the architecture team in the company provided the high-level sketch of a new layered architecture to be used for further refactoring activities. Here, the assumption was that due to the complexity of the software, the large degree of modularity issues, as well as shortage of resources, it was not feasible to have a fully detailed architecture at once. In this phase, we were asked to support by the refactoring of two pilot subsystems, mainly at detail design and code levels.

We defined four goals for this phase: a) Setting up the refactoring infrastructure consisting of suitable tools and metrics, and means for lean architecture knowledge management, b) Adopting and validating these for refactoring two pilot subsystems, c) Defining domain-specific design patterns for improving modularity at the code level, and d) Knowledge transfer via frequent teleconferences and the two-week visit of the consultancy team to the company for face to face architecture discussion/refactoring and another requirements solicitation workshop.

4.1   Tool Selection

There are many static code analysis tools available, which usually support different metrics and detect different issues in the code. We relied on existing studies on assessing these tools [3,8] as well as our field observation in the company to define criteria for selecting a suitable tool for practical usages. Some important criteria are listed below:

- Support for architecture recovery and analysis using different metrics: The company already had one static code analysis tool installed in its build system, which was not actively used by all teams due to its false positive results, among other barriers. Therefore, we decided not to introduce yet another tool that performs analysis at the code level. Nevertheless, since there was no up-to-date architecture picture of the software available, the adoption of a tool that supports architecture recovery and analysis seemed to be necessary.
- Support for stepwise refactoring: In large-scale software system, refactoring will take place in small steps, during different timeframes, by different groups of architects who are expert in specific parts of the software. Therefore, the tool must enable each architect to iteratively apply refactoring only at the desired parts of the software. Naturally, local refactoring is not always sufficient, and the tool must also enable architects to refactor the overall architecture of the software.
- Support for delayed code-level refactoring: The tool must enable the architects to refactor the architecture and the structure of the code, without the need for immediately changing the actual code. This is an important criterion because of two reasons: a) due to resource and time constraints, software developers who should implement the refactoring may not immediately be available, b) since different parts of the architecture are designed by the architects, who may work at different parts of the company with different refactoring priorities, the tool must enable collaborative refactoring at the architecture level before changing the code.
- Support for the integration in the Jenkins' build system: The tool must be integrated in the build system of the company so that architectural metrics and rules can frequently be validated and monitored.
- No reliance on the Git history: Some tools rely on the Git history of commits to identify modularity violations. Such features assume consistent tagging of each Git commit by developers in terms of bug fixes, feature development, refactoring, etc. However, such consistent tagging may not exist across all projects in the company, especially in older projects.
- Consistency of adopted tools in the company: To make sure the project results are transferable to other divisions of the company, we aimed at keeping the adopted tools across divisions consistent.

We selected Lattix [9] among several other tools [5-7,9-12] that we assessed. Tools such as Understand [5], CppDepend [5], SonarQube [5] and TeamScale [6] are mostly at code level, and do not fully fulfill our above-listed criteria. DV8 [11] is an architecture assessment tool; however, it heavily relies on Git history of commits, also the soundness of its metrics is still under validation [13].

4.2   Architecture Knowledge Management and Documentation

The requirement specifications, architectural models and decisions were documented in different formats in the company, although not very consistently nor comprehensively. For example, requirements on each task were documented as part of the task description in Azure DevOps; Microsoft Visio was adopted for architectural modelling, but the models were outdated; Atlassian Confluence was used for collection of technical debt; decision forces are not documented at all, or very inadequately.

We assessed the lean ways of documenting architecture knowledge as well as architecture models. Our study mainly targeted available proposals for Architecture Decision Records [14], as well as other templates such as arch42 [15]. We also assessed various modelling tools such as Enterprise Architect, IBM Rhapsody and Structurizr [16]. Our assessment of the tools was eventually postponed to future, because the requirements of the company on such tools were not clear. Nevertheless, we tailored a template for architecture decision records and adopted it for documenting our new design.

4.3   Refactoring Two Subsystems

The refactoring of two subsystems took almost six months, where we focused on the detail design of two subsystems, proposed new module structures and interfaces, implemented the new modules, and adjusted test cases and build scripts. In this activity, we explored various design patterns that were suitable for the two subsystems, and assessed the alternatives based on various quality attributes such as readability, modularity and testability. Due to confidentiality reasons, we cannot share the details of this activity.

In summary, the major achievements of the phase 2 were: a) The installation of Lattix in the build system of the company, b) The identification of various design patterns for refactoring two subsystems, c) The selection of most suitable design patterns based on various quality attributes, d) Refactoring of the pilot modules to some degree, and e) Gaining more insight on the obstacles to perform technical debt management more effectively.

5   Phase 3: Systematic Technical Debt Management

The decision of our client to put more emphasize on code-level improvements can be interpreted as an example of technical debt prioritization. However, this prioritization was not as effective as we expected, because: a) The actual time spent for refactoring was twice longer than the estimated time, b) Some modularity-related technical debt was resolved in one subsystem, and more or less similar debt had to be introduced in another subsystem, c) The refactored code was not fully integrated into the final software release, d) The proposed tools and documentation templates were not actively used later.

Nevertheless, phase 2 helped us illustrate that a) effective technical debt management at code level cannot be achieved if technical debt at architecture level is not adequately addressed, b) although gut feeling and domain experience are also important in technical debt prioritization, we need to complement them with more systematic approaches, c) there are several other kinds of debt in the company, which impact software quality improvement activities.

Based on our field observation during the phase 2, as well as some internal workshops and interviews with various participants, we developed a set of hypotheses about various categories of debt, their root causes, and their impacts on software quality improvement activities. We started the phase 3 of the project by performing a survey in the company to validate our hypotheses based on the responses of a larger set of colleagues. The survey aimed at collecting information on the impacts of technical debt on the daily work of developers, an estimation of technical debt growth rate, the causes of technical debt, other kinds of debt (e.g., process and infrastructure) in the company, as well as the self-assessment of developers of their software engineering competences.

There were 100 respondents in total, consisting of 70 software developers or architects, and 30 participants in different managerial roles. The survey was active for two months; afterwards we analyzed and normalized the results and presented to large audience in the company. The survey confirmed that most of the participants see technical debt as an obstacle in their everyday work, and technical debt is increasing in various parts of the software. Also, the majority of the participants assessed themselves to have intermediate knowledge of various software engineering topics.

5.1   Causes of Technical Debt

Due to confidentiality reasons, the survey details cannot be published. Nevertheless, based on the results of the survey, we classified the causes of the technical debt as below. This classification is an extension of the proposal by [1].

Changes in Context: This category contains following causes:

- Changes in business context: New hardware products are introduced, but old software is reused and adapted for them. This results in the replication of technical debt across multiple products.
- Aging technology: Where there is good potential for adopting new technologies such as software product lines, old technology is still used for programming, which limits the usage of advanced object-oriented concepts as well as reuse across different products.

  In addition, there is technical debt in the build system, due to the adopted ad-hoc approach for supporting multiple hardware/software variants.
- Natural evolution and aging: Some parts of the software have been developed and extended for many years, with a lot of patches to accommodate new use cases.

Business: This category contains the following causes:

– Time and cost pressure: There is time pressure for developing new features. In addition, cost limitations for hardware development forces developers to resolve some hardware-related issues at the software level; i.e. technical debt in hardware propagates to software.
– Requirements shortfall: Customer requirements are not well-documented and accessible to the developers. The missing history of the requirements makes it rather impossible to identify obsolete parts of the code that are no longer requested.
– Misalignment of business goals: The focus of each team is usually on developing and optimizing a single feature in the code that may be shared across different hardware products. There is no systematic way of aligning and ensuring quality across different hardware products.

Processes and Practices: This category contains the following causes:

– Insufficient processes: Although it was confirmed by the participants that over the past years the organizational/software processes have improved, there are still various possibilities for further improvements. For example, current software processes do not include technical debt management and topics related to it such as templates for technical debt backlog items, quality checklists for assessing technical debt, etc. In addition, current processes to enable systematic cross-team architecture and code review can significantly be improved.
– Insufficient documentations: Missing or outdated architecture and code documentations make it very hard and or even impossible to keep track of previous design decisions. Besides, product roadmaps are not always in hand to help architects identify future changes of the architecture and prepare the architecture to accommodate those changes. As a result, changes are applied in a rather ad-hoc way, leading to more technical debt.
– Inadequate software engineering practices and tools: Current practices for requirements management, architecture design, coding and testing should be updated based on latest developments in respective areas; for example, via adoption of new tools, requirements engineering methods, ATAM (architecture trade-off analysis method), etc.
– Inadequate planning: To achieve desired goals in technical debt repayment, the extent of required refactoring in architecture, code, test cases and build scripts should be identified and considered during the planning phase. Otherwise, as we experienced in the phase 2 of the project, not all planned technical debt can be repaid, or even new technical debt may be introduced due to the time pressure.

People: This category contains the following causes:

– Inexperienced teams: Software competences may not be very strong in companies that historically produce hardware products. Although there are already multiple trainings going on in various areas, it was mentioned that such theoretical trainings must be combined with more practical coaching to become more effective.

- Unclear quality-related roles and responsibilities: There is no clear role in teams for performing quality checks and improvements. Although some colleagues have the role of software architect, they may spend the majority of their time on bug fixing.
- Insufficient motivation with respect to quality improvement: Some participants feel demotivated regarding this topic because of the large number of identified causes as well as previous attempts for improving the quality, which had not fully achieved their goals.
- Coordination and communication shortfall: There are different Scrum teams that focus on different parts of the software within or across multiple products. To manage intra-, and inter-products dependencies, systematic means of coordination and communication across teams must be in place. Otherwise, developers must attend all the meetings of other teams to get informed on relevant decisions, and this is impractical. Likewise, to manage inter-products dependencies and to derive course-grained and futuristic architectural decisions, systematic means of coordination and communication among teams and portfolio managers must be in place. Currently, such communications are not performed systematically, causing teams make sub-optimal decisions based on the information that is available to them.
- Lack of common understanding of technical debt: Some developers believe that technical debt only exists in the older parts of the software, and the growth rate of technical debt in the new parts of the software is fixed or even reducing. However, the above-listed causes of technical debt do not make new software parts immune against technical debt.

5.2 Various Aspects of Technical Debt Management

Based on our survey, there was consensus that debt is not limited to code and architectural levels, and other kinds of debt such as social, process and infrastructure debt also impact the overall quality of products. Accordingly, we derived Fig. 2 that depicts various elements, which we believe play a role in achieving successful debt management at the system level.

The impacts of debt are visible in evolving products, which need to accommodate new customer requirements in certain period. Therefore, clear understanding of current and possibly futuristic customer requirements helps to plan for the evolution of the products better. Likewise, business visions define the roadmaps for future changes of the products, and availability of such roadmaps help architects to prepare the architecture for accommodating the future changes.

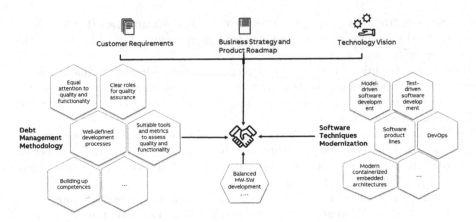

Fig. 2. The scope of technical debt management

Software engineering topics and software technologies are frequently evolving to address the need of industries. Consequently, companies must now and then modernize their technologies and methods to benefit from these advances. Methods such as test-driven software development, software product lines and model-driven software development pave the way to prevent various technical debt.

A systematic debt management methodology must become a mandatory part of a company. Depending on the causes of debt in the company, such a methodology must cover various aspects such as defining suitable processes, competence development, and infrastructure support.

Last but not least, industrial devices are 'systems' that contain both hardware and software components. Therefore, debt management can only be effective if its scope is at the system level, so that the interplay between technical debt in mechanical, electrical software architecture can be taken into account [17].

5.3   Towards Systematic Technical Debt Identification and Prioritization

Naturally, the depicted scope of debt management in Fig. 2 is very large, requires significant investment of time and money, and more importantly requires agreement and approval from different parts of the company.

Since it usually takes some time to achieve such an agreement, we had to narrow down the scope in the phase 3 of the project to the parts that are feasible in short-term. We see this scope definition as a kind of debt prioritization, where we have to identify our focus on the debt that can be paid considering the available constraints. Nevertheless, the awareness about various kinds of debt and their causes helps us mitigate their impacts on the selected scope of work.

We decided to proceed with more systematic architectural-level technical debt identification and prioritization based on available proposals in the literature [3,4,18–20], and adjusting them based on the needs of the company.

We are pursuing the following goals in this phase: a) Defining intermediate architectures to reach to the envisioned one in an iterative manner, b) Proposing a catalog of criteria for more objective prioritization of technical debt based on existing proposals in the literature, c) Quantitative and qualitative assessment of intermediate architectures and the required refactoring effort via Lattix and the ATAM method, d) Defining criteria of the 'Definition of Done' for the respective refactoring activities, e) Proposing a unified template for documenting technical debt at the architectural and code levels, f) Extending existing infrastructure (e.g., Azure DevOps) to incorporate the template, and g) Defining necessary extensions to the existing processes to incorporate the above steps. The results of this experiment will be reported in our future papers.

6   Challenges and Lessons Learnt

Below is the summary of our observed challenges and lessons learnt so far:

Assessing the Product Development Maturity Level: We believe that assessing the maturity of the development processes within a company should be one of the early activities towards software quality improvement in the company. The Capability Maturity Model [21] could be taken as a reference for this matter. Such an assessment helps to gain deeper insight on the impacts of current processes on (technical) debt accumulation.

Finding the Right Balance to Repay Various Debt: It is a well-known believe that software architecture may reflect the organizational structure of a company; meaning that there are more than just technical factors that influence the design of software architecture. Our study also confirms that to achieve the desired outcome in software quality improvement, one has to identify both technical and non-technical debt and their causes (e.g., see Sect. 5.1), identify their impacts on each other and develop a holistic approach to address debt.

Since we cannot address all causes of debt at the same time, there will always be some debt remaining at different levels, which we may revisit in the future if their impacts are high enough. For example, in the phase 2 of our project, it was clear that there is debt at the documentation, architecture, requirements, infrastructure, social and process levels. However, addressing them requires major agreements and effort across the company, which cannot be combined with refactoring the code in parallel. Even if we keep the focus on technical debt management, finding effective ways of prioritizing technical debt at architecture and code levels is already very challenging. Therefore, one must always assess such cases and select the most effective path to follow, knowing that some decisions have to revisited later when other debt is addressed or even is accepted to remain.

Improving Quality-Aware Working Culture: Introducing a methodology for systematic technical debt management in a large-scale company requires adjusting the working culture of the company, which is inherently a long-term activity. Most developers feel the impacts of technical debt on their work, but may not agree on the root causes of it. Especially if there are many causes of technical debt, it is always a challenge to find the right starting point. A major challenge here is to achieve common understanding of technical debt management and its associated topics across the company, as well as raising awareness on the role that each person can play to improve the situation. In addition, allocating dedicated time for quality improvement (e.g., 20% of developers time) is not sufficient, and more support (e.g., competence development, processes and infrastructure improvement) should be provided to help developers use that time more effectively.

Considering Previous/Ongoing Quality Improvement Attempts: In large-scale companies usually there have been several attempts in the past, or even there are ongoing activities for improving the quality of products. This can include introducing a tool that offers some metrics for technical debt measurement, attempts to improve the processes, attempts to harmonize architecture across multiple products, etc. To successfully contribute in the quality improvement activities, one has to familiarize himself with such activities and their positive/negative impacts on the perception of different parties on the various attempts.

Bi-directional Stepwise Competence Development: Introducing yet another tool or method, and providing some theoretical trainings are not enough for developing the competence of teams. Practical coaching to integrate new tools and methods in the working culture of the company is rather mandatory. Based on our experience, a stepwise approach is needed to illustrate the effectiveness of different quality improvement approaches, and to validate the effectiveness of the state-of-the-art methods in practice. This also requires the familiarity of the consultancy team with the daily working culture of the company to be able to effectively adjust existing methods to fit the specifics of the company.

Dealing with Frequently Changing Scope: In working with large-scale companies, we often hear from managers and developers that 'we have to start somewhere'. Finding the right starting point for technical debt management, which can have the desired impacts under dynamically changing external and internal conditions, is a major challenge. For example, where it was already very difficult to receive agreement to invest more time on technical debt management, the impacts of COVID-19 on the availability of resources made it even more difficult. Therefore, we had to adjust the scope so that we would not need extra resources allocated to our project. Considering that introducing systematic technical debt management in a company is a long-term activity, one has to always be prepared for adjusting the scope of the work to cope with such uncertainties.

7   Related Work

Various studies [22, 23] have been performed to provide a better understanding on how teams in large-scale agile organizations coordinate, and show that the coordination of work between teams influences teams' internal processes and how each team makes decisions. The study in [24] focuses on identification of social and process debt in agile companies. The study in [25] confirms that agile practices has positive impact in managing technical debt. We also believe that effective technical debt management at code and architecture levels cannot be achieved if social and process debt is not tackled.

In [4], the authors propose an approach to adopt business process management (BPM) to make the technical debt prioritization decision process more aligned with business expectations. Based on our insight discussed provided in our paper, we believe that the study proposed by [4] should be extended for large-scale embedded systems, where there are different business goals for software and hardware components, as well as there are multiple product variants with not completely aligned business goals.

Systematic technical debt prioritization based on multiple criteria is an active area of research [3,18–20]. In [18], the authors define multiple criteria based on customer, project and nature of technical debt for prioritization of technical debt. In [19], the authors investigated how a model of cost and benefits of incurring technical debt could be part of the change control board's decision process. In [20], by studying multiple large-scale companies, various criteria such as customer needs, lead time, cost/benefit, maintenance costs, and violated quality rules are determined to be considered for technical debt prioritization.

Where the input from these studies are useful for the phase 3 of our project, we found the focus of these studies to be limited to technical debt only, without taking other kinds of debt such as social and process debt into account. To the best of our knowledge, such a comprehensive study of debt prioritization is still missing in the research community. Besides, the cross-disciplinary management of technical debt by considering the impacts of mechanical, electrical and software engineering aspects of technical debt is still open for further research.

8   Conclusions and Future Work

Developing highly reliable software with low maintenance costs is ultimately the goal of most companies. Since software engineering is an evolving field, there is always the likelihood that advanced methods and techniques are not fully adopted in large-scale companies, which have long-living software with strong time to market requirements. Therefore, if a company requires support to improve the quality of its software, one may quickly strive for adopting various advanced software architecture and coding topics in the company. However, there are usually many challenges and obstacles along the way, which one has to find an effective solution to cope with.

In this paper, we reported on our ongoing experience in introducing technical debt management in a large-scale industrial company as our client. We explained that even if the classical steps for technical debt management are known, one has to take a stepwise approach to build common understanding on the relevant topics inside the company, to validate different approaches of technical debt prioritization, and to deal with various challenges that appear along the way. As for future work, we will continue assessing and adjusting our current methodology based on the lessons that we learnt along the way. In addition, we would like to adopt existing metrics and invest on various company-specific metrics to monitor quality improvement trends at various levels such as planning, architecture, code, and testing.

References

1. Kruchten, P., Nord, R., Ozkaya, I.: Managing Technical Debt: Reducing Friction in Software Development. Addison-Wesley Professional, Boston (2019)
2. Li, Z., Avgeriou, P., Liang, P.: A systematic mapping study on technical debt and its management. J. Syst. Softw. **101**, 193–220 (2015)
3. Lenarduzzi, V., Besker, T., Taibi, D., Martini, A., Fontana, F.A.: Technical debt prioritization: state of the art. A systematic literature review, ArXiv, vol. abs/1904.12538 (2019)
4. de Almeida, R.R., Kulesza, U., Treude, C., Feitosa, D.C., Lima, A.H.G.: Aligning technical debt prioritization with business objectives: a multiple-case study (2018)
5. SciTools - Understand. https://scitools.com/
6. TeamScale. https://www.cqse.eu/en/products/teamscale/landing/
7. CppDepend. https://www.cppdepend.com/
8. Fontana, F.A., Roveda, R., Zanoni, M.: Technical debt indexes provided by tools: a preliminary discussion. In: 2016 IEEE 8th International Workshop on Managing Technical Debt (MTD), pp. 28–31 (2016)
9. Lattix. https://www.lattix.com/
10. Structure101. https://structure101.com/
11. Cai, Y., Kazman, R.: Dv8: automated architecture analysis tool suites. In: 2019 IEEE/ACM International Conference on Technical Debt (TechDebt) (2019)
12. SonarQube: SonarQube. https://www.sonarqube.org/
13. Nayebi, M., et al.: A longitudinal study of identifying and paying down architecture debt. In: 2019 IEEE/ACM 41st International Conference on Software Engineering: Software Engineering in Practice (ICSE-SEIP), pp. 171–180 (2019)
14. Parker-Hernderson, J.: Architecture Decision Record (ADR). https://github.com/joelparkerhenderson/architecture_decision_record
15. arch42. https://arc42.org/
16. structurizr. https://structurizr.com/
17. Dong, Q.H., Ocker, F., Vogel-Heuser, B.: Technical debt as indicator for weaknesses in engineering of automated production systems. Prod. Eng. Res. Devel. **13**, 273–282 (2019). https://doi.org/10.1007/s11740-019-00897-0
18. Ribeiro, L.F., Souza Rios Alves, N., Gomes De Mendonca Neto, M., Spínola, R.O.: A strategy based on multiple decision criteria to support technical debt management. In: 2017 43rd Euromicro Conference on Software Engineering and Advanced Applications (SEAA), pp. 334–341 (2017)
19. Snipes, W., Robinson, B., Guo, Y., Seaman, C.: Defining the decision factors for managing defects: A technical debt perspective. In: 2012 Third International Workshop on Managing Technical Debt (MTD), pp. 54–60 (2012)
20. Besker, T., Martini, A., Bosch, J.: Technical debt triage in backlog management. In: IEEE/ACM International Conference on Technical Debt (TechDebt) (2019)
21. Paulk, M.C., Weber, C.V., Curtis, B., Chrissis, M.B.: The Capability Maturity Model: Guidelines for Improving the Software Process. Addison-Wesley Professional, Boston (1994)

22. Dingsøyr, T., Moe, N.B., Fægri, T.E., Seim, E.A.: Exploring software development at the very large-scale: a revelatory case study and research agenda for agile method adaptation. Empir. Softw. Eng. **23**(1), 490–520 (2017). https://doi.org/10.1007/s10664-017-9524-2

23. Bjørnson, F.O., Wijnmaalen, J., Stettina, C.J., Dingsøyr, T.: Inter-team coordination in large-scale agile development: a case study of three enabling mechanisms. In: Garbajosa, J., Wang, X., Aguiar, A. (eds.) XP 2018. LNBIP, vol. 314, pp. 216–231. Springer, Cham (2018). https://doi.org/10.1007/978-3-319-91602-6_15

24. Martini, A., Stray, V., Moe, N.B.: Technical-, social- and process debt in large-scale agile: an exploratory case-study. In: Hoda, R. (ed.) XP 2019. LNBIP, vol. 364, pp. 112–119. Springer, Cham (2019). https://doi.org/10.1007/978-3-030-30126-2_14

25. Holvitie, J., Leppänen, V., Hyrynsalmi, S.: Technical debt and the effect of agile software development practices on it - an industry practitioner survey. In: 2014 Sixth International Workshop on Managing Technical Debt, pp. 35–42 (2014)

Architecting Contemporary Distributed Systems

Determining Microservice Boundaries: A Case Study Using Static and Dynamic Software Analysis

Tiago Matias[1], Filipe F. Correia[1,2(✉)], Jonas Fritzsch[4,5], Justus Bogner[4,5], Hugo S. Ferreira[1,2], and André Restivo[1,3]

[1] Faculty of Engineering, University of Porto, Porto, Portugal
{up201700421,filipe.correia,hugosf,arestivo}@fe.up.pt
[2] INESC TEC, FEUP Campus, Porto, Portugal
[3] LIACC, FEUP Campus, Porto, Portugal
[4] Institute of Software Technology, University of Stuttgart, Stuttgart, Germany
{jonas.fritzsch,justus.bogner}@iste.uni-stuttgart.de
[5] University of Applied Sciences Reutlingen, Reutlingen, Germany

Abstract. A number of approaches have been proposed to identify service boundaries when decomposing a monolith to microservices. However, only a few use systematic methods and have been demonstrated with replicable empirical studies. We describe a systematic approach for refactoring systems to microservice architectures that uses static analysis to determine the system's structure and dynamic analysis to understand its actual behavior. A prototype of a tool was built using this approach (MonoBreaker) and was used to conduct a case study on a real-world software project. The goal was to assess the feasibility and benefits of a systematic approach to decomposition that combines static and dynamic analysis. The three study participants regarded as positive the decomposition proposed by our tool, and considered that it showed improvements over approaches that rely only on static analysis.

Keywords: Microservices · Refactoring · Software architecture

1 Introduction

The *microservices* architecture steadily gained popularity over the last years. Nowadays, it is often used in greenfield projects, but a lot of the times, systems are first developed as monoliths, which are quicker to develop and to test than microservices. Monoliths can then be broken up into microservices, when and if the need arises [1]. Doing this may promise high scalability, shorter release cycles or better maintainability. However, missing to identify the right boundaries may hinder reaching these benefits [2]. Therefore, an essential part of such a refactoring is the decomposition approach [3], which has the end-goal to identify contextually-related functionality and encapsulate it into different services. These should be characterized by a high cohesion inwards and loose coupling

© Springer Nature Switzerland AG 2020
A. Jansen et al. (Eds.): ECSA 2020, LNCS 12292, pp. 315–332, 2020.
https://doi.org/10.1007/978-3-030-58923-3_21

outwards. To optimally leverage from the microservices architectural pattern, existing functionality has to be split up with appropriate granularity as well.

There have been a number of approaches proposed already to decompose monoliths into microservices [4,5]. However, Fritzsch et al. found that such refactoring approaches were often not considered by practitioners and that identifying suitable service cuts is still perceived as a major challenge [3]. They asked 16 practitioners from 10 companies who were in the process of migrating their systems. Participants were either not aware of such tools or even convinced that it would be impossible to automate such a complex task. In a review of refactoring approaches, the same authors ascribed a lack of automation and missing tool support to most approaches proposed by academia [5]. This lack of tools inhibits adoption in industrial contexts and makes empirical studies more challenging to conduct.

We address this gap by *a)* identifying a systematic approach that combines principles of the previously proposed methods, *b)* using it to create a prototypical implementation, and *c)* conducting an industry case study with the prototype.

In the remainder of the paper, we discuss **related work** to provide an overview of other approaches, and describe our own **approach**, which relies on static and dynamic analysis. We introduce a **prototype** – MonoBreaker – that embodies this approach, and that identifies service boundaries for monoliths based on the Django web framework. Afterward, we present a **case study**, in which we contrast the results of MonoBreaker with ServiceCutter by surveying three developers of the project.

2   Related Work

The subject of decomposing and migrating monolithic applications to microservices is addressed in books such as *Building Microservices* [6], *Monolith to Microservices* [7] and *Microservices Patterns* [8]. Likewise, a variety of research papers describe ways to tackle such transformations.

Building microservices ideally means to create services that are highly cohesive and loosely coupled. Tyszberowicz [9] confirms that Domain-Driven Design (DDD) is the most common technique for modeling microservices. With DDD, the software mirrors business domains and sub-domains as well as the related domain models and bounded contexts. Each bounded context implements a small set of strongly-related behaviors and conforms to the Common Closure Principle [10]. These sets of behaviors shape individual units, resulting in cohesive designs of loosely-coupled services [11]. A system following DDD supports a higher degree of team independence as well as better scalability, testability and changeability [12].

Meta-studies. Ponce et al. provide an up-to-date overview in their review of 20 papers of migration and refactoring techniques [4]. Their study focuses on the approaches, the applicability to certain system types, validations of the techniques, and the associated challenges. The authors group works by their underlying decomposition approaches: *model-driven* (involving design elements, e.g.,

DDD), *static analysis* (based on source code) and *dynamic analysis* (based on runtime data).

Fritzsch et al. similarly compare 10 refactoring approaches and likewise provide a classification [5]. They distinguish decompositions based on *Static Code Analysis*, *Meta-Data*, *Workload-Data*, and *Dynamic Microservice Composition*. While the first three classes imply a fixed decomposition result, a dynamic composition of services would be continuously re-calculated, e.g., based on workload constraints. The study moreover reveals that most approaches are only applicable to certain types of applications, require significant amounts of input, or have limited and prototypical tool support.

Concrete Approaches and Tools. Nunes et al. pursue an approach based on identifying transactional contexts of business applications and using a clustering algorithm to determine service candidates [13]. Chen et al. similarly base the decomposition on the data flow of the business logic [14]. They compare the resulting service cut with the output of ServiceCutter [15], a freely-available tool implementing the approach by Gysel et al. [16]. ServiceCutter applies a clustering algorithm to identify new services and currently supports the *Girvan-Newman* and *Leung* algorithms for this purpose. To calculate the service cut, it requires that an *Entity-Relationship Model* (ERM) of the system is given in a specific format along with *User Representations* and *Coupling Criteria*. The collection of these partly-exhaustive system specifications is done in a manual process and requires the help of domain experts.

Ren et al. acknowledge the inadequacy of approaches only relying on static analysis [17]. They recognize that not analyzing the runtime behavior would hinder the calculation of a complete and accurate service cut. Therefore, they combine static and dynamic analysis based on the applications' runtime behavior. A subsequent clustering calculates the candidate service cut. Likewise, Taibi et al. propose a combined approach based on dependency analysis and process mining techniques [18]. The decomposition encompasses execution path and frequency analysis. After removing circular dependencies, additionally specified decomposition options are ranked based on coupling and granularity metrics to produce the candidate service cut. The authors employ a tool[1] that is capable of generating graphical visualizations to represent the business processes. Although a tool is referenced to capture the dynamic behavior of the system, the suggestion of service cuts is outside the scope of the work and must be done by experts, even if the authors mention that the process can somehow be automated.

Implications for our Approach. The methods described by Richardson [8] (*Decompose by business capability* and *Decompose by subdomain*) provide general guidelines for a partly-automated decomposition process. They support architects in choosing appropriate input values and assessing the resulting candidate service cuts.

The two meta-studies by Ponce and Fritzsch yield a variety of strategies to break down a monolith. Most do not combine static and dynamic analysis

---

[1] More information is found at the tool's website – https://fluxicon.com/disco/.

to steer the decomposition. As such, the works by Ren et al. and Taibi et al. comprise the core concepts of the approach described in our work. These works do not provide tools for service decomposition, or for any form of automation, but we will build on the concept of gathering runtime behavior and its analysis.

ServiceCutter is also of importance to our work, as it too implements the deterministic *Girvan-Newman* algorithm. In some aspects, our work is less sophisticated than ServiceCutter, as it does not yet consider quality attributes like security, scalability, and business ownership. However, it trades that for the benefit of being independent from extraneous, subjective, information provided by experts to determine the service cuts.

3   Approach

Decomposing a monolith is often done based on insights from software developers on the specific context of the *problem domain* and of the *application's architecture*. The challenge that we aim to address is to reduce subjectivity, making the process more systematic and automated. The approach described below is based on ideas that have been documented before [16–18], but are employed here for determining service boundaries with minimal to no manual input, which so far has not been feasibly demonstrated. Therefore, the approach is described as a hypothesis, and the case study in Sect. 5 as a first step to provide support for its effectiveness.

In more concrete terms, this approach aims to be data-driven and to be independent of sophisticated input from experts. To do this, we do not take into account all the intricacies of the process as it is often done manually today. Instead, we focus on what information can be obtained from the application itself via *static* and *dynamic* analysis to find beneficial service cuts. We rely on the availability of *a)* static software artifacts, namely source code, and *b)* operational data, such as the use of API endpoints, of datastores, and of issued method calls.

Static Analysis. Software artifacts are analyzed and the collected information used to build a graph-like model of the system, representing components as *nodes* and the dependencies between them as *edges*. Components and dependencies can be of different types, and identifying them will depend on the used programming languages, frameworks and environments. For example, components can refer to *classes*, *packages* or *modules*, and dependencies to *imports* or *method calls*.

Each edge is assigned a *weight* to represent the strength of the dependency. This is a function of the number and quality of connections between the two components. The weight of edges after static analysis can, for example, be the sum of the number of imports and method calls between its two components.

Dynamic Analysis. The system is then monitored at runtime to gather *operational data*, which is analyzed to identify how the dependencies are exercised during execution, and gain an understanding of how the system is actually used. Such information is used to compute a new weight for each edge of the graph. The *final weight* values are a function of the *static* and *dynamic weights*, and are a measure for how the components in the system are mutually bound. The underlying assumption is that a high amount of interaction between two components correlates with belonging to a common bounded context. Including them in different microservices would imply higher costs in latency and in maintaining resilience and fault tolerance.

Clustering. A graph of the service composition will support identifying different clusters of components. The nodes connected by the edges with higher weight values will be grouped to form clusters of relatively *high cohesion*. These clusters will depend on each other through edges with low weight values, representing relatively *low coupling*. The clusters can, therefore, be used to determine a set of possible *service cuts*. The specific clustering algorithm to be used is outside the scope of this approach, but would be interesting to explore (see Sect. 6).

Decomposition Suggestion. The identified service cuts serve as a foundation for assigning existing *software artifacts* to each of the new services and advise on the architectural *refactoring process*.

4   The MonoBreaker Tool

MonoBreaker aims to demonstrate the feasibility of the approach and was used in the **case study** described in Sect. 5. It is a prototype[2] and currently works with applications using the Django web framework. It takes a project's directory as input and does a **static analysis** of the source code to identify the overall project structure. This information is mapped to a graph-like model together with associated files and their dependencies. The same graph is populated with data collected through **dynamic analysis** to quantify the strength of the dependencies. The graph is then traversed to suggest a decomposition into new services, highlighting the source code files that will be involved and how the resulting services should communicate. This workflow is depicted in Fig. 1 and the several steps are exemplified below.

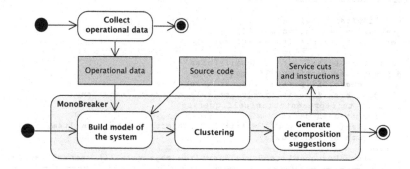

Fig. 1. Operation flow of MonoBreaker with inputs and outputs.

---

[2] MonoBreaker is freely available at https://github.com/tiagoCMatias/monoBreaker.

4.1 Collect Operational Data

Operational data is gathered using Silk, which is a profiling tool for Django[3]. The tool is capable of supplying information about the usage of entrypoint methods (the ones invoked when a URL is requested), and the model classes and queries involved in the process of returning results from the database. It uses this information to infer some of the internal method calls, as we will see in the next section.

4.2 Build Model of the System

The static analysis inspects the domain model, the views, and the dependencies between them. In particular, it tracks the use of Django's `Model` class, identifying its subclasses (i.e., the *domain model* of the application) and how they are connected through the declared *foreign keys*. It also tracks the use of the `ModelViewSet` class by identifying its subclasses (i.e., the *views* of the application) as well as the connections between these views and the model classes, via the `import` statements.

To illustrate the process, we present a minimalist example and the steps involved in suggesting a service decomposition using MonoBreaker. The file exemplified in Listing 1.1 results in the extraction of the `ViewItem` class as a new graph node. The imports of `Attribute` (line 4) and `Item` (line 6) refer to subclasses of Django's `Model` class, therefore, these are also extracted as nodes, with graph edges connecting them to the `ViewItem` node. Both the model subclasses `Attribute` and `Item` have a connection to `ViewItem` because it imports them and invokes their methods.

```
1   from rest_framework.decorators import action
2   from rest_framework.response import Response
3   from rest_framework.viewsets import ModelViewSet
4   from ..models.Attribute import Attribute
5   from ..serializers.ItemSerializer import ItemSerializer
6   from ..models.Item import Item
7
8   class ViewItem(ModelViewSet):
9     queryset = Item.objects.all()
10    serializer_class = ItemSerializer
11
12    @action(methods=['get'], detail=False)
13    def get_item_details(self, request):
14      if request.GET.get('attributes', None):
15        data = self.serializer_class(self.queryset, many=True).
              to_representation(self.queryset)
16        for item in data:
17          item['attributes'] = Attribute.objects.get_by_item(item['id'])
18        return Response(data)
19      else:
20        return Response(ItemSerializer(Item.objects.all(), many=True).data)
```

Listing 1.1. The `ViewItem` class, an example of a *view* in a Django application.

---

[3] See https://github.com/jazzband/django-silk for more information.

Monobreaker uses the graph resulting from the analysis described thus far to generate the visual representation depicted by Fig. 2a. The *weight* values associated to the edges represent the strength of the dependencies and are determined by:

$$StaticEdgeWeight = NumImports + NumMethodCalls$$

After the analysis of all source code files, a global dependency graph of the project is built. In this example, these files would also include Listing 1.2.

```
1   from rest_framework.decorators import action
2   from rest_framework.response import Response
3   from rest_framework.viewsets import ModelViewSet
4   from ..serializers.OrderSerializer import OrderSerializer
5   from ..models.Order import Order
6
7   class ViewOrder(ModelViewSet):
8       queryset = Order.objects.all()
9       serializer_class = OrderSerializer
10
11      @action(methods=['get'], detail=False)
12      def get_order_details(self, request):
13          if request.GET.get('items', None):
14              data = self.serializer_class(self.queryset, many=True).
                    to_representation(self.queryset)
15              for order in data:
16                  order['items'] = Order.objects.get_order_items(order['id'])
17              return Response(data)
18          else:
19              return Response(OrderSerializer(self.queryset, many=True).data)
20
21      def list(self):
22          return Response(OrderSerializer(Order.objects.all(), many=True).data)
```

Listing 1.2. The `ViewOrder` class, an example of a *view* in a Django application.

Figure 2b represents the updated version of the graph after the static analysis of the second *view* class. Note also the dependency between `ViewOrder` and `Item` via the call to the `get_order_items()` method. Detecting it could be attempted through deeper static analysis, in particular of chains of method calls that jump into framework code. The static detection of this dependency is a limitation of the current implementation of MonoBreaker, but it is one of little consequence, as it can still be detected through dynamic analysis, as we will see next.

The static analysis of the system is followed by the runtime analysis. The operational data that was previously collected (see Sect. 4.1) is processed and the result used to update the graph with *a)* previously undetected dependencies (in this example, the one between `ViewOrder` and `Item`) and *b)* with updated weight values. This ensures that we also consider the existence and the strength of dependencies that cannot be determined solely by inspecting the source code.

The requests received by the application may result in multiple method calls that eventually touch specific model classes. These are determined by Mono-Breaker via the database queries that are issued during the processing of a specific request. Table 1 shows some of the data resulting from the dynamic analysis, which is used to compute the dynamic weights.

Table 1. Data determined through dynamic analysis for this example.

View	Method	# Calls	Related models
ViewOrder	list()	2	Order
ViewOrder	get_order_details()	4	Order, Item
ViewItem	list()	4	Item
ViewItem	get_item_details()	8	Item, Attribute

To keep the weight values calculated by the dynamic analysis in the same order of magnitude as those calculated from static analysis, MonoBreaker normalizes them – the highest weight determined from the dynamic analysis will be at most as high as the highest one calculated from static analysis. Therefore, the equation representing the weight that arises from dynamic analysis becomes:

$$DynaEdgeWeight = NumMethodCalls \times \frac{MaxStaticWeight}{MaxNumMethodCalls}$$

In this implementation, the weights from the static and dynamic analyses were considered in equal parts for determining the final weights, resulting in:

$$EdgeWeight = StaticEdgeWeight + DynaEdgeWeight$$

Figure 2c depicts the resulting graph, showing the computed *DynaEdge Weight* in green and the final *EdgeWeight* in black.

4.3   Clustering

The dependencies collected through the static and dynamic analyses are used by MonoBreaker to create a graph-like model of the system. Nodes consist mainly of Django *model* and *view* classes. A clustering algorithm is then applied to break

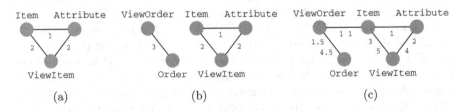

Fig. 2. Each graph shows a different stage of the example, (a) is after analysing the ViewItem class, (b) after analysing the ViewOrder class, and (b) after incorporating the results from the dynamic analysis. Values in green are the weights determined by dynamic analysis alone, and those in black are the total weight produced up to that stage.

the network down into smaller communities, thus grouping nodes according to the weights of the edges. We have chosen the Girvan-Newman algorithm[4] [19] given its apparent successful use in tools such as ServiceCutter. The resulting clusters indicate a set of potential service cuts.

4.4   Generate Decomposition Suggestions

After clustering the nodes, MonoBreaker provides an overview of the decomposition. It obtains the service cuts through the Girvan-Newman algorithm and provides the lists of the classes that will be needed for each service. These can be used by the developers to guide the refactoring process. Listing 1.3 shows the output for our simple example.

```
Total Files: 19
Django_Views: 2
Django_Models: 3

GraphNumber: 0
list_of_files: [
    'models.Attribute',
    'models.Item',
    'serializers.ItemSerializer',
    'views.ViewItems'
]

GraphNumber: 1
list_of_files: [
    'models.Item',
    'models.Order',
    'serializers.OrderSerializer',
    'views.ViewOrder'
]
```

Listing 1.3. Example of an output of MonoBreaker.

4.5   Limitations

The approach described in Sect. 3 is designed to apply to a wide range of contexts. The tool described in this section, on the other hand, was designed with a narrower scope and it is worth highlighting some of its limitations.

Technologies. The opportunity, of using a fully developed monolith built with Django to conduct a case study in the industry, led us to develop MonoBreaker specifically for Django-based monoliths that use the object-relational mapper. At this point, the tool will work only for systems developed using these technologies.

Design Assumptions. The implementation makes simplistic assumptions about the system to decompose, such as that it was designed around a domain model, and that it avoids cyclic dependencies and other kinds of unnecessary complexity. Such design problems should be approached before running MonoBreaker.

---

[4] Connectivity-based clustering algorithm, such as Girvam-Newman, are based on the idea that nodes have more affinity to nearby nodes than to those farther way.

Operational Time Frame. The quality of the decomposition is sensible to the choice of an appropriate time frame for collecting operational data, as it should be representative of how the system is normally used. Functionality not used during the dynamic analysis time frame will not be considered for calculating dynamic weights.

Balancing Quality Attributes. Another assumption is that there is a single *optimal* set of service cuts, but we know that there are often trade-offs when refactoring. Users of MonoBreaker are still not able to specify, for e.g., how the maintainability of the resulting system should be weighed against its scalability.

5   Case Study

To assess the feasibility and benefits of a systematic approach to decomposition that combines static and dynamic analysis, we conducted an industry case study using the developed prototype. We were interested in generating insights about the approach, in particular, in understanding its effectiveness for identifying good service boundaries when refactoring a monolith, and the impact that *dynamic* analysis has on the decomposition result. For the latter part of the study, we turned to ServiceCutter for a comparison.

5.1   Context

The case study focused on a web application for supporting the collaboration between two centers of a logistics startup company. The application had 15 KLOC and more than 40 domain-model elements, and had recently gone through significant growth in its use, making it an interesting candidate for the study.

We achieved the participation of three of the four developers that form the team responsible for this application. Their professional experience was in the range of 1–5 years for two of the developers and 5–15 years for the third developer.

5.2   Process

MonoBreaker was used to analyze the project and produced a suggestion for decomposing it into different services. The process consisted of four steps:

a) **Run MonoBreaker** – We gathered the project source code and the runtime data collected through Silk and provided them as input to MonoBreaker, which used both *static* and *dynamic* analysis to produce a suggestion of how the system could be decomposed.
b) **Run ServiceCutter** – The data statically-collected in step **a)** was transformed to the ERM format expected by ServiceCutter and was provided as input to produce an alternative decomposition using *static* analysis only.
c) **Present MonoBreaker** – A session was scheduled with the development team and included an introduction that explained the goal of the experiment and a showcase of MonoBreaker using an example project.

Table 2. Questions and answers in the *approach* group.

Question *[It's important ...]*	Answers
... to know what methods are called between the components of the monolith	5, 4, 3
... to know how frequently each method is called when the monolith is run in production	4, 3, 3
... to identify what the domain objects of the monolith are	5, 5, 5
... to identifying what are the relationships between the monolith components	5, 5, 5
... to know how the relationships between the components are used when the monolith is run in production	5, 5, 5
... to identify what imports are made by each software component of the monolith	5, 4, 3
... to identify what the schema of the database/datastore is	5, 5, 5
... to know the operations made to the database/datastore	5, 4, 4
... to identify how frequently the operations made to the database/datastore are executed when the monolith is run in production	4, 3, 4

d) **Questionnaire** – Following the MonoBreaker demo, a questionnaire was handed out to the participants. It aimed to assess how the feasibility of the approach and the impact of *dynamic* analysis on the quality of the results were perceived by the team. The participants did not have access to the source code during the questionnaire, and the two service decompositions were presented visually as dependency graphs. Participants were given 30 min to analyze the graphs and answer the questionnaire.

Table 3. Questions and answers in the *feasibility* group.

Question *[The proposed decomposition as microservices ...]*	Answers
... is the best one possible	4, 3, 2
... is easier to scale (performance)	4, 3, 2
... is easier to deploy new versions of the system	4, 3, 2
... is easier for maintainability by the existing team(s)	4, 3, 2

Fig. 3. MonoBreaker decomposition result as depicted in the questionnaire.

5.3 Data Sources

The case study used as data sources: *a)* the source code of the project, *b)* operational data collected through Silk during one week in a production environment and *c)* the answers to the questionnaire that were given by the team of the project.

The source code was obtained from the company's code repository. The operational information was collected in two tables created by Silk in the application's database (`silk_request` and `silk_sqlquery`). The questionnaire was built using Google Forms and the answers were gathered in a spreadsheet.

5.4 Data Analysis

Most questions were based on a Likert scale [20], ranging from (1) *Strongly Disagree* to (5) *Strongly Agree*. Questions were organized into four groups. Below, we summarize the answers provided by the three interviewees for each group of questions.

Personal Experience. These questions support understanding the team's professional experience, its familiarity with the case study project and with the process of migrating monoliths to microservices. The answers reveal that all team members have some experience migrating monoliths to microservices (3, 4, 3)[5] and that they were very familiar with the case study project (5, 5, 5), as expected. This ensures their ability to evaluate the decomposition approach.

Approach. The questions in this group aim to assess the perceived importance of different aspects when decomposing a monolith into microservices. If

---

[5] Throughout this section, we'll use this notation to represent the answers of the three team members to a questionnaire item using a five-level Likert scale.

the understanding of these aspects by the study participants revealed to be different from our own, it could explain differences in the answers to questions in the next groups of questions. The questions and answers from the three developers are shown in Table 2. The results show unanimous agreement in that identifying the *domain objects*, the *relationships between components*, how these *relationships are used in production* and the *schema of the data store* are very important factors when determining potential new services (5,5,5).

The answers to the remaining questions were not unanimous, but still show that significant importance is attributed to knowing *what operations are made to the database/datastore* (5,4,4).

These results show the relevance, as perceived by the members of this team, of both structural and behavioral information for service decomposition, and therefore are aligned with the concepts that we used to define our approach.

Feasibility. The questions in this group evaluate the perceived feasibility of the approach regarding the quality attributes of the application. Namely, the questions focus on the scalability, ease of deployment, and ease of maintenance. They are supported by the decomposition created by MonoBreaker, which was visually presented as depicted by Fig. 3. Both the questions and the answers are shown in Table 3.

The participants did not agree in their answer to these questions but answered consistently to all the questions (4,3,2). This led us to inspect more closely the answers for the *justification* question (the open-ended question where they could provide further context to their answers) and conclude that the decomposition was perceived as a good basis, but insufficient. Namely, the decomposition consists of 3 services, but team members argued in favor of a more aggressive decomposition. Looking closely at Fig. 3, we can see clusters around three different classes – `CargoMovement`, `MasterdataProducts` and `ShippingTransfer`. From their answers, we understood that the team was expecting the `ShippingTransfer` cluster to be further decomposed into two distinct services. Section 6 outlines a few factors that can be explored in future work to improve the decomposition.

Comparison With Using Only Static Analysis. This group has two Likert-scale questions, each accompanied by an open-ended *justification* question.

The first question compared the decomposition using both *dynamic* and *static* analysis with the one using only *static* analysis. To ease the comparison between the outputs, we transported the information to Gephi[6] and extracted both graphs. The graphs were depicted in the beginning of this group of questions as *Decomposition A* and *Decomposition B* (respectively, Fig. 4 and Fig. 3).

The second question directly addressed the usefulness of the output provided by MonoBreaker, listing the classes that would be required by each service.

Table 4 shows the two questions and the associated answers.

---

[6] Gephi is a tool for graph analysis and visualization – https://gephi.org.

Table 4. Questions and answers in the "comparing with the state-of-the-art" group.

Question	Answers
The decomposition A is better than the decomposition B	2, 2, 1
A tool to support decomposing a monolith into microservices would be useful if it provided this output	5, 5, 5

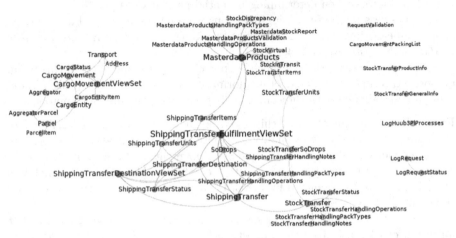

Fig. 4. ServiceCutter decomposition result as depicted in the questionnaire.

The answers dismiss *Decomposition A* as the best, concluding that combining *static* and *dynamic* analysis provided a better decomposition when compared to using *static* only.

Regarding the output provided by MonoBreaker for guidance on the refactoring, the answers were unanimous in that it would be helpful.

5.5 Threats to Validity

The purpose of this case study is to gather evidence to support the approach. The design described in Section 5 tries to minimize possible threats to validity, but those that exist need a closer look.

Projects and Participants. The sample of our case study was limited to one project and three software developers. The answers to the questionnaire's *approach* group can be used to confirm if this team valued both structural and behavioral information when decomposing services, as these were base assumptions used to design our approach, but the small scale doesn't allow to generalize conclusions. We would certainly like to see this case study replicated for other products and larger organizations with different backgrounds, to verify if these preliminary results hold in other contexts.

Possible Biases from Respondents. The partnership with the startup company for this case study was only possible due to good working and personal relationships and commitment between the company and the researchers. Therefore, there is always the possibility that the participants may have been inadvertently influenced. During the MonoBreaker presentation (Sect. 5.2), we took particular caution to take an impartial stance regarding the merits of the tool and of its underlying approach and to not interfere in any way when participants were responding to the questionnaire. Moreover, they didn't know which decomposition had been made using only *static* analysis or using both *static* and *dynamic* analysis. For these reasons, we are confident in discarding this as a threat to validity.

Representativeness of Sampled Data. The company supplied the project source code and allowed to alter it to enable the collection of operational data that otherwise would not be possible. As already mentioned, the operational data covered only one week of the application's run time information and collecting data for a longer period may have led to different results. All the relevant functionality of the application seems to have been used during this time, and we believe the amount of data to be sufficient to base a decomposition decision on. For this reason, we are confident in discarding this a threat to validity.

Suboptimal Baseline. To assess the impact of *dynamic* analysis in the decomposition, we compared the result of MonoBreaker (using *static* and *dynamic* analysis) with that of ServiceCutter (using *static* analysis only). The choice of ServiceCutter stemmed from the intention to compare MonoBreaker with leading tools from the current state of the art. ServiceCutter is the only freely-available tool that we could run to automate the decomposition process with minimal manual input[7].

However, we realized that the specific purpose of assessing the impact of dynamic analysis would have been better served by comparing the output of MonoBreaker when run with *static* and *dynamic* analysis with its output when run with *static* analysis only. We believe that when the Girvan-Newman algorithm is chosen when running ServiceCutter, the resulting output should be identical to MonoBreaker's if only *static* analysis is used, as MonoBreaker uses the same algorithm for clustering dependent components. Notwithstanding, running MonoBreaker with and without dynamic analysis would provide more robust evidence that no other factors had a significant influence on the decomposition result.

6   Conclusions and Future Work

In this work we contribute, *a)* a systematic **approach** to decompose monolithic applications to microservices, *b)* a **tool** prototype (MonoBreaker) that implements this approach and *c)* the design and results of an industry **case study**.

---

[7] This was possible by synthesizing a part of the inputs that it requires – namely, the ERM – and omitting the remaining inputs, which we were unable to create without resourcing to software developers – namely, the *User Representations* and the *Coupling Criteria*.

The approach is based on previous ideas but differs in its focus on fully automating the process of determining service boundaries. It does so by relying on static and dynamic software analysis. The case study uses MonoBreaker to assess the feasibility and merits of the approach. The decomposition obtained by the tool was regarded positively by the participants and seen as an improvement over using only static analysis. MonoBreaker is freely available, and the methodological design is documented to enable the replication of the case study by other researchers.

To improve these contributions, several aspects will be addressed in future work:

Model Building. The approach doesn't define a specific way to build the model of the application using the results of *static* and *dynamic* analysis. Future work will evaluate if other algorithms for calculating the weight of dependencies may perform better than our current implementation, which is currently based on a set of simple heuristics.

Clustering Algorithms. The approach is also not prescriptive of a particular clustering algorithm. It will be interesting to evaluate if others render better results than Girvan-Newman, the one currently used by MonoBreaker.

Evaluation Metrics. To enable a more objective evaluation of the proposed decomposition, the approach could be extended with service-based metrics – e.g., coupling and cohesion [21]. The approach of Taibi et al. [18] already includes metrics to rank decomposition candidates. A set of suitable service-based metrics for our approach would have to be determined, and can help to drive the search for better *model-building* and *clustering* algorithms.

Comparison with Human Experts. Future studies will evaluate if a data-driven approach such as ours is, not only able to automate the decomposition process fully, but will also provide a better decomposition than human experts.

Further Studies. More industry case studies will need to be conducted to improve our understanding of the effectiveness and limitations of the approach, ideally with a diverse and significant number of applications and participants.

Representativeness of Sampled Data. Future studies will compare the number of requests – per request type – that are received during the collection of operational data with those of more extended periods where operational data wasn't captured, but for which we are able to collect request statistics nonetheless. This will reinforce our confidence that the operational data collected is representative enough of a *normal* use of the application.

Fully Automatic Decomposition. MonoBreaker can identify file contents affected by the suggested decomposition, e.g., which class has to be extracted for each resulting service. The next step could be to suggest a sequence of lower-level refactorings required for the decomposition or even to automatically apply such refactorings to decompose the system.

Acknowledgment. João Paiva Pinto and Isabel Azevedo discussed different forms of this work with us. We thank them for all the precious feedback.

This work is financed by National Funds through the Portuguese funding agency, FCT - Fundação para a Ciência e a Tecnologia within project UIDB/50014/2020.

References

1. Fowler, M.: Monolith first. Martin Fowler's Bliki (2015). https://martinfowler.com/bliki/MonolithFirst.html. Accessed 27 Nov 2019
2. Balalaie, A., Heydarnoori, A., Jamshidi, P.: Migrating to cloud-native architectures using microservices: an experience report. In: Celesti, A., Leitner, P. (eds.) ESOCC Workshops 2015. CCIS, vol. 567, pp. 201–215. Springer, Cham (2016). https://doi.org/10.1007/978-3-319-33313-7_15
3. Fritzsch, J., Bogner, J., Wagner, S., Zimmermann, A.: Microservices migration in industry: intentions, strategies, and challenges. In: 2019 IEEE International Conference on Software Maintenance and Evolution (ICSME), pp. 481–490 (2019)
4. Ponce, F., Márquez, G., Astudillo, H.: Migrating from monolithic architecture to microservices: a rapid review. In: Proceedings of 38th International Conference of the Chilean Computer Science Society (SCCC 2019), Chile (2019)
5. Fritzsch, J., Bogner, J., Zimmermann, A., Wagner, S.: From monolith to microservices: a classification of refactoring approaches. In: Bruel, J.-M., Mazzara, M., Meyer, B. (eds.) DEVOPS 2018. LNCS, vol. 11350, pp. 128–141. Springer, Cham (2019). https://doi.org/10.1007/978-3-030-06019-0_10
6. Newman, S.: Building Microservices: Designing Fine-Grained Systems, 1st edn. O'Reilly Media, Sebastopol (2015)
7. Newman, S.: Monolith to Microservices: Evolutionary Patterns to Transform Your Monolith, 1st edn. O'Reilly Media, Sebastopol (2019)
8. Richardson, C.: Microservices Patterns: With examples in Java. Manning, Shelter Island (2018)
9. Tyszberowicz, S., Heinrich, R., Liu, B., Liu, Z.: Identifying microservices using functional decomposition. In: Feng, X., Müller-Olm, M., Yang, Z. (eds.) SETTA 2018. LNCS, vol. 10998, pp. 50–65. Springer, Cham (2018). https://doi.org/10.1007/978-3-319-99933-3_4
10. Martin, R.C.: Clean Architecture: A Craftsman's Guide to Software Structure and Design. Prentice Hall, Upper Saddle River (2017)
11. Evans, E.: Domain-Driven Design. Addison-Wesley Professional, Boston (2003)
12. Millett, S., Tune, N.: Patterns, Principles, and Practices of Domain-driven Design. Wiley, Hoboken (2015)
13. Nunes, L., Santos, N., Rito Silva, A.: From a monolith to a microservices architecture: an approach based on transactional contexts. In: Bures, T., Duchien, L., Inverardi, P. (eds.) ECSA 2019. LNCS, vol. 11681, pp. 37–52. Springer, Cham (2019). https://doi.org/10.1007/978-3-030-29983-5_3
14. Chen, R., Li, S., Li, Z.: From monolith to microservices: a dataflow-driven approach. In: Proceedings of the 24th Asia-Pacific Software Engineering Conference – APSEC 2017, pp. 466–475. IEEE (2018)
15. Kälbener, L., Gysel, M.: Service cutter: a structured way to service decomposition. https://servicecutter.github.io/

16. Gysel, M., Kölbener, L., Giersche, W., Zimmermann, O.: Service cutter: a systematic approach to service decomposition. In: Aiello, M., Johnsen, E.B., Dustdar, S., Georgievski, I. (eds.) ESOCC 2016. LNCS, vol. 9846, pp. 185–200. Springer, Cham (2016). https://doi.org/10.1007/978-3-319-44482-6_12

17. Ren, Z., et al.: Migrating web applications from monolithic structure to microservices architecture. In: Proceedings of the Tenth Asia-Pacific Symposium on Internetware, series ICPS, Internetware 2018. ACM, New York (2018)

18. Taibi, D., Systä, K.: From monolithic systems to microservices: a decomposition framework based on process mining. In: Proceedings of the 9th International Conference on Cloud Computing and Services Science—CLOSER 2019 (2019)

19. Newman, M.E.J., Girvan, M.: Finding and evaluating community structure in networks. Phys. Rev. E **69**(2) (2004). https://journals.aps.org/pre/abstract/10.1103/PhysRevE.69.026113

20. Likert, R.: A technique for measurement of attitudes. Arch. Psychol. **22**, 5–55 (1932)

21. Bogner, J., Wagner, S., Zimmermann, A.: Automatically measuring the maintainability of service- and microservice-based systems: a literature review. In: Proceedings of the 27th International Workshop on Software Measurement and 12th International Conference on Software Process and Product Measurement, series ICPS, IWSM Mensura 2017, pp. 107–115. ACM, New York (2017)

IAS: An IoT Architectural Self-adaptation Framework

Mahyar T. Moghaddam[1]($\boxtimes$), Eric Rutten[1], Philippe Lalanda[2], and Guillaume Giraud[3]

[1] Univ. Grenoble Alpes, Inria, CNRS, LIG, 38000 Grenoble, France
{mahyar.tourchi-moghaddam,eric.rutten}@inria.fr
[2] Univ. Grenoble Alpes, LIG, 38058 Grenoble, France
philippe.lalanda@imag.fr
[3] RTE, 92073 Paris, France
guillaume-np.giraud@rte-france.com

Abstract. This paper develops a generic approach to model control loops and their interaction within the Internet of Things (IoT) environments. We take advantage of *MAPE-K* loops to enable architectural self-adaptation. The system's architectural setting is aligned with the adaptation goals and the components run-time situation and constraints. We introduce an integrated framework for IoT Architectural Self-adaptation (*IAS*) where *functional* control elements are in charge of environmental adaptation and *autonomic* control elements handle the functional system's architectural adaptation. A *Queuing Networks (QN)* approach was used for modeling the *IAS*. The *IAS-QN* can model control levels and their interaction to perform both architectural and environmental adaptations. The *IAS-QN* was modeled on a smart grid system for the Melle-Longchamp area (France). Our architectural adaptation approach successfully set the propositions to enhance the performance of the electricity transmission system. This industrial use-case is a part of *CPS4EU* European industrial innovation project (CPS4EU is a three years project funded by the H2020-ECSEL-2018-IA. The project develops four vital IoT technologies, namely computing, connectivity, sensing, and cooperative systems. It incorporates those IoT technologies through pre-integrated architectures and design tools. It instantiates the architectures in dedicated use-cases from a strategic application viewpoint for automotive, smart grid, and industrial automation https://cps4eu.eu).

Keywords: IoT · Software architecture · Self-adaptation · Autonomic control · Functional control · Performance · Queuing networks

1 Introduction

Internet of Things (*IoT*) systems are composed of distributed smart elements that are pervasively installed to affect the environment. Like most software systems, *IoT* is exposed to changes that occur in both their state and their surrounding environment. The changes cause uncertainties during system operation.

© Springer Nature Switzerland AG 2020
A. Jansen et al. (Eds.): ECSA 2020, LNCS 12292, pp. 333–351, 2020.
https://doi.org/10.1007/978-3-030-58923-3_22

Control loops are introduced to facilitate self-adaptation to handle changes and uncertainties. *IoT* sensors supply raw data (*M*) to central or distributed computational components to be refined and analyzed (*A*) towards further actuation planning (*P*) and execution (*E*). This process within comprehensive knowledge (*K*) forms the *MAPE-K* control loop. Control loops can be designed and developed in many different ways. Architecture-based adaptation is an example that focuses on the role of architectures in engineering self-adaptive systems. Typically, modeling architectural self-adaptation imposes separating the concerns about system functionality from adaptation [1].

In contrast to most of the architecture-based adaptation models, we propose an approach that considers the adaptation internal to the system functionality. More specifically, we regard functional control elements (*FCE*) in charge of managing the system functionality and autonomic control elements (*ACE*) responsible for monitoring the functional system's situation and handling the architectural composition. In our **IoT A**rchitectural **S**elf-adaptation (**IAS**) framework, we are concerned with the interaction among various levels of control loops that are driven by the system adaptation goals. Our focus is on reasoning and modeling various *IoT* architectural patterns and their run-time architectural transitions managed by the autonomic control logic. The *IAS* conceptual framework, while inspired by the *IEEE/ISO/IEC 42010* architecture description standard [2], comprises both functional and autonomic control elements as well as their interaction mechanisms.

We define the *IAS* conceptual framework, and we model it on a real smart grid application: the Melle-Longchamp area (France). Since the area expands renewable energy generation using several wind-farms as sources of energy, the voltage and current of the system sometimes become hard to forecast. Therefore, to avoid the risk of overloading the lines and creating danger for people's safety, the peak current has to be managed. Instead of developing new installations, the French Transmission System Operator policy is to investigate new exploitation methods of the existing electrical installations and favor their optimal operation. Wind-farm generation can be limited by opening their feeder's circuit breaker, or more efficiently, by modulating their generation. Additional means can also be used, such as batteries, power electronics, and *IoT*. The heterogeneity and variation of sensors, actuators, and processing elements of power systems increase the concerns on reliability and performance. In our use-case, while the circuit breakers are the safe and quick solution to avoid overloading of lines, their usage should be minimized to prevent imposing indirect costs. Modulating wind-farms' generation is a solution exposed to a high actuation time, and batteries can store electricity for a few seconds. Thus, the system needs to make quick decisions on its own composition to keep the performance within an adequate threshold.

Putting the self-adaptation control at the center of the software process, we started by analyzing the problem and selecting the data to see what factors affect the system response time. Then we upgraded the software architecture from local centralized to hierarchical, which enables all types of architectural transition. We further modeled the *IAS* approach by queuing networks (QNs) that facilitate designing the various levels of control for performance evaluation.

The paper makes the following contributions: *i)* presenting an IoT architectural self-adaptation framework that focuses on functional and autonomic control components and their run-time interaction; *ii)* modeling the proposed framework with queuing networks to estimate the performance of IoT systems and to support architectural decisions and transitions; *iii)* applying our framework to a smart grid system by analyzing its various components and their run-time behavior, for establishing performant operations.

The paper is organized as follows. Relevant literature is discussed in Sect. 2. The IAS framework is thoroughly explained in Sect. 3. The approach is applied to a real case in Sect. 4, and conclusions are finally drawn in Sect. 5.

2   Related Work

In software engineering, works on self-adaptation typically focus on functional control elements that interact with the environment to provide a service. Here we find works on using feedback control loops (such as *MAPE-K*) and their interaction that can be presented as patterns [3], in which the functions from multiple loops are coordinated in different ways. Such interactive coordination mechanisms are indeed crucial to model ever-growing distributed systems. Each interaction pattern can satisfy several non-functional requirements while guaranteeing the functionality of the system [4]. To quote an example, *QoSMOS* [5] is an adaptive service-based platform that enables dynamic adaptation to run-time changes to achieve some quality of service (*QoS*) requirements. Some studies [6] take advantage of layered queuing networks (*LQNs*) while considering run-time *QoS* to automatically generate adaptation policies. Each element of *MAPE-K* loop should dynamically react [7] to changes that occur in system's goals and requirements. Current research on goal modeling takes into account uncertainty [8], but the goals' dynamic transition [1] and multiple dynamic goals' satisfaction [9] has not received much attention. We believe that the self-adaptive software systems' goals are highly influenced by the limitations and constraints imposed by the non-controllable environment. Various modes of functional requirement satisfaction should be engineered to enable the system to pick, synthesize, and verify those modes dynamically.

Such a challenge is even bolder in IoT systems, which comprise heterogeneous devices that dynamically interact through the internet. The problem can be tackled by designing self-managing devices that can adapt their state to changes in the system context and environment [10,11]. However, realizing the IoT devices is challenging because of inherent uncertainties in their operation contexts, such as interferences and dynamic traffic in the network [12]. Often these uncertainties are difficult to predict by architects at development time and often lead to indecisiveness.

Several studies propose the use of software architectures to address self-adaptation [13,14]. An architecture model provides a global view of the system and its properties and behavior [15]. While architectures can give a global idea of the system, the heterogeneity of software systems makes it challenging to design a set of self-adaptation architectural patterns. Some studies argue that architectural adaptation includes an architectural model of the controllable software components that allows the feedback loop to reason about various system configurations and adapt it based on goals [16]. However, considering the feedback loop running on *FCE* as an external mechanism to the system minimizes the dynamicity of the self-adaptive system. We believe that the functional control mechanism should be monitored and adapted by autonomic control components [17,18], which gets input from both dynamic goals and real-time state of the system.

3   IAS Framework

This section introduces the conceptual foundations of *IAS*, comprising a metamodel that focuses on the *FCE* and *ACE* interaction. The framework is inspired by the *IEEE/ISO/IEC 42010* standard [2], but focuses on architecture self-adaptation rather than architecture description. The metamodel (Fig. 1) depicts vital concepts of systems and the control mechanism as a process to be considered in the software design and adaptation process. The metamodel is divided into two parts: the right side depicts *functional control* component and its inputs and dependencies, and the left side deals with *autonomic control* component and its correlation with other elements of the system. Software system **stakeholders** comprise users, developers/clients/managers, and citizens/occupants. Stakeholders have concerns regarding the system-of-interest [2]. As the focus of this paper, developers and managers are concerned with the **architecture variant**, including the life cycle from system needs and requirements, design choices and implementation, and operating considerations.

IEEE/ISO/IEC 42010 standard [2] specifies that the system goals and concerns are traditionally formed of functional and non-functional requirements, design constraints, assumptions, dependencies, and architecture decisions. A system contains both **functional** and **adaptation goals** that are set by stakeholders. Functional goals specify the system's functionality under various environmental constraints, and adaptation goals mostly concern the quality of the system. In the *IAS* approach, we argue that self-adaptation is a goal-directed process and its goals should be captured. As shown in Fig. 1, the goals are generally affected by the **environment**. In other words, the environment context might enforce prioritizing a set of goals or ignoring another set of goals. For instance, if the goal of a self-adaptive smart grid system is performance improvement, a disaster may prioritize taking adequate measures to prevent the emergency by, e.g., activating circuit breakers.

Thus, a system is situated in the environment. The environment is the real world, by which the software system interacts. The environment might include both physical and virtual elements [1], that the system does not directly control their functionality. The system interacts with the environment and is influenced by it. A system can also interact with other systems in the environment.

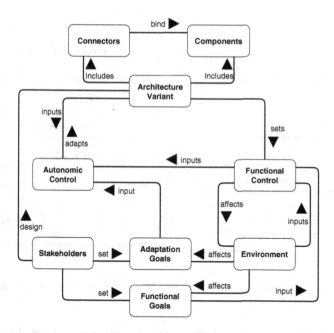

Fig. 1. Conceptual model of IoT Architectural Self-adaptation (*IAS*).

The environment can be sensed and affected through *sensors* and *actuators*, respectively, which locate within *IoT elements* subsystem and perform the functionality of the IoT system. As shown in Fig. 2/right, the *sense* elements frequently retrieve raw data [19] to input the control components, and *actuate* elements receive periodic commands to affect environment. The mentioned data transmission is continuous since the environment is not under full control of the software system, and the dynamics of the environment should be tackled.

The **functional control** comprises the adaptation logic that allows the system to perform the intended adaptation within the environment. The *FCE* has a *MAPE-K* (*Monitor, Analysis, Plan, Execute and comprehensive knowledge*) approach behind [14,17,19]. The *Monitor* element aggregates and refines the data to be analyzed and updates the *knowledge* base of the control component. The *Analyze* element interprets the monitored data based on the *functional goals*. The *Plan* element builds actuation strategies, and the *Execute* element processes the actuation strategies and prepares the type of message to be set to each set of actuators.

The left side of the metamodel (Fig. 1) shows the **autonomic control** that is more extensively described within Fig. 2/left. The autonomic control supports a continuous self-adaptation process [17]. It enables the system to monitor itself continuously and perform necessary adaptation to achieve the adaptation goals. The *ACE* takes advantage of the *MAPE-K* concept as well. It *monitors* the system's situation (including *functional control*) and assesses both the system functionality and quality to update the *knowledge* base. The *ACE* further

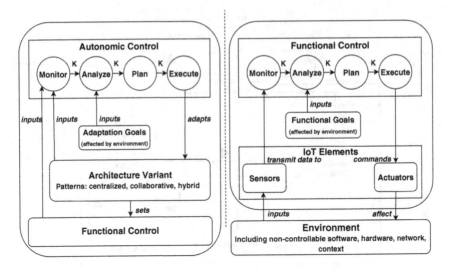

Fig. 2. IAS autonomic control (right) and functional control (left) mechanisms.

analyzes the data and compares it with real-time adaptation goals. Afterward, an adequate strategy will be *planned* to be *executed* by architecture variant adaptation. For instance, suppose that the adaptation goal is to keep the performance in a proper threshold, and the high CPU time on a local controller is preventing such a purpose. In this situation, the autonomic control component adapts the architecture based on a specific strategy, e.g., switching from local to the remote control.

Architecture variant determines variations in both software and hardware architectures [20]. The hardware architecture includes *IoT* hardware elements, i.e., sensors, network facilities, controllers, and actuators. The software architecture that is run on hardware elements includes a set of **components** that are bounded by **connectors** based on specific rules and constraints. These architectures are designed by stakeholders and self-adapted by *ACE* during system execution [21].

It is worth mentioning that, from a software architecture point of view, *FCE* and *ACE* and *architecture variant* are all part of the architecture. Architecture variant determines multiple functional deployment types, which appear as architectural patterns shown in Fig. 3. The patterns are composed of *IoT elements* layer and one or several *functional control* layers. The functional control can perform locally and/or centrally and remotely. Here is the point in which a centralized cloud and distributed edge and fog can form the *hierarchical* pattern. Thus, the patterns [22] characterize *IoT* systems based on their levels of *distribution* and *collaboration* [20,22]. Distribution specifies whether data analysis software ought to be deployed on a single node (*centralized*) or on several nodes (*distributed* and *hierarchical*) that are dispersed across the *IoT* system. The collaboration deals with interaction among functional control components to satisfy

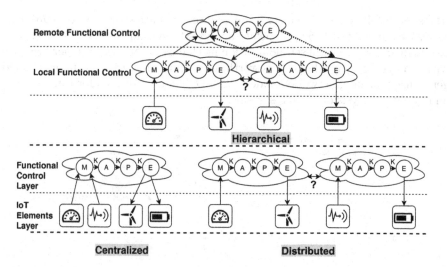

Fig. 3. *IoT* architectural patterns based on functional control components composition. The *centralized* pattern comprises processing on a *central local* or *remote* controller. The *distributed* pattern includes the processing on *independent* or *collaborative* controllers. The *Hierarchical* pattern contains *independent* or *hybrid* (i.e., with distributed collaborative) controllers.

the goals, requirements, and strategies. This collaboration may appear as a level of information sharing, coordinated analysis or planning, or synchronized execution [14].

The *IAS-based* architectures contain the mechanisms to determine the required architectural adaption, based on intended *QoS* satisfaction level. Our conceptual framework does not rely on any specific tool; thus, practical modeling solutions can be mapped within it. The following section describes the steps taken to map a smart grid system within *IAS*, to improve its performance indices.

4 Application

We model our *IAS* framework on the performance improvement for *RTE*[1] *Company's* transmission network, located in the Melle-Longchamp area (France). Figure 4 shows the smart grid network that includes 35 substations connected by 30 lines. The grid has some constraints regarding current and voltage. In addition to the power flowing through the network, it contains wind-farms with a total peak production capacity of 700 MW. Melle-Longchamp area's control network is being upgraded from a traditional centralized control to an *IoT* distributed control system to enhance the performance of the software system.

---

[1] Electricity Transmission Network, usually known as RTE, is the electricity transmission system operator of France.

The system follows the usual sense - compute - actuate structure from *IoT* systems. We applied the *IAS* approach to analyze the system and its objectives, and to design an architectural self-adaptation mechanism that keeps the performance within a desirable threshold. It is worth mentioning that *IAS* and its associated generalized queuing networks models (*IAS-QN*) can be re-used for functionality and quality analysis of all IoT systems.

Fig. 4. Smart grid network for Melle-Longchamp. It includes 35 substations connected with 30 lines.

4.1   Problem and Goals Analysis

Renewable energy systems that convert wind and sun's rays into electricity are growing as the primary source of energy. Such renewable generation is mainly connected to the distribution grid but has an impact on the transmission grid as well. In the example presented in Fig. 5/lower, a high percentage of the required electricity to distribute is being supplied from RTE substation, e.g. B and a small percentage form distribution substation D. If a strong wind blows and the generation in D becomes excessive, an overload will occur on the transmission line between B and A. To deal with this problem, the functional controller can activate different levers: *i)* the battery in E can be charged, *ii)* the production in D can be limited, *iii)* the circuit breaker on B can be activated (less desirable option). Practically, a combination of the actions mentioned above is required. Dealing with transmission overload risk necessitates considering some information from sensors such as values of currents and voltages on every line, state of the network circuit breakers, state of battery's charge, and also a set of parameters such as time to limit production of the wind farms, current overload thresholds on every line and eventually generator merit order.

Having such sensory input, *FCE* must ensure the safe operation of the network by sending: *i)* topological orders to the network circuit breakers, *ii)* modulation orders to the generators, *iii)* set-point orders to the storage batteries. The adaptive management of such smart transmission systems is exposed to performance issues since: *i)* some types of sensors and actuators need a significant service time, *ii)* enhanced forecasting algorithms for generation require a notable computation time, *iii)* network transmission and propagation delays sometimes become long, and *iv)* the collaboration pattern among local and remote control resources (with various processing power) is not always efficiently designed.

The typical application needs the delay between data acquisition and actuation to be less than *five seconds*, but shorter operation times seek. Within the next subsections, we design the RTE's *IAS*-based system that enables the smart grid to tackle both functional and performance problems.

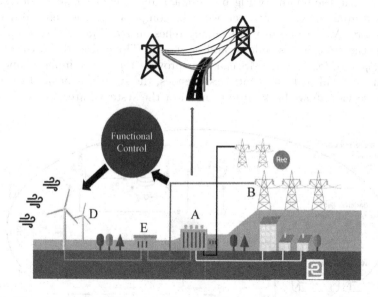

Fig. 5. The smart grid problem specification. The overloading of the lines because of e.g. a strong wind can create danger for people's safety.

4.2   Architecture

Figure 6 shows the architecture we designed for the Melle-Longchamp case by taking advantage of the *New Automated Adaptive Zone (*NAZA) platform [23]. The architecture follows a hierarchical pattern with distributed collaborative controllers (see Fig. 3) that can turn into centralized or distributed patterns if needed. As shown at the bottom of the figure, each of the 35 substations acquires data from two types of sensors: *i)* current and voltage transducers, and *ii)* position relays. This function can include aggregation or basic combination of acquired data (e.g., turning high-frequency sample values into root mean square values). Data from the sensors is sent to the control level, eventually after filtering. Each substation has a gateway that is in collaboration with other areas' gateways. Gateway are servers *Advantech ECU-4787* or *MOXA 681-C*. Current and voltage measurements (in protocol *IEC61850*) are sent every second to the local gateway. The position of circuit breaker (in protocol *IEC60780-5-104*) is sent to the local gateway on every event.

Each gateway can act as the central controller of the whole network, with limited CPU capacity that is five times less than the central remote controller. The gateway on *substation 1* acts as the *autonomic control element (ACE)* that plans the combination of *functional control elements (FCE)* in use. The *ACE* can be moved to any other substation's gateway or the cloud. The *ACE* implements the control logic given the states, conditions, and behaviors of the functional controllers.

As shown in the middle of Fig. 6, the main functional element retrieves and stores data from the gateways, performs the computation, and sends orders to the actuators. *NAZA* platform principally relies on *RESTful API* to communicate with the transducers, relays, and actuators. The collected data is stored in a *MySql DBMS*. The DBMS can also provide the solver inner-component with summary and real-time statistics. Besides, the system associated with the simulator service allows back-office to monitor the system state.

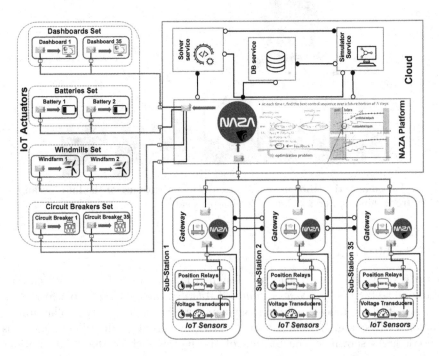

Fig. 6. The proposed hierarchical architecture for RTE. The architecture includes sense, process and actuating layers. *NAZA* platform can be run on gateways, local controller, and cloud.

The solver implements a Model Predictive Control (*MPC*) model to optimize a cost function to use levers such as batteries set-points and generation limit values. It gets real-time data from the gateways and calculates the values for actuators every 5 s. In some cases that the algorithm finds no solution or computation takes too long; simple flow charts enforce safety rules such as curtailing all necessary generations. *NAZA* platform can be run on RTE substation gateways, local controller, and cloud. Cloud has an unlimited processing power but causes 2 or 3 times more network delay than local servers mode. The left side of Fig. 6 shows the actuators. Circuit breakers that are the fastest mode to stop the current in a line are located in every substation. The batteries can store the electricity for dozens of seconds to give some time to wind-farms to shut down. The dashboards show controllers' state, the values measured by sensors, and the set-points or limits sent to batteries and generators.

Our main architectural challenges are related to the combination and location of the computation components, i.e., gateways, RTE controllers, and cloud. The challenge mainly arises when the intended *QoS* (here performance) is not satisfied, and a run-time architectural pattern switch is required. Such run-time dynamic adaptation and reconfiguration is set by *ACE*. The architectural patterns and their adaptation can be modeled by the Queuing Networks *(QNs)* concept. In the following section, we introduce a *QNs* modeling approach that can facilitate dealing with computation components' combination and location issues.

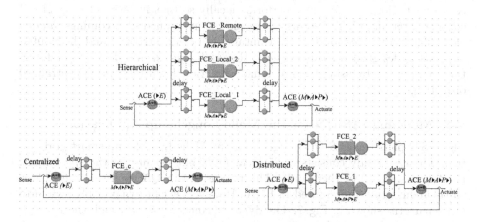

Fig. 7. *IAS-QN* patterns based on Fig. 3. These generalized patterns can be re-used for functionality and quality analysis of all *IoT* systems.

4.3   Modeling IAS Using QNs

In this section, we model the *IAS* within Queuing Networks (*QNs*) to introduce a generalized set of *IAS-QN* models. Our approach provides a pattern-based performance modeling of the entire self-adaptive system. The patterns can be re-used to model various self-adaptive *IoT* systems. In *IAS-QN*, the architectural components are represented by *QN* stations, and various sensing, computing, and actuating activities are represented by job classes that flow through the *QN*. In our *MAPEK-based* approach, the activities are performed both within and between components.

Figure 7 shows the IAS-QN patterns corresponding to the *IoT* architectural patterns shown in Fig. 3. Data coming from *sense* elements feed the *controllers* to plan for specific *actuation*. The computation on sensed data is performed by the functional control elements (shown as *FCE*), while the composition of *FCE* is set by the autonomic control elements (shown as *ACE*). The *ACE* adopts a *MAPE-K* loop to assess the conformity between the *FCE* situation and the goals. Based on the locality of *ACE* and *FCE*, the communication between them suffers form some *delay*. *Centralized* pattern benefits from only one *FCE* so that the architectural adaptation can only take place on other elements, i.e., sense, actuate, and network. A centralized pattern can be associated with using a central server or cloud as the *FCE*.

Distributed pattern benefits from a minimum of two *FCE* that might share some information. Here the *ACE* can also enforce adaptation on *FCE* level by heading data toward a controller that enhances system quality. A distributed pattern is generally associated with the local processing and storage, which take place in *fog* nodes. Fog brings a degree of cloud functionality to the network edge. The computation capacity of fog is lower than the cloud, but it reduces a significant point of failure by shifting towards more than one computational component. However, fog only performs locally so that it does not have global coverage over large IoT systems. To tackle the mentioned shortcomings, *hierarchical* pattern that contains the advantages of both centralized and distributed patterns is designed. In this pattern, the *ACE* can execute dynamic architectural adaptation by using local or remote functional controllers in a centralized or distributed way.

4.4 Modeling IAS-QN for the Melle-Longchamp Application

Figure 8 depicts the *IAS-QN* designed for the Melle-Longchamp smart grid system. The case study consists of 35 local *FCE*, but because of the space limit, the figure shows 2 of them only. The proposed *IAS-QN* conforms the *hierarchical* architecture represented in Fig. 6. However, it can dynamically switch to other patterns shown in Fig. 7. The dynamic control flows through the *IAS-QN* components are specified as follows:

1. Environmental data are sampled by *sampling* nodes in charge of specifying the sampling rate. Our system has two types of sensors with different sampling rates; thus, tow sampling nodes are required. The effect of the system on the environment is shown by *done* node. The mentioned nodes are located on the environment side (shown in Fig. 2).
2. The *sense* nodes represent various types or clusters of sensors, which take as input specific kinds of sampled data. In our smart grid system, the transducers sample voltage and current every second, while the relays sample the

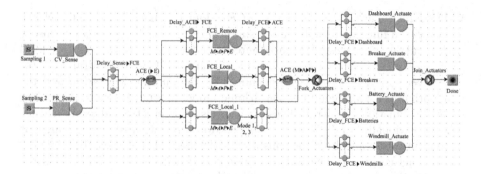

Fig. 8. *IAS-QN* for the Melle-Longchamp application. It conforms to the architecture shown in Fig. 6. The case study consists of 35 local *FCE*, but 2 of them are shown here.

circuit breakers position in an event-based manner. The sensory data is forwarded through a network to the controller(s). The network is exposed to both transmission delay (*td*) and propagation delay (*pd*).

3. The *autonomic control element (ACE)* is represented by *class-switches* nodes ($A \rightarrow B$) which use the *MAPE-K* logic. As we pointed out previously, the *ACE* class-switches, monitor the situation of the *FCE*, analyze its situation based on system goals, and plan for architectural adaptation execution in line with system goals (shown as $ACE: M \rightarrow A \rightarrow P$). The adaptation specifies where the sensory data should be routed for specific processing. When the feedback from the *FCE* goes back to the *ACE*, the composition of controllers to which the next job should be sent is decided (shown as $ACE: \rightarrow E$). Such decisions can be based on various control selection strategies:

- *Probabilities*: the destination controller is chosen according to predefined probabilities that, in general, are different for each controller.
- *Random*: the destination controller is chosen randomly; i.e., each controller has the same probability of selecting.
- *Round-Robin*: controllers are cyclically and circularly chosen as the destination controller.
- *Join the Shortest Queue*: the task is routed to the controller with the minimum number of tasks. The controller may be able to process the tasks immediately or with a queuing delay.
- *Shortest Response Time*: the task is instantly routed to the controller, which implies the minimum response time for the corresponding task type.
- *Least Utilization*: the controller with the smallest instant utilization is chosen as the destination controller.
- *Fastest Service*: the task is routed to the controller with the minimum service time for the corresponding task type.

Due to both the *RTE* preferences and the smart network configurations, we set the *ACE* logic based on *Probabilities* and keep the other strategies for future work. The following subsection clarifies the use of such probabilities.

4. The *Functional Control elements (FCE)* adopt the *MAPE-K* loop to achieve the system functional goals. In our smart grid system, the aggregated sensory data might be processed in distributed collaborative gateways and/or local or remote central controllers. The transition from local to central *FCE* (or vice versa) is a mode-switch dependent on the autonomic control, and the adoption of a more complex algorithmic model is a mode switch dependent on the functional control. These two levels of interactive adaptation drive the functionality of *IAS*-based systems. Mode transition in *IAS-QN* aims at adapting the control mechanisms and deployment of their execution by adequate actuation. In this example of application, a powerful *RTE* processor is used in the centralized pattern, while in the distributed pattern, the gateways with lower processing power collaborate to manage the situation. In the hierarchical pattern, hierarchies among central cloud and collaborative gateways are designed.

The *FCE* of the Melle-Longchamp area should deal with three modes:

- **Mode 1:** *Fast action mode.* Due to a critical situation of the transmission network, a simple flow chart logic is used to activate the circuit breakers only. This mode is a fall-back plan of mode 2 as well. The computation consumes a <u>low CPU</u>.
- **Mode 2:** *Normal mode.* The *MPC* solver base the computation on a cost function to give the optimal use of all levers (wind-farms modulation, batteries, and circuit breakers) on a 60 s horizon. If no solution is found in the allocated time slot, it switches to mode 1. The computation consumes <u>medium CPU</u>).
- **Mode 3:** *Enhanced forecasting mode.* A more sophisticated *MPC* provides data-driven forecasts which enhance the predictions on generation. The computation consumes <u>high CPU</u>).

It is worth mentioning that the system's situation is shown on the operators' dashboards in all three modes. Each of the modes has an occurrence probability. The probabilities that come from the *RTE* data-driven estimation specify the amount of time each mode is in operation. The probabilities are stipulated as 10% for Mode 1, 60% for mode 2, and 30% for mode 3.

5. The *fork/join* nodes split the sampled data for different sensors and/or actuators sets. These nodes facilitate adaptation in *sense* and/or *actuate* levels by, e.g., specifying the routing probabilities for each brand-new task type heading to sensors and/or actuators.

6. The actuation plan is implemented by actuators to achieve common goals. In our smart grid system, the dashboard components receive the data every second, but other actuation types perform in an event-based manner. The loop is complete when the actuation on the environment is perceived again by sensors.

Table 1. *IAS-QN* task types and CPU times for the Melle-Longchamp case.

IAS-QN Layer	Service Center	Task Type Name	Mean Service time (milliseconds)		
			Centralized (RTE)	Distributed (Gateways)	Hierarchical (Fog-Cloud)
IoT Eelements (sensors)	Current/voltage	CVSense		200	
	Position Relays	PRSense		500	
Network	Sense to Gateways (td+pd)	CVSense and PRSense		1	
	Gateways to Controllers (td+pd)	CVSense and PRSense	400	-	1200
Processing	ACE	Model, 2, 3	10	25	1
	FCE	Model	15	35	1
		Mode 2	200	440	1
		Mode 3	800	1760	1
Network	Control to Dashboard (td+pd)	DashboardActuate		150	
	Control to Circuit Breakers (td+pd)	BreakerActuate		150	
	Control to Batteries (td+pd)	Battery Actuate		300	
	Control to Windmills (td+pd)	WindmillActuate		300	
IoT Elements (actuators)	Dashboards	DashboardActuate		1	
	Circuit Breakers	BreakerActuate		100	
	Batteries	Battery Actuate		1000	
	Windmills	WindmillActuate		20000	

4.5   Simulation

The *IAS-QN* is modeled and simulated in *JMT 1.0.5* [24]. We ran all the experiments on a *Corei7 2.7* GHz computer with *16* GB of RAM memory under Windows 10 pro *64-bits*. While flowing through the *IAS-QN*, each task takes a certain amount of service (CPU) demand on each visited station. The CPU depends on the job class associated with the tasks. Table 1 shows mean service time on each *IAS-QN* component and layer. Workload intensities that are the entry rate of job classes to *IAS-QN*, must be specified as well. In our application scenarios, the workloads associated with transducers and relays are 1 s and event-based, respectively. As already mentioned, the architectural self-adaptation within our process is addressed by mode adaptation. Mode adaptation relies on class-switch routing probabilities, i.e., the probability of monitoring tasks routed to functional controllers. In this study, we are mainly concerned with *mean system response time*, which is the mean time spent from sampling to the time that actuation ends.

We tested three architectural patterns (see Fig. 7) and their transition to assess their impact on the system's performance. Figure 9 shows the mean response time associated with the smart transmission network managed by our self-adaptive pattern transition approach. We considered 21 different scenarios resulted from the architectural patterns' combinations for handling the three modes. 18 out of 27 scenarios address the transition between patterns (i.e., run-time adaptation), each being in charge of managing a specific computation mode of the Melle-Longchamp *IoT* architecture.

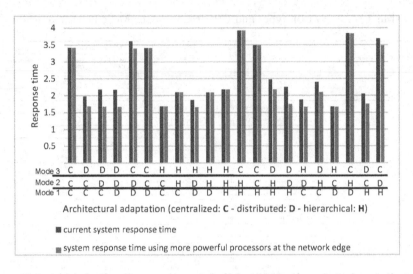

Fig. 9. The experimental results: response time (seconds).

4.6   Architectural Design Decisions

Experimental results on system response time (blue bars of Fig. 9) show that managing the fast action mode (*mode 1*) and the normal mode (*mode 2*) with the centralized, and the enhanced forecasting mode (*mode 3*) with the hierarchical architecture minimizes system response time (1.66 s). Furthermore, adapting the architecture from distributed (for *mode 1*) to centralized (for *mode 2*), and hierarchical (for *mode 3*) provides the same optimal response time (1.66 s).

In several *IoT* systems, the architectural adaptation can take place only on sensors and actuators levels. This might happen, e.g., due to the restrictions on algorithm distribution, hardware resources availability, or middleware design. Thus, if we ignore pattern transition for our smart grid system, we see that, compared with only distributed or only hierarchical, managing the situation with only the centralized pattern increases the delay by 58%. Apart from the fact that the performance depends on how much the processing and storage components are pushed to the edge in a decentralized way, other *QoS* consideration may entirely change the story. If we prioritize, e.g., the *fault-tolerance* of the system, using a centralized pattern causes a single point of failure. Thus, a hierarchical architecture can guarantee the fault-tolerance [22] since if one fog node fails, the *IoT* system can shift the computation to another fog to avoid the single point of failure.

Furthermore, we tested using the more powerful computing resource (i.e., the same as RTE central control element) distributed at the edge of the network (i.e., gateways). The corresponding result is shown as the orange bars in Fig. 9. The results show an improvement in response time in all pattern transitions where the distributed pattern is involved. This upgrade highlights the *only distributed* pattern as the optimal solution, by an 11% response time improvement over the previous optimal solution. Thus, taking advantage of our *IAS-QN*, we proposed the RTE company to *i)* re-design their software architecture adaptation policy to manage their *mode 2* with centralized and *mode 3* with hierarchical, while choosing among centralized and distributed patterns for mode 1; *ii)* push the powerful *FCE* to the edge of the network in a distributed collaborative way.

Lessons Learned. The modeling and development of the Melle-Longcham area smart grid system are still ongoing. However, we learned that adopting a run-time architectural adaptation mechanism is crucial, specially to set the propositions to enhance the performance of the system. We believe that applying *IAS* could bring various benefits to *IoT* systems. We notably learned that Internet of Things architectures require containing the mechanisms to determine the architectural adaption based on their *QoS* satisfaction level. In our use-case, the architectural adaptation performed by changing the computational components' combination to satisfy the performance requirements. However, the adaptation can also take place in sensing, network, and actuating components. The adaptation can be considered internal to the system. The autonomic control element can analyze the situation of functional control elements in run-time, and plan for specific architecture variant adaptation. Architecture variant determines multiple functional deployment types as patterns. In our use-case, this process was executed by class-switch in *QNs*, which enabled a run-time pattern adaptation for performance improvements.

5   Conclusion

This paper presents a conceptual framework for *IoT* Architectural Self-adaptation (*IAS*). The approach facilitates architectural adaptation by correlating it with autonomic and functional control elements. The method is further modeled within Queueing Networks to provide architecture-based performance assessments. We took advantage of the *IAS* framework to design and improve the architecture of *RTE Company*'s transmission network, located in the Melle-Longchamp area (France). By modeling the interaction among autonomic and functional control elements, we designed and further improved a set of *IAS-QN* models that take advantage of *MAPE-K* approach for desirable run-time adaptation. We observed that a proper architecture could keep the response time in a level that is compliant with real-time requirements. We also noticed that some architecture patterns and their switch provide similar response times. Thus in future work, we will consider other complementary criteria (e.g., resiliency) to make architectural design-decisions. We will also apply our approach to test other performance indices. Another improvement that can be performed in future work is formalizing both the run-time pattern selection process and sampling rate settings.

References

1. Weyns, D.: Software engineering of self-adaptive systems: an organised tour and future challenges. In: Chapter in Handbook of Software Engineering (2017)
2. ISO/IEC/IEEE: ISO/IEC/IEEE 42010, systems and software engineering - architecture description (2011)
3. Weyns, D., et al.: On patterns for decentralized control in self-adaptive systems. In: de Lemos, R., Giese, H., Müller, H.A., Shaw, M. (eds.) Software Engineering for Self-Adaptive Systems II. LNCS, vol. 7475, pp. 76–107. Springer, Heidelberg (2013). https://doi.org/10.1007/978-3-642-35813-5_4
4. Calinescu, R., Gerasimou, S., Banks, A.: Self-adaptive software with decentralised control loops. In: Egyed, A., Schaefer, I. (eds.) FASE 2015. LNCS, vol. 9033, pp. 235–251. Springer, Heidelberg (2015). https://doi.org/10.1007/978-3-662-46675-9_16
5. Calinescu, R., Grunske, L., Kwiatkowska, M., Mirandola, R., Tamburrelli, G.: Dynamic QoS management and optimization in service-based systems. IEEE Trans. Softw. Eng. 37(3), 387–409 (2010)
6. Jung, G., Joshi, K.R., Hiltunen, M.A., Schlichting, R.D., Pu, C.: Generating adaptation policies for multi-tier applications in consolidated server environments. In: 2008 International Conference on Autonomic Computing, pp. 23–32. IEEE (2008)
7. Zavala, E., Franch, X., Marco, J., Berger, C.: HAFLoop: an architecture for supporting highly adaptive feedback loops in self-adaptive systems. Future Gen. Comput. Syst. 105, 607–630 (2020)
8. Cheng, B.H.C., Sawyer, P., Bencomo, N., Whittle, J.: A goal-based modeling approach to develop requirements of an adaptive system with environmental uncertainty. In: Schürr, A., Selic, B. (eds.) MODELS 2009. LNCS, vol. 5795, pp. 468–483. Springer, Heidelberg (2009). https://doi.org/10.1007/978-3-642-04425-0_36
9. Shevtsov, S., Weyns, D.: Keep it simplex: satisfying multiple goals with guarantees in control-based self-adaptive systems. In: Proceedings of the 2016 24th ACM SIGSOFT International Symposium on Foundations of Software Engineering, pp. 229–241 (2016)
10. Athreya, A.P., DeBruhl, B., Tague, P.: Designing for self-configuration and self-adaptation in the Internet of Things. In: 9th IEEE International Conference on Collaborative Computing: Networking, Applications and Worksharing, pp. 585–592. IEEE (2013)
11. Iftikhar, M.U., Ramachandran, G.S., Bollansée, P., Weyns, D., Hughes, D.: DeltaIoT: a self-adaptive Internet of Things exemplar. In: 2017 IEEE/ACM SEAMS, pp. 76–82. IEEE (2017)
12. Weyns, D., Ramachandran, G.S., Singh, R.K.: Self-managing Internet of Things. In: Tjoa, A.M., Bellatreche, L., Biffl, S., van Leeuwen, J., Wiedermann, J. (eds.) SOFSEM 2018. LNCS, vol. 10706, pp. 67–84. Springer, Cham (2018). https://doi.org/10.1007/978-3-319-73117-9_5
13. Garlan, D., Cheng, S.-W., Huang, A.-C., Schmerl, B., Steenkiste, P.: Rainbow: architecture-based self-adaptation with reusable infrastructure. Computer 37(10), 46–54 (2004)
14. Muccini, H., Spalazzese, R., Moghaddam, M.T., Sharaf, M.: Self-adaptive IoT architectures: an emergency handling case study. In: Proceedings of the 12th European Conference on Software Architecture: Companion Proceedings, pp. 1–6 (2018)
15. Garlan, D., Schmerl, B., Cheng, S.-W.: Software architecture-based self-adaptation. In: Zhang, Y., Yang, L., Denko, M. (eds.) Autonomic Computing and Networking, pp. 31–55. Springer, Boston (2009). https://doi.org/10.1007/978-0-387-89828-5_2

16. Weyns, D., Iftikhar, M.U., Hughes, D., Matthys, N.: Applying architecture-based adaptation to automate the management of Internet-of-Things. In: Cuesta, C.E., Garlan, D., Pérez, J. (eds.) ECSA 2018. LNCS, vol. 11048, pp. 49–67. Springer, Cham (2018). https://doi.org/10.1007/978-3-030-00761-4_4

17. Rutten, E., Marchand, N., Simon, D.: Feedback control as MAPE-K loop in autonomic computing. In: de Lemos, R., Garlan, D., Ghezzi, C., Giese, H. (eds.) Software Engineering for Self-Adaptive Systems III. Assurances. LNCS, vol. 9640, pp. 349–373. Springer, Cham (2017). https://doi.org/10.1007/978-3-319-74183-3_12

18. Lalanda, P., McCann, J.A., Diaconescu, A.: Autonomic Computing: Principles Design and Implementation. Springer, London (2013). https://doi.org/10.1007/978-1-4471-5007-7

19. Arbib, C., Arcelli, D., Dugdale, J., Moghaddam, M., Muccini, H.: Real-time emergency response through performant IoT architectures. In: International Conference on Information Systems for Crisis Response and Management, ISCRAM (2019)

20. Muccini, H., Moghaddam, M.T.: IoT architectural styles. In: Cuesta, C.E., Garlan, D., Pérez, J. (eds.) ECSA 2018. LNCS, vol. 11048, pp. 68–85. Springer, Cham (2018). https://doi.org/10.1007/978-3-030-00761-4_5

21. Dugdale, J., Moghaddam, M.T., Muccini, H.: Human behaviour centered design: developing a software system for cultural heritage. In: International Conference on Software Engineering, ICSE-SEIS 2020, pp. 85–94. ACM (2020)

22. Moghaddam, M.T., Muccini, H.: Fault-tolerant IoT. In: Calinescu, R., Di Giandomenico, F. (eds.) SERENE 2019. LNCS, vol. 11732, pp. 67–84. Springer, Cham (2019). https://doi.org/10.1007/978-3-030-30856-8_5

23. Olaru, S., Maeght, J., Straub, C., Panciatici, P.: Zonal congestion management mixing large battery storage systems and generation curtailment. In: IEEE Conference on Control Technology and Applications (CCTA), pp. 988–995. IEEE (2018)

24. Casale, G., Bertoli, M., Serazzi, G.: JMT: performance engineering tools for system modeling. In: ACM SIGMETRICS Performance Evaluation Review, pp. 10–15. ACM (2009)

A Comparison of MQTT Brokers
for Distributed IoT Edge Computing

Heiko Koziolek$^{(\boxtimes)}$, Sten Grüner, and Julius Rückert

ABB Corporate Research Center Germany, Ladenburg, Germany
{heiko.koziolek,sten.gruener,julius.rueckert}@de.abb.com

Abstract. Many enterprise IoT application scenarios, such as connected cars, smart cities, and cloud-connected industrial plants require distributed MQTT brokers to achieve high scalability and availability. With a market of over 20 MQTT brokers, it is hard for software architects to make a good selection. Existing MQTT comparisons often include only non-distributed brokers, focus exclusively on performance, or are difficult to generalize. We compared three distributed MQTT brokers for performance, scalability, resilience, security, extensibility, and usability in an enterprise IoT scenario deployed to an edge gateway cluster. We found that EMQX provided the best performance (28K msg/s), while only HiveMQ showed no message loss in our test scenario. VerneMQ offers similar features as the other brokers but is fully available as open source. The paper includes decision guidance for software architects, listing six major decision points regarding MQTT brokers.

Keywords: IoT · MQTT · Distributed messaging · Edge computing · Virtualization · Software containers · Benchmarking · GQM · Performance

1 Introduction

The global Internet-of-Things (IoT) market has an estimated volume of 190 BUSD and is expected to grow to more than 1100 BUSD by 2026 [6]. There are many application areas where connected devices provide value-adding functions: smart cities, industrial plants, smart home, connected cars, smart energy grids, etc. These devices often send telemetry data to edge gateways and cloud platforms, where the data is used for monitoring, supervision, predictive maintenance, and optimization. One of the most popular protocols for this type of communication is MQTT (Message Queuing Telemetry Transport, ISO/IEC 20922), which implements a publish-subscribe pattern [11]. MQTT is specifically suited for IoT applications, since it is designed for unstable network connections and bandwidth saving [13].

There are more than 20 MQTT broker implementations available, making a selection hard for software architects. Software architects need to balance and prioritize different quality attributes of MQTT brokers to make an informed

© Springer Nature Switzerland AG 2020
A. Jansen et al. (Eds.): ECSA 2020, LNCS 12292, pp. 352–368, 2020.
https://doi.org/10.1007/978-3-030-58923-3_23

decision. There is a lack of evaluation criteria for such messaging brokers specifically in enterprise IoT scenarios. Such scenarios require scalable, high available MQTT brokers deployed to a cluster, which brings special challenges for capacity planning and configuration.

Researchers and practitioners have studied different aspects of MQTT communication in the past. There are comparisons to other protocols, such as CoAP, AMQP, and Kafka [5,12,21,22], as well as small-scale performance tests of different, non-clustered MQTT brokers [2,15,21]. However, there is no comprehensive comparison between *distributed* MQTT brokers available, which are deployed in highly scalable and redundant edge clusters for enterprise IoT. Practitioner experience reports have demonstrated impressive scalability of MQTT brokers on cloud platforms [4,17], but are often difficult to generalize since they are geared towards specific contexts. Furthermore these tests often focus exclusively on performance, neglecting other quality attributes.

The contribution of this paper is a comparison of three representative, distributed MQTT brokers using evaluation criteria systematically defined using a Goal/Question/Metric (GQM) scheme [3]. We report on evaluation results for five quantitative metrics and provide additional qualitative analyses for security, usability, and extensibility. We found that EMQX showed the best throughput, while only HiveMQ achieved no message loss in our test scenarios. VerneMQ is fully available as open source, while providing similar features and quality as the commercial brokers. To obtain the previously defined metrics, we deployed the selected MQTT brokers in redundant edge gateway servers running the open-source edge virtualization platform StarlingX. This allowed analyzing the interplay with software containers and container orchestration using Kubernetes (K8s).

The remainder of this paper is structured as follows: Sect. 2 sets the context for Enterprise IoT messaging, for which Sect. 3 defines metrics and a representative experiment scenario. Section 4 provides a brief overview of distributed MQTT brokers to rationalize the selected candidates. Section 5 presents the analysis results for performance, scalability, resilience, security, extensibility, and usability. Section 6 summarizes the results and decision points as guidance for software architects. Finally, Sect. 7 investigates related work and Sect. 8 concludes the paper.

2   Background: Enterprise IoT Messaging

Figure 1 shows an enterprise-scale, generic edge gateway cluster architecture that can be useful in different application domains. IoT **Devices** are for example sensors and actuators mainly publishing telemetry data to the edge gateway cluster and occasionally consuming control signals. Due to potential temporal network failures, possibly involving cellular connections and resource-constrained devices, the MQTT protocol [13] is well suited as it is resilient against temporal disconnects and has a low message size overhead thus saving bandwidth.

Message Broker Instances on the edge gateway cluster ingest messages from the IoT Devices and enable different applications to consume them. Distributed MQTT brokers with multiple instances, each residing on a separate

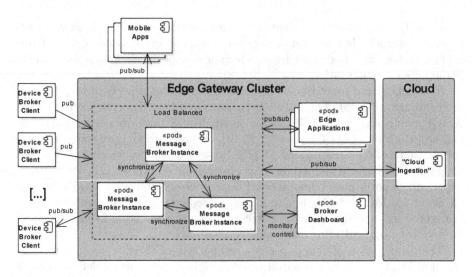

Fig. 1. Distributed message brokers on edge gateway cluster

physical or virtual node, may scale horizontally (i.e., with the number of available nodes) to cope with a high number of connected devices and message workloads. The instances exchange messages and client session information, so that the overall system may survive crashes of individual instances of nodes and support high-availability scenarios. A load balancer provides network endpoints of available broker instances to clients interested in messaging, for example in a round-robin fashion. Many MQTT brokers provide a **Broker Dashboard** for monitoring and supervision of the clustered instances.

Mobile Apps subscribe for message topics, for example to display an alarm list to a field operator in an industrial plant or to provide car telemetry data to a car owner. **Edge Applications** may utilize messaging data to execute data analytics algorithms on premises, for example to enable predictive maintenance of individual devices or derive optimizations for the entire system. For larger analysis tasks or cross-site statistics, cloud applications in public data centers ingest the messages via Internet connections.

In enterprise IoT, the edge gateway cluster may contain multiple physical nodes that run multiple layers of virtualization. There are several platforms available supporting different aspects of such an edge gateways, e.g., EdgeX-Foundry, Fledge, KubeEdge, Azure IoT Edge, and StarlingX.

3   IoT Messaging Requirements

We define metrics and evaluation criteria for distributed MQTT brokers (Sect. 3.1) and specify the basic scenario used in later tests (Sect. 3.2).

3.1   Goal/Question/Metric

The goal of our study (according to GQM [3]) is to evaluate the quality attributes of distributed MQTT brokers in enterprise IoT scenarios from the software architect's perspective. The following questions with corresponding metrics to answer them shall support achieving this evaluation for each broker:

What is the Performance? Metric **M1** is the maximum sustainable throughput (MST) [24] at which the broker is able to process all communicated messages. In this case, both publishers and subscribers are able to maintain stable message queues for an agreed reference workload. Metric **M2** is the average latency from publisher to subscriber in a given scenario. Short latencies are important for many IoT applications, where live monitoring of telemetry data is desired. Practical limits are set by network connections, which introduce latencies outside of the control of the broker.

What is the Scalability? Metric **M3** is the maximum number of supported concurrent connections, each issuing a reference workload to the broker. Large-scale IoT scenarios involving smart cities, power distribution grids or fleets of connected cars may include millions of IoT devices. Metric **M4** is the time to start a new broker instance in case of a high load on the already running instances. This metrics pertains the dynamic scalability (elasticity) to cope with changing workloads without wasting computing resources.

What is the Resilience? Metric **M5** is the message loss count in case of a broker instance crashing for a reference scenario. While losing individual sensor readings may be acceptable in some scenarios (e.g., temperature values in a smart home), it may be harmful in others (e.g., missing an emergency shutdown signal of a plant). This metric is influenced by the queue lengths configuration of a broker in relation to a particular workload.

What is the Security? Security of a broker is largely determined by the user configuration and only to a lesser extent by the broker's security features. These include authentication and authorization mechanisms, as well as encryption support and overload protection procedures. We refrain from defining a potentially misleading, quantitative metric for security and instead provide a qualitative discussion in the evaluation section. Metric **M6** is only a side-aspect of security and measures the overhead of enabled TLS encryption on the maximum sustainable throughput (as percentage).

What is the Extensibility? MQTT brokers offer plug-in mechanisms allowing third-party extensions, e.g., logging messages to a database. The evaluation section provides a qualitative discussion on the extensibility of the brokers.

What is the Usability? The usability of a distributed MQTT broker includes both installation and operation. Easy deployment on container orchestration systems may be valued. We again refrain from defining a quantitative measure for usability, but instead provide a qualitative discussion.

3.2   Basic Experiment Scenario

MQTT performance tests can be categorized into "fan-in"-driven, "fan-out"-driven, and symmetric tests. Fan-in tests reflect typical IoT applications scenarios with a high number of IoT devices (e.g., 10,000s) acting as publishers, but only a few or a single subscriber (e.g., an analytics application). Fan-out tests are the opposite, e.g., a high number of mobile applications consuming data from few or a single publisher (e.g., weather station). We decided to use a symmetric test scenario with 10 publishers and 10 subscribers, as our goal was to assess quality differences of different brokers in a mostly representative scenario. This also avoids the need to optimize broker queue size configurations. We refer to other scalability tests [4, 9, 17] for specific fan-in/fan-out tests.

In our scenario, publishers try to send as many messages as possible to the broker instances and ultimately the subscribers. We tested in a range between 1,000 and 50,000 messages per second, which is higher than many real cases. For example, BMW's connected car platform processes 1,500 messages per second on HiveMQ, while Bose's messaging backend using VerneMQ ran up to 9,700 messages per second [17]. The workload expected for an industrial plant equipped with automation by ABB is within our experimentation range.

We used a fixed message payload size of 150 Bytes with random binary content. While a single telemetry datum (e.g., a temperature value) may be encoded with only 4 Bytes, we assume that messages provide additional meta data (e.g., identification, timestamps, etc.) in a realistic scenario. Payloads of 64 Bytes or 128 Bytes have been used in other benchmarks and a previous work [21] has found that payload sizes up to 4,096 Bytes have limited influence on the maximum sustainable throughput. Batching messages may improve overall throughput, but leads to more complexity on the consumer side, where the batches needs to be de-grouped as part of the application logic.

All publishers and subscribers use MQTT QoS 1 assuring no message loss, but requiring message acknowledgments (i.e., implying an extra network round trip). QoS level 2 would also exclude duplicated messages, but is considered to imply a too high overhead for most IoT scenarios, while QoS level 0 is risky in terms of message loss.

4   Distributed MQTT Brokers

Comprehensive feature comparison tables are available for more than 20 MQTT brokers[1]. There are also MQTT plug-ins available for message brokers originally designed for other protocols, such as RabbitMQ or Apache Kafka. However these plug-ins may be limited in their support of MQTT features. One of the most popular MQTT brokers is Eclipse Mosquitto (implemented in C). It supports MQTT versions 3.1 and 5.0 and has a low footprint, but provides no multi-threading and no native cluster support. AWS IoT and Microsoft Azure IoT provide basic MQTT support, but lack some features [10].

---

[1] https://en.wikipedia.org/wiki/Comparison_of_MQTT_implementations.

For our evaluation, we selected three representative, native MQTT brokers that provide cluster support and are available as open source (at least in feature-reduced "community-versions"). All of them support the full MQTT version 3.1 and 5.0 protocols, SSL/TLS, and all MQTT QoS levels.

EMQX[2]: The Erlang/Enterprise/Elastic MQTT Broker (EMQX) started as an open source project in China in 2013. The developers created the company EMQ Technologies Co., Ltd. in 2017 for commercial support and services. The company claims having more than 5,000 enterprise users and customers from various application domains. EMQX is now available in multiple variants, as pure open source broker (1.5M docker pulls), as Enterprise broker, and as private cloud solution. There is also a lightweight variant (15 MB installation) called "EMQ X Edge" for resource-constrained IoT gateways, which may interface with KubeEdge[3]. The open-source variant is available under Apache License 2.0 for all major operating system and processor architectures.

HiveMQ[4]: The company dc-square started the development of the commercial MQTT broker HiveMQ in Germany in 2012. dc-square was renamed to HiveMQ in 2019 and created an open-source variant (Community Edition, Apache License 2.0, 0.5M docker pulls). The company claims having more than 130 customers for HiveMQ, among them BMW with a connected car platform and Mattenet with a platform providing the real-time flight status of drones. HiveMQ is implemented in Java and now available as community, professional, and enterprise edition, in addition to an IoT cloud platform variant with hourly subscription fees. The HiveMQ DNS discovery plug-in uses DNS service discovery to add or remove brokers instances to the cluster at runtime.

VerneMQ[5]: Octavo Labs AG from Switzerland is developing the VerneMQ MQTT broker since 2015. It is an open-source project (Apache License 2.0, 7.1M docker pulls) with two main developers that started after they had been working on an energy marketplace project. They discovered that AMQP and XMPP did not scale well enough for a large number of devices and started implementing VerneMQ using Erlang/OTP. There are no commercial variants with licensing fees, but the company offers commercial support around VerneMQ. There are several featured customers, among them Microsoft and Volkswagen.

5 Analysis of Distributed MQTT Brokers

5.1 Test Infrastructure

Our testbed is a StarlingX[6] all-in-one duplex bare metal installation running on two identical servers in a redundant, high-available fashion. Each server has a

---

[2] https://www.emqx.io/.

[3] https://kubeedge.io/.

[4] https://www.hivemq.com/.

[5] https://vernemq.com/.

[6] https://www.starlingx.io/.

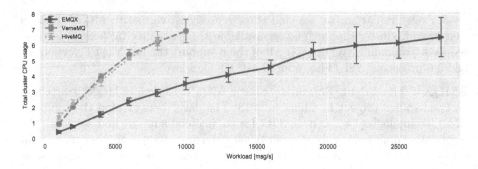

Fig. 2. Stable throughput compared to aggregated CPU usage of all broker pods

Dual Intel Xeon CPU E5-2640 v3 running at 2.60 GHz with 8×2 physical cores (32 threads), 128 GB of RAM and Gigabit connectivity.

StarlingX v3.0 is an open-source virtualization platform for edge clusters and runs on top of CentOS 7.6. All tested brokers run in Docker CE orchestrated by K8s. Prometheus monitoring tools measure CPU load among other metrics. For the broker installations we used helm charts (VerneMQ 1.10.2, EMQX 4.0.5) or public tutorials from broker vendors (Enterprise HiveMQ 4.3.2 evaluation). In K8s, the brokers use replication controllers (HiveMQ), stateful sets (VerneMQ, EMQX) and load balancer services (metalLB as Level 2 Load Balancer).

A dedicated node in the same Ethernet segment as the StarlingX controllers acts as load driver (CentOS 8.1, Intel Xeon CPU E5-2660 v4 @ 2.00 GHz, 16 cores (32 threads) and 8 GB of RAM). We evaluated different load driver applications, including mqtt-stresser, paho-clients, Locust/MQTT, JMeter/MQTT and MZBench. We decided to use MZBench[7] due to a low resource footprint, convenient Web UI allowing to monitor and export metrics, and also a possibility to define load scenarios in a simple Benchmark Definition Language (BDL). We utilized custom MZBench MQTT workers provided by VerneMQ[8]. We spawn MQTT workers locally in a Docker CE environment on the load driver node.

In addition to metrics from Prometheus and MZBench, we used broker dashboards provided by brokers to validate throughput measurements. A generic graphical MQTT client MQTTExplorer[9] was also used to validate topic lists.

5.2 Performance

To obtain the metrics **M1** (maximum sustainable throughput) and **M2** (average latency), we conducted experiments as described in Sect. 3.2.

During each experiment run, the publishers first established a defined publishing rate (e.g., 4,000 msg/s), held this for two minutes to assure stability, and then increased the publishing rate (e.g., by 2,000 msg/s) in two minute intervals.

---

[7] https://satori-com.github.io/mzbench/.

[8] https://github.com/vernemq/vmq_mzbench.

[9] http://mqtt-explorer.com/.

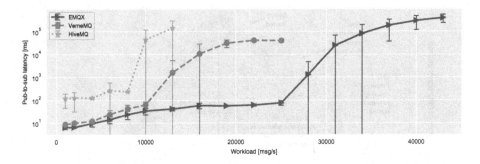

Fig. 3. Stable throughput compared to average publisher-to-subscriber latency

Table 1. Performance metrics

Performance		EMQX	HiveMQ	VerneMQ
Maximum sustainable throughput (msg/s)	**M1**	28,000	8,000	10,000
Average latency at 1000 msg/s (ms)	**M2**	6.4	119.4	8.7

To avoid interference with background noise from other processes running on the edge gateway cluster, we configured each broker pod to utilize at most *four* CPU cores. This leaves other cores to execute edge analytics applications or broker dashboards and provides a fair comparison between the brokers.

Figure 2 shows the aggregated CPU utilization (y-axis) over the messaging rate (x-axis) for the three analyzed brokers. We repeated each experiment three times and report the average utilizations to exclude outliers. 95%-confidence intervals are shown as indication for variations across experiments. The figure shows the CPU utilization curves leveling out at around 4 CPU cores per pod (2 pods per broker). At this point the broker cannot sustainably handle the message load and the message queues run full. We defined an instability point where the average message consumption differs from the published messages by more than 100 msg/s. The plots only include the measurements before reaching this instability point after which, eventually, the message broker starts to drop messages.

Our measurement confirmed that the CPU was the bottleneck in this test scenario. Scenarios with substantially larger message payloads could however run into network bottlenecks, while fan-in and fan-out scenarios could overwhelm the publisher or subscriber queues. In our specific scenario, EMQX managed the highest MST with 28K msg/s, while VerneMQ managed 10K msg/s, and HiveMQ managed 8K msg/s. We confirmed these throughput numbers with independent measurements by MZBench and the respective broker dashboards. It should be noted that each broker allows for much higher message throughput in other scenarios if provided more CPU power (e.g., uncapped CPU assignment, and deployment to more nodes).

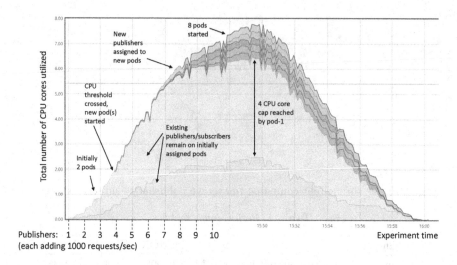

Fig. 4. Kubernetes autoscaling applied to broker pods (VerneMQ)

Figure 3 shows the average publisher-to-subscriber latency for the same scenario. Before reaching CPU bottlenecks, the average latencies are below 150 ms for all brokers. At 28K msg/s for EMQX the bottleneck is reached, so that the average latency quickly increases beyond acceptable levels. A similar effect is visible for the other brokers when reaching their CPU bottlenecks.

Our scenario enables a rough performance comparison of the brokers. Table 1 summarizes the GQM metrics. The Erlang-based MQTT brokers outperform HiveMQ, which is implemented in Java. Each broker had equally configured message queues sizes. There may be additional configuration options to tune each broker's performance including broker specific and system-wide parameters.

5.3 Scalability

Our tests showed that all evaluated brokers are multi-threaded and utilize as many CPU cores as available on a given host (tested up to 16 cores). Thus they support vertical scaling with more powerful CPUs. Software architects need to define their expected workload profile in the application scenario and can then perform capacity planning for the required number of nodes. Other authors have conducted MQTT scalability tests with millions of connections in larger clusters (see Sect. 7), demonstrating theoretically unlimited scalability (metric **M3**).

In an edge gateway cluster also horizontal scaling by creating additional broker instances is possible. We minimally tested horizontal scalability, since our testbed included only two physical servers. We configured K8s auto-scaling for a minimum number of 2 pods (1 per node) and a maximum of 8 pods. A CPU threshold was defined which triggered the instantiation of new pods.

Figure 4 shows the CPU utilization per pod instance in a stacked line chart over the course of an autocaling experiment with VerneMQ. In the experi-

Table 2. Scalability metrics

Scalability		EMQX	HiveMQ	VerneMQ
Maximum number of connections	M3	Unlimited (tests up to 50 mio)	Unlimited (tests up to 10 mio)	Unlimited (tests up to 5 mio)
Time to start new broker instance (s)	M4	18.6	20.2	14.2
Container image sized (MB)		89.2	298.6	82.5

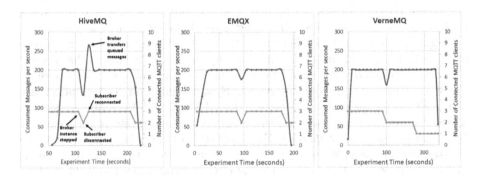

Fig. 5. Consumption rate and number of connections during resilience test

ment, one new publisher connected every minute and added a publishing rate of 1000 msg/s to the overall publishing rate. At the peak, the experiment had 10 publishers with a total of 10,000 msg/s, and 10 subscribers consuming each message. Initially, 10 subscribers and 1 publisher are assigned by the load balancer to two active pod instances. Once three publishers have connected to the broker, the pre-defined CPU utilization threshold is crossed and K8s starts new pods.

We also observe that the load balancer assigns new connection requests to the newly started pods, but existing connections are not shifted between pods. Thus, the autoscaling is only effective if there are new connections. For a constant number of connections but a higher messaging rate, the cluster cannot benefit from autoscaling without disconnecting clients.

Metric **M4** is the start-up time of new broker pods, since load peaks below this time can only be handled by vertical scaling. We measured the duration of the transition between the "PodSheduled" and the "Ready" condition of the pod. Table 2 shows the average time of ten pod starts, excluding the time of downloading the container image when it is run on the node for the first time.

5.4 Availability/Resilience

We assessed resilience by modifying the scenario described in Sect. 3.2 to avoid high queue lengths. The modified scenario contains one publisher (100 msg/s), two subscribers, and two broker pods (B_1, B_2). B_1 had the publisher P and subscriber S_1 connected. B_2 had subscriber S_2 connected. Both subscribers consume all messages (total consumption rate of 200 msg/s). Furthermore, the scenario used QoS 1 and persistent sessions. We configured the broker queues to an in-flight message queue of 1,000 and on-/offline message queue of 50,000.

After a stabilization phase of each experiment, we forcefully stopped the broker process on B_2, i.e., Java VM or Erlang BEAM VM to simulate a crash. Subscriber S_2 was expected to reconnect to B_1 via the load balancer immediately, i.e., before B_2 pod is restarted by K8s. Furthermore, S_2 is supposed to resume its session, and receive messages that the broker buffered during the disconnect.

Figure 5 shows that HiveMQ exhibits the expected behavior, resulting in zero message loss. The dark lines show the consumption rate of 200 msg/s that is temporarily disturbed due the subscriber disconnect upon broker pod B_2 stopping. We observe an immediate re-connection of S_2 and a temporary consumption rate *above* 200 msg/s for queued messages. Both EMQX and VerneMQ performed unexpectedly: the temporary decrease of the consumption rate is not equalized by a later increase over 200 msg/s. For VerneMQ also note the number of clients constantly decreasing. We repeated each experiment three times to exclude temporary distortions but arrived at the same result summarized in Table 3. This unexpected behavior requires further investigations in future work.

Table 3. Average message loss during resilience test

Resilience		EMQX	HiveMQ	VerneMQ
Average messages loss in reference scenario	**M5**	580	0	82

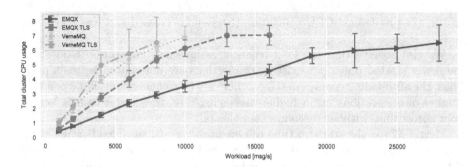

Fig. 6. CPU utilization with and without TLS encryption

5.5   Security

MQTT security can be tackled at the network level (e.g., using VPN), the transport layer (e.g., using TLS) and the application layer (e.g., authentication and authorization). In the following, we focus on the security at the transport layer.

We conducted tests using TLS encryption to measure CPU and bandwidth overhead. We configured each broker to use TLS v1.2, where encryption was terminated directly at the broker instance. Please note, we were not able to connect MZBench MQTT workers to HiveMQ due to reported SSL errors. Tests with other MQTT clients, e.g., MQTTExplorer, worked fine.

Figure 6 shows the impact of TLS encryption on the CPU utilization for one representative broker (EMQX). The CPU utilization levels out at the cap of four CPU cores already at 16,000 msg/s when using TLS, compared to 28,000 msg/s without TLS. Installing certificates on the broker was similar between all the brokers and can be performed, e.g., by using K8s secrets mounted into the pod. An overview of additional security features of brokers can be found in Table 4.

5.6   Extensibility

All brokers offer plug-in mechanisms for developing extensions to the basic broker functionality. For example, plug-ins allow special authentication mechanisms or integration with monitoring frameworks.

VerneMQ provides hooks for changing protocol flow, events, and conditional events. Developers can write plug-ins in Erlang, Elixir, or Lua and load them during runtime. VerneMQ also provides webhooks, where a VerneMQ plugin dispatches an HTTP post request to a registered endpoint. This mechanism allows implementing extensions in any programming language.

Table 4. Security metrics

Security		EMQX	HiveMQ	VerneMQ
Authentication/authorization		Files, database	Files, database, OAuth, LDAP	Files, database
Certificate-based authentication		Yes	Yes	Yes
TLS version support		v1.1, v1.2	v1.1, v1.2, v1.3	v1.1, v1.2
Maximum sustainable throughput (TLS off)		28,000	8,000	10,000
Maximum sustainable throughput (TLS on)		16,000	?	8,000
Overhead of enabled TLS on MST	**M6**	43%	n/a	20%

HiveMQ plug-ins are Java JAR files and shall be integrated using dependency injection (using Google Guice). HiveMQ provides more than 30 callback types besides services to interact with the HiveMQ core (e.g., publish services to send new messages to clients). There is also a "RestService", which allows to create a REST API to be consumed by other applications. The HiveMQ marketplace provides a few open source plug-ins (e.g., Prometheus monitoring) and commercial plug-ins (e.g., HiveMQ for Kafka).

EMQX can also be extended with Erlang code, 25 plug-ins are already available from the vendor (e.g,. web dashboard, rule engine, Lua hooks, STOMP support). Plug-ins can be loaded at runtime, and there are also webhooks available. EMQ provides 15 hooks, chaining plug-ins on these hooks is possible.

In summary, the extensibility of all brokers is deemed good. HiveMQ has the most extensive developer guides and the most hooks, while being geared towards Java development. VerneMQ and EMQX may have more active communities due to their longer open source history, offer fewer hooks, and are geared towards Erlang development.

5.7   Usability

The installation of all brokers is smooth, which allows software architects to quickly perform experiments with their intended workloads configured in a load driver. All of them offer Docker containers, VerneMQ and EMQX provide helm charts for K8s. EMQX and HiveMQ are available as Amazon Machine Images. Users can configure the brokers via files and environment variables. All brokers provide a web-based dashboard for monitoring and troubleshooting, where connected clients and performance metrics can be investigated. The dashboards of HiveMQ and EMQX offer the most information. All brokers have command line interfaces. HiveMQ has the most comprehensive documentation and developer guides, including several MQTT tutorials, although the documentation of the other brokers is also good.

6   Architecture Decision Guidance

Figure 7 shows a preliminary problem space modelled with ADMentor[10] and intended as architect decision guidance. In an enterprise IoT scenario, software architects first (1) need to decide whether the MQTT protocol is appropriate. This choice is beyond the scope of our paper (see [16,18,21]). To decide for a clustered broker (2), a detailed specification of the expected workload profile should be created. This includes the number of publishers, subscribers, payload sizes, topics, expected QoS levels, publication/subscription rates,etc. Non-trivial scenarios likely benefit from a cluster.

A potentially business-driven choice (3) is the selection of an open-source or commercial MQTT broker, which may largely limit the available alternatives.

---

[10] https://github.com/IFS-HSR/ADMentor.

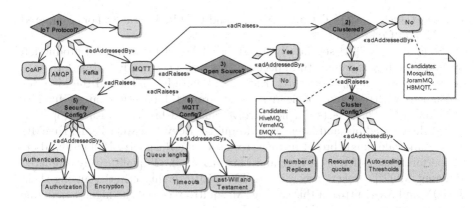

Fig. 7. Architecture decision guidance: IoT/MQTT problem space

Here, it needs to be traded-off whether licensing fees, commercial support, and advanced features are well invested compared to own development efforts and community support.

In a containerized edge cluster, the software architect may decide **(4)** on the number of required pod replicas, resource quotas, and auto-scaling parameters (if needed at all). Another decision point is the security configuration **(5)**. The MQTT configuration itself is a set of fine-granular decisions based the expected workload profile **(6)**.

The design of the MQTT topic space may also be in control of the software architect and there are guides available with best practices for topic spaces[11]. Here, the software architect does not have discrete options.

We found that the comparably easy installation of the brokers and the availability of powerful MQTT load drivers allow software architects to quickly evaluate MQTT brokers for a given application scenario. If the target deployment hardware is already available for testing, we recommend specifying the expected workload for a given load driver (e.g., in the simple Benchmark Definition Language of MZBench[12]) and then quickly running a few experiments to get a feeling on the performance and availability to expect. This exercise has been reported by others [4,17] and also allows familiarizing with the usability and documentation of the brokers, which then supports making a final decision.

7 Related Work

A broad survey of IoT technologies, among them MQTT, was provided by Al-Fuquaha et al. [1]. Several books describe the protocol, applications, and usage scenarios in detail [8,13,14]. Naik [16] discusses criteria for selecting messaging

---

[11] https://pi3g.com/2019/05/29/mqtt-topic-tree-design-best-practices-tips-examples/.

[12] https://satori-com.github.io/mzbench/scenarios/tutorial/.

protocols, such as MQTT, CoAP, AMQP, and HTTP. Several authors compared MQTT and CoAP [5,12,22].

Sommer et al. [21] specifically investigated MOM for industrial production systems, aiming at architectural decision support. They conducted performance tests with Mosquitto, RabbitMQ, Kafka, and JeroMQ and found the MST for Mosquitto with different payload sizes at around 1000 msg/s on an Intel i7 Windows-PC. These tests did not involve clustered brokers. Mishra [15] compared the throughput and latency of Mosquitto, BevyWiseMQTT, and HiveMQ in a small-scale, single broker instance scenario on a Raspberry Pi, but found little performance differences. Bertrand-Martinez et al. [2] qualitatively evaluated different MQTT brokers according to ISO 25010 quality criteria, among them EMQX and Mosquitto. In this scoring, Mosquitto received the highest rank due to simplicity and lightweightness.

There are also practitioner reports of performance tests with specific MQTT brokers: Mahony et al. [17] set up a Kubernetes cluster on AWS and deployed VerneMQ in up to 80 nodes to open 5 million messaging connections and more than 9500 msg/s (measured with Locust). The company Hotstar [4] evaluated the open source MQTT brokers VerneMQ and EMQX for distributing a social feed to mobile applications. They set the brokers up on up to 5 AWS extra-large node instances, ran performance tests with MZBench, and reached up to 50 million connections with EMQX. The HiveMQ team [9] demonstrated up to 10 million connections to HiveMQ deployed to 40 AWS EC2 instances.

Most broker vendors provide whitepapers on performance tests with their own brokers. HiveMQ conducted performance tests on AWS including fan-in and fan-out scenarios. For example, in a fan-in scenario with QoS1 they achieved up to 60K msg/s on an 8-core CPU. ScaleAgent [20] compared JoramMQ, Apollo, Mosquitto, and RabbitMQ at up to 44K msg/s and concluded that their JoramMQ broker performed best. HiveMQ provides several customer case studies on their website, for example BMW's connected car scenario with 1500 msg/s or a scenario involving 1000 connected air quality sensors with 1100 msg/s.

There are more general works related to our study: The SPECjms2007 benchmark [19] provided an agreed workload to test messaging systems (supermarket chain scenario), but has been retired as of 2016. Thean et al. [23] shows Mosquitto running in Docker Swarm. Architecture decision guidance models have been proposed for example for SOA [25], cloud computing [26], and microservices [7].

8   Conclusions

This paper analyzed distributed MQTT brokers deployed to an edge gateway cluster. We found that EQMX showed the highest throughput with 28K msg/s, while VerneMQ managed 10K msg/s and HiveMQ managed 8K msg/s, respectively. The test scenario was intentionally limited to a maximum of eight CPU cores). We found that the scalability of the brokers is potentially unlimited, since they are multi-threaded and can be horizontally scaled. Only HiveMQ managed our test scenario without message loss. All brokers have similar security features and offer extensions in any programming language using webhooks.

Our paper provides decision guidance for software architects in enterprise IoT scenarios. They can use the results in our paper as an orientation and quickly set up their own experiments using the tools referenced in the paper. Researchers can derive reference enterprise IoT scenarios from our paper, conduct additional tests, and build constructive models for IoT messaging.

As a next step, we intend to deepen our analysis with additional metrics and scenarios and broaden it by integrating additional messaging solutions. In addition to StarlingX, a complementary evaluation on more resource-constrained edge gateways is warranted. It is conceivable to construct predictive performance models for quick forecasting and to work an automated experiment generator as a software service utilizing cloud computing resources.

References

1. Al-Fuqaha, A., Guizani, M., Mohammadi, M., Aledhari, M., Ayyash, M.: Internet of Things: a survey on enabling technologies, protocols, and applications. IEEE Commun. Surv. Tutor. **17**(4), 2347–2376 (2015)
2. Bertrand-Martínez, E., Feio, P., Nascimento, V., Pinheiro, B., Abelém, A.: A methodology for classification and evaluation of IoT brokers. In: 9th Latin American Network Operations and Management Symposium, LANOMS. IFIP (2019)
3. Basili, V.R., Caldiera, G., Rombach, H.D.: The goal question metric approach. In: Encyclopedia of Software Engineering, pp. 528–532 (1994)
4. Chaudhari, M., Gupta, P.: Building pubsub for 50m concurrent socket connections, June 2019. https://blog.hotstar.com/building-pubsub-for-50m-concurrent-socket-connections-5506e3c3dabf
5. De Caro, N., Colitti, W., Steenhaut, K., Mangino, G., Reali, G.: Comparison of two lightweight protocols for smartphone-based sensing. In: Symposium on Communications and Vehicular Technology in the Benelux (SCVT), pp. 1–6. IEEE (2013)
6. Fortune Business Insights: Internet-of-Things market research report, July 2019. https://www.fortunebusinessinsights.com/industry-reports/internet-of-things-iot-market-100307
7. Haselböck, S., Weinreich, R.: Decision guidance models for microservice monitoring. In: International Conference on Software Architecture Workshops (ICSAW), pp. 54–61. IEEE (2017)
8. Hillar, G.C.: MQTT Essentials-A Lightweight IoT Protocol. Packt Publishing Ltd., Birmingham (2017)
9. HiveMQ-Team: 10,000,000 MQTT clients: HiveMQ cluster benchmark paper, October 2017. https://www.hivemq.com/benchmark-10-million/
10. HiveMQ-Team: Comparison of MQTT support by IoT cloud platforms, May 2020. https://www.hivemq.com/blog/hivemq-cloud-vs-aws-iot/
11. Hohpe, G., Woolf, B.: Enterprise Integration Patterns: Designing, Building, and Deploying Messaging Solutions. Addison-Wesley Professional, Boston (2004)
12. Iglesias-Urkia, M., Orive, A., Barcelo, M., Moran, A., Bilbao, J., Urbieta, A.: Towards a lightweight protocol for industry 4.0: an implementation based benchmark. In: International Workshop of Electronics, Control, Measurement, Signals and their Application to Mechatronics (ECMSM), pp. 1–6. IEEE (2017)
13. Lampkin, V., et al.: Building Smarter Planet Solutions with MQTT and IBM WebSphere MQ Telemetry. IBM Redbooks (2012)

14. Mesnil, J.: Mobile and Web Messaging: Messaging Protocols for Web and Mobile Devices. O'Reilly Media Inc., Sebastopol (2014)
15. Mishra, B.: Performance evaluation of MQTT broker servers. In: Gervasi, O., et al. (eds.) ICCSA 2018. LNCS, vol. 10963, pp. 599–609. Springer, Cham (2018). https://doi.org/10.1007/978-3-319-95171-3_47
16. Naik, N.: Choice of effective messaging protocols for IoT systems: MQTT, CoAP, AMQP and HTTP. In: International Systems Engineering Symposium (ISSE), pp. 1–7. IEEE (2017)
17. O'Mahony, D., Doyle, D.: Reaching 5 million messaging connections: our journey with kubernetes, December 2018. https://www.slideshare.net/ConnectedMarketing/reaching-5-million-messaging-connections-our-journey-with-kubernetes-126143229
18. Profanter, S., Tekat, A., Dorofeev, K., Rickert, M., Knoll, A.: OPC UA versus ROS, DDS, and MQTT: performance evaluation of industry 4.0 protocols. In: IEEE International Conference on Industrial Technology (ICIT) (2019)
19. Sachs, K., Kounev, S., Bacon, J., Buchmann, A.: Performance evaluation of message-oriented middleware using the SPECjms2007 benchmark. Performance Evaluation **66**(8), 410–434 (2009)
20. ScaleAgent: benchmark of MQTT servers, January 2015. https://bit.ly/2WsTw0Z
21. Sommer, P., Schellroth, F., Fischer, M., Schlechtendahl, J.: Message-oriented middleware for industrial production systems. In: International Conference on Automation Science and Engineering (CASE), pp. 1217–1223. IEEE (2018)
22. Thangavel, D., Ma, X., Valera, A., Tan, H.X., Tan, C.K.Y.: Performance evaluation of MQTT and CoAP via a common middleware. In: International Conference on Intelligent Sensors, Sensor Networks and Information Processing (ISSNIP), pp. 1–6. IEEE (2014)
23. Thean, Z.Y., Yap, V.V., Teh, P.C.: Container-based MQTT broker cluster for edge computing. In: International Conference and Workshops on Recent Advances and Innovations in Engineering (ICRAIE), pp. 1–6. IEEE (2019)
24. Tran, P., Greenfield, P., Gorton, I.: Behavior and performance of message-oriented middleware systems. In: International Conference on Distributed Computing Systems Workshops, pp. 645–650. IEEE (2002)
25. Zimmermann, O., Grundler, J., Tai, S., Leymann, F.: Architectural decisions and patterns for transactional workflows in SOA. In: Krämer, B.J., Lin, K.-J., Narasimhan, P. (eds.) ICSOC 2007. LNCS, vol. 4749, pp. 81–93. Springer, Heidelberg (2007). https://doi.org/10.1007/978-3-540-74974-5_7
26. Zimmermann, O., Wegmann, L., Koziolek, H., Goldschmidt, T.: Architectural decision guidance across projects-problem space modeling, decision backlog management and cloud computing knowledge. In: Working IEEE/IFIP Conference on Software Architecture, pp. 85–94. IEEE (2015)

Author Index

Aerts, Ad T. M. 247
Aleti, Aldeida 182
Almeida, João Franscisco 39
Araújo, Camila 101
Arcelli, Davide 139
Astudillo, Hernán 231, 281

Babar, Muhammad Ali 165
Batista, Thais 101
Berger, Christian 73
Bogner, Justus 315

Capilla, Rafael 231
Caporuscio, Mauro 57, 265
Carrillo, Carlos 231
Cavalcante, Everton 101
Chondamrongkul, Nacha 21
Correia, Filipe F. 315
Cruz, Pablo 281

D'Angelo, Mirko 57
Dajsuren, Yanja 247
De Sanctis, Martina 118
Dias, Fagner 101

Edrisi, Farid 265

Ferreira, Hugo S. 315
Fritzsch, Jonas 315

Geiger, Sebastian 3
Giaimo, Federico 73
Giraud, Guillaume 333
Goodwin, Sarah 182
Grassi, Vincenzo 57
Gratzl, Samuel 182
Grüner, Sten 352

Hallberg, Margrethe 265
Herold, Sebastian 193

Iovino, Ludovico 118
Islam, Chadni 165

Jamshidi, Pooyan 182
Johannesson, Anton 265

Kaplan, Angelika 220
Keim, Jan 220
Kopf, Claudia 265
Koziolek, Anne 148, 220
Koziolek, Heiko 352
Kruchten, Philippe 202

Lago, Patricia 202
Lalanda, Philippe 333
Leite, Jair 101

Malakuti, Somayeh 296
Matias, Tiago 315
Meixner, Sebastian 3
Mirakhorli, Mehdi 220
Mirandola, Raffaela 57
Moghaddam, Mahyar T. 333

Nepal, Surya 165
Ntentos, Evangelos 3

Oliveira, Marcel 101
Oquendo, Flavio 101
Ostroumov, Sergey 296

Perez-Palacin, Diego 265
Plakidas, Konstantinos 3
Poll, Erik 89

Restivo, André 315
Rossi, Maria Teresa 118

Rückert, Julius   352
Rutten, Eric   333

Salinas, Luis   281
Seifermann, Stephan   148
Serban, Alex   89
Silva, António Rito   39
Sun, Jing   21

Trubiani, Catia   182

van Hoorn, Andre   182
Verdecchia, Roberto   202
Visser, Joost   89

Warren, Ian   21
Werle, Dominik   148
Wimmer, Manuel   118

Zdun, Uwe   3
Zimmermann, Olaf   231

ited in the United States

ookmasters